Waiting for Spring 2

Anashin

Waiting
for Spring
vol.2

Presented by
Anashin

period 6
"Aya-chan Shock"

5

period 7
"Wishing Basket"

41

period 8
"Straight Talk"

76

period 9
"Heart-Pounding Time"

113

period 10
"Aya-chan Attack"

147

CONTENTS

WAITING FOR SPRING
Harumatsu Bokura

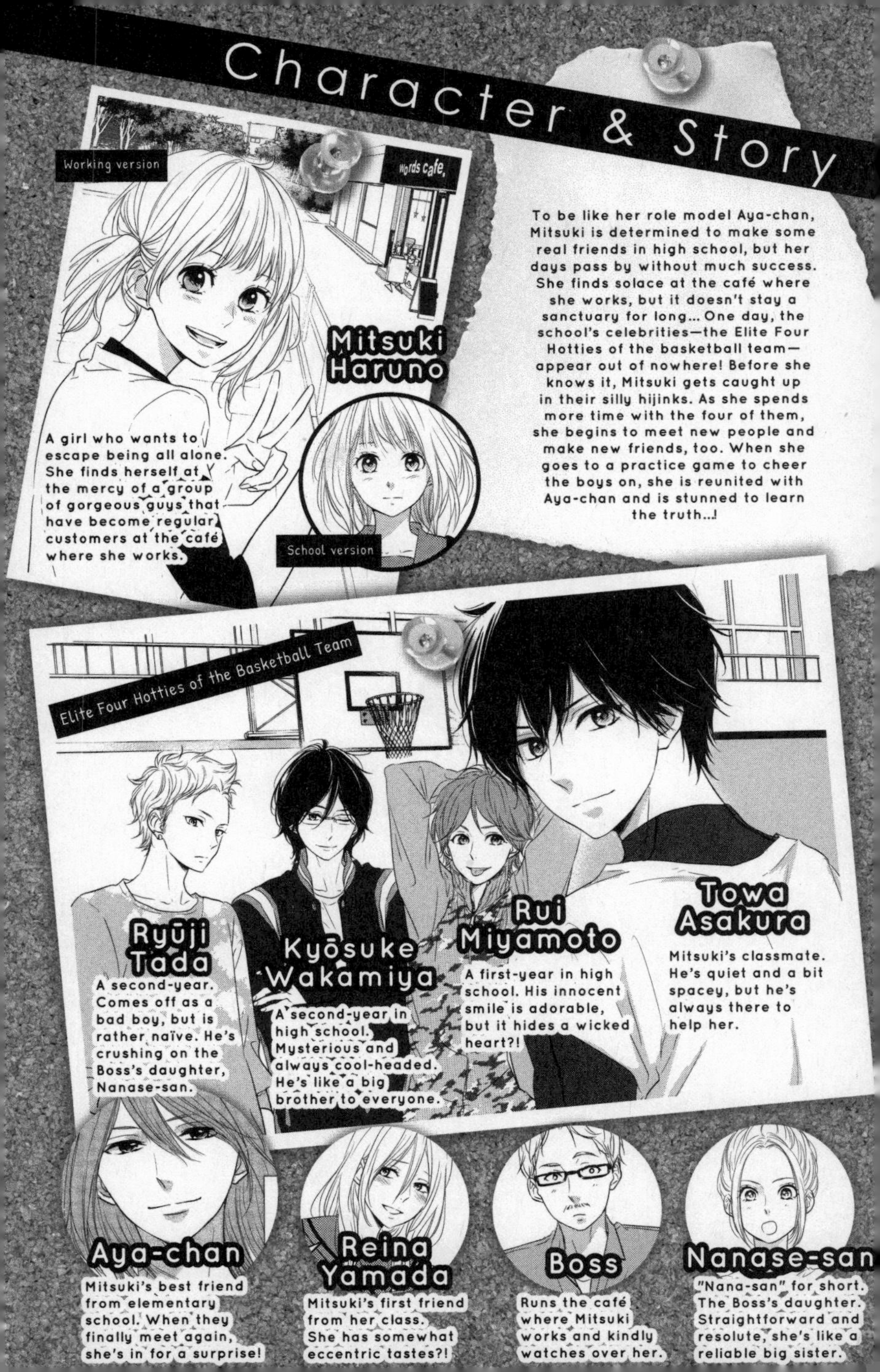
Character & Story
Working version
words cafe.
Mitsuki Haruno
A girl who wants to escape being all alone. She finds herself at the mercy of a group of gorgeous guys that have become regular customers at the café where she works.
School version
To be like her role model Aya-chan, Mitsuki is determined to make some real friends in high school, but her days pass by without much success. She finds solace at the café where she works, but it doesn't stay a sanctuary for long... One day, the school's celebrities—the Elite Four Hotties of the basketball team—appear out of nowhere! Before she knows it, Mitsuki gets caught up in their silly hijinks. As she spends more time with the four of them, she begins to meet new people and make new friends, too. When she goes to a practice game to cheer the boys on, she is reunited with Aya-chan and is stunned to learn the truth...!
Elite Four Hotties of the Basketball Team
Towa Asakura
Mitsuki's classmate. He's quiet and a bit spacey, but he's always there to help her.
Rui Miyamoto
A first-year in high school. His innocent smile is adorable, but it hides a wicked heart?!
Kyōsuke Wakamiya
A second-year in high school. Mysterious and always cool-headed. He's like a big brother to everyone.
Ryūji Tada
A second-year. Comes off as a bad boy, but is rather naïve. He's crushing on the Boss's daughter, Nanase-san.
Aya-chan
Mitsuki's best friend from elementary school. When they finally meet again, she's in for a surprise!
Reina Yamada
Mitsuki's first friend from her class. She has somewhat eccentric tastes?!
Boss
Runs the café where Mitsuki works and kindly watches over her.
Nanase-san
"Nana-san" for short. The Boss's daughter. Straightforward and resolute, she's like a reliable big sister.

Hello! Anashin here.

Thank you very much for picking up Volume 2.

A lot of happy things have happened because

so many people read Volume 1.

I'll talk more about one of those things later.

...First, let's tell the story.

Enjoy!

Pleeeease enjoy!

Mitsuki

Rabbit

Volume 2!

period 6: “Aya-chan Shock”

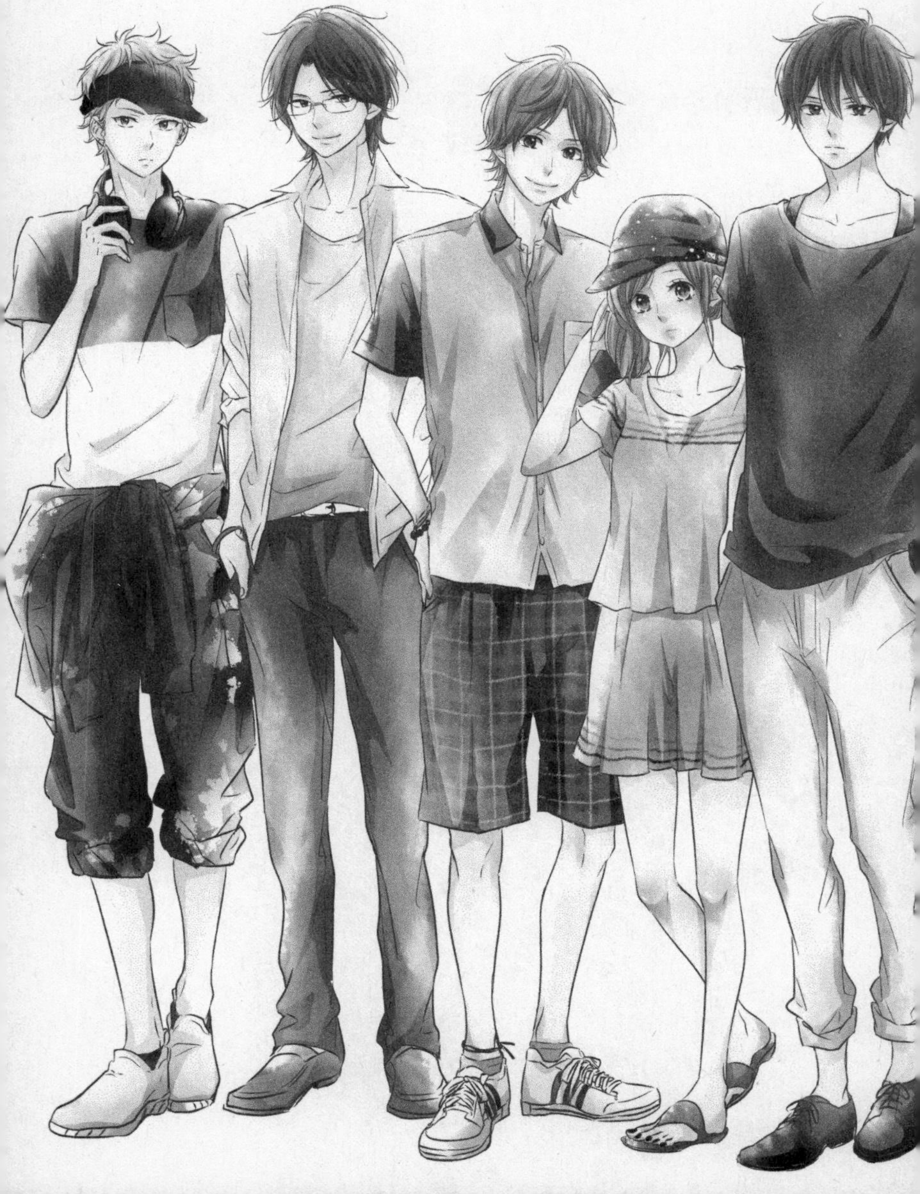

...but before that...

Returning for Volume 2! Silhouette Pop Quiz!! (ha ha)

Who is holding this ball?

Answer on page 75.

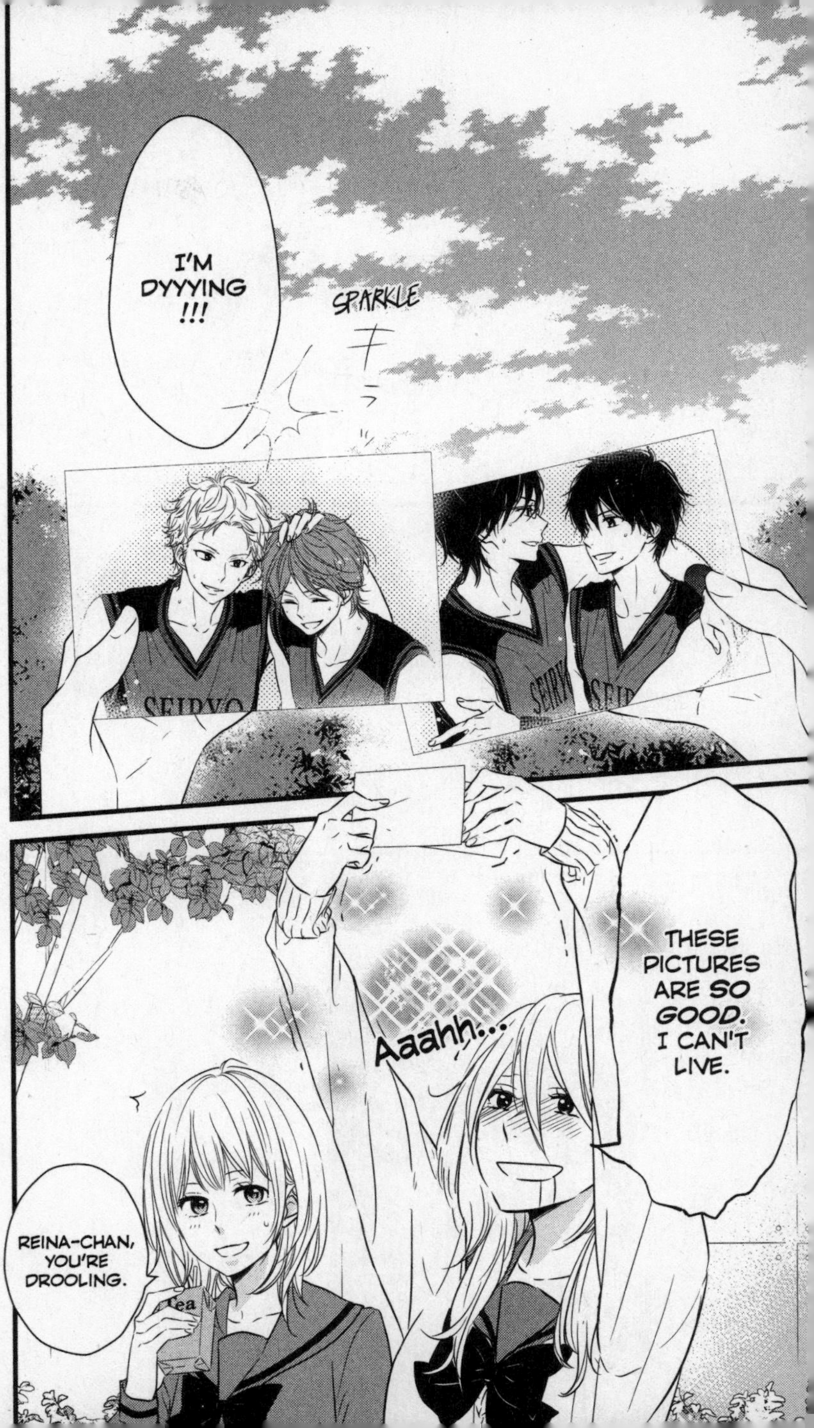
I'M DYYYING!!!
SPARKLE
THESE PICTURES ARE SO GOOD. I CAN'T LIVE.
Aaahh...
REINA-CHAN, YOU'RE DROOLING.
Tea

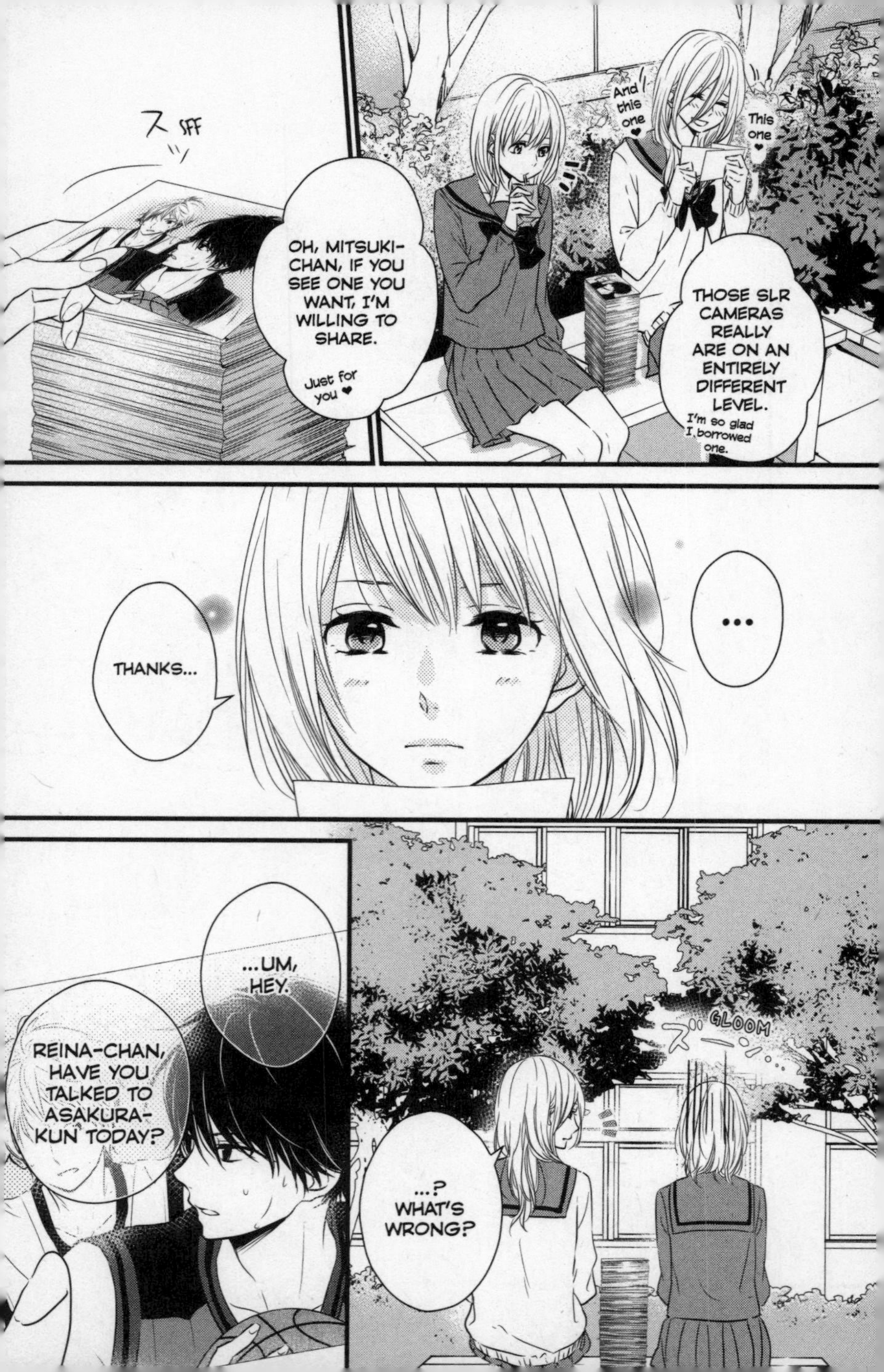
This one ♥
And this one ♥
THOSE SLR CAMERAS REALLY ARE ON AN ENTIRELY DIFFERENT LEVEL.
I'm so glad I borrowed one.
OH, MITSUKI-CHAN, IF YOU SEE ONE YOU WANT, I'M WILLING TO SHARE.
Just for you ♥
SFF
...
THANKS...
GLOOM
...? WHAT'S WRONG?
...UM, HEY.
REINA-CHAN, HAVE YOU TALKED TO ASAKURA-KUN TODAY?

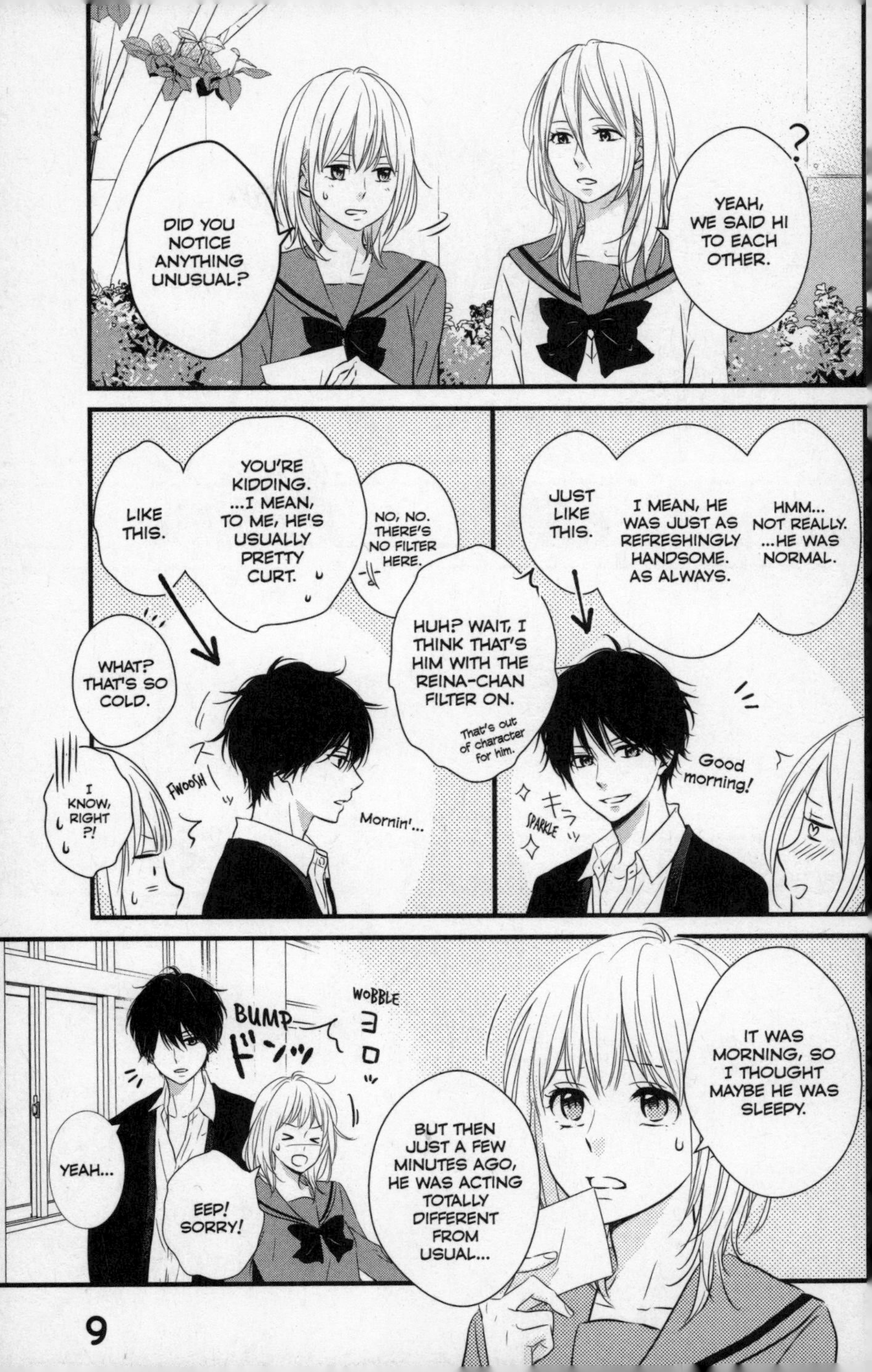
?
YEAH, WE SAID HI TO EACH OTHER.
DID YOU NOTICE ANYTHING UNUSUAL?
HMM... NOT REALLY. ...HE WAS NORMAL.
I MEAN, HE WAS JUST AS REFRESHINGLY HANDSOME. AS ALWAYS.
JUST LIKE THIS.
Good morning!
SPARKLE
キラッ
HUH? WAIT, I THINK THAT'S HIM WITH THE REINA-CHAN FILTER ON.
That's out of character for him.
NO, NO. THERE'S NO FILTER HERE.
YOU'RE KIDDING. ...I MEAN, TO ME, HE'S USUALLY PRETTY CURT.
LIKE THIS.
Mornin'...
FWOOSH
WHAT? THAT'S SO COLD.
I KNOW, RIGHT?!
IT WAS MORNING, SO I THOUGHT MAYBE HE WAS SLEEPY.
BUT THEN JUST A FEW MINUTES AGO, HE WAS ACTING TOTALLY DIFFERENT FROM USUAL...
WOBBLE
ヨロッ
BUMP
ドンッ
EEP! SORRY!
YEAH...

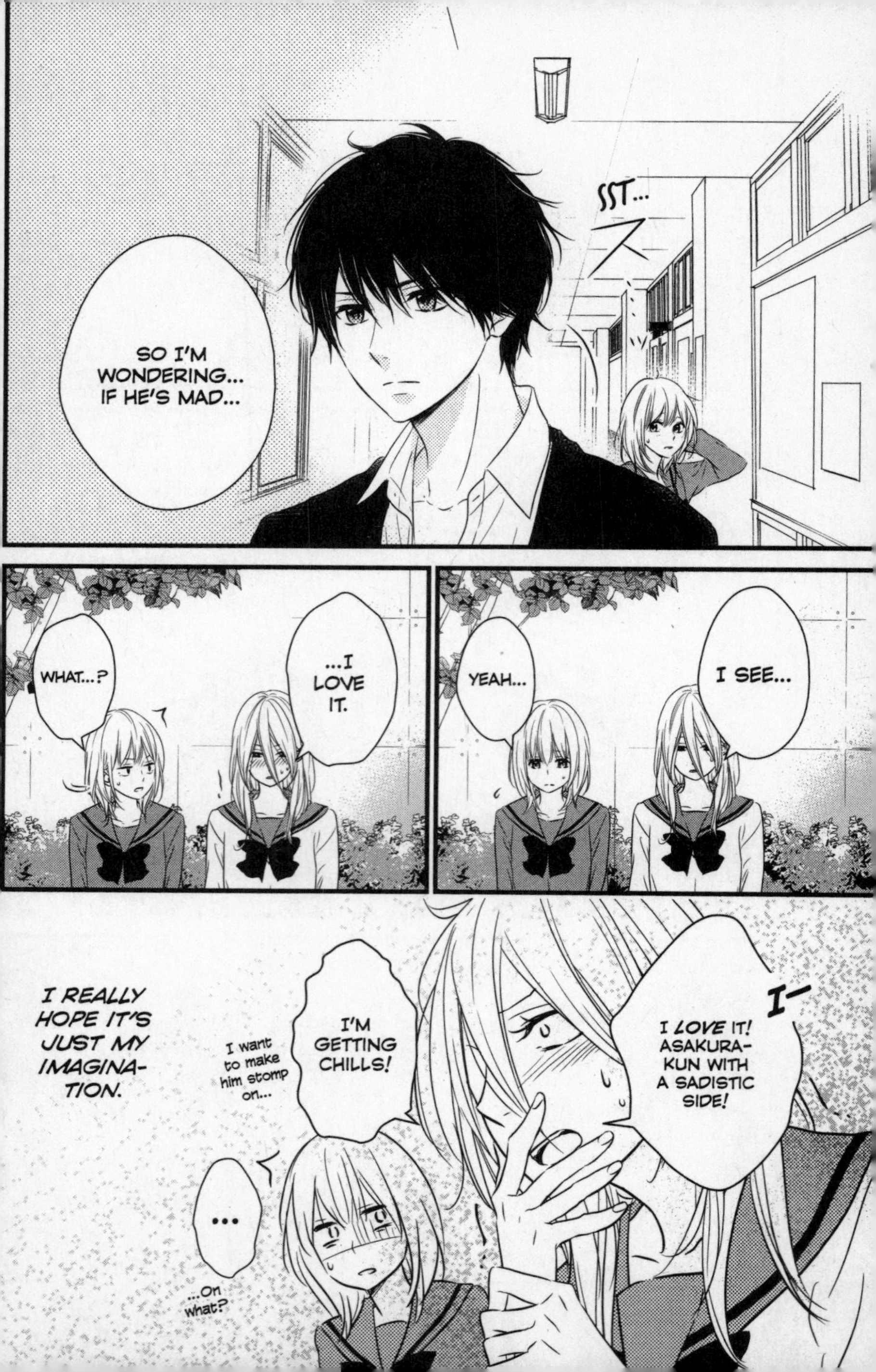
SST...
SO I'M WONDERING... IF HE'S MAD...
I SEE...
YEAH...
...I LOVE IT.
WHAT...?
I—
I LOVE IT! ASAKURA-KUN WITH A SADISTIC SIDE!
I'M GETTING CHILLS!
I want to make him stomp on...
I REALLY HOPE IT'S JUST MY IMAGINATION.
...
...On what?

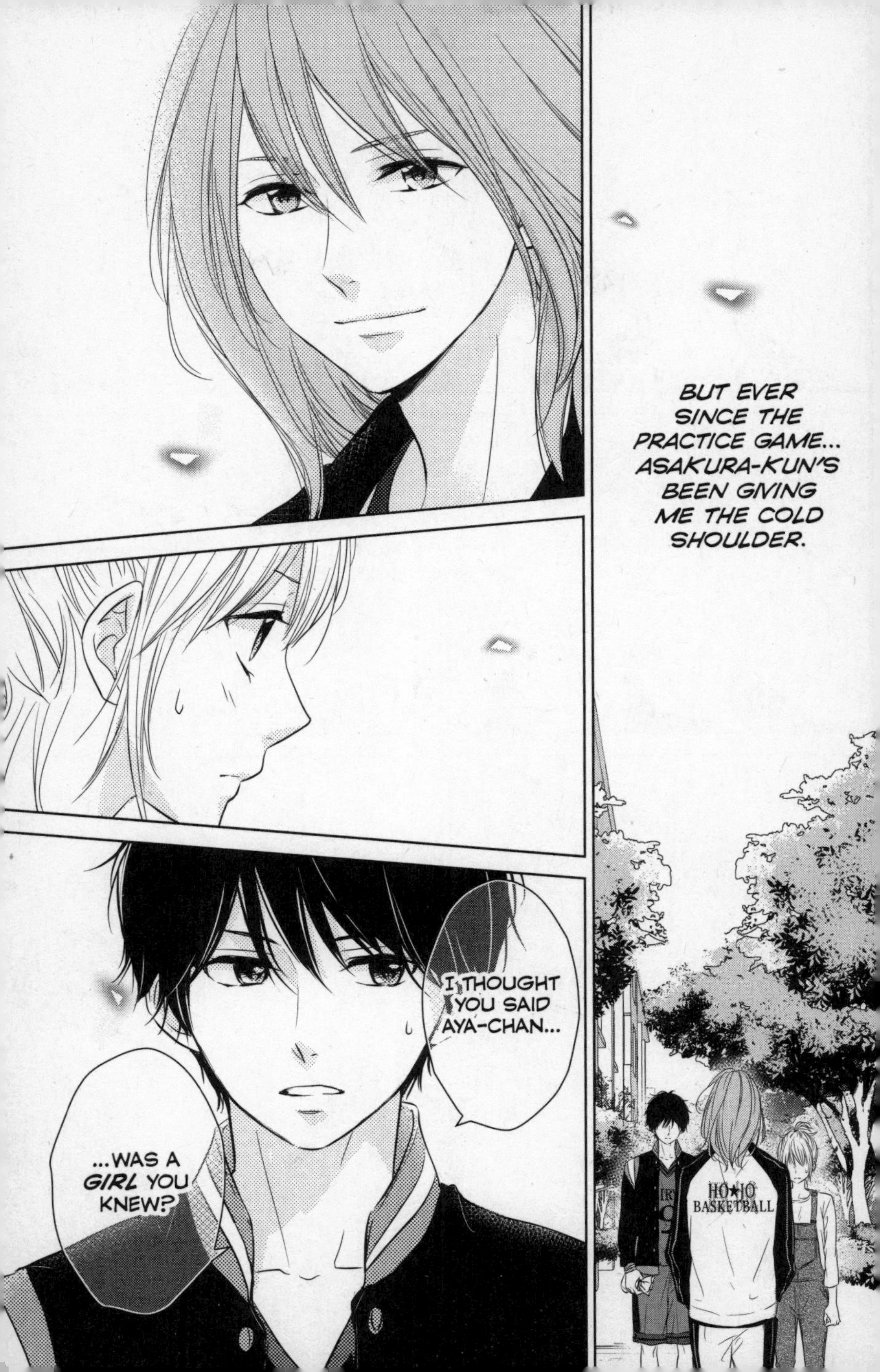
BUT EVER SINCE THE PRACTICE GAME... ASAKURA-KUN'S BEEN GIVING ME THE COLD SHOULDER.
HO★JO BASKETBALL
I THOUGHT YOU SAID AYA-CHAN...
...WAS A *GIRL* YOU KNEW?

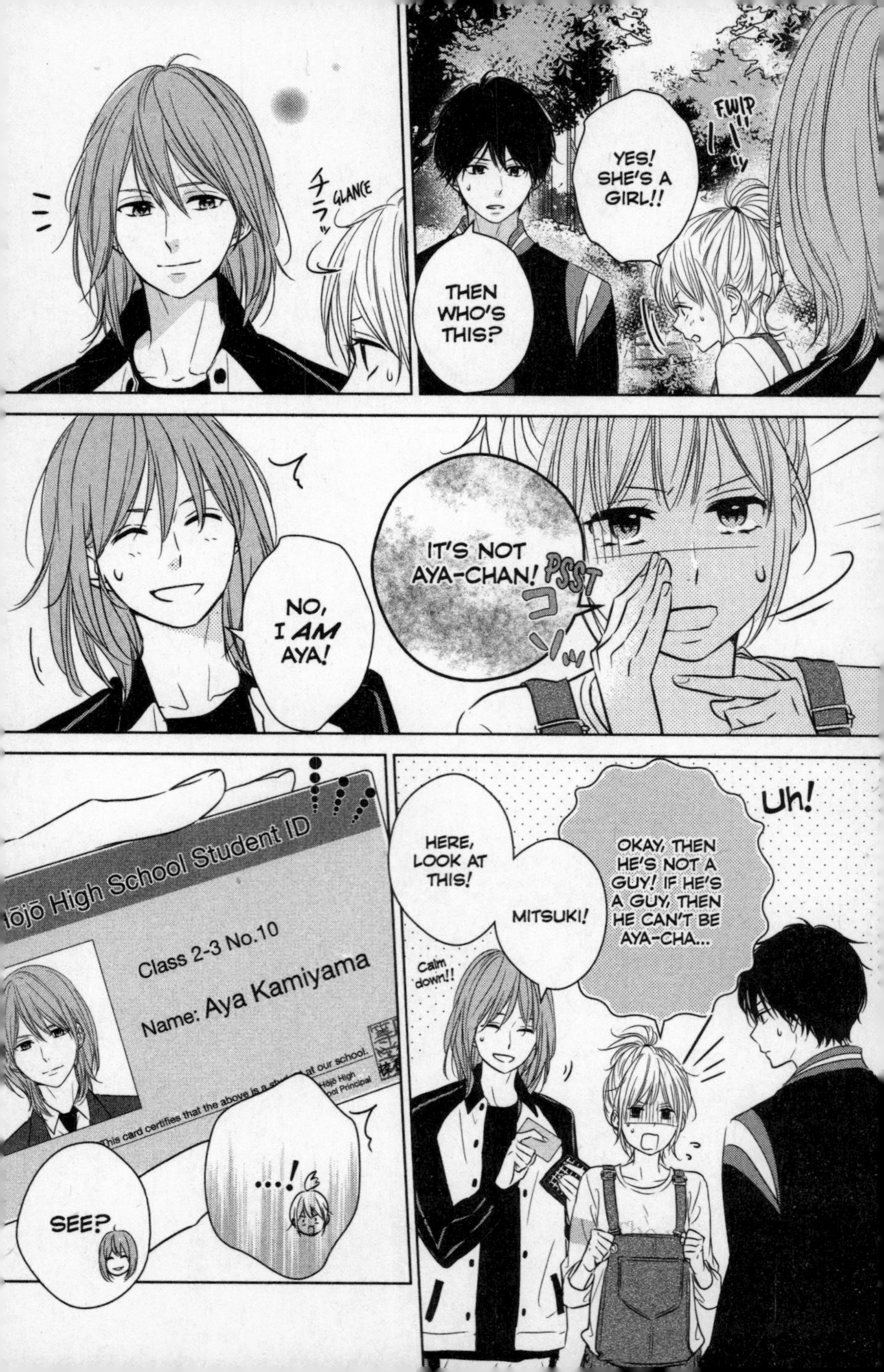
FWIP
YES! SHE'S A GIRL!!
THEN WHO'S THIS?
GLANCE
IT'S NOT AYA-CHAN!
PSST
NO, I *AM* AYA!
Uh!
OKAY, THEN HE'S NOT A GUY! IF HE'S A GUY, THEN HE CAN'T BE AYA-CHA...
MITSUKI!
Calm down!!
HERE, LOOK AT THIS!
ōjō High School Student ID
Class 2-3 No.10
Name: Aya Kamiyama
...!
SEE?

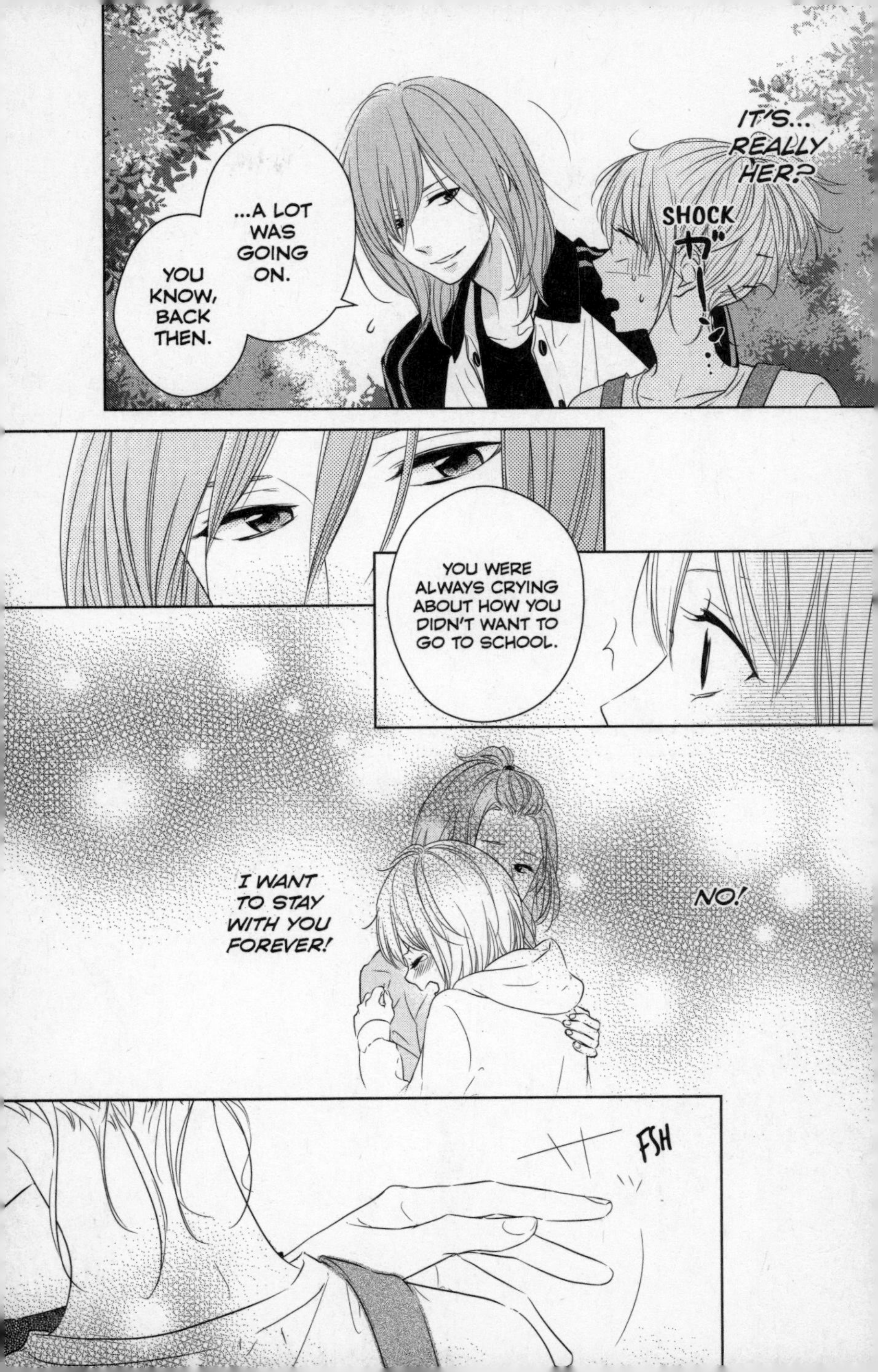
IT'S... REALLY HER?
SHOCK
ガー
...A LOT WAS GOING ON.
YOU KNOW, BACK THEN.
YOU WERE ALWAYS CRYING ABOUT HOW YOU DIDN'T WANT TO GO TO SCHOOL.
NO!
I WANT TO STAY WITH YOU FOREVER!
FSH

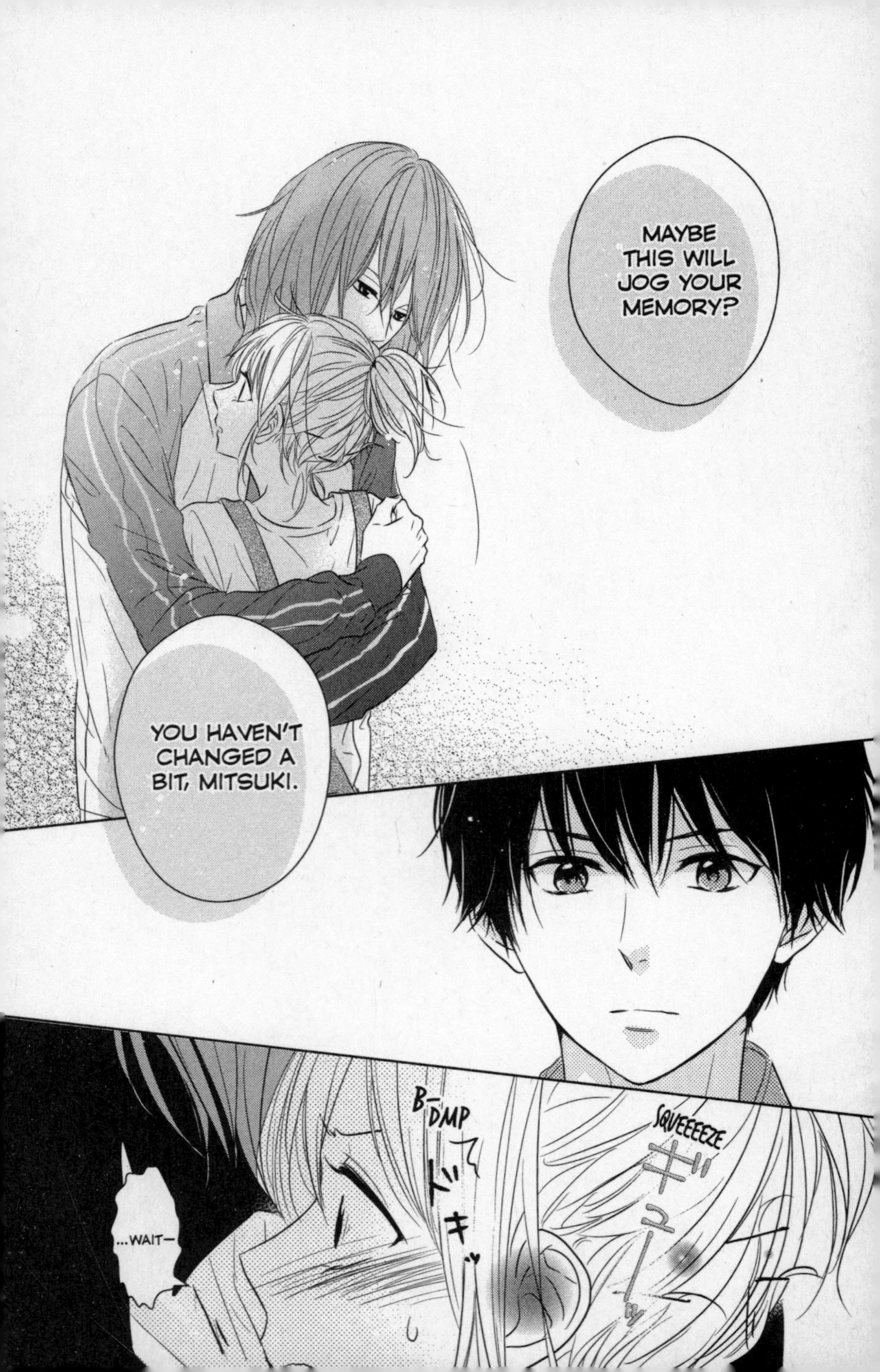
MAYBE THIS WILL JOG YOUR MEMORY?
YOU HAVEN'T CHANGED A BIT, MITSUKI.
SQUEEEEZE
ギュー
B-DMP
ドキ
...WAIT—

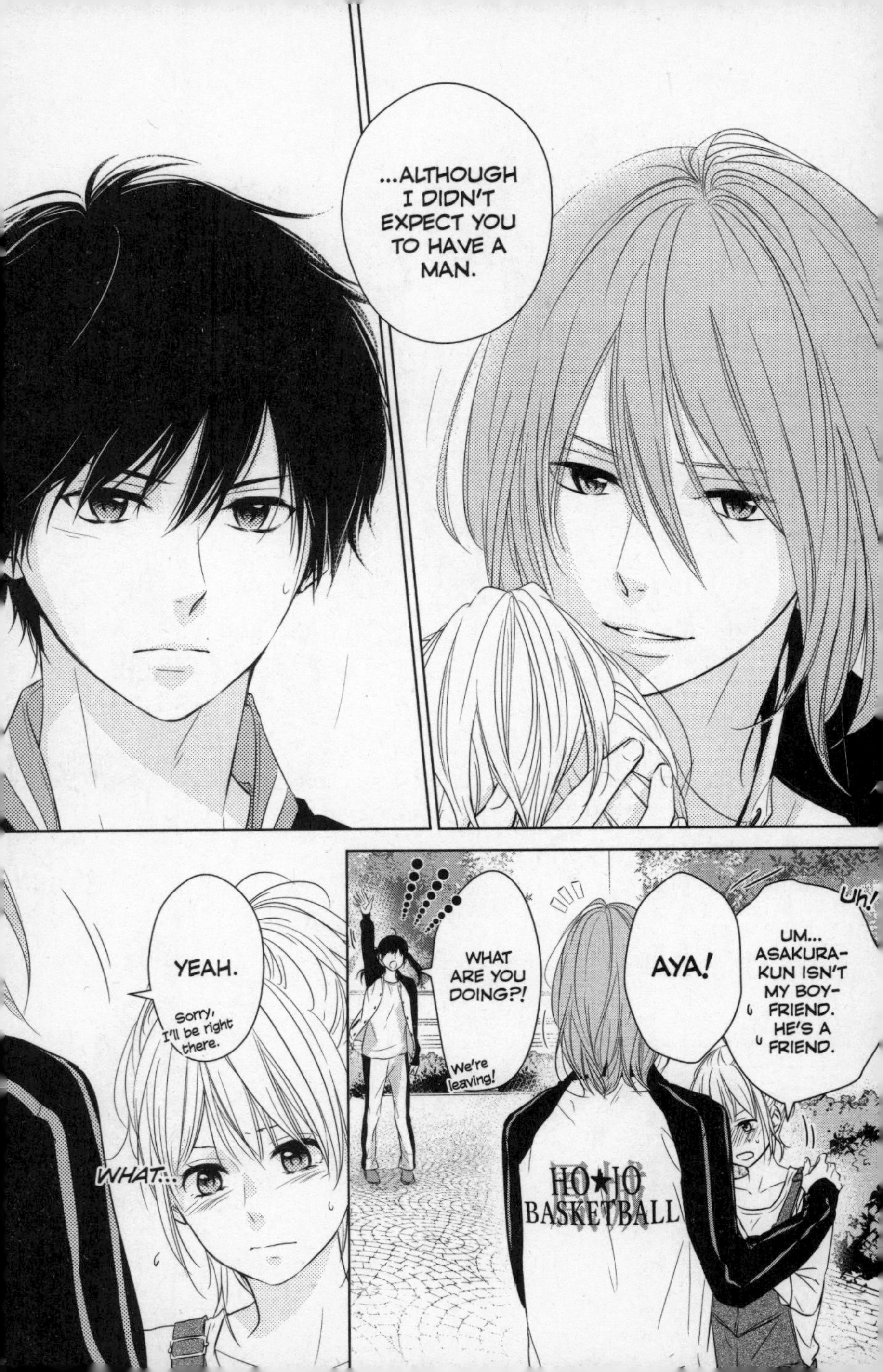
...ALTHOUGH I DIDN'T EXPECT YOU TO HAVE A MAN.
Uh!
UM... ASAKURA-KUN ISN'T MY BOY-FRIEND. HE'S A FRIEND.
AYA!
WHAT ARE YOU DOING?!
We're leaving!
HO★JO BASKETBALL
YEAH.
Sorry, I'll be right there.
WHAT...

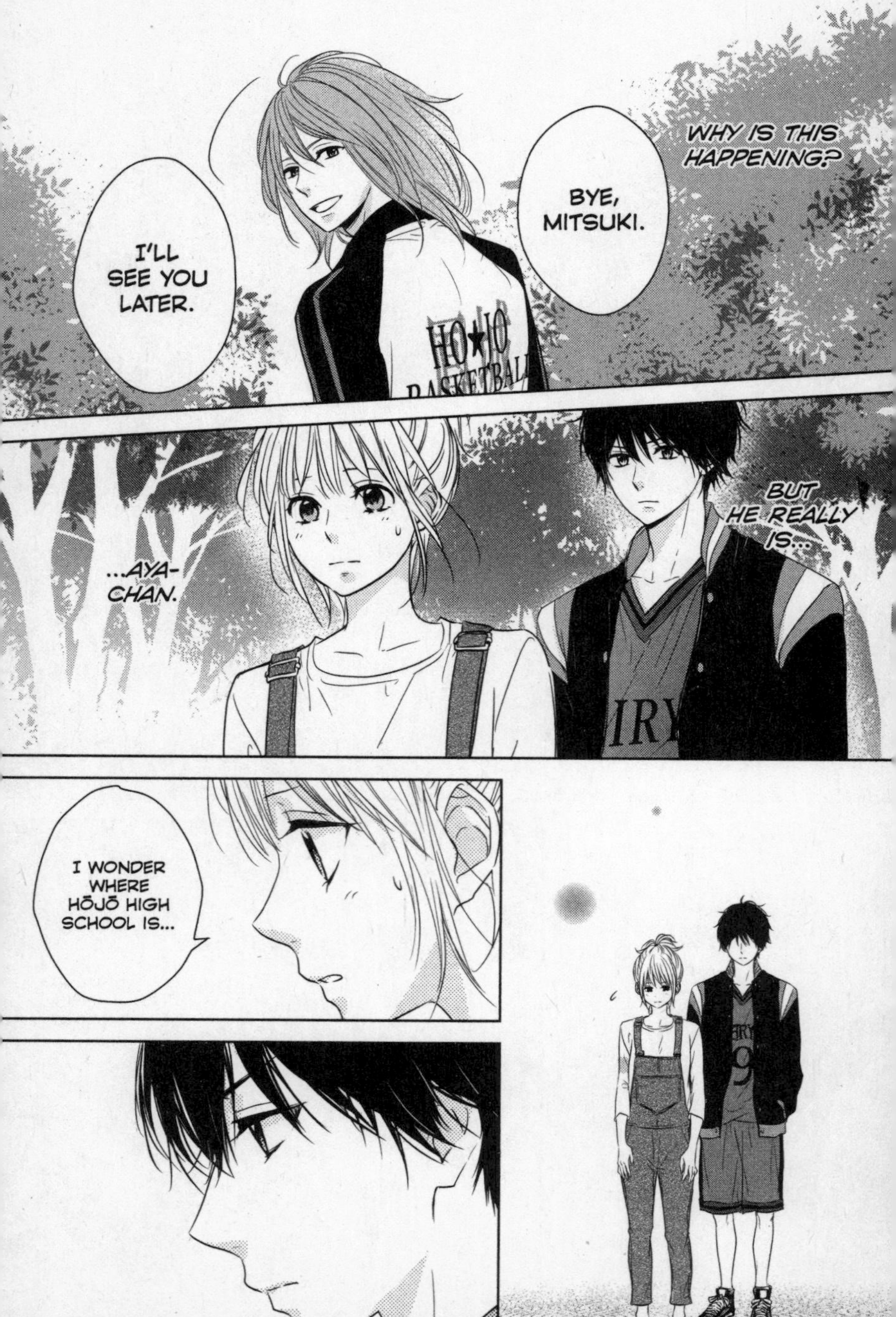
WHY IS THIS HAPPENING?
BYE, MITSUKI.
I'LL SEE YOU LATER.
BUT HE REALLY IS...
...AYA-CHAN.
I WONDER WHERE HŌJŌ HIGH SCHOOL IS...

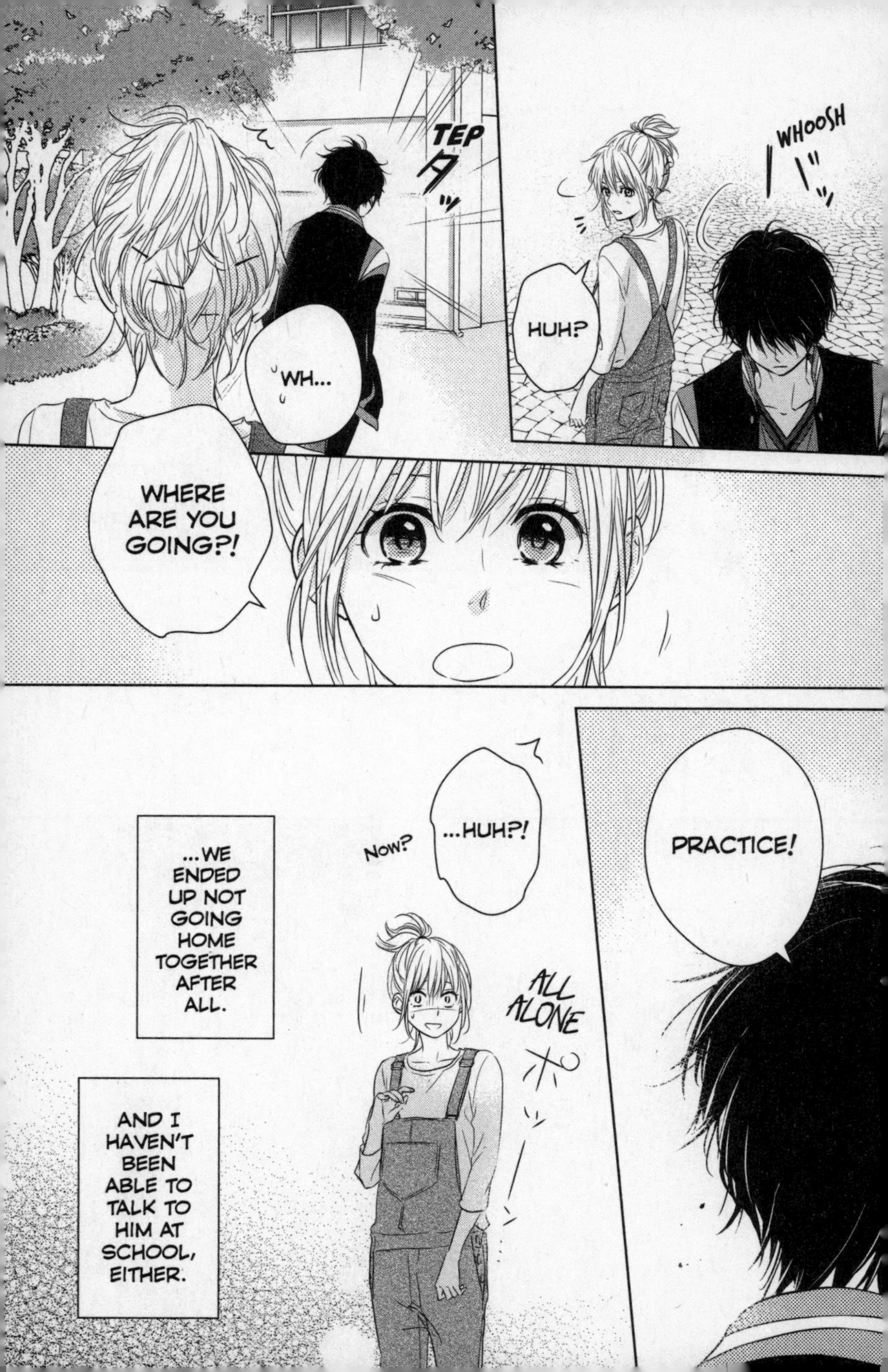
WHOOSH
HUH?
TEP
WH...
WHERE ARE YOU GOING?!
PRACTICE!
...HUH?!
Now?
ALL ALONE
...WE ENDED UP NOT GOING HOME TOGETHER AFTER ALL.
AND I HAVEN'T BEEN ABLE TO TALK TO HIM AT SCHOOL, EITHER.

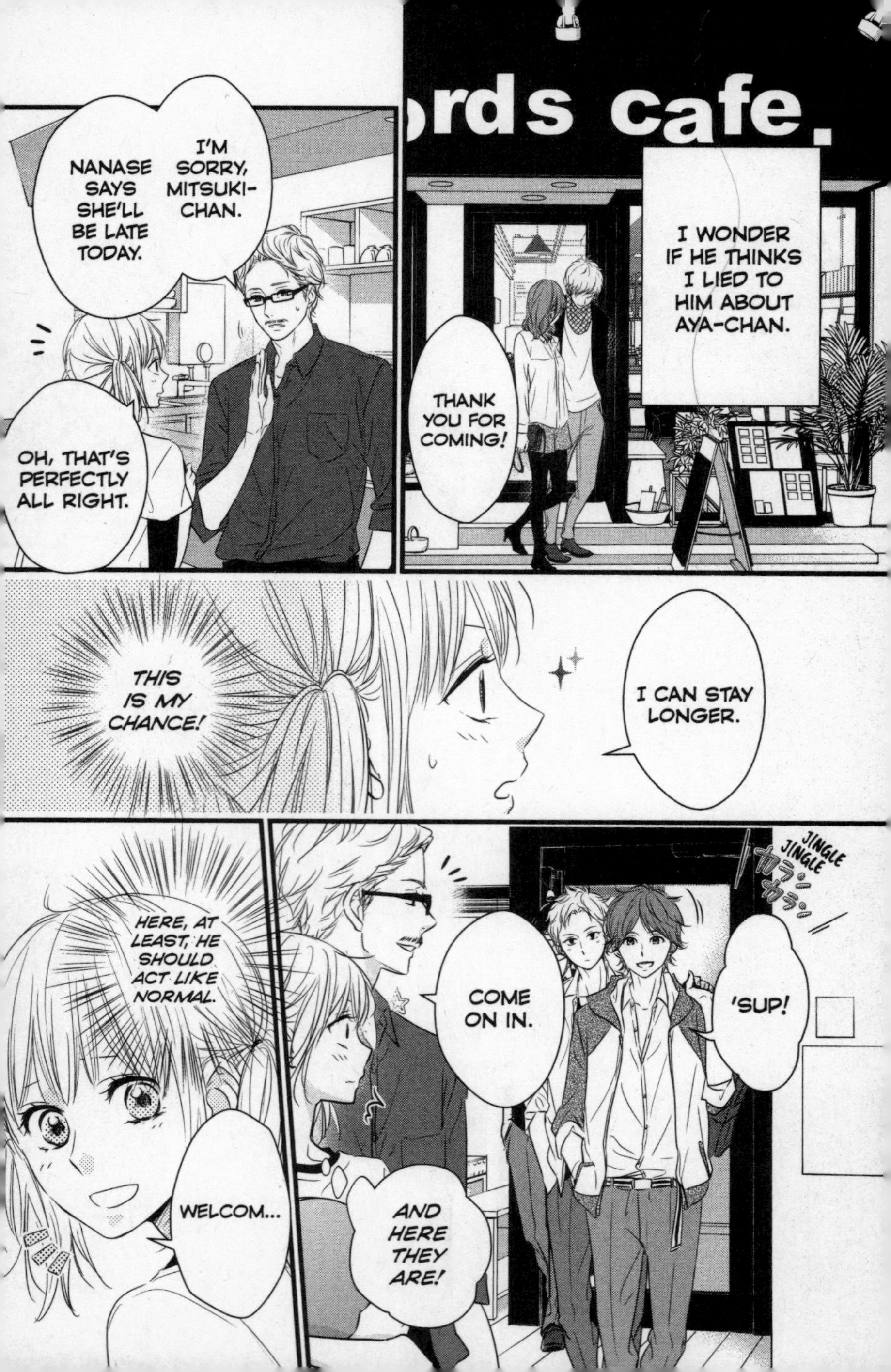

ords cafe.
I WONDER IF HE THINKS I LIED TO HIM ABOUT AYA-CHAN.
THANK YOU FOR COMING!
I'M SORRY, MITSUKI-CHAN.
NANASE SAYS SHE'LL BE LATE TODAY.
OH, THAT'S PERFECTLY ALL RIGHT.
I CAN STAY LONGER.
THIS IS MY CHANCE!
JINGLE JINGLE
カラ カラ
'SUP!
COME ON IN.
AND HERE THEY ARE!
HERE, AT LEAST, HE SHOULD ACT LIKE NORMAL.
WELCOM...

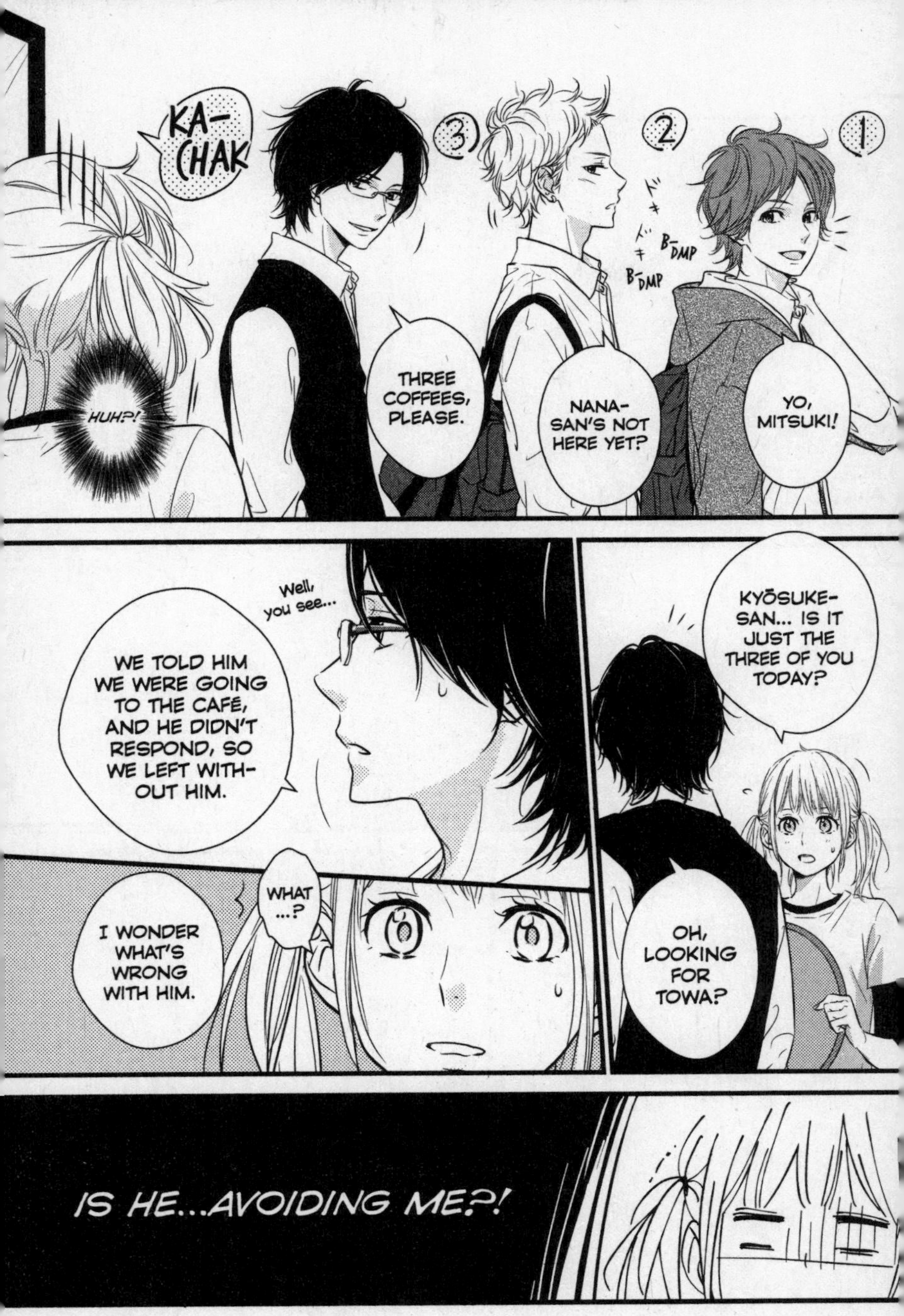
1
YO, MITSUKI!
2
ドキ ドキ
B-DMP
B-DMP
NANA-SAN'S NOT HERE YET?
3
THREE COFFEES, PLEASE.
KA-CHAK
HUH?!
KYŌSUKE-SAN... IS IT JUST THE THREE OF YOU TODAY?
OH, LOOKING FOR TOWA?
Well, you see...
WE TOLD HIM WE WERE GOING TO THE CAFÉ, AND HE DIDN'T RESPOND, SO WE LEFT WITH-OUT HIM.
WHAT ...?
I WONDER WHAT'S WRONG WITH HIM.
IS HE...AVOIDING ME?!

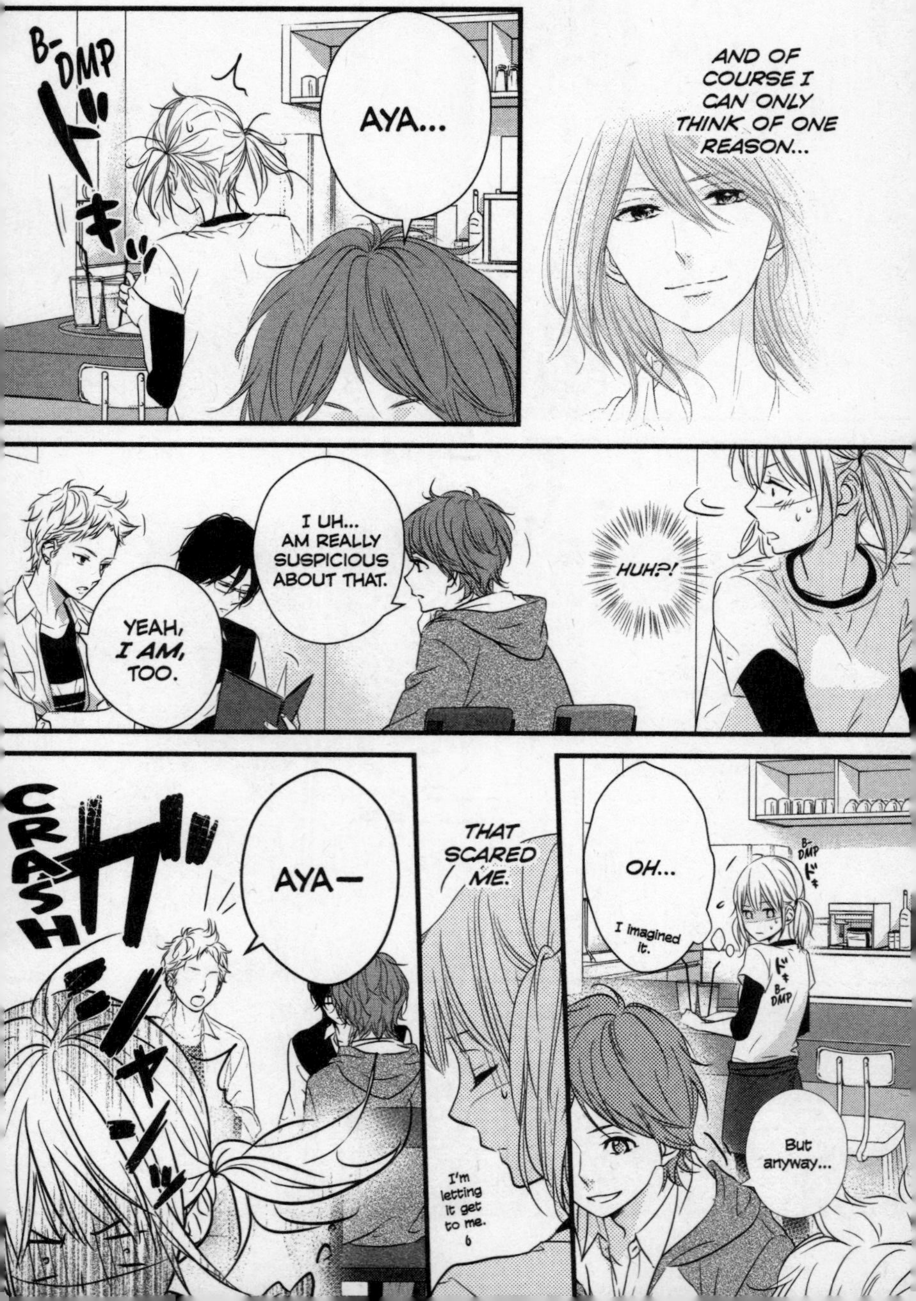
AND OF COURSE I CAN ONLY THINK OF ONE REASON...
B-DMP
AYA...
HUH?!
I UH... AM REALLY SUSPICIOUS ABOUT THAT.
YEAH, I AM, TOO.
OH...
I imagined it.
B-DMP
B-DMP
But anyway...
THAT SCARED ME.
I'm letting it get to me.
AYA—
CRASH

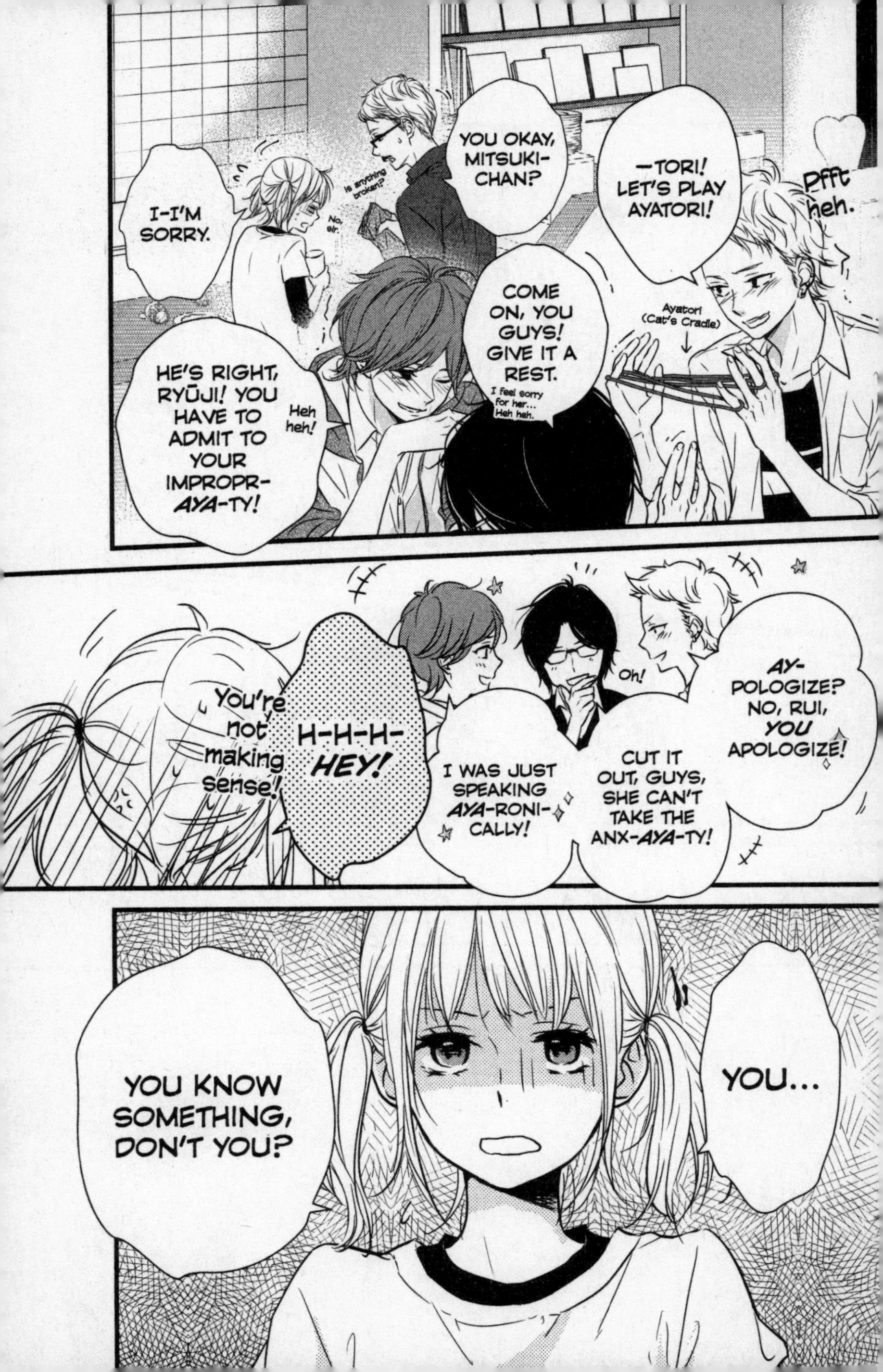
Pfft heh.
—TORI! LET'S PLAY AYATORI!
YOU OKAY, MITSUKI-CHAN?
Is anything broken?
No, sir.
I-I'M SORRY.
Ayatori (Cat's Cradle)
COME ON, YOU GUYS! GIVE IT A REST.
I feel sorry for her... Heh heh.
Heh heh!
HE'S RIGHT, RYŪJI! YOU HAVE TO ADMIT TO YOUR IMPROPR-AYA-TY!
AY-POLOGIZE? NO, RUI, YOU APOLOGIZE!
Oh!
CUT IT OUT, GUYS, SHE CAN'T TAKE THE ANX-AYA-TY!
I WAS JUST SPEAKING AYA-RONI-CALLY!
H-H-H-HEY!
You're not making sense!
YOU...
YOU KNOW SOMETHING, DON'T YOU?

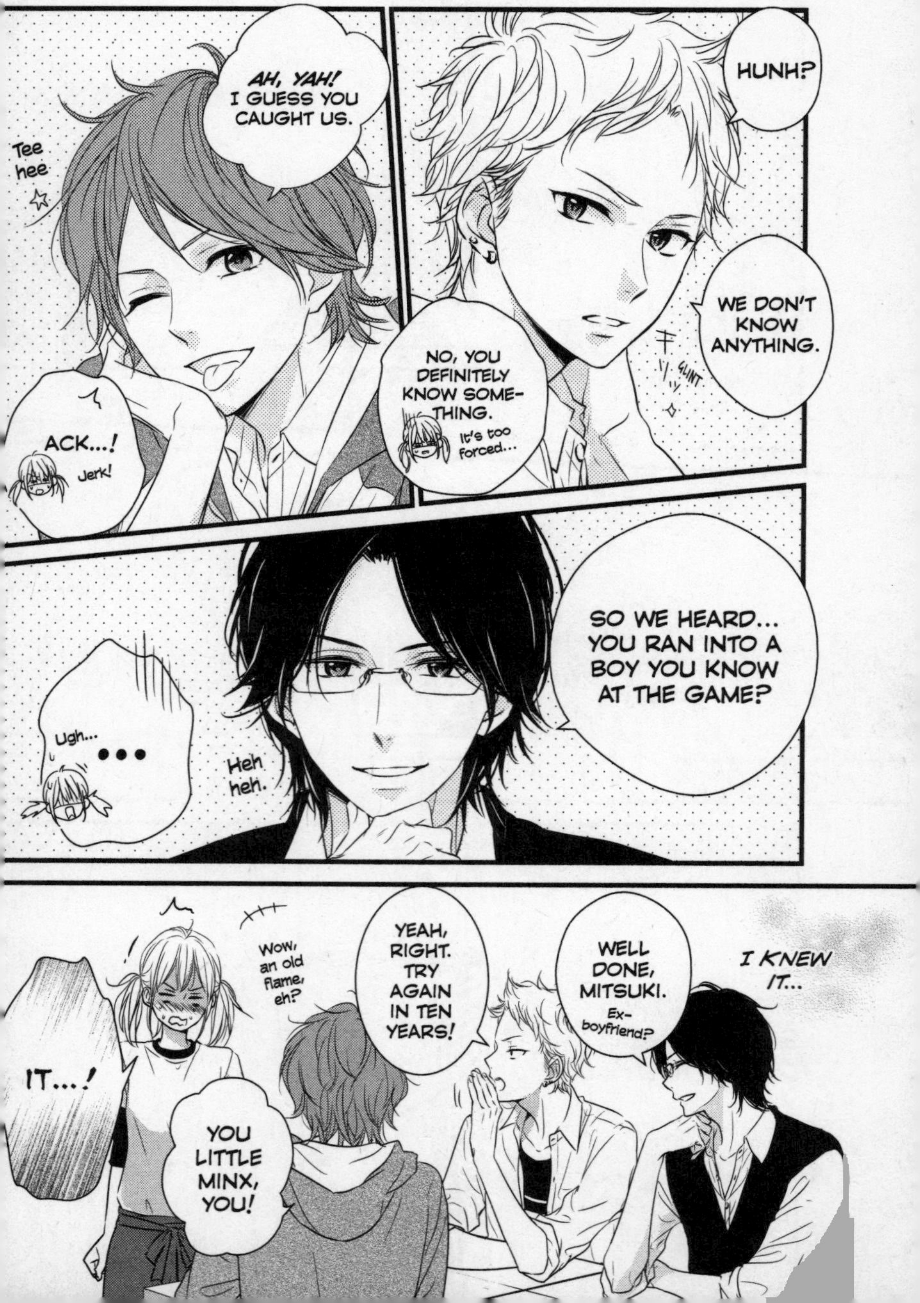
HUNH?
WE DON'T KNOW ANYTHING.
GLINT
NO, YOU DEFINITELY KNOW SOME-THING.
It's too forced...
AH, YAH! I GUESS YOU CAUGHT US.
Tee hee
ACK...!
Jerk!
SO WE HEARD... YOU RAN INTO A BOY YOU KNOW AT THE GAME?
Heh heh.
...
Ugh...
I KNEW IT...
WELL DONE, MITSUKI.
Ex-boyfriend?
YEAH, RIGHT. TRY AGAIN IN TEN YEARS!
Wow, an old flame, eh?
YOU LITTLE MINX, YOU!
IT...!

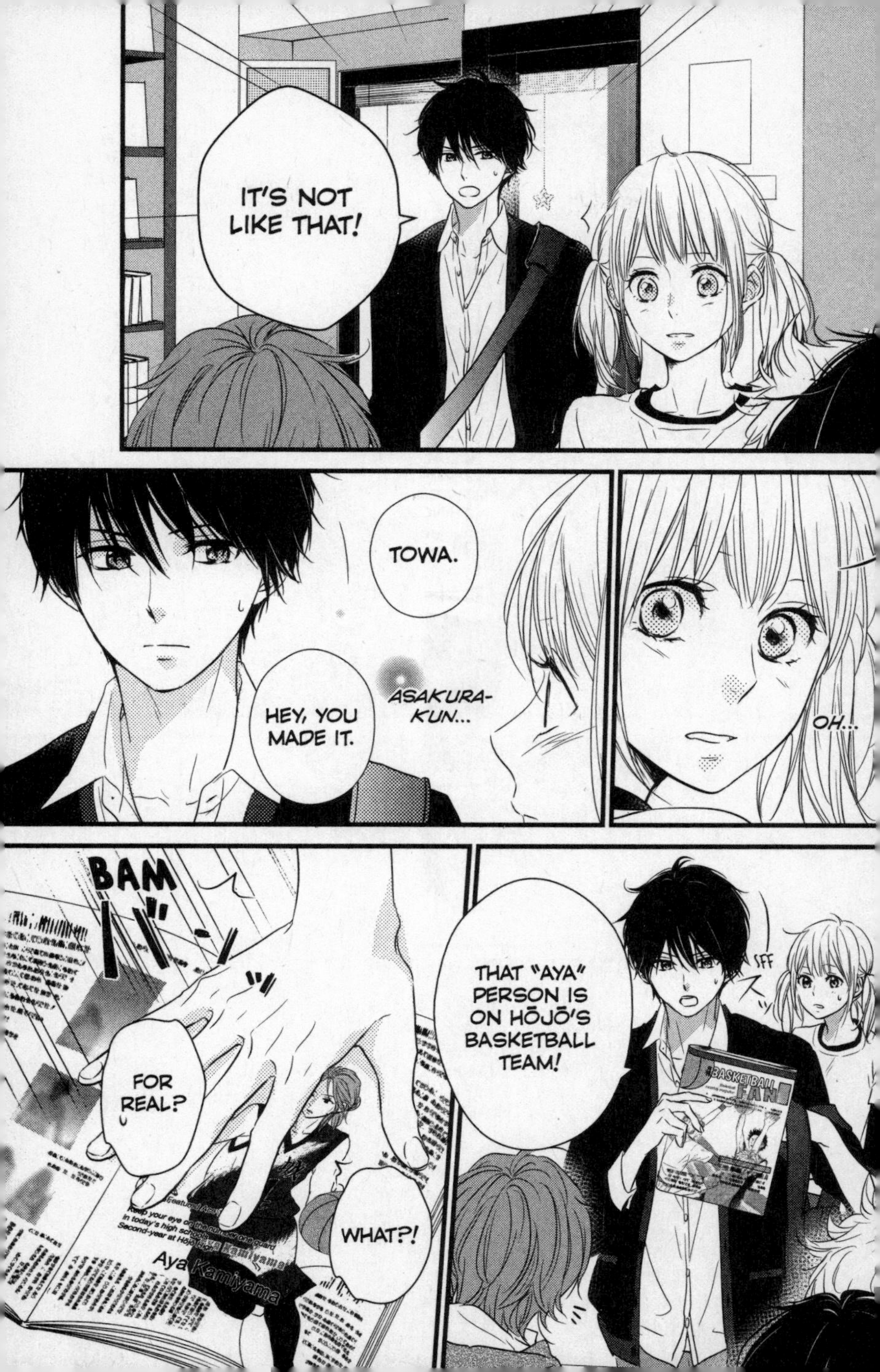
IT'S NOT LIKE THAT!
OH...
TOWA.
ASAKURA-KUN...
HEY, YOU MADE IT.
SFF
THAT "AYA" PERSON IS ON HŌJŌ'S BASKETBALL TEAM!
BASKETBALL FAN
BAM
WHAT?!
FOR REAL?
Aya Kamiyama

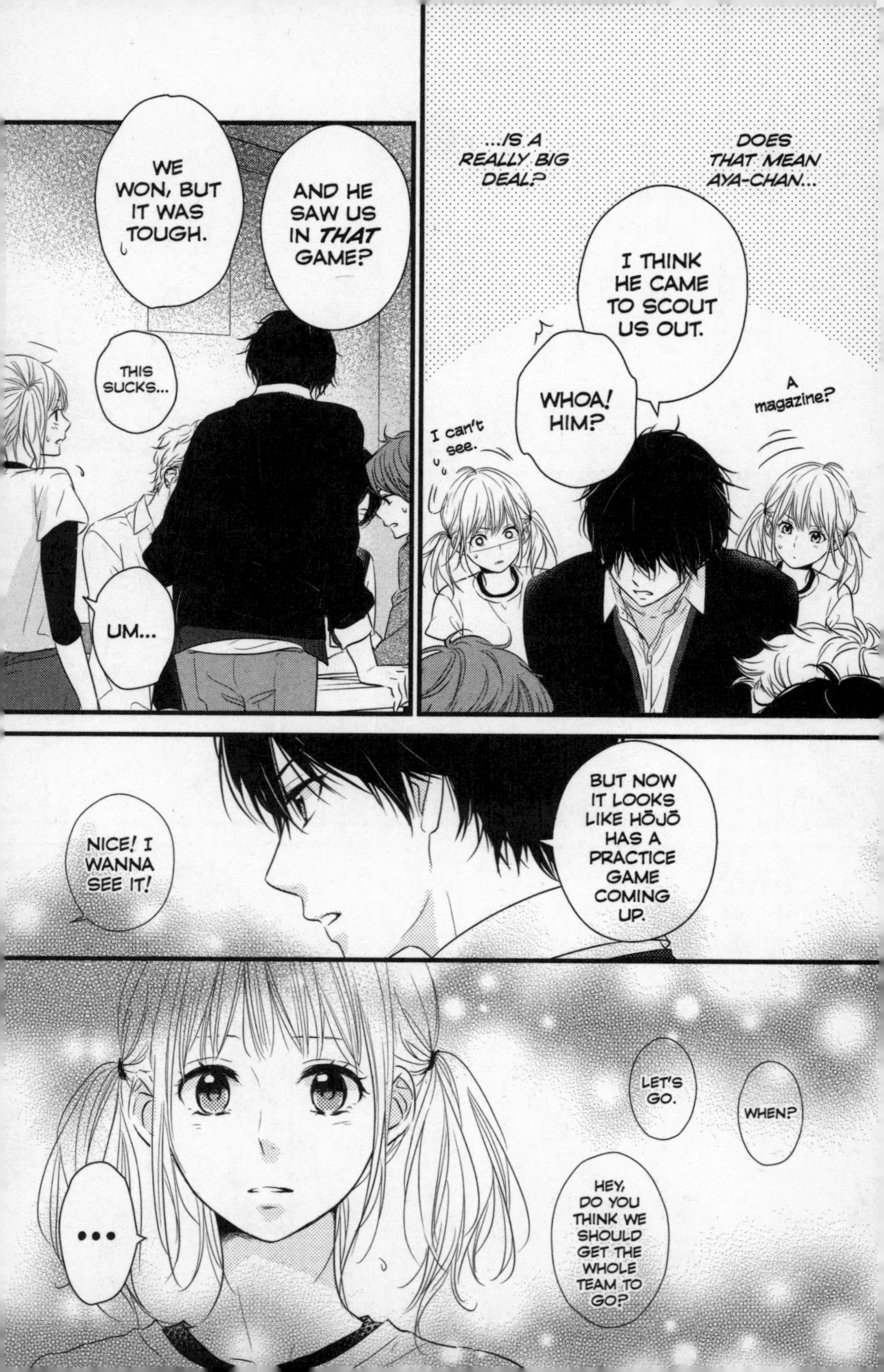
DOES THAT MEAN AYA-CHAN...
...IS A REALLY BIG DEAL?
I THINK HE CAME TO SCOUT US OUT.
WHOA! HIM?
A magazine?
I can't see.
AND HE SAW US IN *THAT* GAME?
WE WON, BUT IT WAS TOUGH.
THIS SUCKS...
UM...
BUT NOW IT LOOKS LIKE HŌJŌ HAS A PRACTICE GAME COMING UP.
NICE! I WANNA SEE IT!
WHEN?
LET'S GO.
HEY, DO YOU THINK WE SHOULD GET THE WHOLE TEAM TO GO?
...

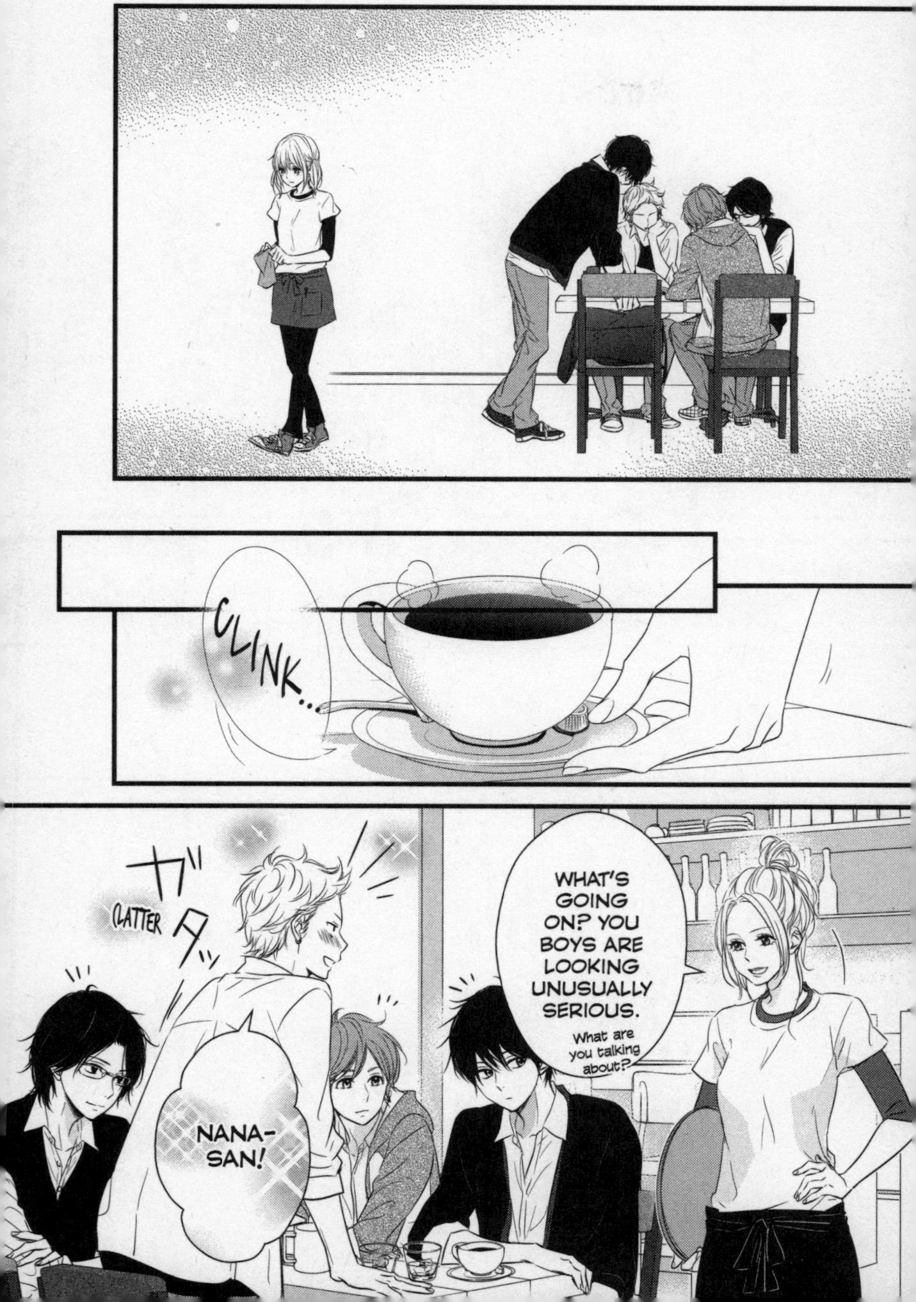
CLINK...
WHAT'S GOING ON? YOU BOYS ARE LOOKING UNUSUALLY SERIOUS.
What are you talking about?
NANA-SAN!
ガタッ
CLATTER

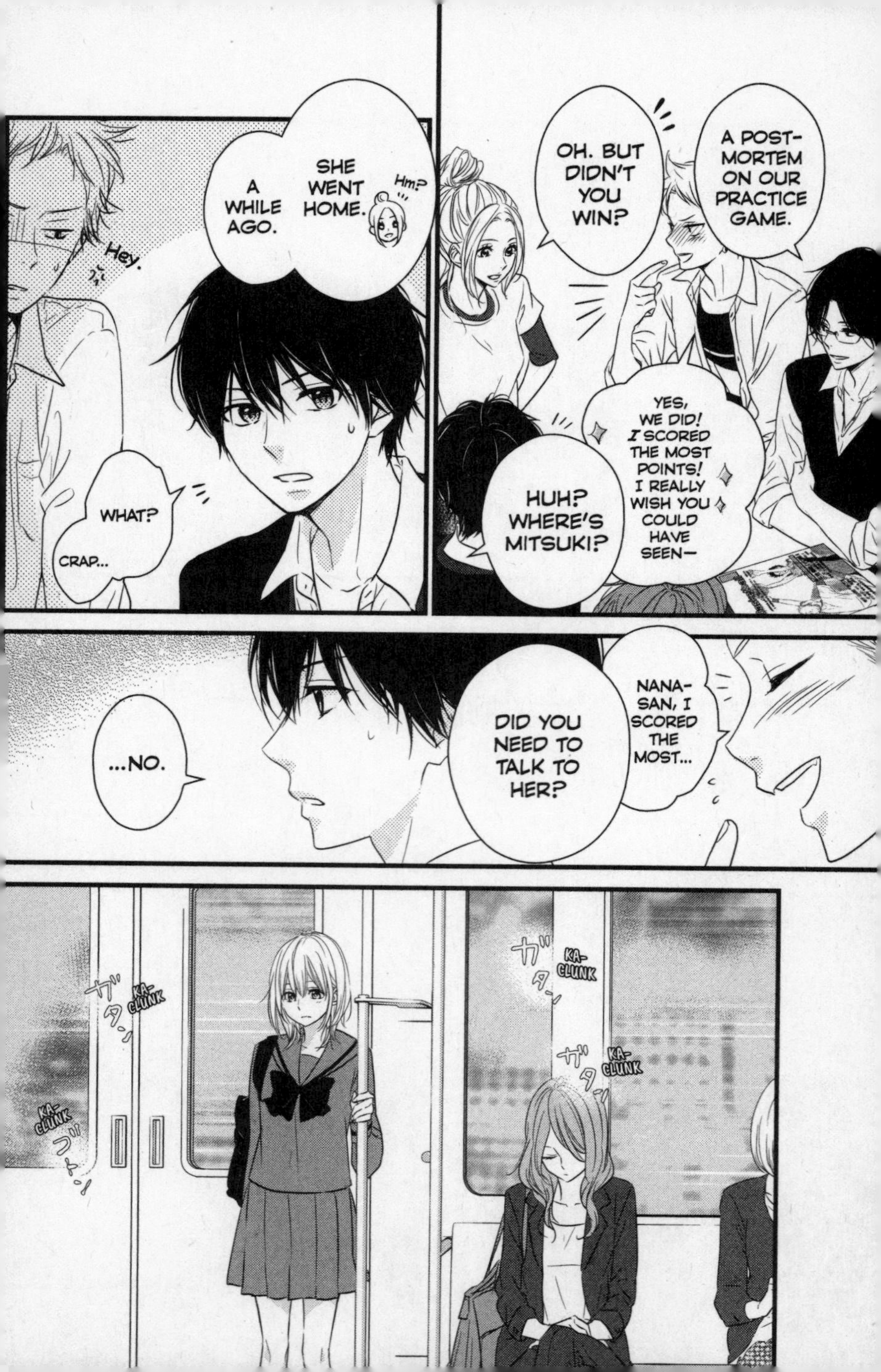
A POST-MORTEM ON OUR PRACTICE GAME.
OH. BUT DIDN'T YOU WIN?
YES, WE DID! I SCORED THE MOST POINTS! I REALLY WISH YOU COULD HAVE SEEN—
HUH? WHERE'S MITSUKI?
Hm?
SHE WENT HOME.
A WHILE AGO.
Hey.
WHAT?
CRAP...
NANA-SAN, I SCORED THE MOST...
DID YOU NEED TO TALK TO HER?
...NO.
KA-CLUNK
KA-CLUNK
KA-CLUNK
KA-CLUNK

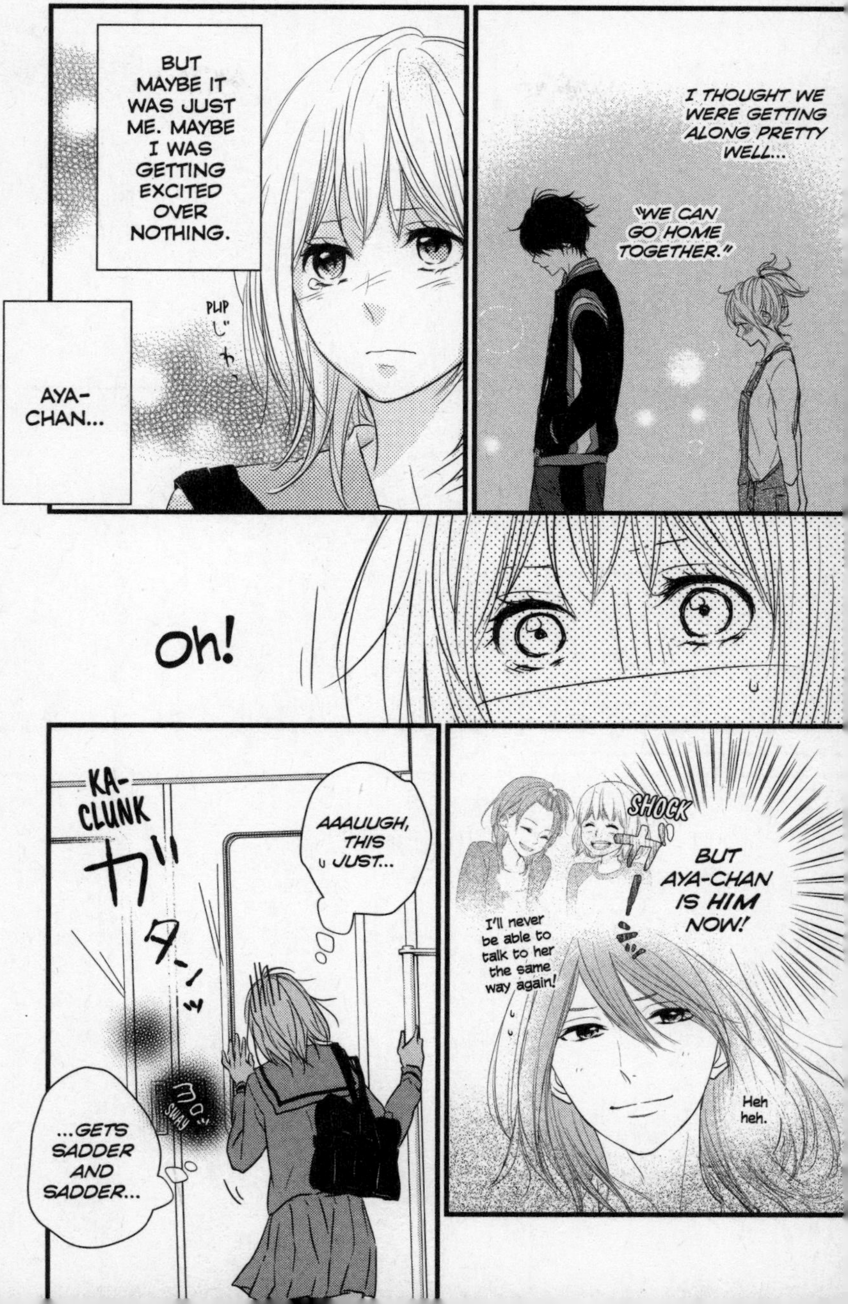
I THOUGHT WE WERE GETTING ALONG PRETTY WELL...
"WE CAN GO HOME TOGETHER."
BUT MAYBE IT WAS JUST ME. MAYBE I WAS GETTING EXCITED OVER NOTHING.
PLIP
AYA-CHAN...
Oh!
SHOCK
BUT AYA-CHAN IS HIM NOW!
I'll never be able to talk to her the same way again!
Heh heh.
KA-CLUNK
AAAUUGH, THIS JUST...
SWAY
...GETS SADDER AND SADDER...

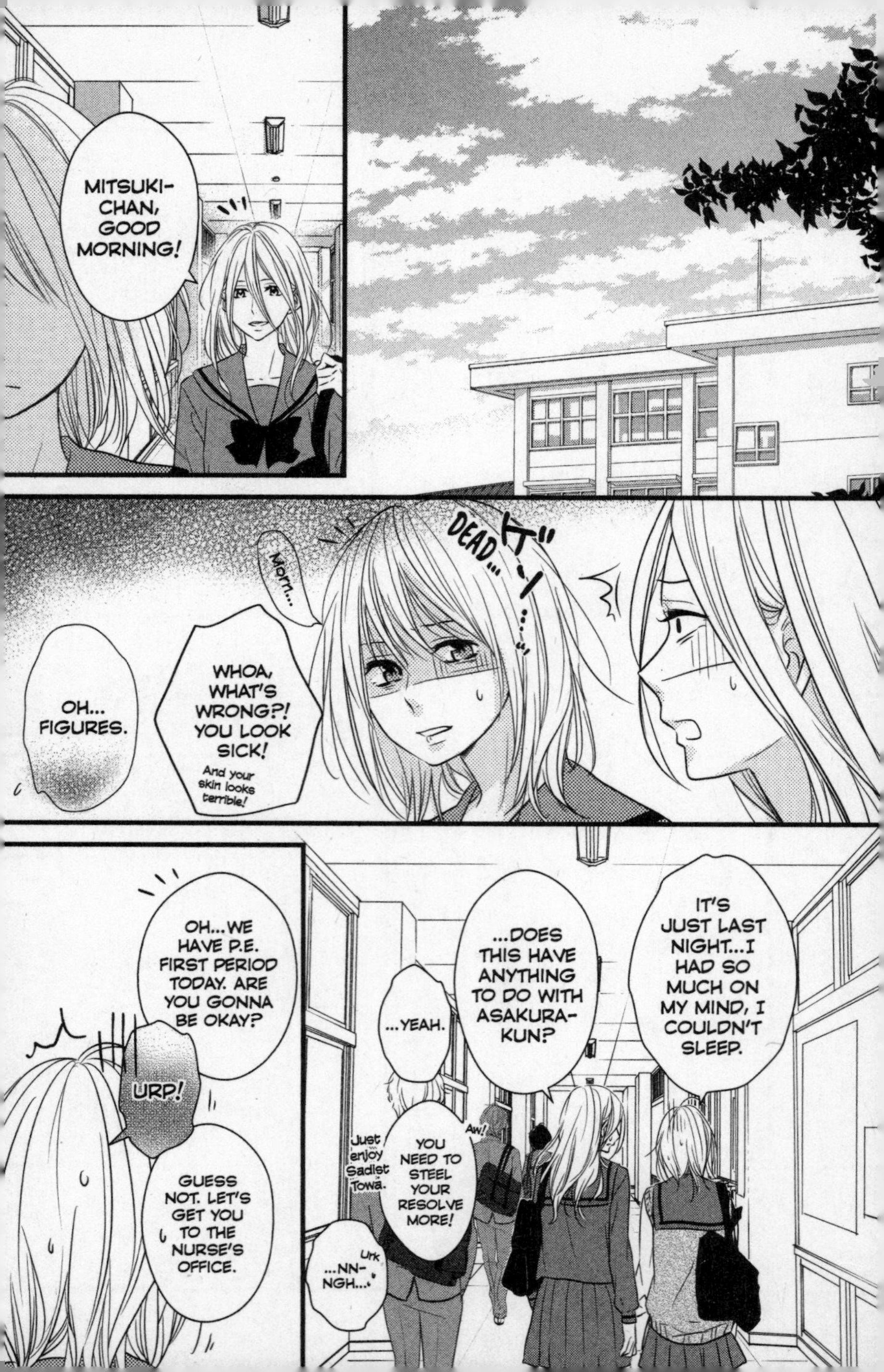
MITSUKI-CHAN, GOOD MORNING!
DEAD...
Morn...
WHOA, WHAT'S WRONG?! YOU LOOK SICK!
And your skin looks terrible!
OH... FIGURES.
IT'S JUST LAST NIGHT...I HAD SO MUCH ON MY MIND, I COULDN'T SLEEP.
...DOES THIS HAVE ANYTHING TO DO WITH ASAKURA-KUN?
...YEAH.
Aw!
YOU NEED TO STEEL YOUR RESOLVE MORE!
Just enjoy Sadist Towa.
Urk
...NN-NGH...
OH...WE HAVE P.E. FIRST PERIOD TODAY. ARE YOU GONNA BE OKAY?
URP!
GUESS NOT. LET'S GET YOU TO THE NURSE'S OFFICE.

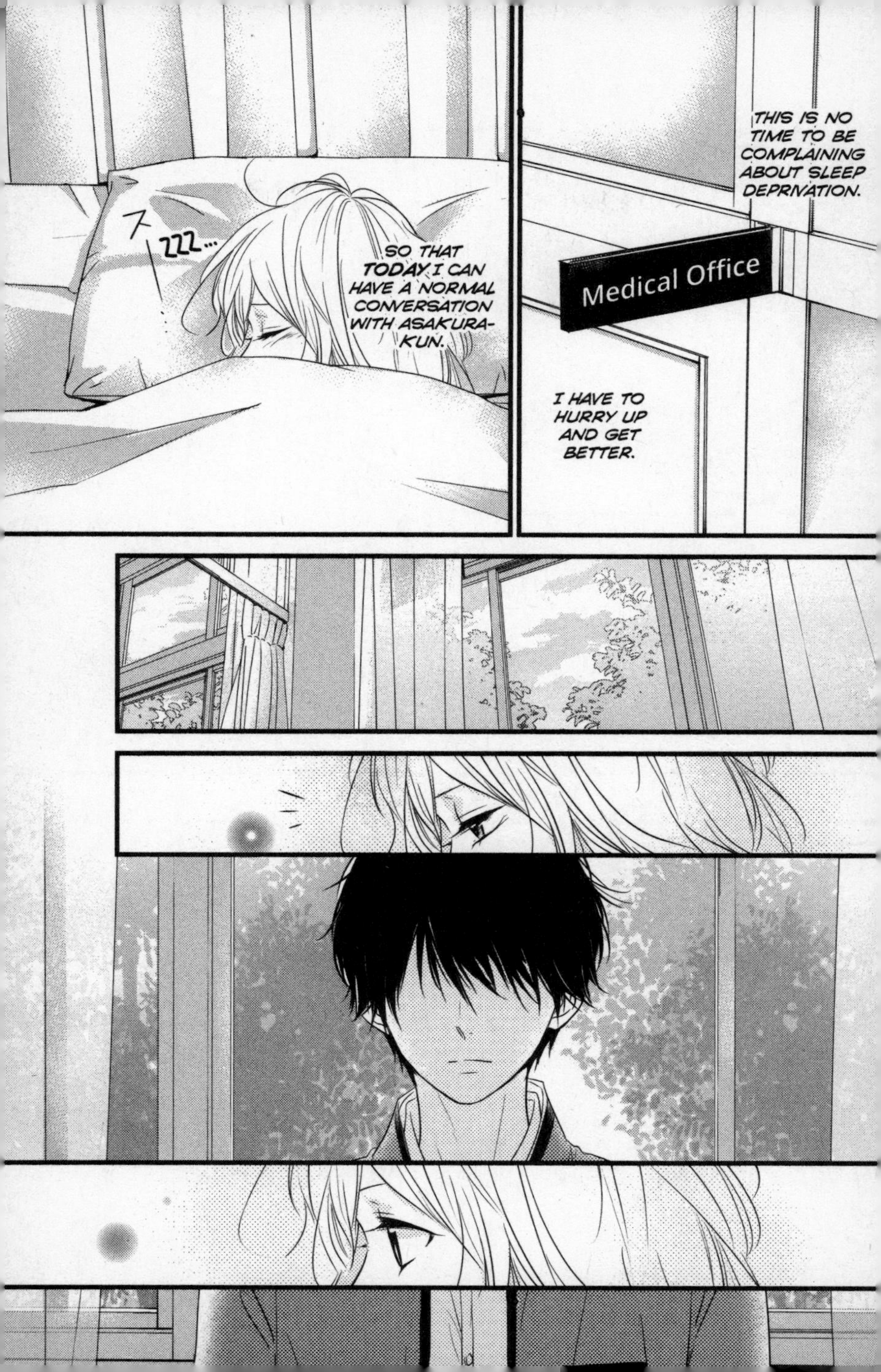
THIS IS NO TIME TO BE COMPLAINING ABOUT SLEEP DEPRIVATION.
Medical Office
I HAVE TO HURRY UP AND GET BETTER.
ZZZ...
SO THAT TODAY I CAN HAVE A NORMAL CONVERSATION WITH ASAKURA-KUN.

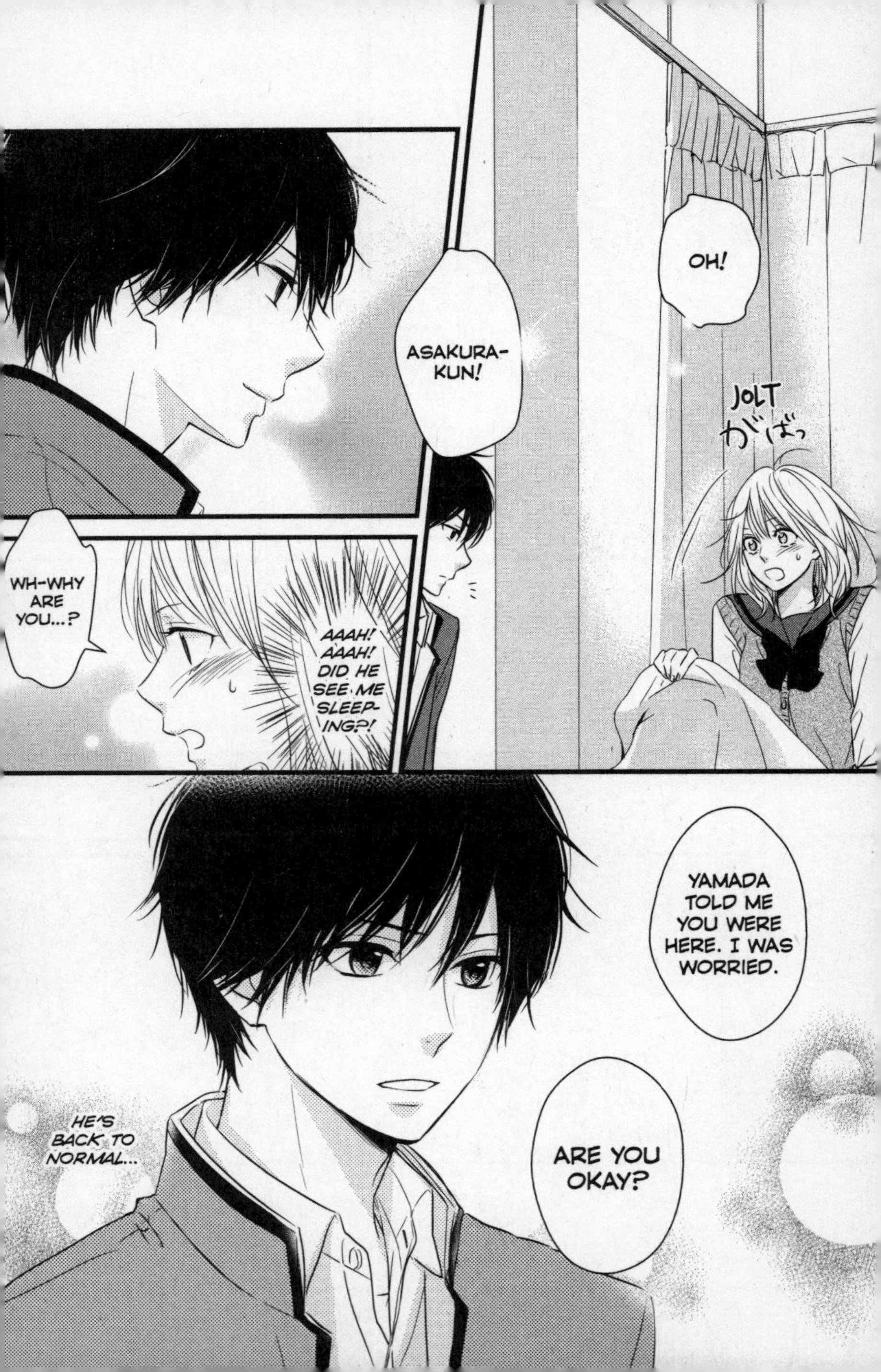
OH!
JOLT
がばっ
ASAKURA-KUN!
AAAH! AAAH! DID HE SEE ME SLEEPING?!
WH-WHY ARE YOU...?
YAMADA TOLD ME YOU WERE HERE. I WAS WORRIED.
ARE YOU OKAY?
HE'S BACK TO NORMAL...

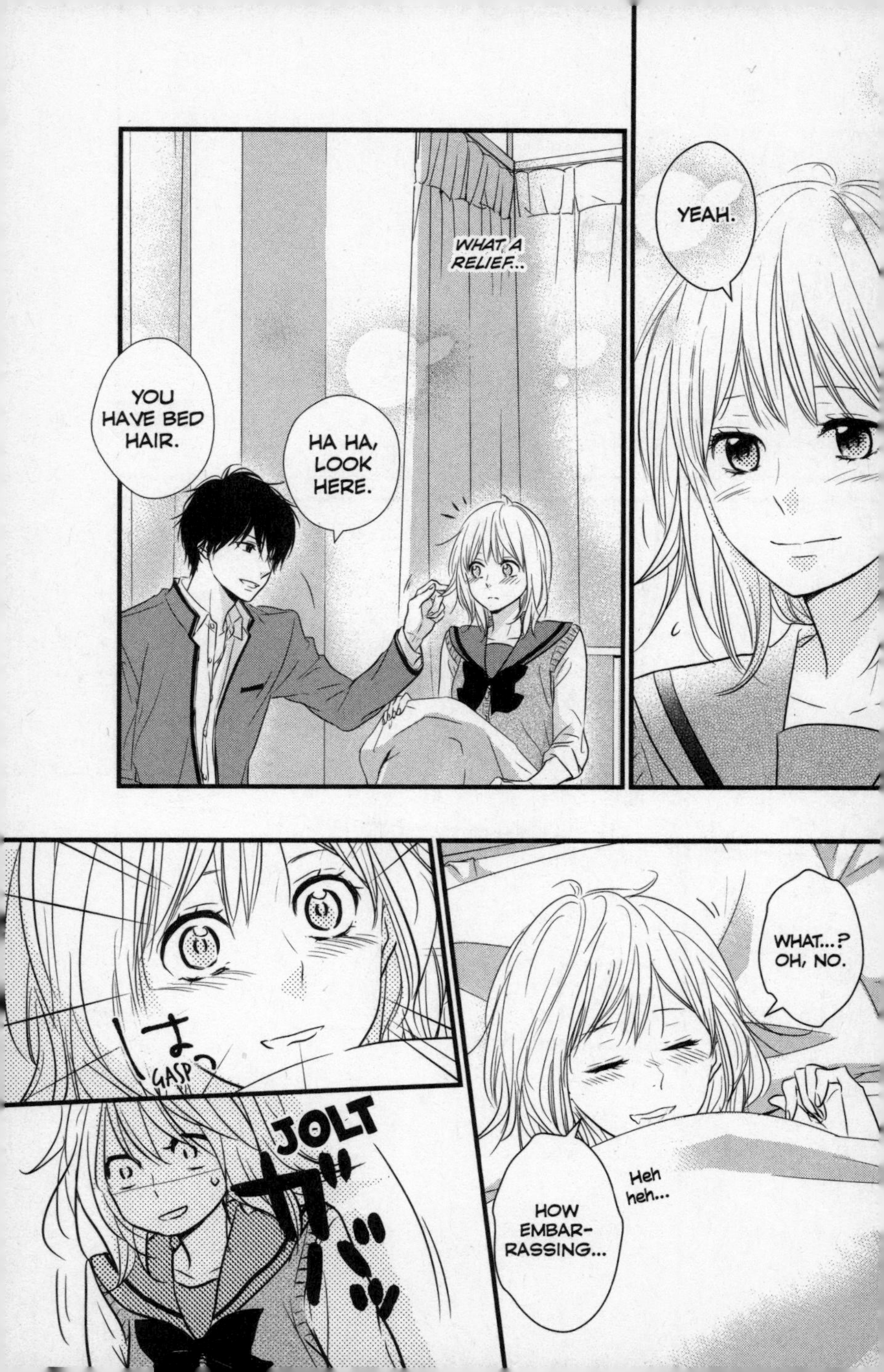
YEAH.
WHAT A RELIEF...
HA HA, LOOK HERE.
YOU HAVE BED HAIR.
WHAT...? OH, NO.
Heh heh...
HOW EMBARRASSING...
はっ
GASP
JOLT

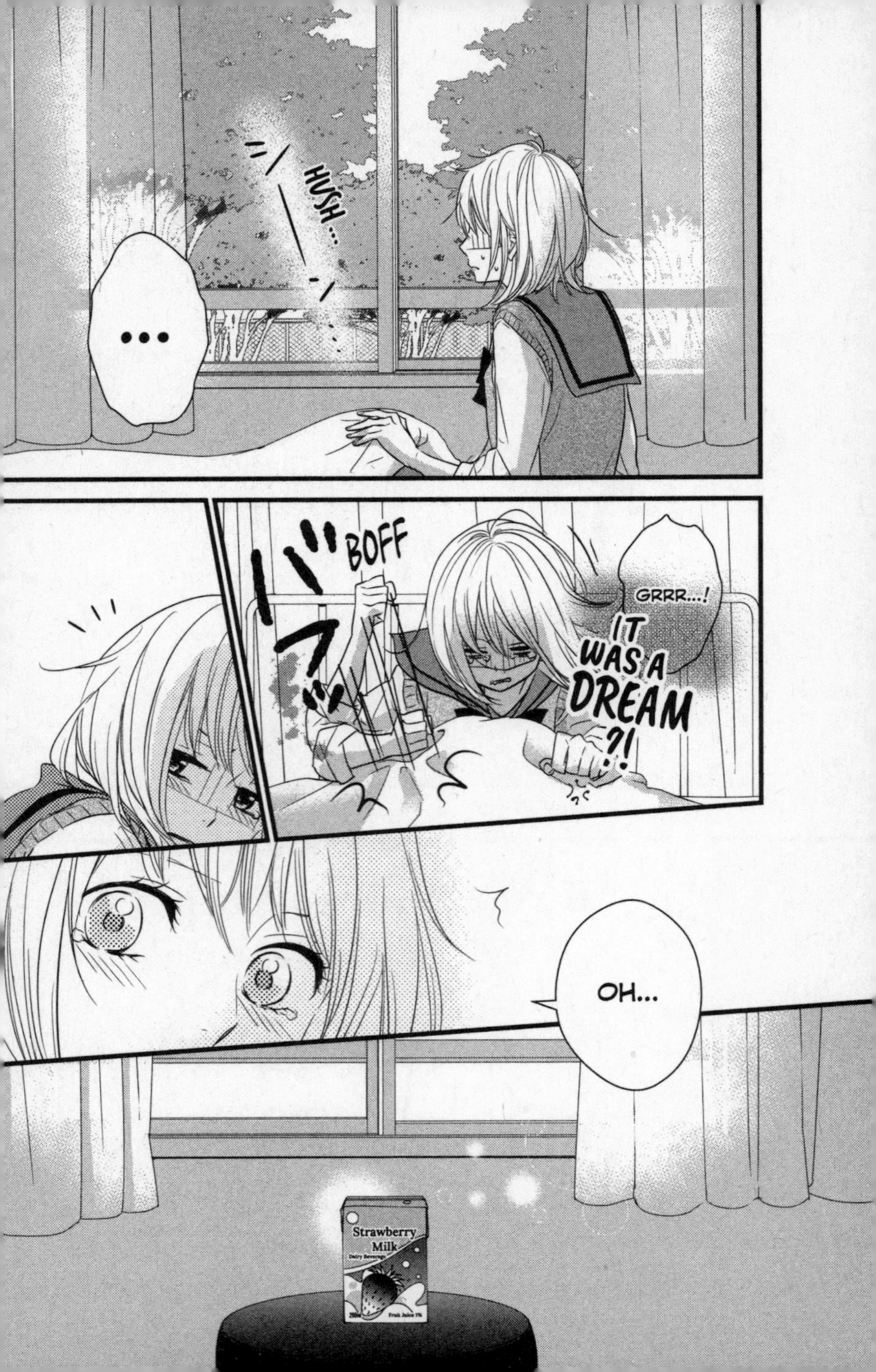
HUSH...
...
バッ
BOFF
GRRR...!
IT WAS A DREAM?!
OH...
Strawberry Milk
Dairy Beverage
Fruit Juice 1%

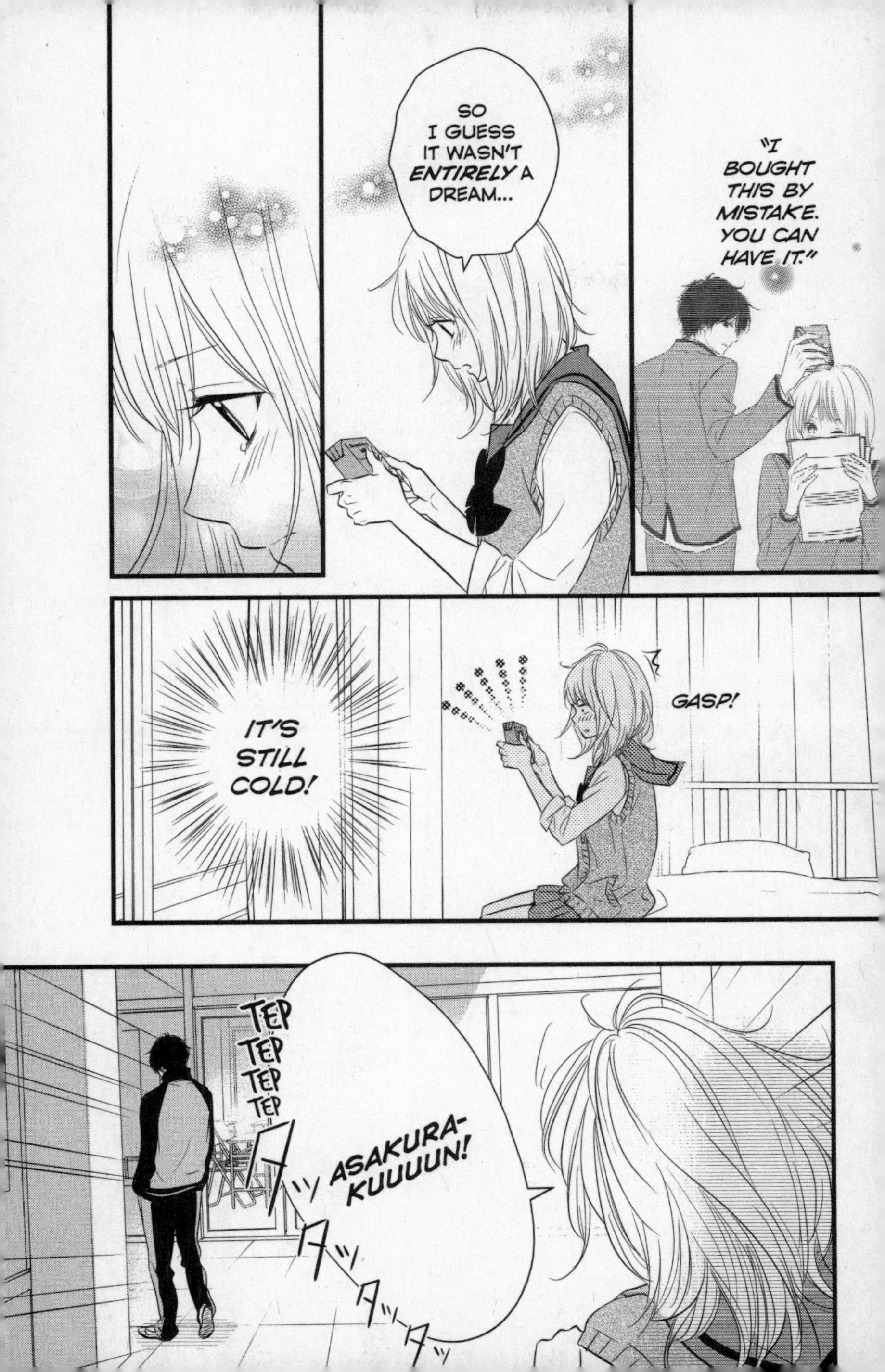
"I BOUGHT THIS BY MISTAKE. YOU CAN HAVE IT."
SO I GUESS IT WASN'T *ENTIRELY* A DREAM...
GASP!
IT'S STILL COLD!
ASAKURA-KUUUUN!
TEP TEP TEP TEP

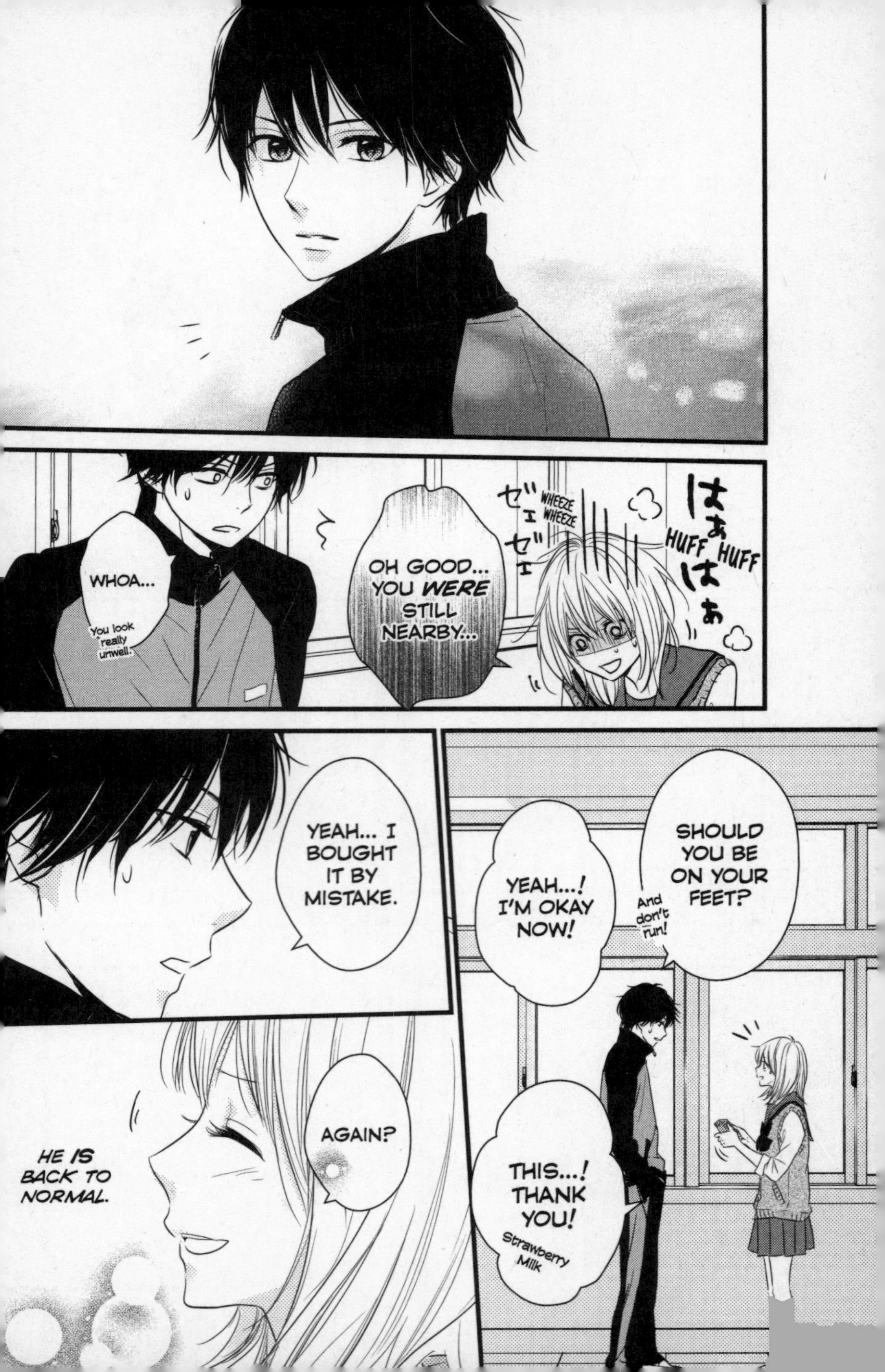
はぁはぁ
HUFF HUFF
ゼェゼェ
WHEEZE WHEEZE
OH GOOD... YOU *WERE* STILL NEARBY...
WHOA...
You look really unwell.
SHOULD YOU BE ON YOUR FEET?
And don't run!
YEAH...! I'M OKAY NOW!
THIS...! THANK YOU!
Strawberry Milk
YEAH... I BOUGHT IT BY MISTAKE.
AGAIN?
HE IS BACK TO NORMAL.

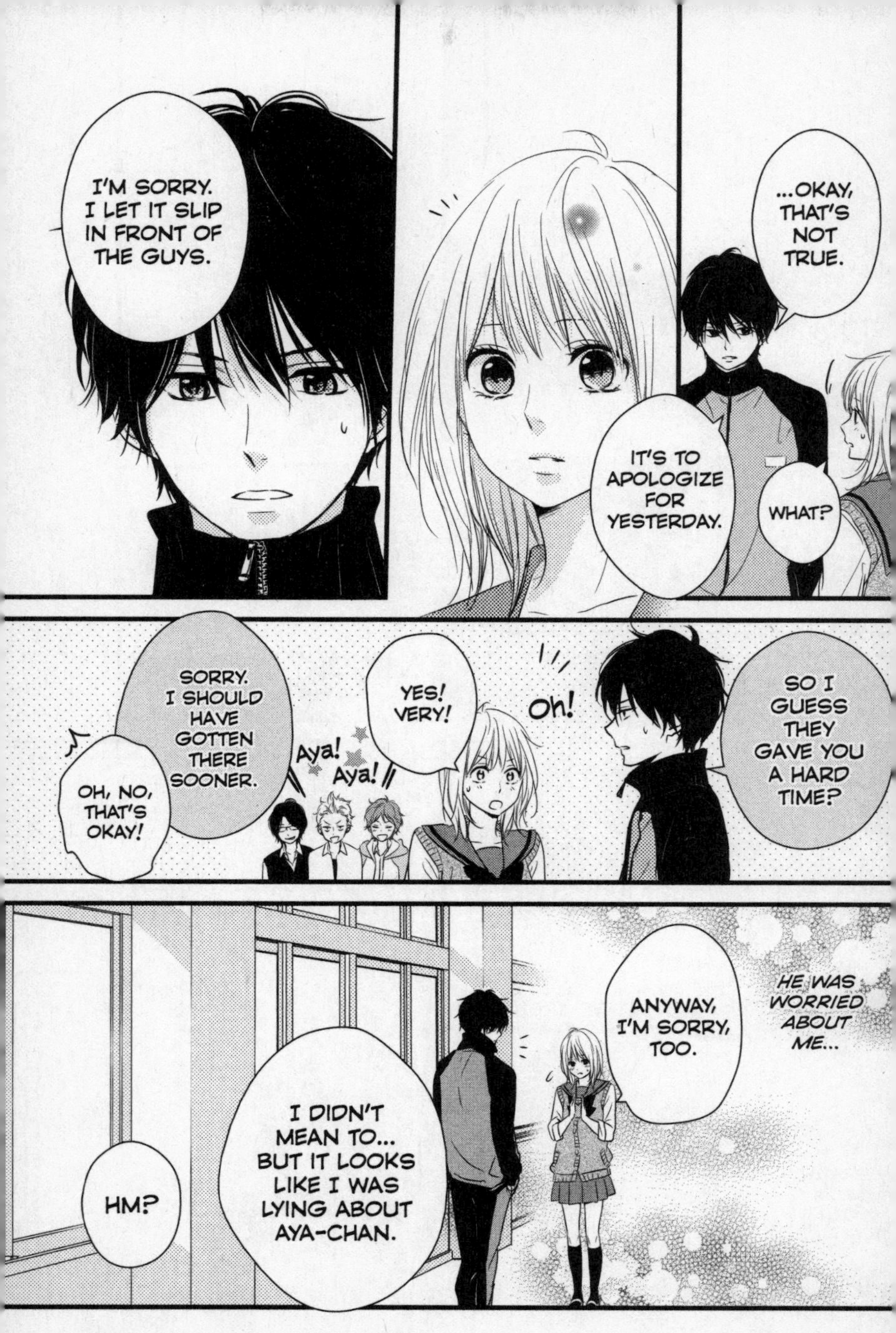
...OKAY, THAT'S NOT TRUE.
WHAT?
IT'S TO APOLOGIZE FOR YESTERDAY.
I'M SORRY. I LET IT SLIP IN FRONT OF THE GUYS.
SO I GUESS THEY GAVE YOU A HARD TIME?
Oh!
YES! VERY!
Aya!
Aya!
SORRY. I SHOULD HAVE GOTTEN THERE SOONER.
OH, NO, THAT'S OKAY!
HE WAS WORRIED ABOUT ME...
ANYWAY, I'M SORRY, TOO.
I DIDN'T MEAN TO... BUT IT LOOKS LIKE I WAS LYING ABOUT AYA-CHAN.
HM?

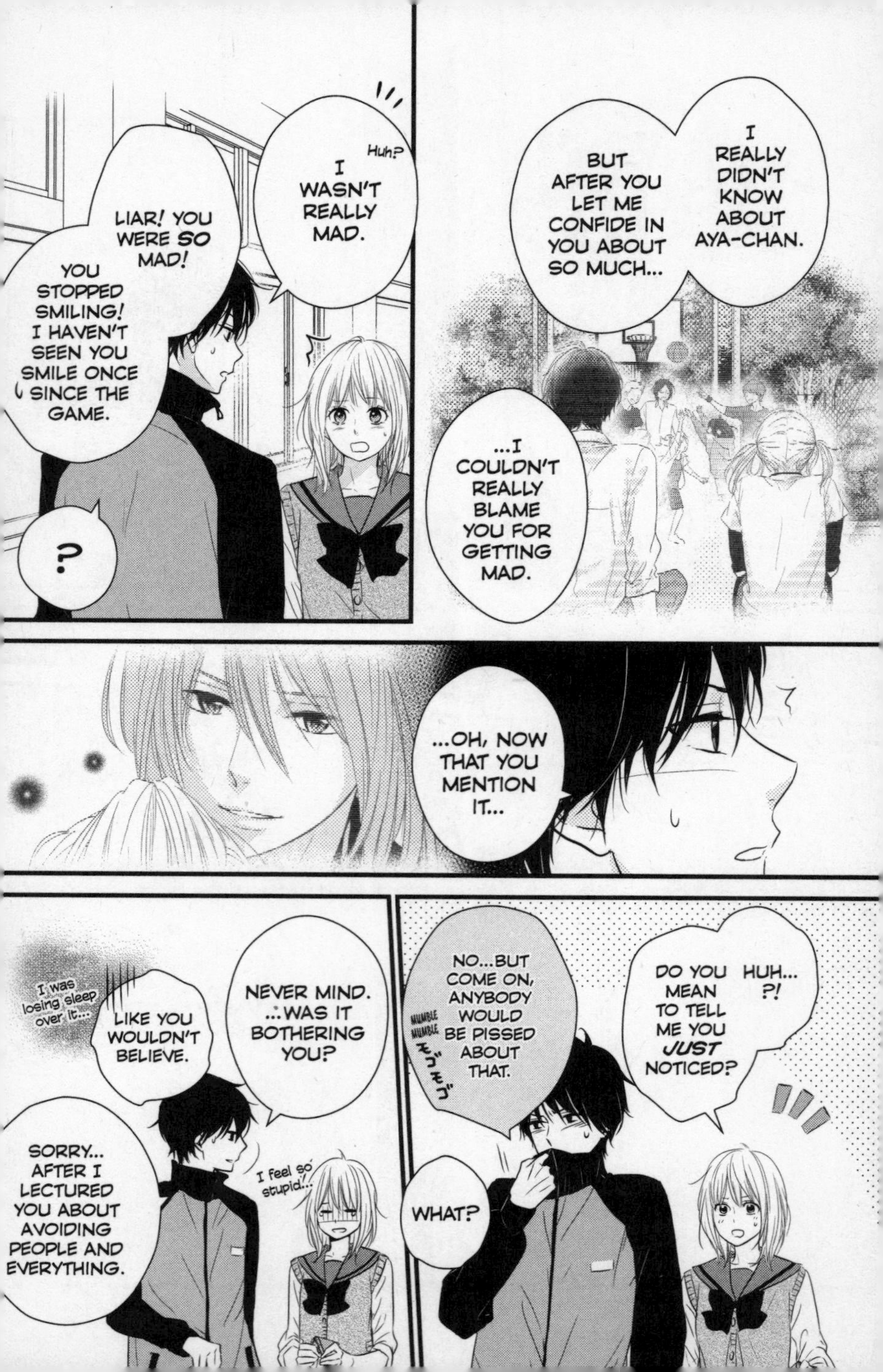
I REALLY DIDN'T KNOW ABOUT AYA-CHAN.
BUT AFTER YOU LET ME CONFIDE IN YOU ABOUT SO MUCH...
...I COULDN'T REALLY BLAME YOU FOR GETTING MAD.
Huh?
I WASN'T REALLY MAD.
LIAR! YOU WERE SO MAD!
YOU STOPPED SMILING! I HAVEN'T SEEN YOU SMILE ONCE SINCE THE GAME.
?
...OH, NOW THAT YOU MENTION IT...
HUH...?!
DO YOU MEAN TO TELL ME YOU JUST NOTICED?
NO...BUT COME ON, ANYBODY WOULD BE PISSED ABOUT THAT.
MUMBLE MUMBLE
WHAT?
NEVER MIND. ...WAS IT BOTHERING YOU?
I was losing sleep over it...
LIKE YOU WOULDN'T BELIEVE.
SORRY... AFTER I LECTURED YOU ABOUT AVOIDING PEOPLE AND EVERYTHING.
I feel so stupid...

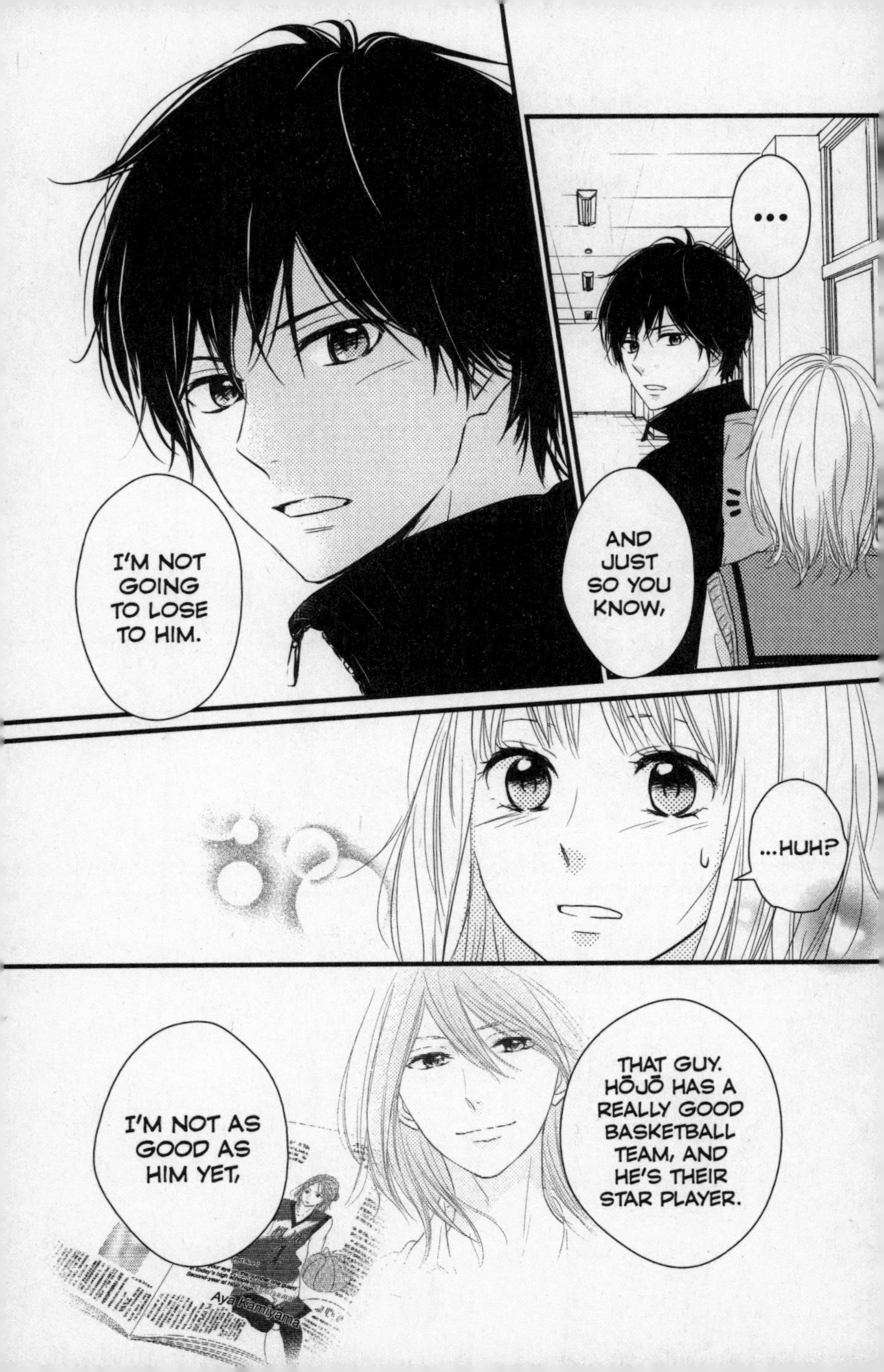
...
AND JUST SO YOU KNOW,
I'M NOT GOING TO LOSE TO HIM.
...HUH?
THAT GUY. HŌJŌ HAS A REALLY GOOD BASKETBALL TEAM, AND HE'S THEIR STAR PLAYER.
I'M NOT AS GOOD AS HIM YET,
Aya Kamiyama

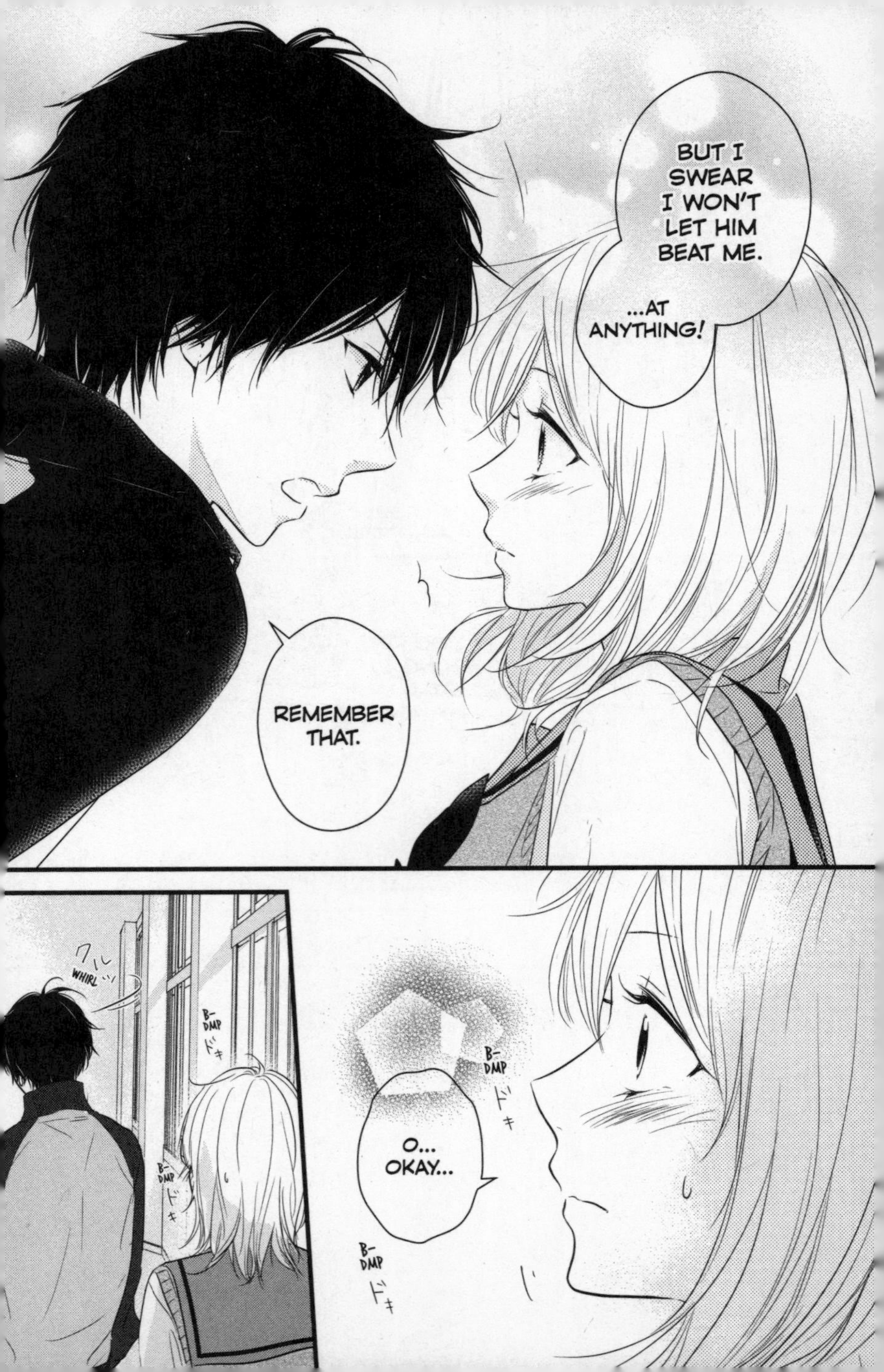
BUT I SWEAR I WON'T LET HIM BEAT ME.
...AT ANYTHING!
REMEMBER THAT.
B-DMP
ドキ
O... OKAY...
B-DMP
ドキ
WHIRL
B-DMP
ドキ
B-DMP
ドキ

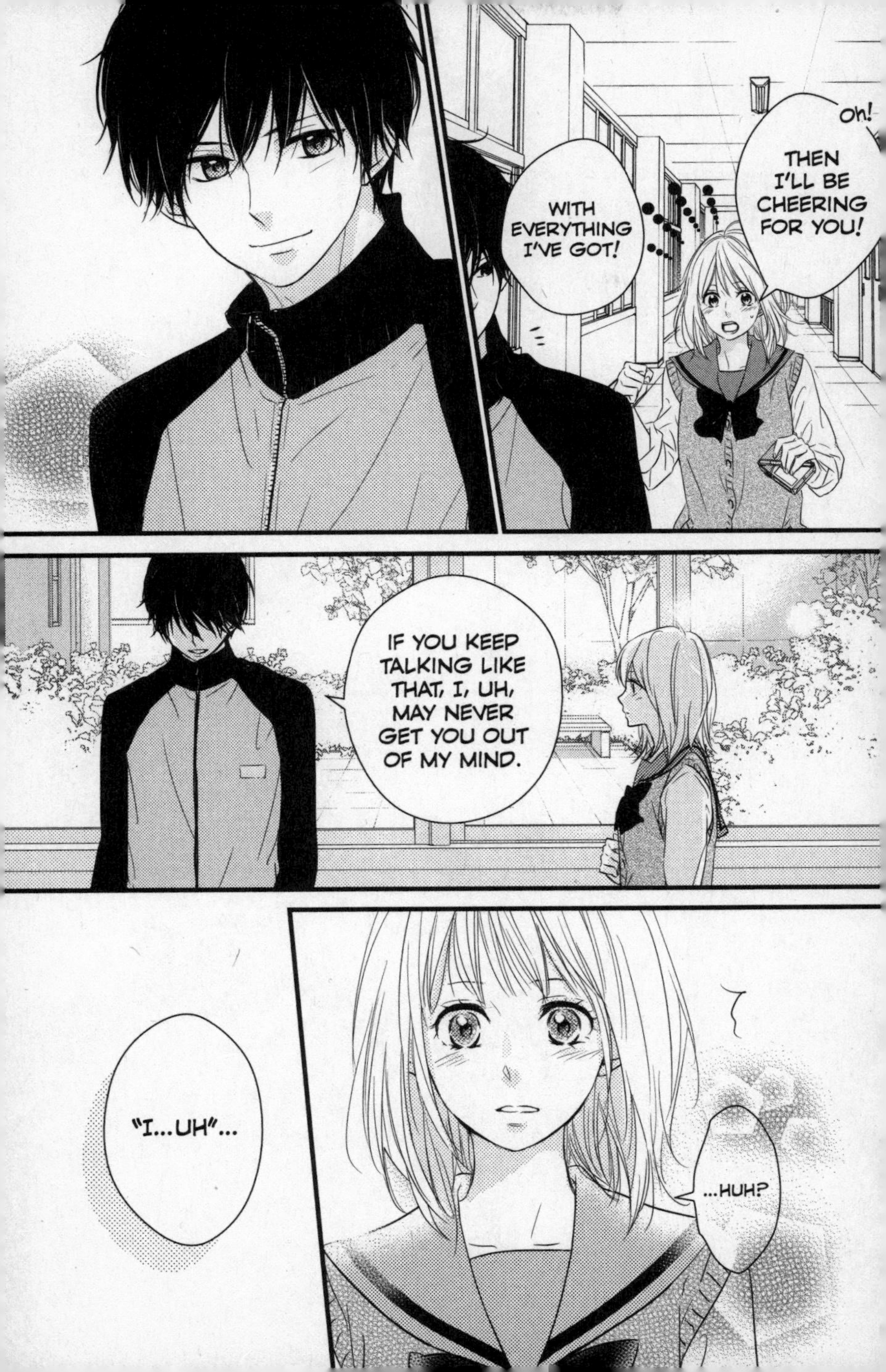
Oh!
THEN I'LL BE CHEERING FOR YOU!
WITH EVERYTHING I'VE GOT!
IF YOU KEEP TALKING LIKE THAT, I, UH, MAY NEVER GET YOU OUT OF MY MIND.
...HUH?
"I...UH"...

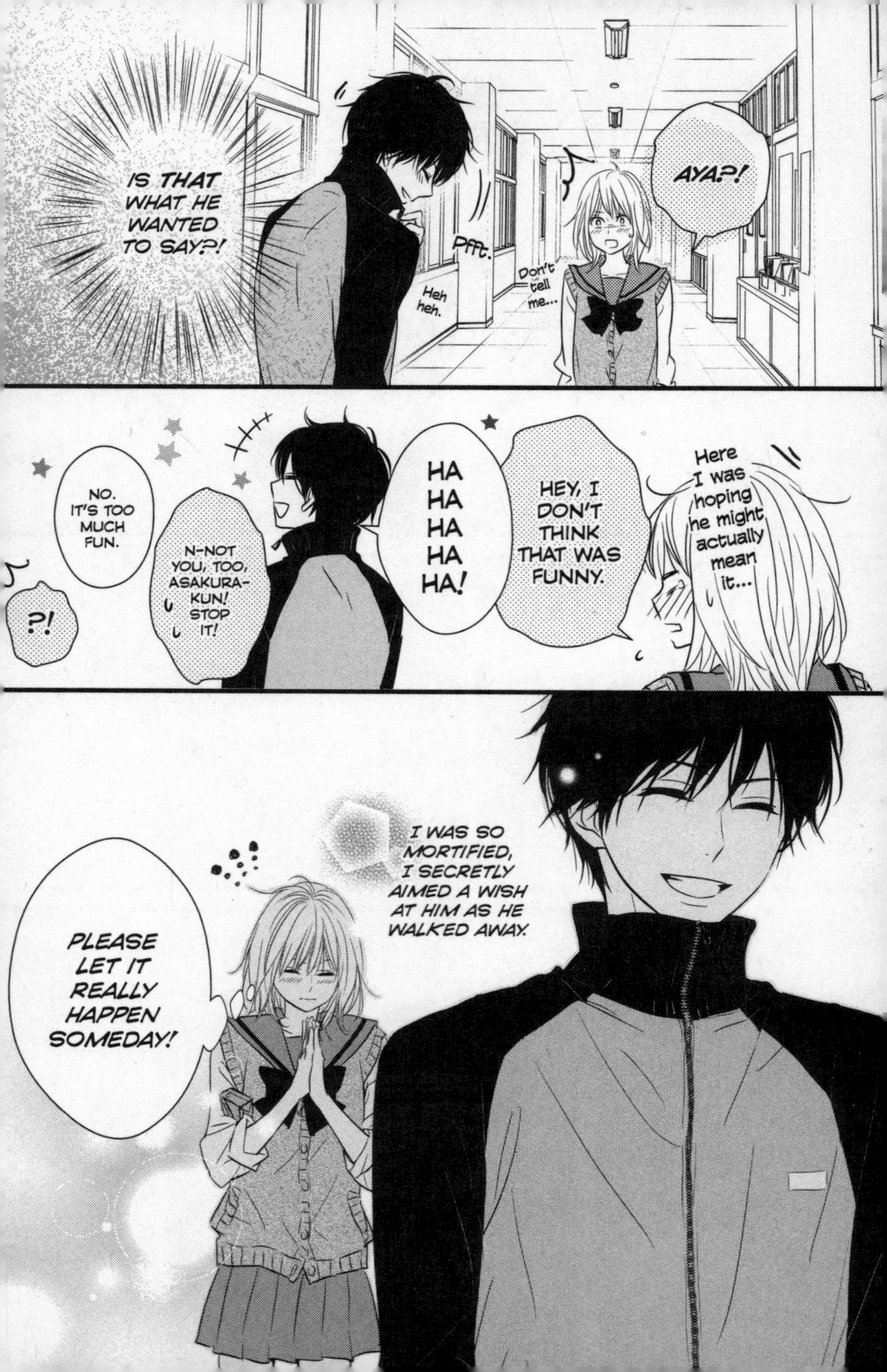
AYA?!
Don't tell me...
Pfft.
Heh heh.
IS THAT WHAT HE WANTED TO SAY?!
Here I was hoping he might actually mean it...
HEY, I DON'T THINK THAT WAS FUNNY.
HA HA HA HA HA!
N-NOT YOU, TOO, ASAKURA-KUN! STOP IT!
NO. IT'S TOO MUCH FUN.
?!
I WAS SO MORTIFIED, I SECRETLY AIMED A WISH AT HIM AS HE WALKED AWAY.
PLEASE LET IT REALLY HAPPEN SOMEDAY!

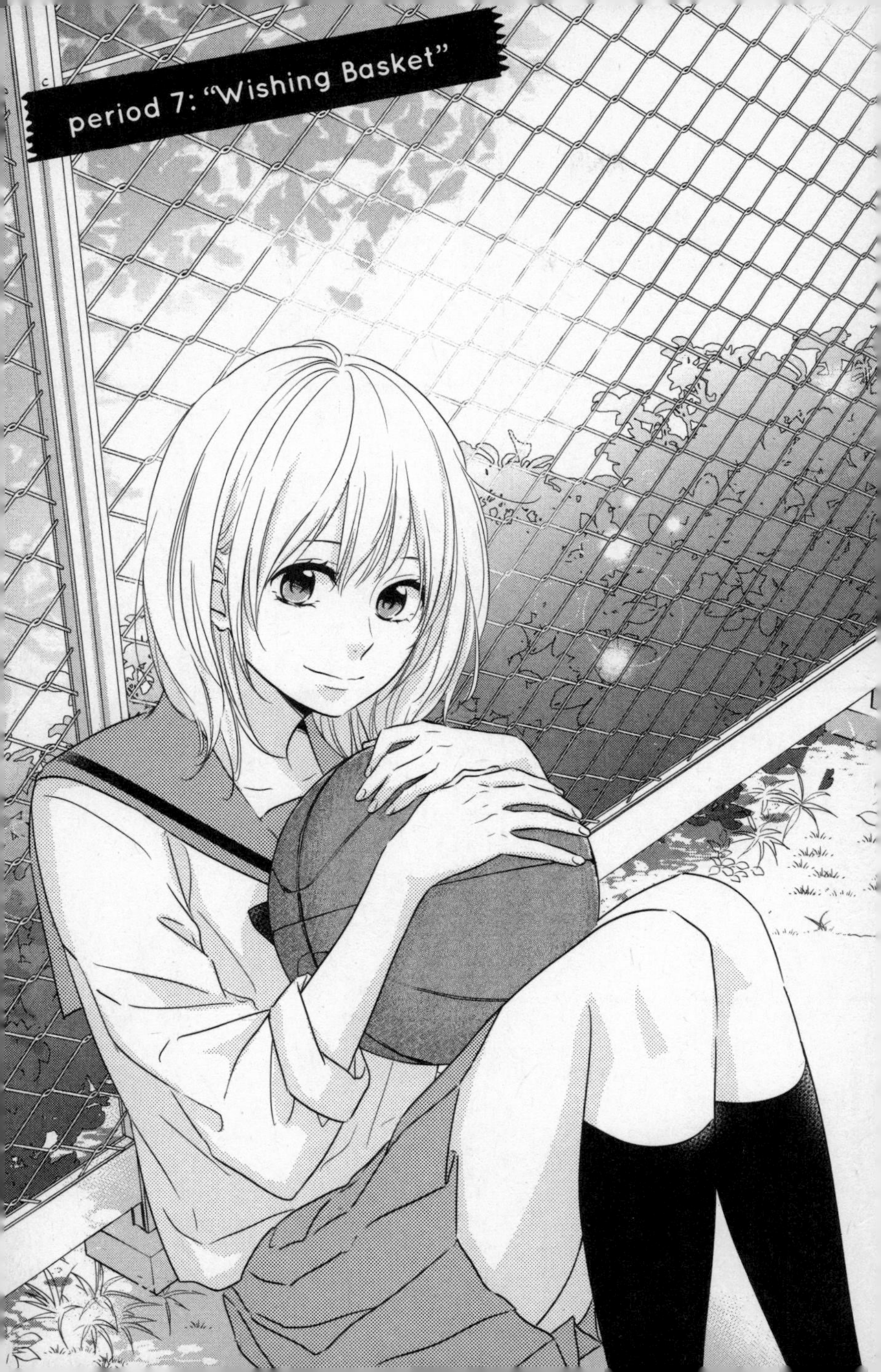
period 7: "Wishing Basket"

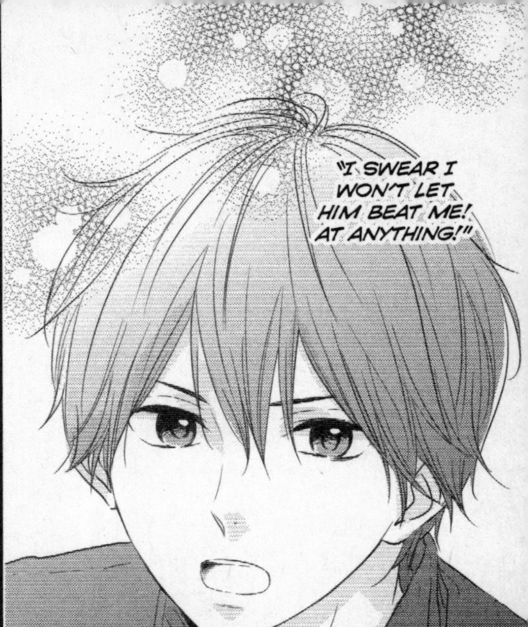
"I SWEAR I WON'T LET HIM BEAT ME! AT ANYTHING!"
"REMEMBER THAT."

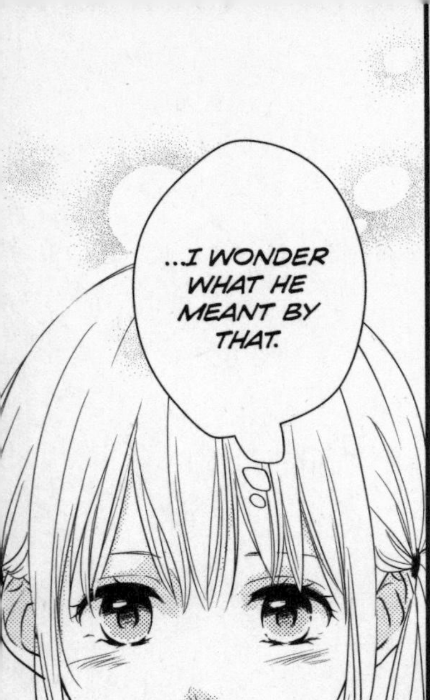
...I WONDER WHAT HE MEANT BY THAT.
CLINK...

Rui Miyamoto	175cm/60kg	Blood type	Born	Favorite food:
	[5'9"/132lbs.]	B	February 14	cream puffs

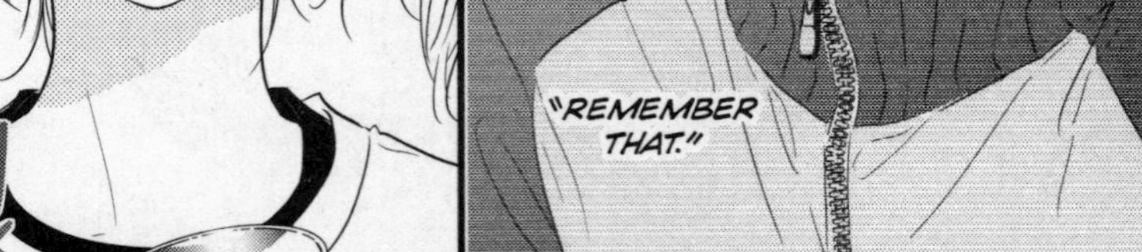
I'm not even really in the story, but I got the cover! Woohoo ☆
I like him; he's the easiest to draw.
Anashin

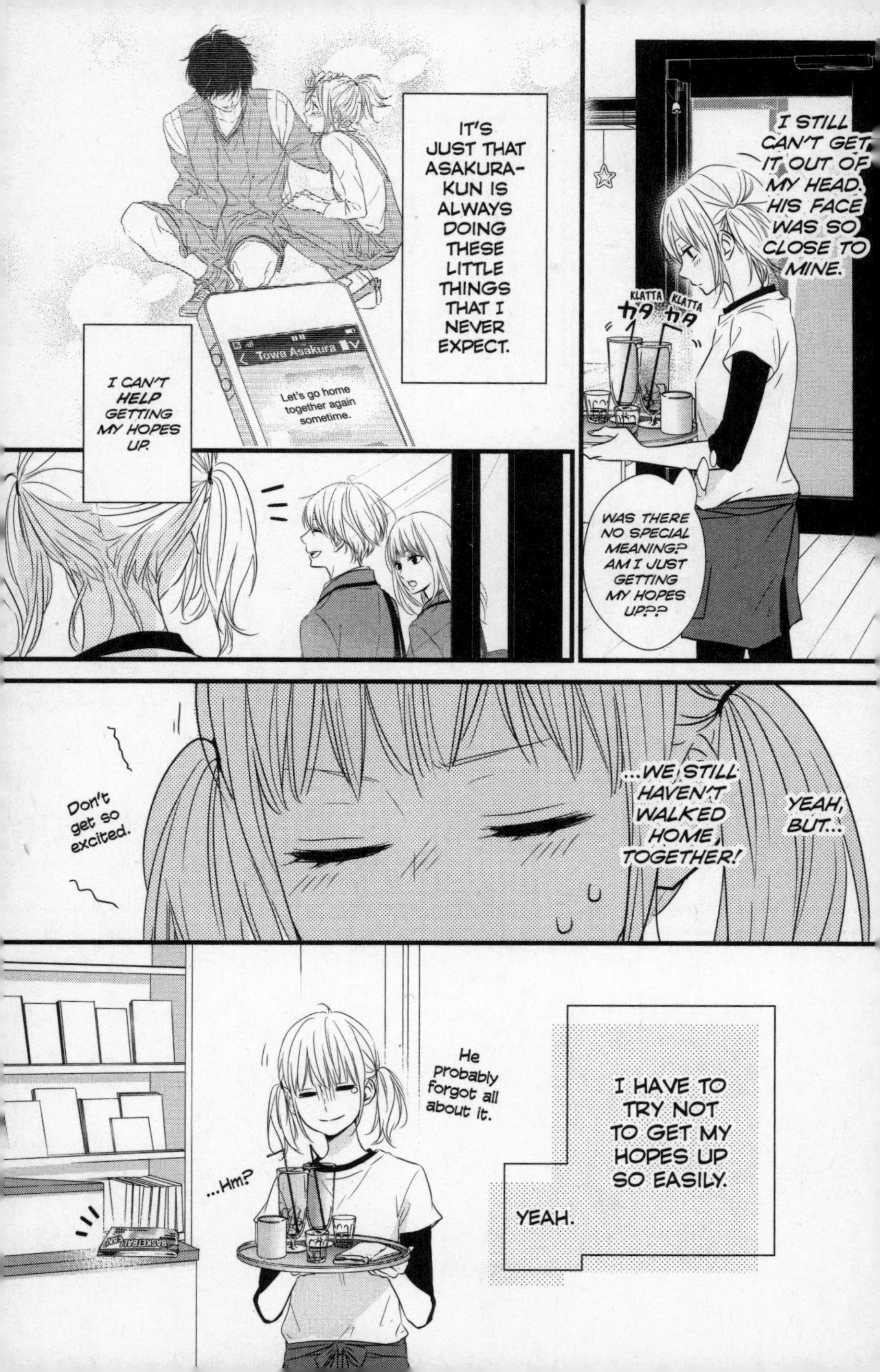
I STILL CAN'T GET IT OUT OF MY HEAD. HIS FACE WAS SO CLOSE TO MINE.
KLATTA カタ
KLATTA カタ
WAS THERE NO SPECIAL MEANING? AM I JUST GETTING MY HOPES UP??
IT'S JUST THAT ASAKURA-KUN IS ALWAYS DOING THESE LITTLE THINGS THAT I NEVER EXPECT.
Towa Asakura
Let's go home together again sometime.
I CAN'T HELP GETTING MY HOPES UP.
YEAH, BUT...
...WE STILL HAVEN'T WALKED HOME TOGETHER!
Don't get so excited.
I HAVE TO TRY NOT TO GET MY HOPES UP SO EASILY.
YEAH.
He probably forgot all about it.
...Hm?

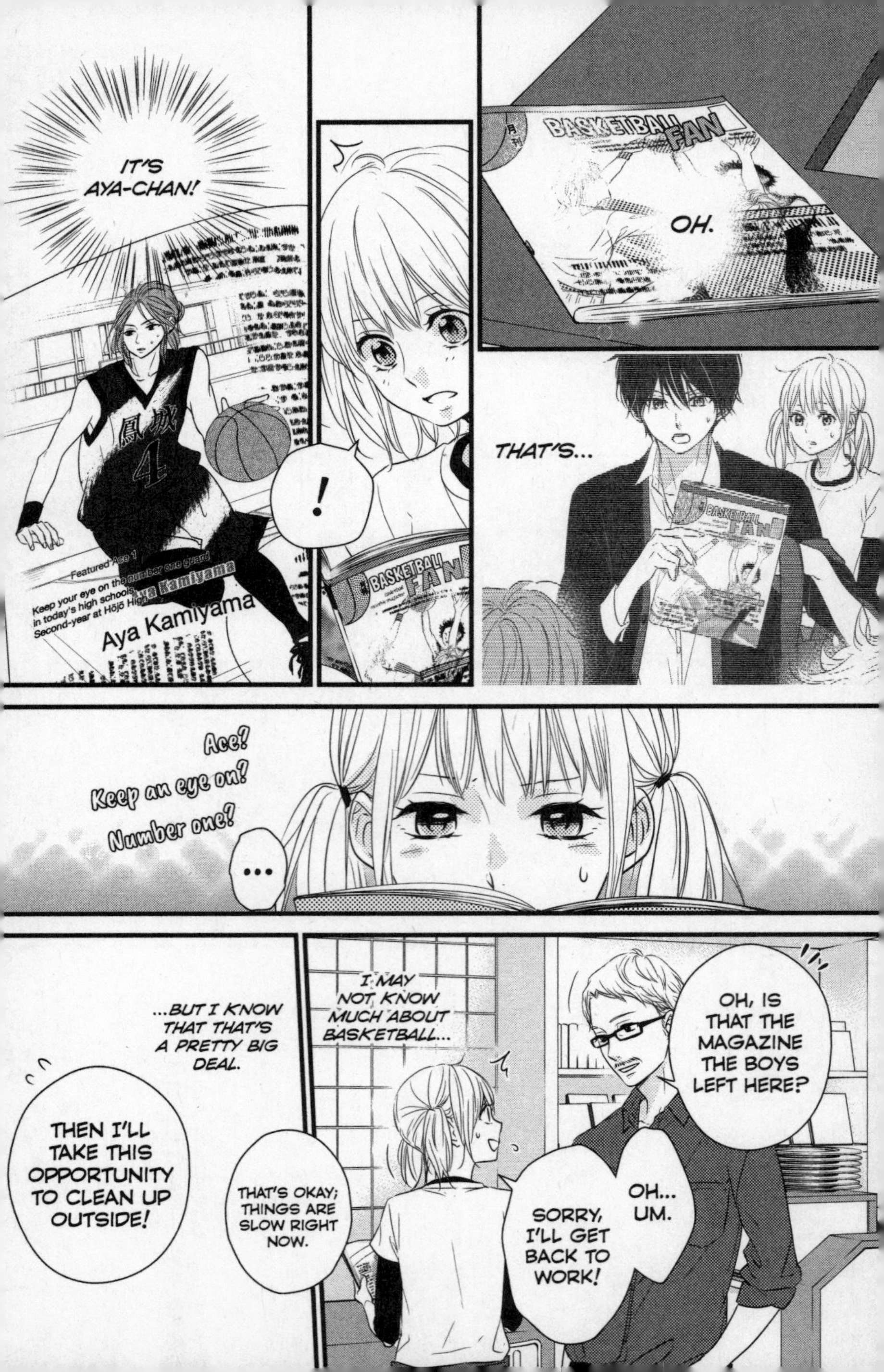
BASKETBALL FAN
OH.
BASKETBALL FAN
THAT'S...
!
BASKETBALL FAN
IT'S AYA-CHAN!
Featured Ace 1
Keep your eye on the number one guard
in today's high schools.
Second-year at Hōjō High
Aya Kamiyama
Ace?
Keep an eye on?
Number one?
...
OH, IS THAT THE MAGAZINE THE BOYS LEFT HERE?
OH... UM.
SORRY, I'LL GET BACK TO WORK!
THAT'S OKAY; THINGS ARE SLOW RIGHT NOW.
I MAY NOT KNOW MUCH ABOUT BASKETBALL...
...BUT I KNOW THAT THAT'S A PRETTY BIG DEAL.
THEN I'LL TAKE THIS OPPORTUNITY TO CLEAN UP OUTSIDE!

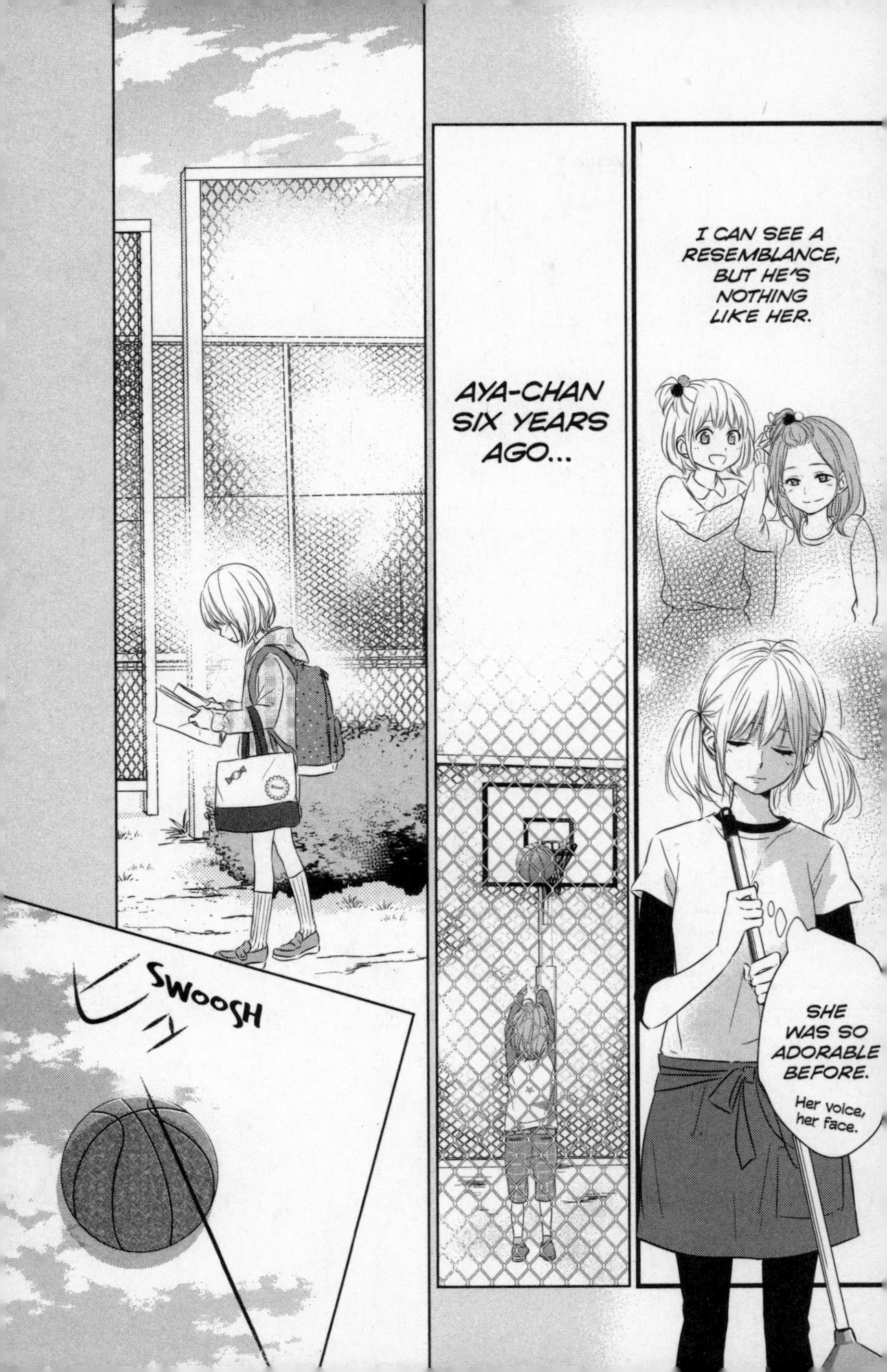
I CAN SEE A RESEMBLANCE, BUT HE'S NOTHING LIKE HER.
SHE WAS SO ADORABLE BEFORE.
Her voice, her face.
AYA-CHAN SIX YEARS AGO...
SWOOSH

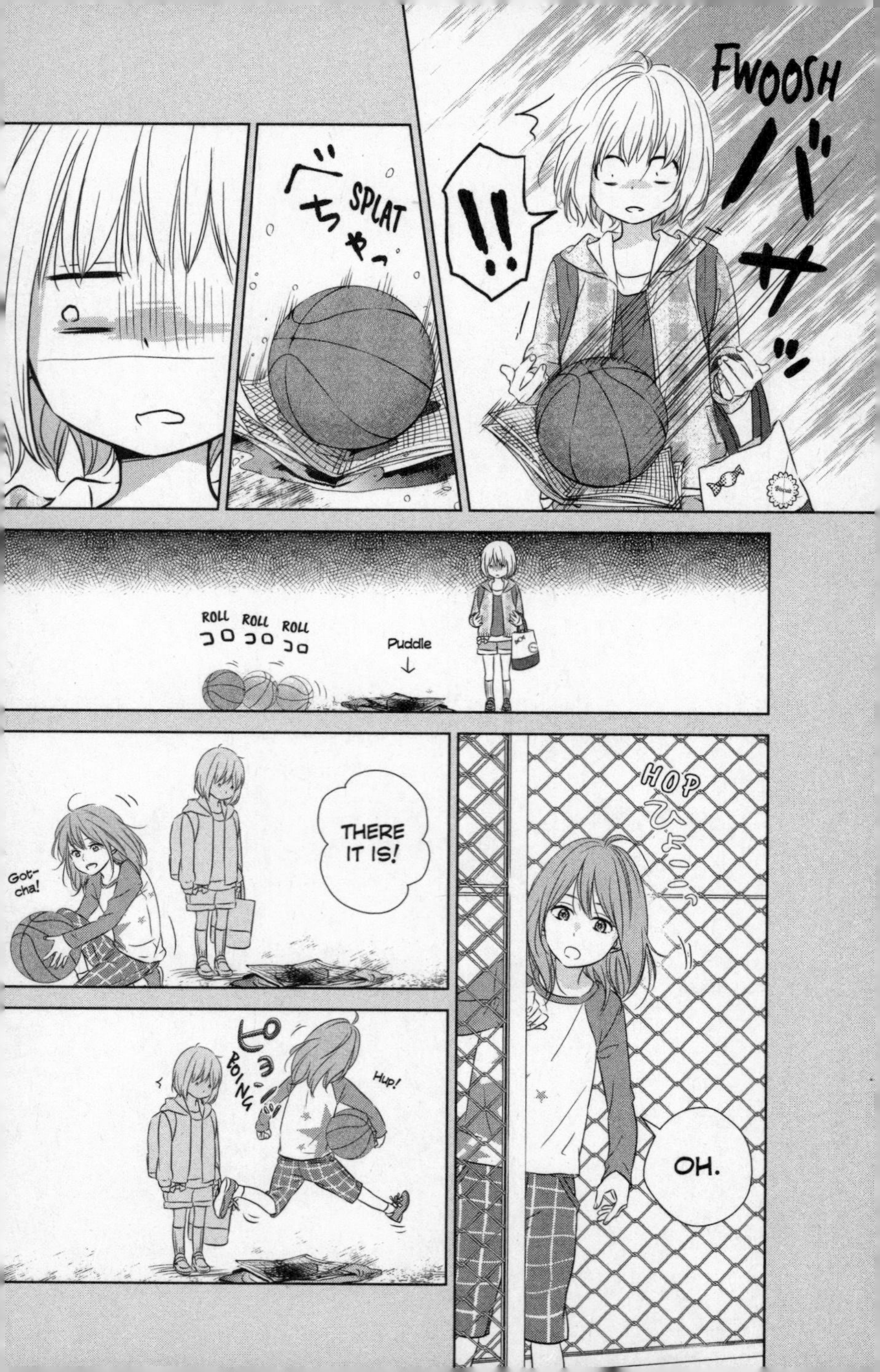
FWOOSH
バサッ
!!
SPLAT
べちゃっ
ROLL ROLL ROLL
コロコロコロ
Puddle
HOP
ひょこっ
OH.
THERE IT IS!
Got-cha!
ピョ
BOING
Hup!

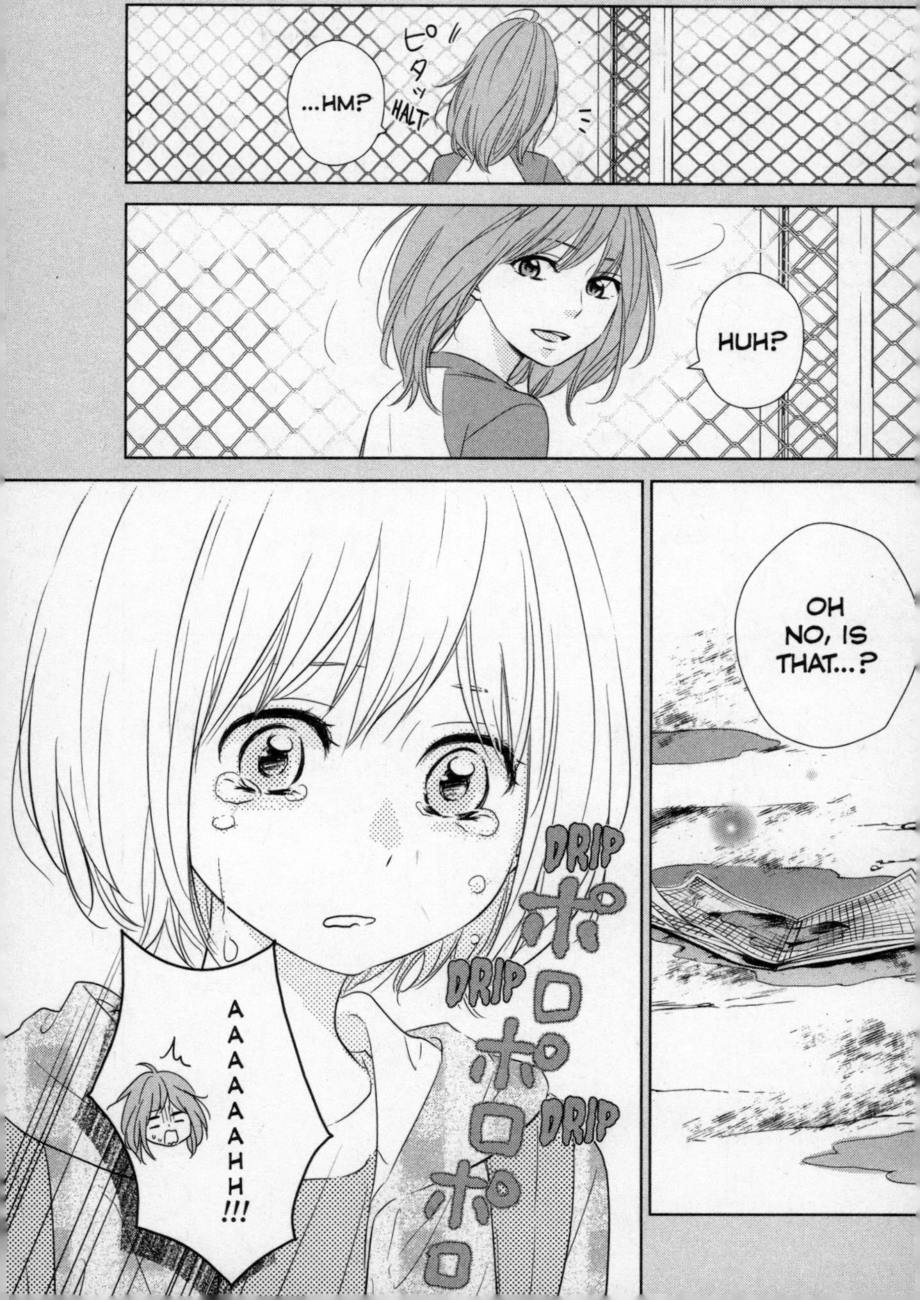
ピタッ
HALT
...HM?
HUH?
OH NO, IS THAT...?
DRIP
DRIP
DRIP
ポロポロポロ
AAAAAAAAAHH!!!

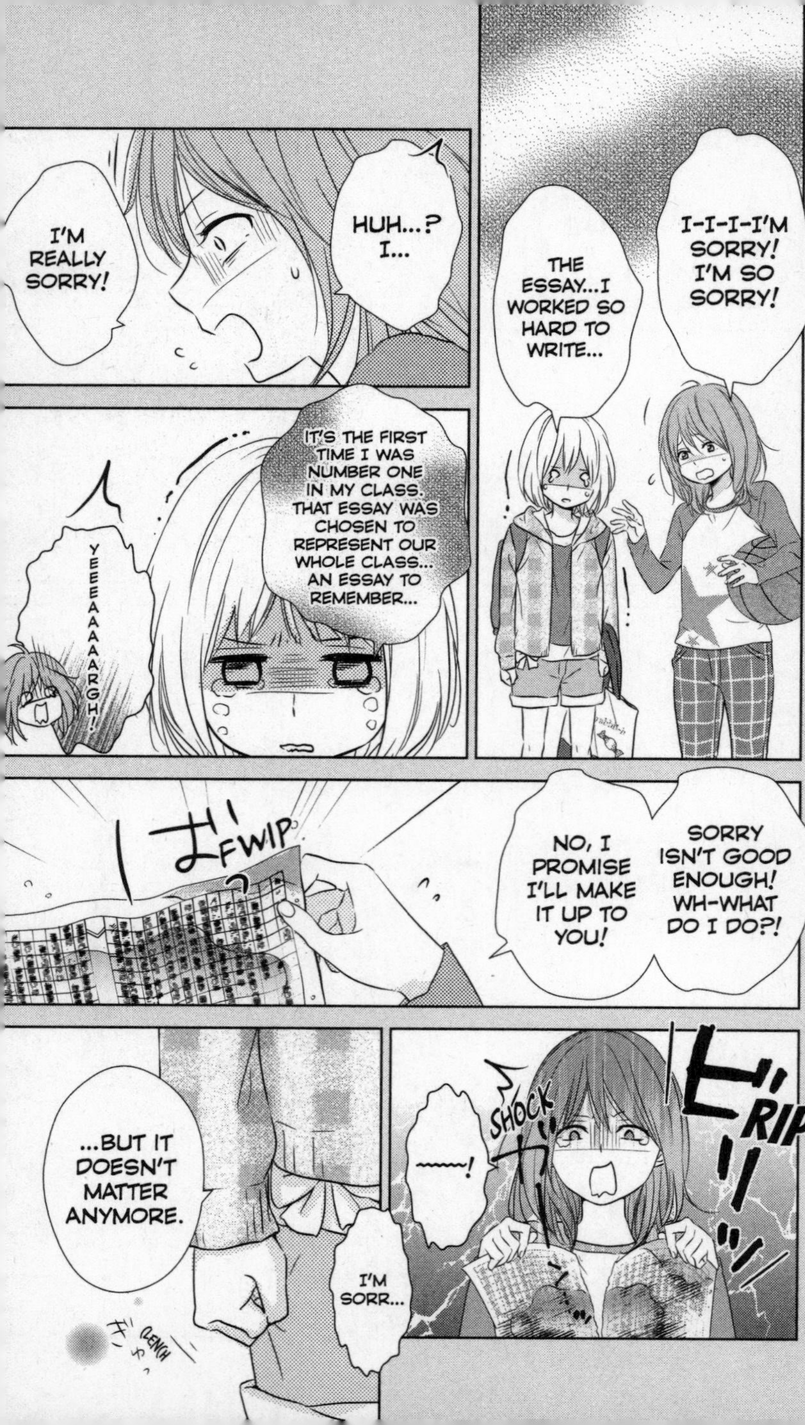
I-I-I-I'M SORRY! I'M SO SORRY!
THE ESSAY...I WORKED SO HARD TO WRITE...
HUH...? I...
I'M REALLY SORRY!
IT'S THE FIRST TIME I WAS NUMBER ONE IN MY CLASS. THAT ESSAY WAS CHOSEN TO REPRESENT OUR WHOLE CLASS... AN ESSAY TO REMEMBER...
YEEEAAAAAARGH!
SORRY ISN'T GOOD ENOUGH! WH-WHAT DO I DO?!
NO, I PROMISE I'LL MAKE IT UP TO YOU!
FWIP
RIP
SHOCK
~~~~~!
I'M SORR...
...BUT IT DOESN'T MATTER ANYMORE.
CLENCH
~~~~~

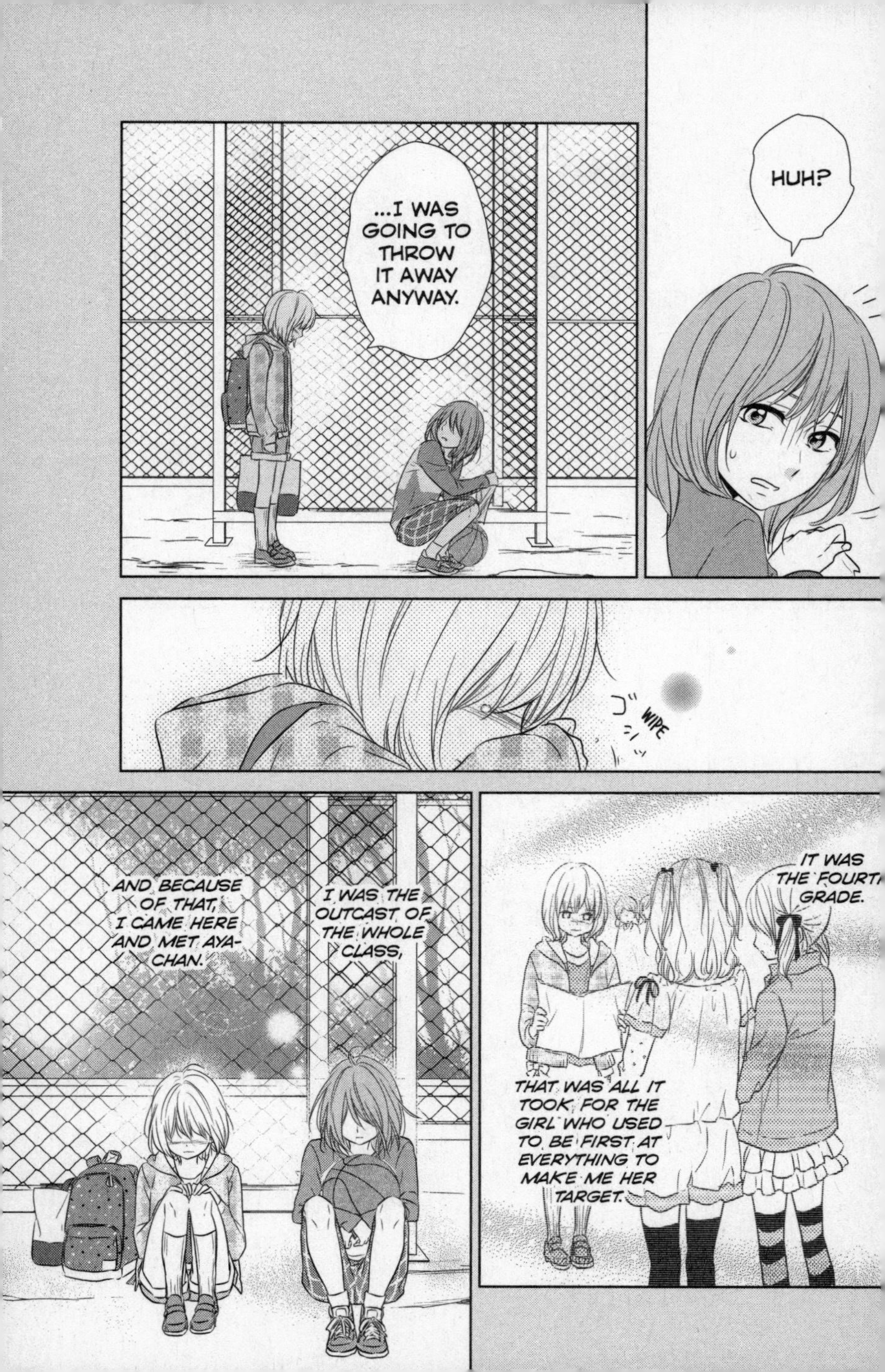
HUH?
...I WAS GOING TO THROW IT AWAY ANYWAY.
WIPE
IT WAS THE FOURT GRADE.
THAT WAS ALL IT TOOK FOR THE GIRL WHO USED TO BE FIRST AT EVERYTHING TO MAKE ME HER TARGET.
I WAS THE OUTCAST OF THE WHOLE CLASS,
AND BECAUSE OF THAT, I CAME HERE AND MET AYA-CHAN.

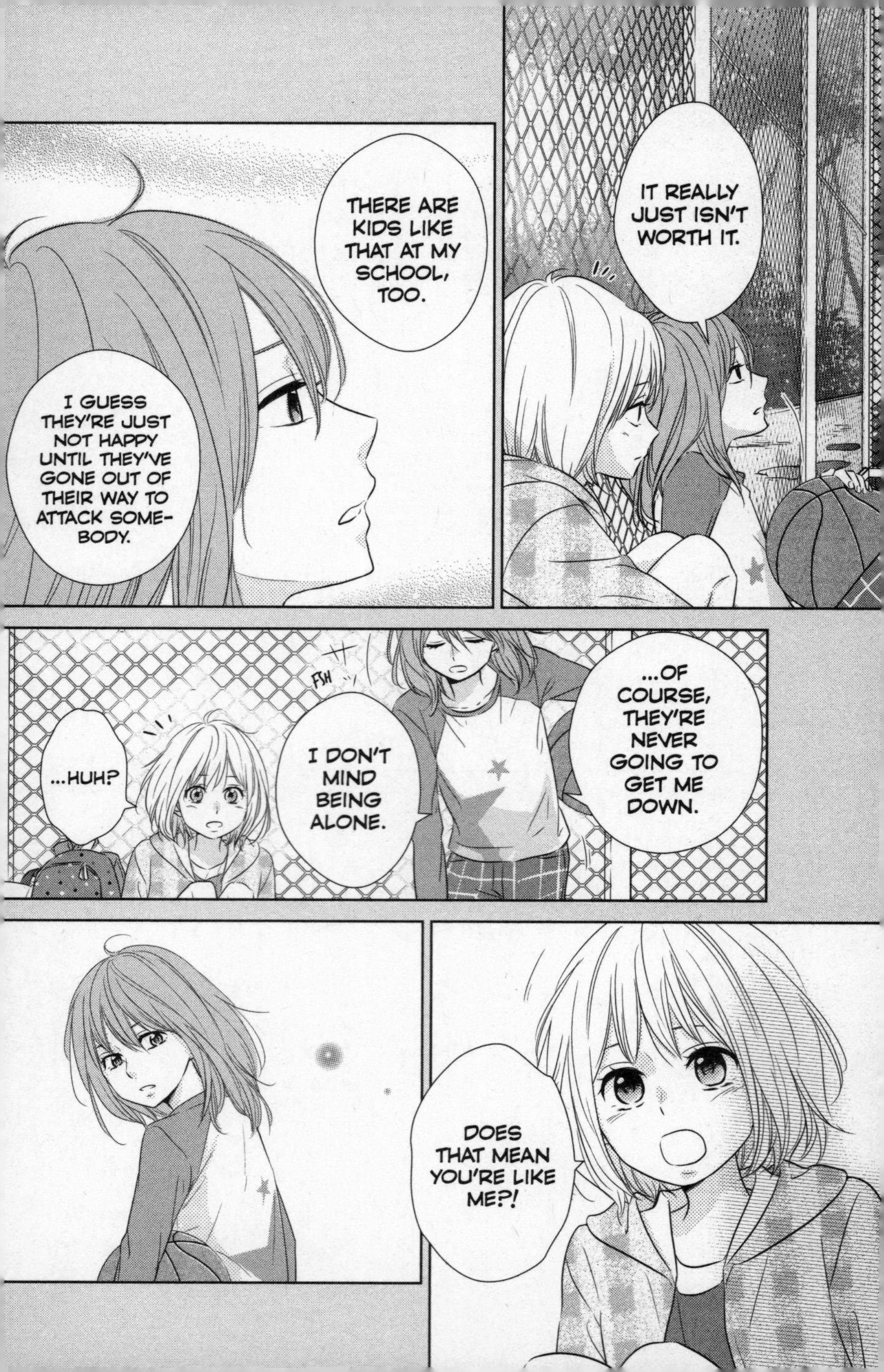
IT REALLY JUST ISN'T WORTH IT.
THERE ARE KIDS LIKE THAT AT MY SCHOOL, TOO.
I GUESS THEY'RE JUST NOT HAPPY UNTIL THEY'VE GONE OUT OF THEIR WAY TO ATTACK SOME-BODY.
...OF COURSE, THEY'RE NEVER GOING TO GET ME DOWN.
FSH
I DON'T MIND BEING ALONE.
...HUH?
DOES THAT MEAN YOU'RE LIKE ME?!

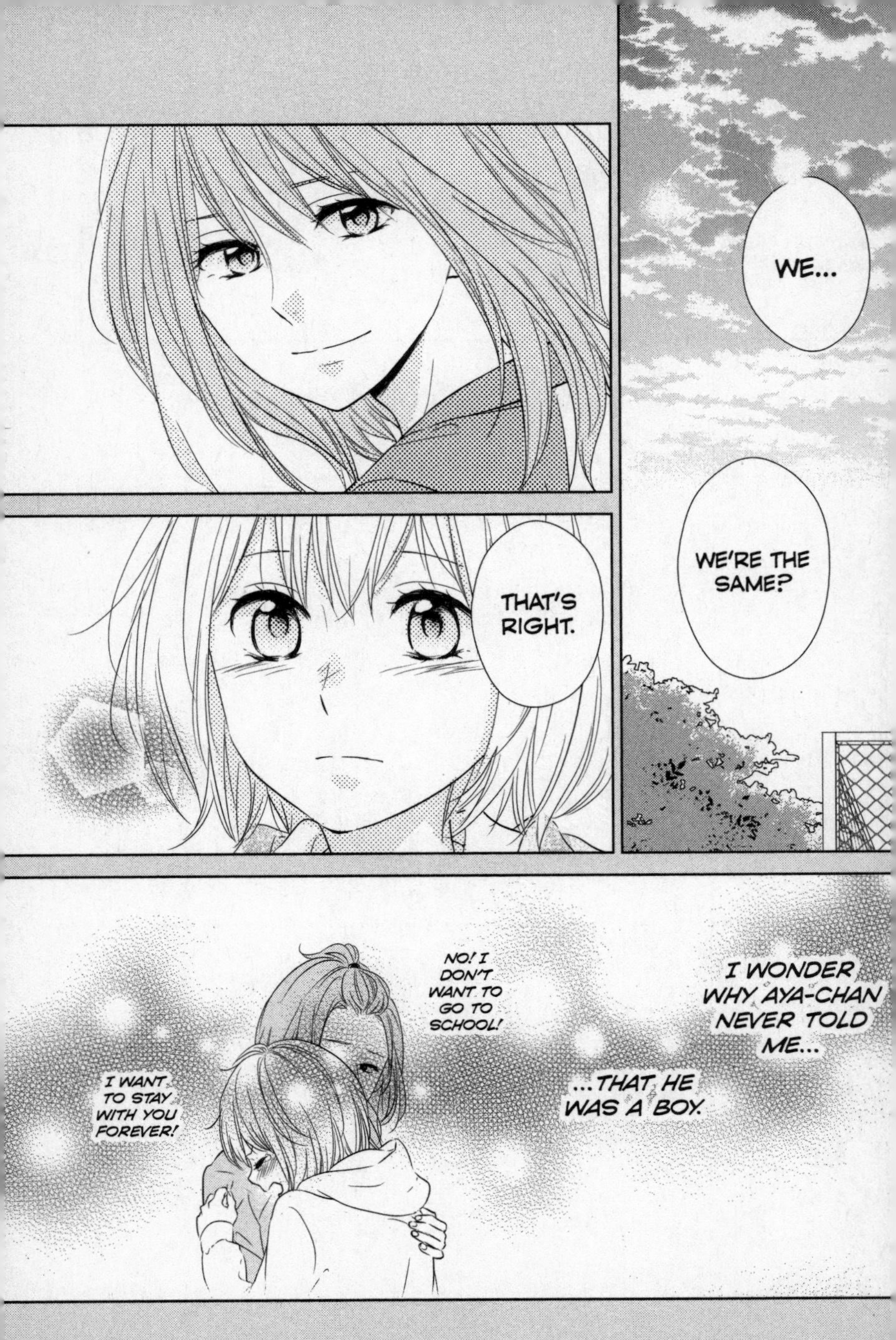
WE...
WE'RE THE SAME?
THAT'S RIGHT.
I WONDER WHY AYA-CHAN NEVER TOLD ME...
...THAT HE WAS A BOY.
NO! I DON'T WANT TO GO TO SCHOOL!
I WANT TO STAY WITH YOU FOREVER!

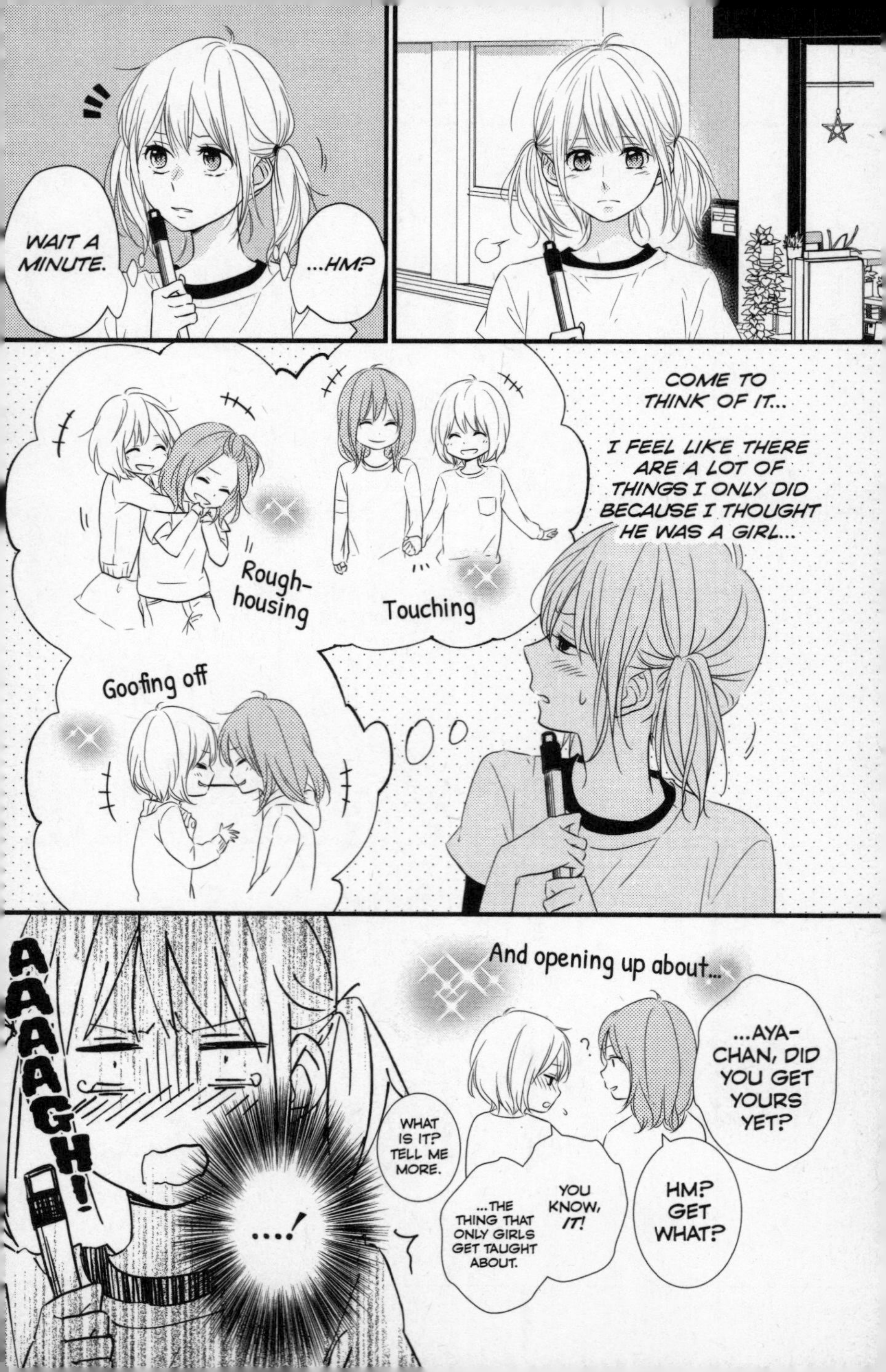
...HM?
WAIT A MINUTE.
COME TO THINK OF IT...
I FEEL LIKE THERE ARE A LOT OF THINGS I ONLY DID BECAUSE I THOUGHT HE WAS A GIRL...
Touching
Rough-housing
Goofing off
And opening up about...
...AYA-CHAN, DID YOU GET YOURS YET?
HM? GET WHAT?
YOU KNOW, IT!
...THE THING THAT ONLY GIRLS GET TAUGHT ABOUT.
WHAT IS IT? TELL ME MORE.
...!
AAAAGH!

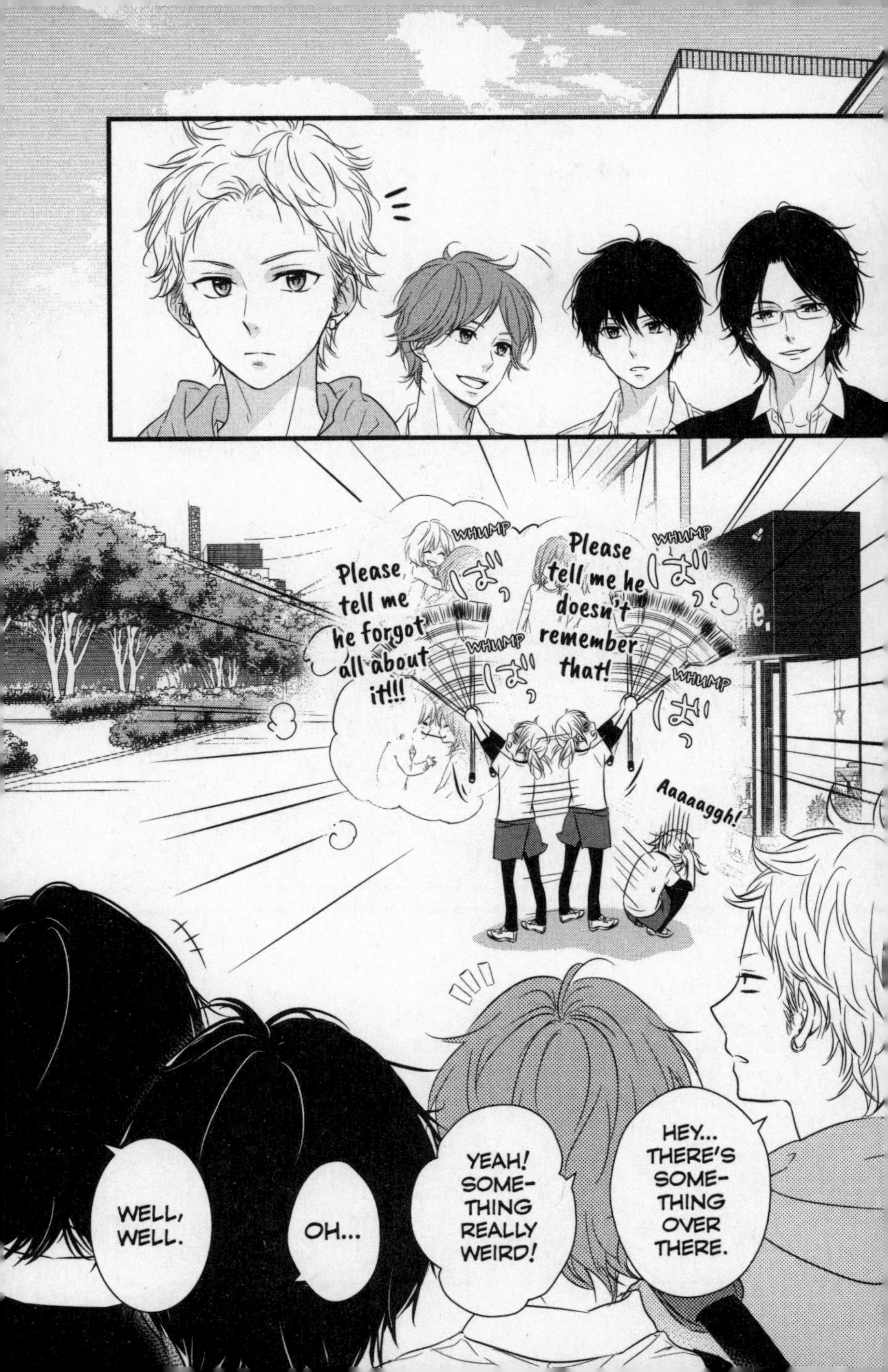
WHUMP
ばっ
Please tell me he doesn't remember that!
WHUMP
ばっ
Please tell me he forgot all about it!!!
WHUMP
ばっ
WHUMP
ばっ
Aaaaaggh!
HEY... THERE'S SOME-THING OVER THERE.
YEAH! SOME-THING REALLY WEIRD!
OH...
WELL, WELL.

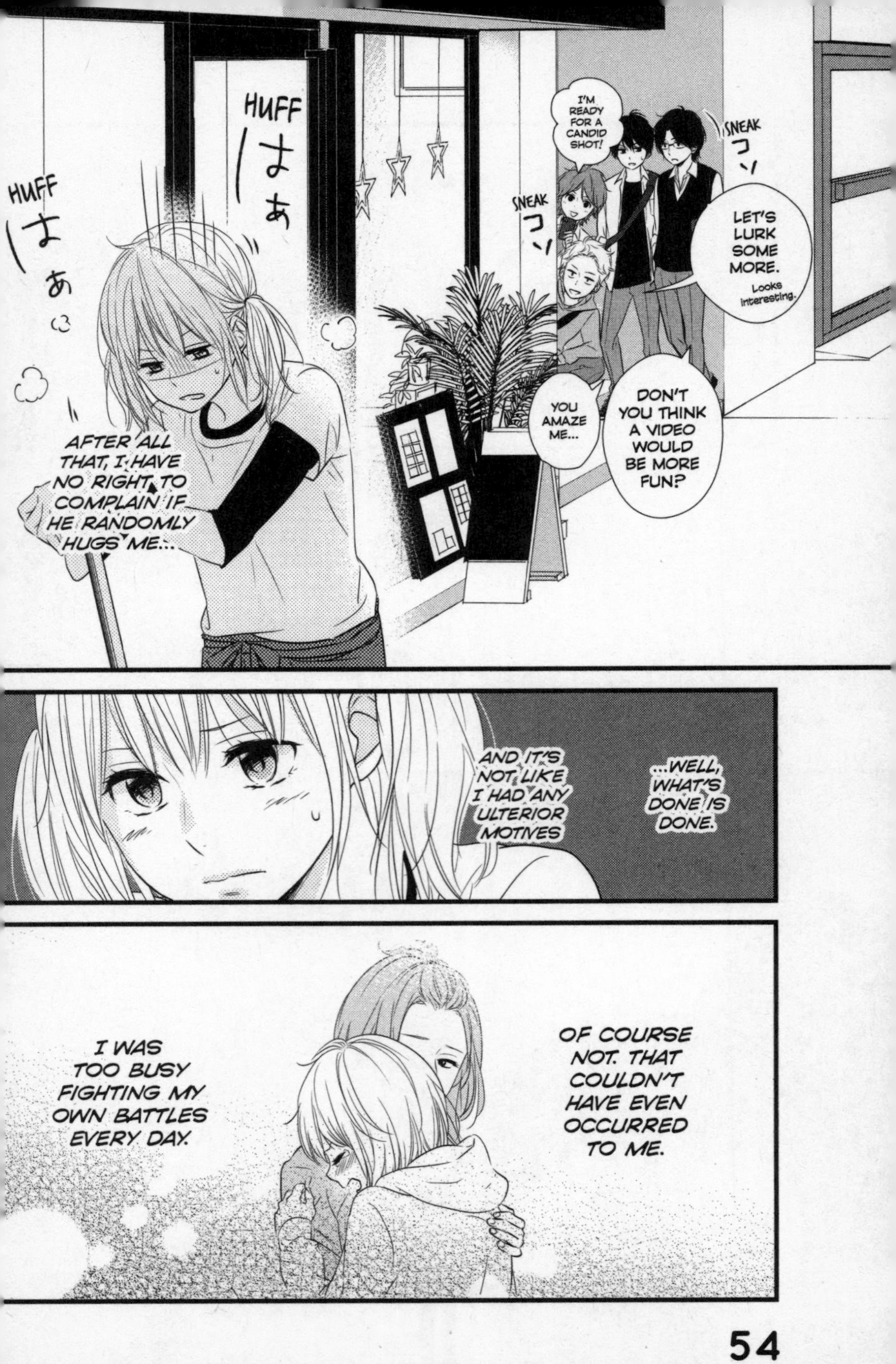

SNEAK
コソ
I'M READY FOR A CANDID SHOT!
LET'S LURK SOME MORE.
Looks interesting.
SNEAK
コソ
DON'T YOU THINK A VIDEO WOULD BE MORE FUN?
YOU AMAZE ME...
HUFF
はぁ
HUFF
はぁ
AFTER ALL THAT, I HAVE NO RIGHT TO COMPLAIN IF HE RANDOMLY HUGS ME...
...WELL, WHAT'S DONE IS DONE.
AND IT'S NOT LIKE I HAD ANY ULTERIOR MOTIVES
OF COURSE NOT. THAT COULDN'T HAVE EVEN OCCURRED TO ME.
I WAS TOO BUSY FIGHTING MY OWN BATTLES EVERY DAY.

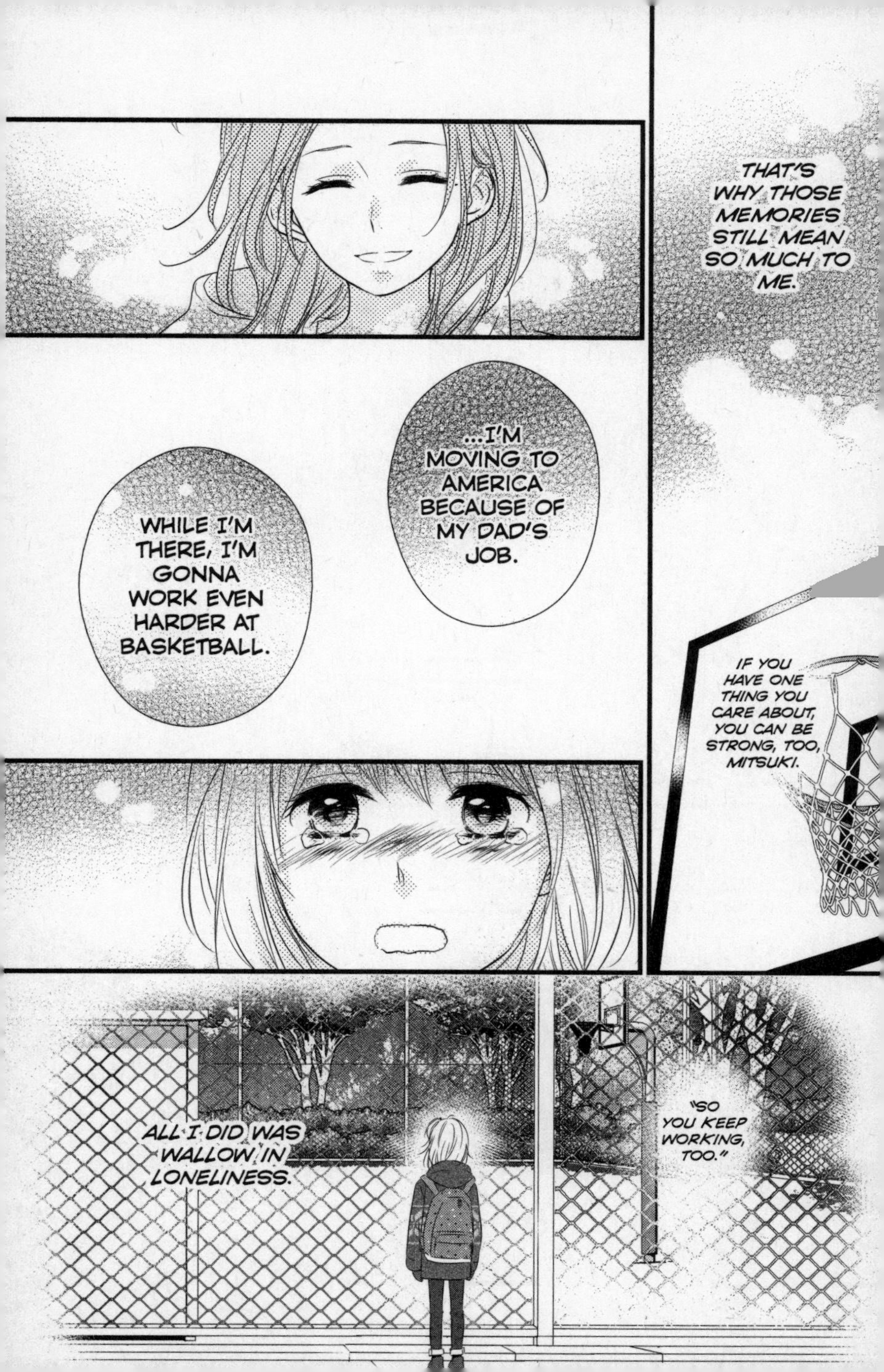
THAT'S WHY THOSE MEMORIES STILL MEAN SO MUCH TO ME.
...I'M MOVING TO AMERICA BECAUSE OF MY DAD'S JOB.
WHILE I'M THERE, I'M GONNA WORK EVEN HARDER AT BASKETBALL.
IF YOU HAVE ONE THING YOU CARE ABOUT, YOU CAN BE STRONG, TOO, MITSUKI.
"SO YOU KEEP WORKING, TOO."
ALL I DID WAS WALLOW IN LONELINESS.

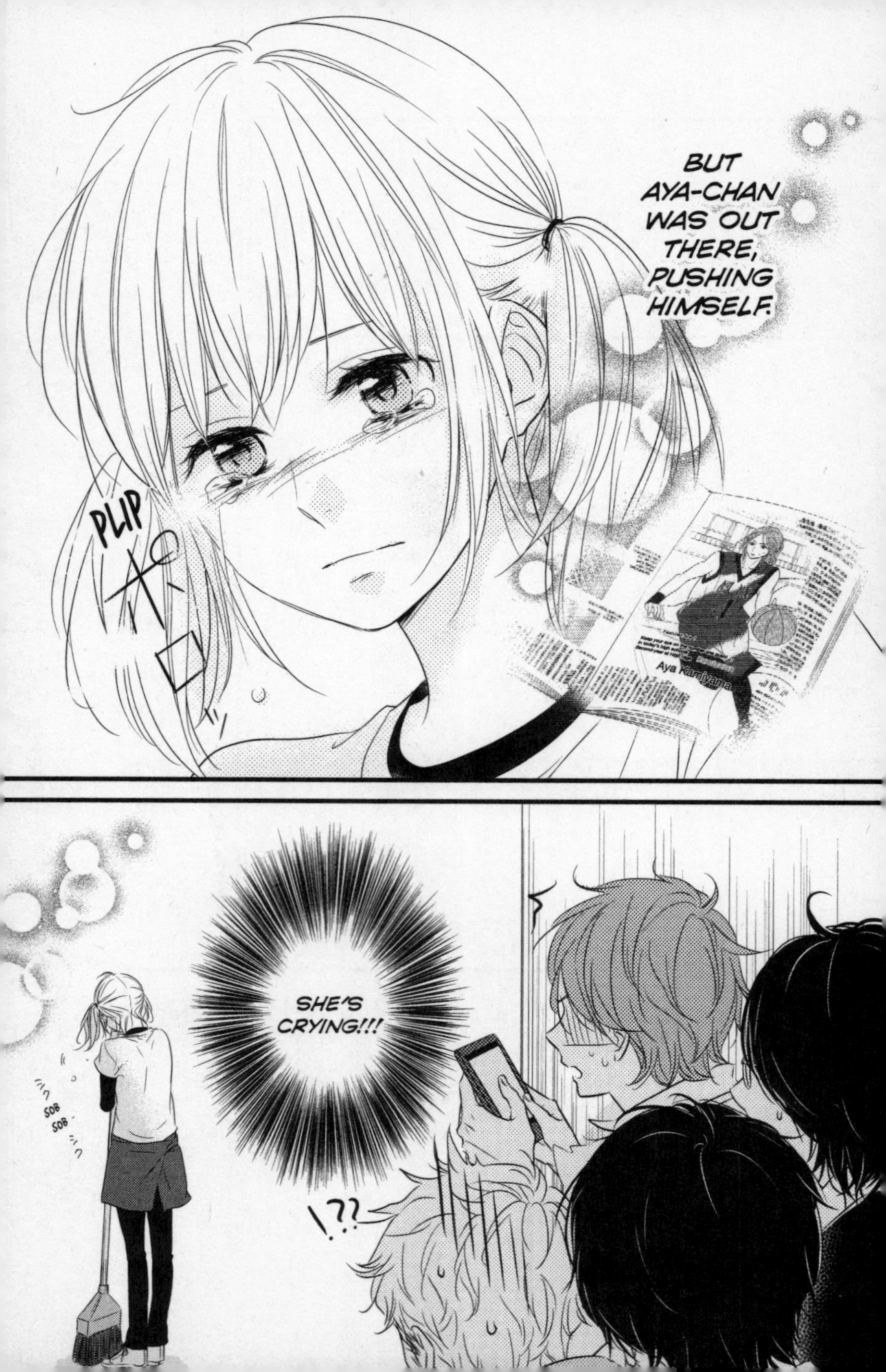
BUT AYA-CHAN WAS OUT THERE, PUSHING HIMSELF.
PLIP
Aya Kamiyama
!??
SHE'S CRYING!!!
SOB SOB

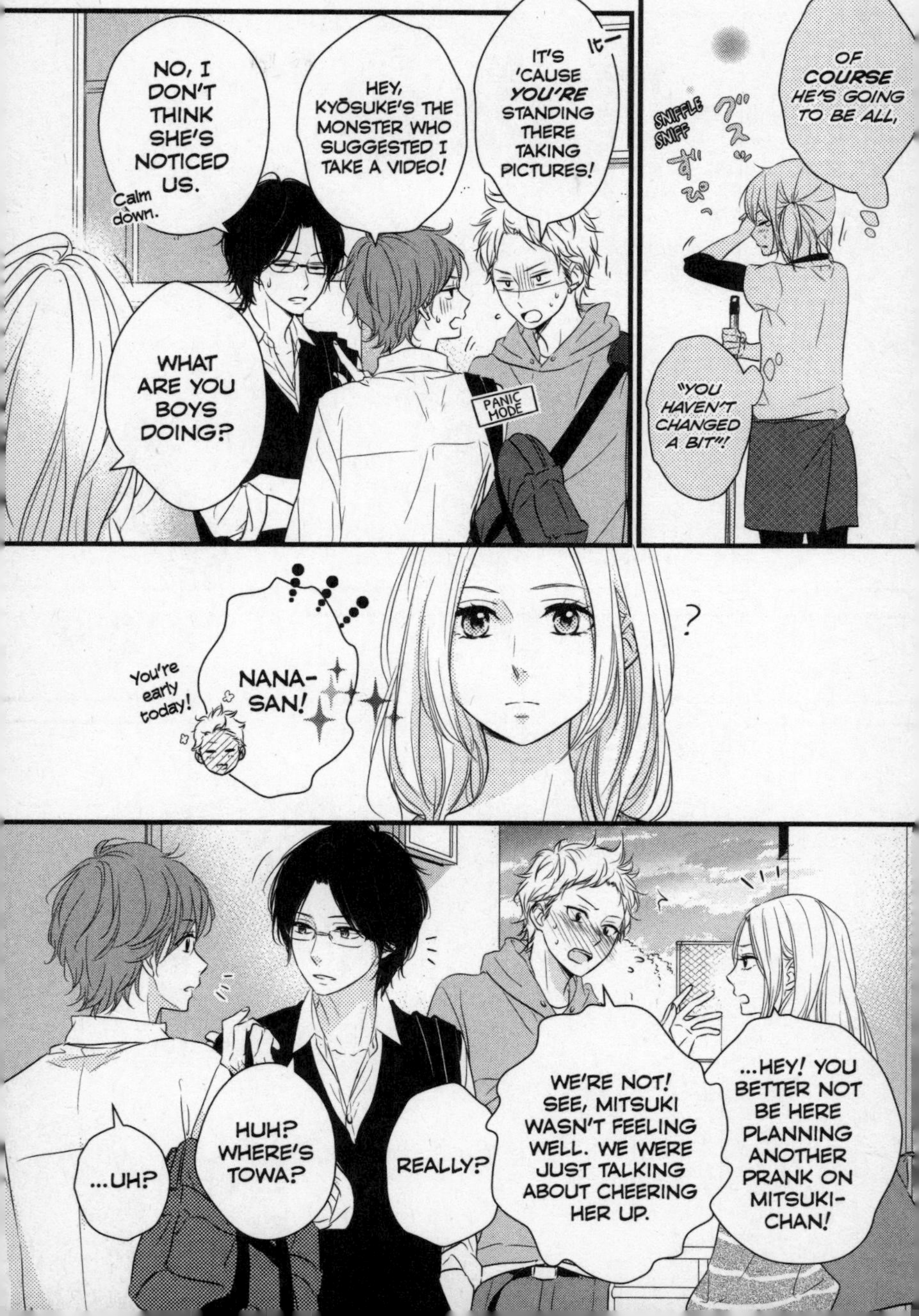
OF COURSE HE'S GOING TO BE ALL,
SNIFFLE SNIFF
"YOU HAVEN'T CHANGED A BIT"!
IT'S 'CAUSE YOU'RE STANDING THERE TAKING PICTURES!
HEY, KYŌSUKE'S THE MONSTER WHO SUGGESTED I TAKE A VIDEO!
NO, I DON'T THINK SHE'S NOTICED US.
Calm down.
PANIC MODE
WHAT ARE YOU BOYS DOING?
?
NANA-SAN!
You're early today!
...HEY! YOU BETTER NOT BE HERE PLANNING ANOTHER PRANK ON MITSUKI-CHAN!
WE'RE NOT! SEE, MITSUKI WASN'T FEELING WELL. WE WERE JUST TALKING ABOUT CHEERING HER UP.
REALLY?
HUH? WHERE'S TOWA?
...UH?

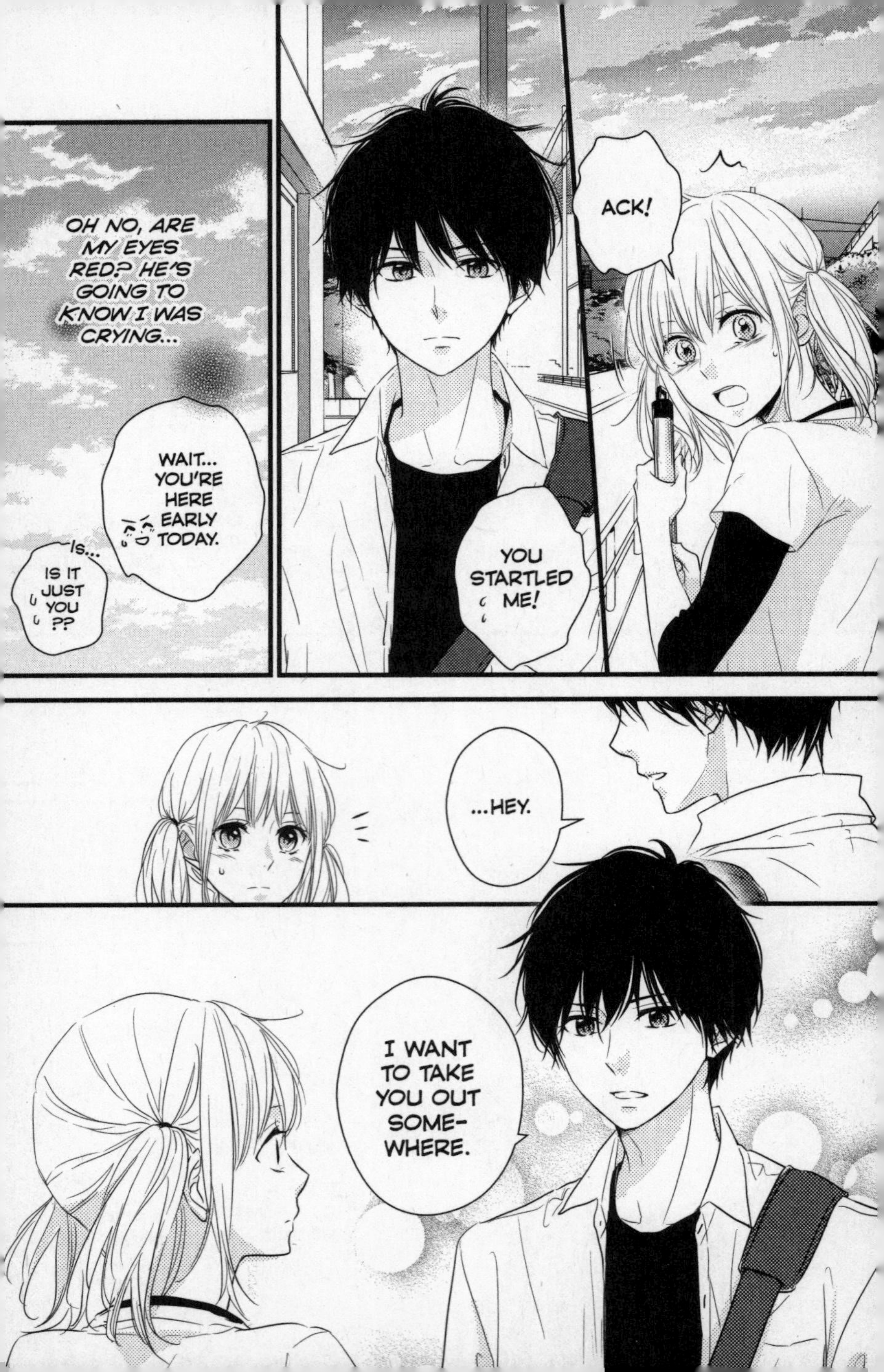
ACK!
YOU STARTLED ME!
OH NO, ARE MY EYES RED? HE'S GOING TO KNOW I WAS CRYING...
WAIT... YOU'RE HERE EARLY TODAY.
IS... IS IT JUST YOU??
...HEY.
I WANT TO TAKE YOU OUT SOME-WHERE.

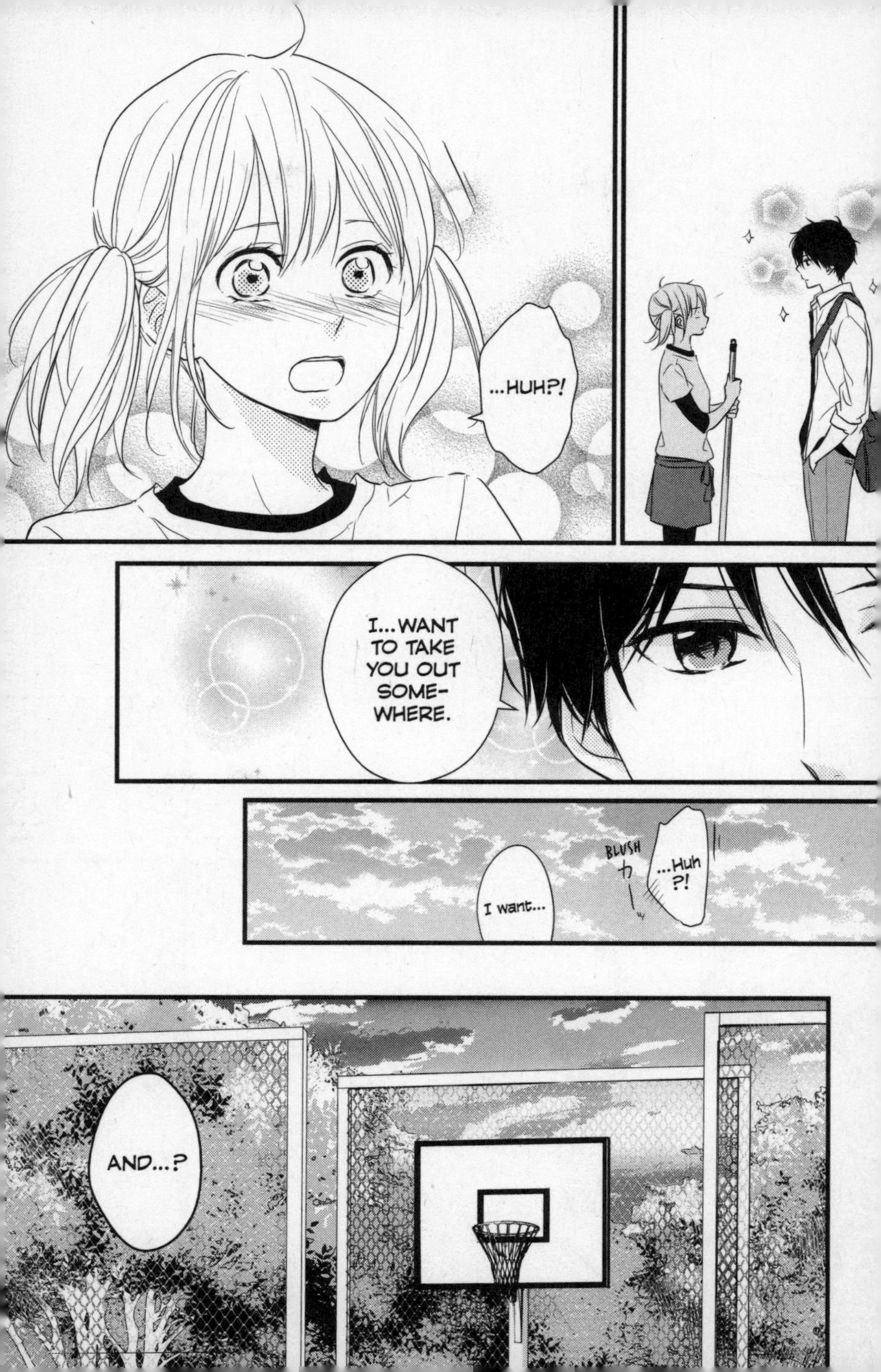
...HUH?!
I...WANT TO TAKE YOU OUT SOME-WHERE.
...Huh ?!
BLUSH
I want...
AND...?

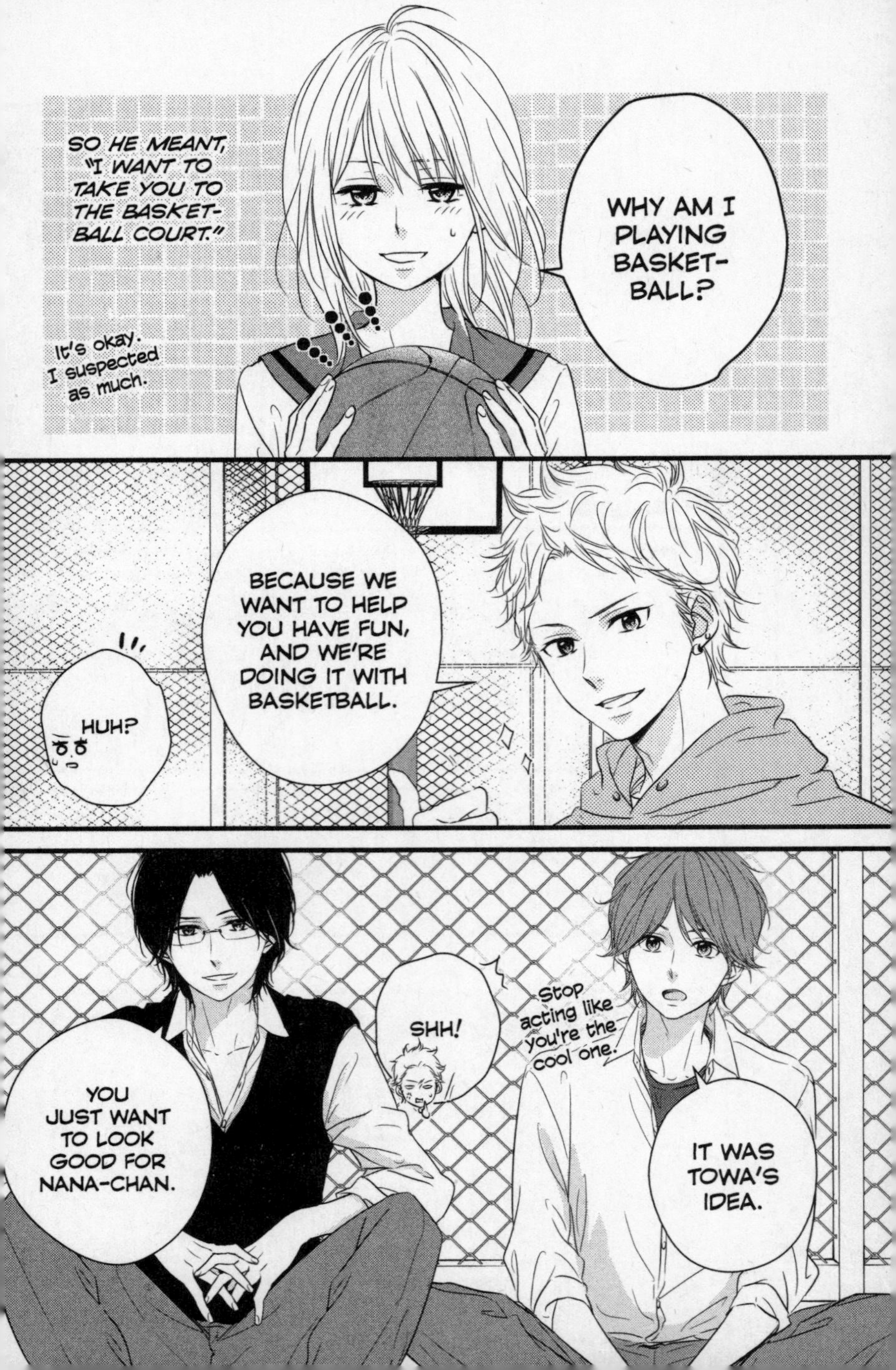
WHY AM I PLAYING BASKETBALL?
SO HE MEANT, "I WANT TO TAKE YOU TO THE BASKETBALL COURT."
It's okay. I suspected as much.
BECAUSE WE WANT TO HELP YOU HAVE FUN, AND WE'RE DOING IT WITH BASKETBALL.
HUH?
IT WAS TOWA'S IDEA.
Stop acting like you're the cool one.
SHH!
YOU JUST WANT TO LOOK GOOD FOR NANA-CHAN.

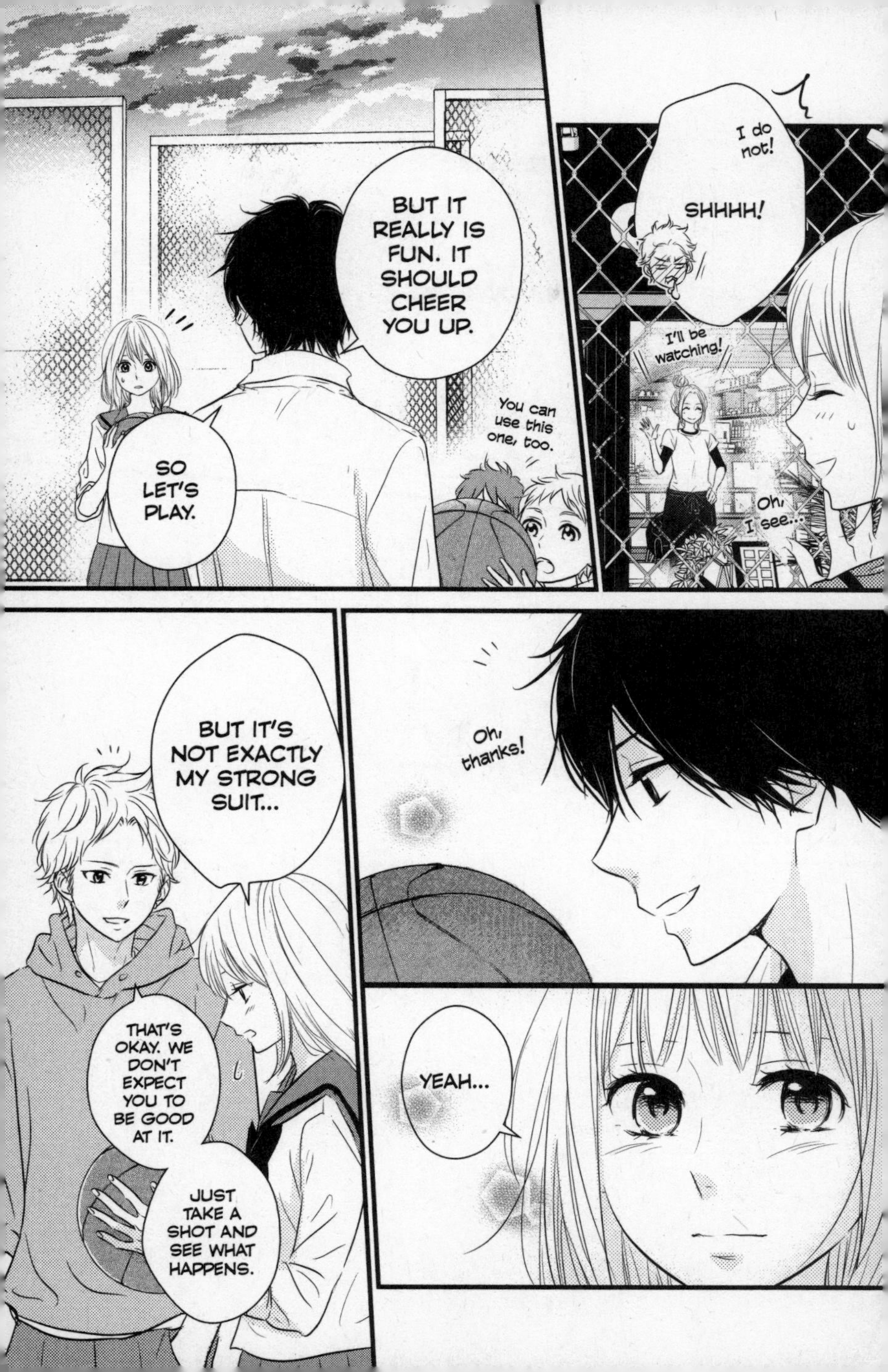
I do not!
SHHHH!
I'll be watching!
Oh, I see...
BUT IT REALLY IS FUN. IT SHOULD CHEER YOU UP.
You can use this one, too.
SO LET'S PLAY.
Oh, thanks!
YEAH...
BUT IT'S NOT EXACTLY MY STRONG SUIT...
THAT'S OKAY. WE DON'T EXPECT YOU TO BE GOOD AT IT.
JUST TAKE A SHOT AND SEE WHAT HAPPENS.

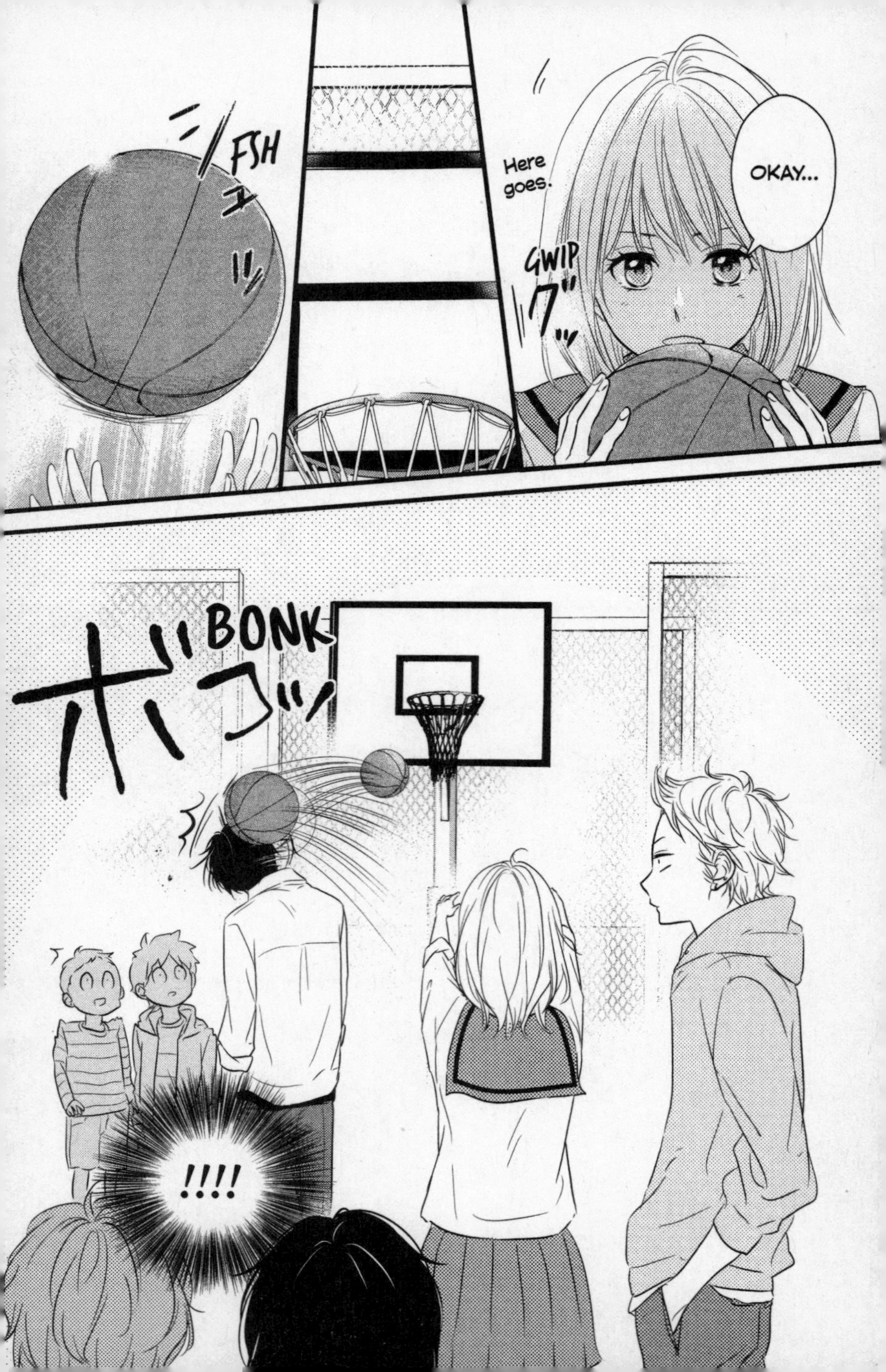
OKAY...
Here goes.
GWIP
FSH
BONK
!!!!

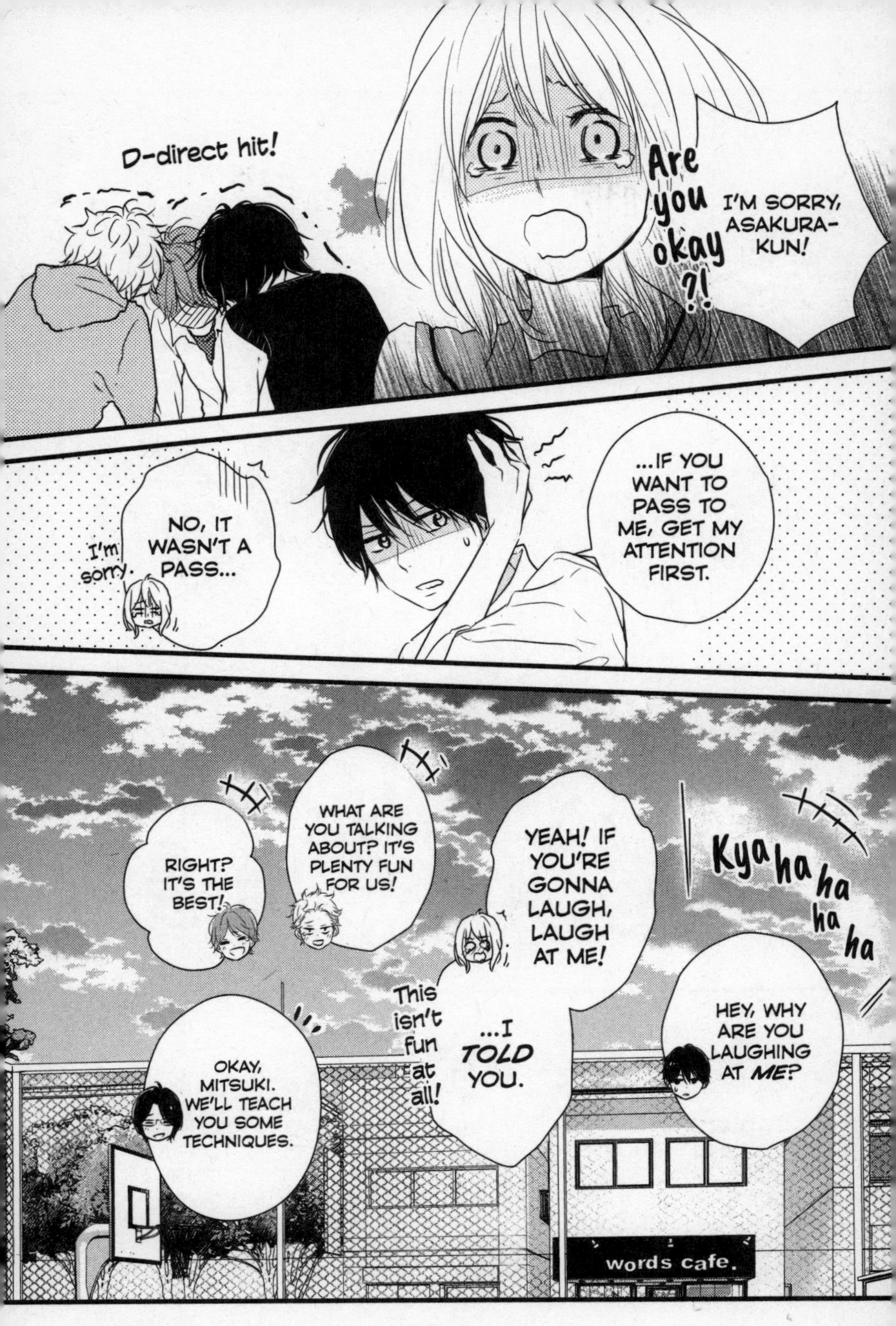
I'M SORRY, ASAKURA-KUN!
Are you okay?!
D-direct hit!
...IF YOU WANT TO PASS TO ME, GET MY ATTENTION FIRST.
NO, IT WASN'T A PASS...
I'm sorry.
Kyahahahaha
YEAH! IF YOU'RE GONNA LAUGH, LAUGH AT ME!
WHAT ARE YOU TALKING ABOUT? IT'S PLENTY FUN FOR US!
RIGHT? IT'S THE BEST!
HEY, WHY ARE YOU LAUGHING AT *ME*?
...I *TOLD* YOU.
This isn't fun at all!
OKAY, MITSUKI. WE'LL TEACH YOU SOME TECHNIQUES.
words cafe.

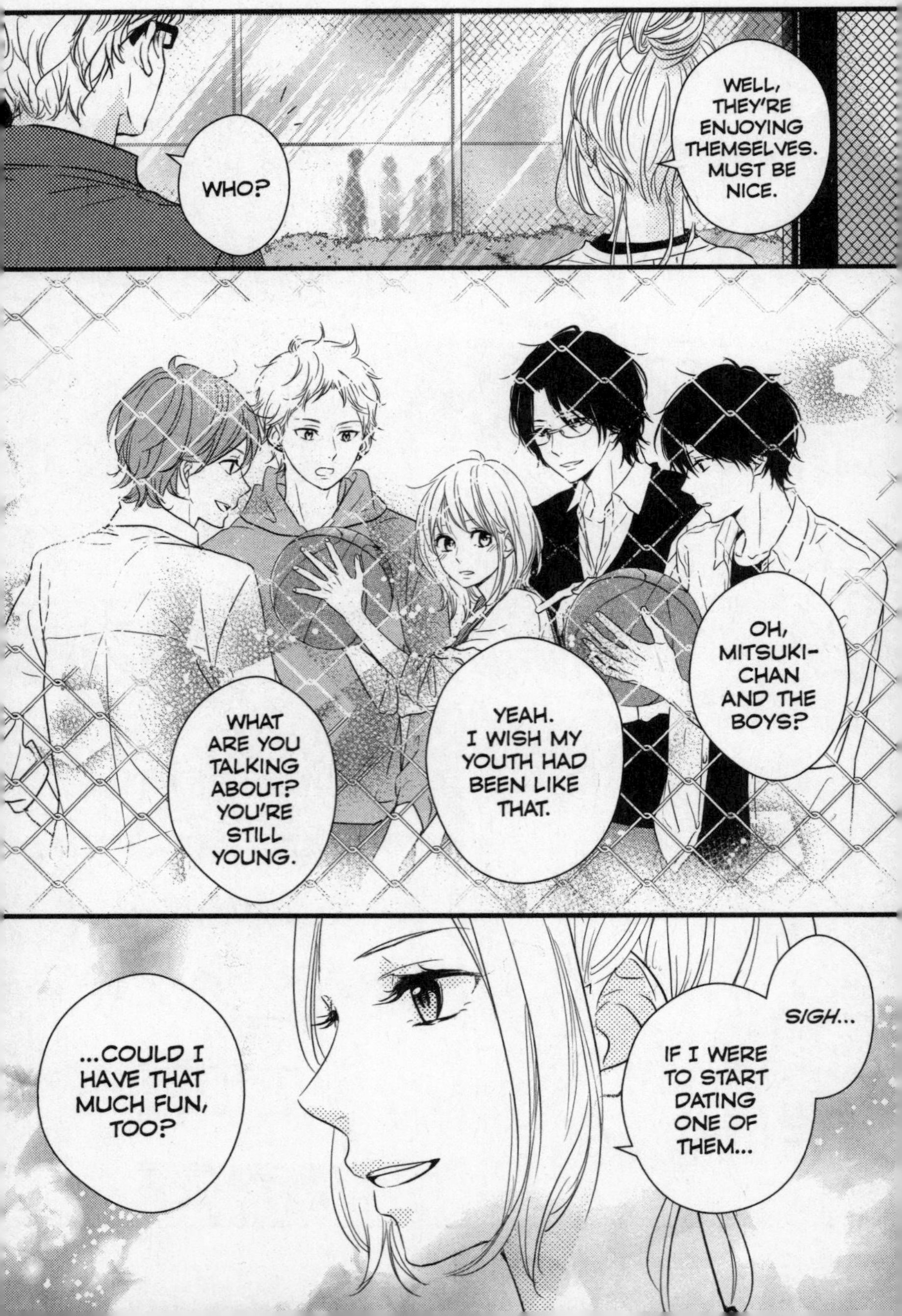
WELL, THEY'RE ENJOYING THEMSELVES. MUST BE NICE.
WHO?
OH, MITSUKI-CHAN AND THE BOYS?
YEAH. I WISH MY YOUTH HAD BEEN LIKE THAT.
WHAT ARE YOU TALKING ABOUT? YOU'RE STILL YOUNG.
SIGH...
IF I WERE TO START DATING ONE OF THEM...
...COULD I HAVE THAT MUCH FUN, TOO?

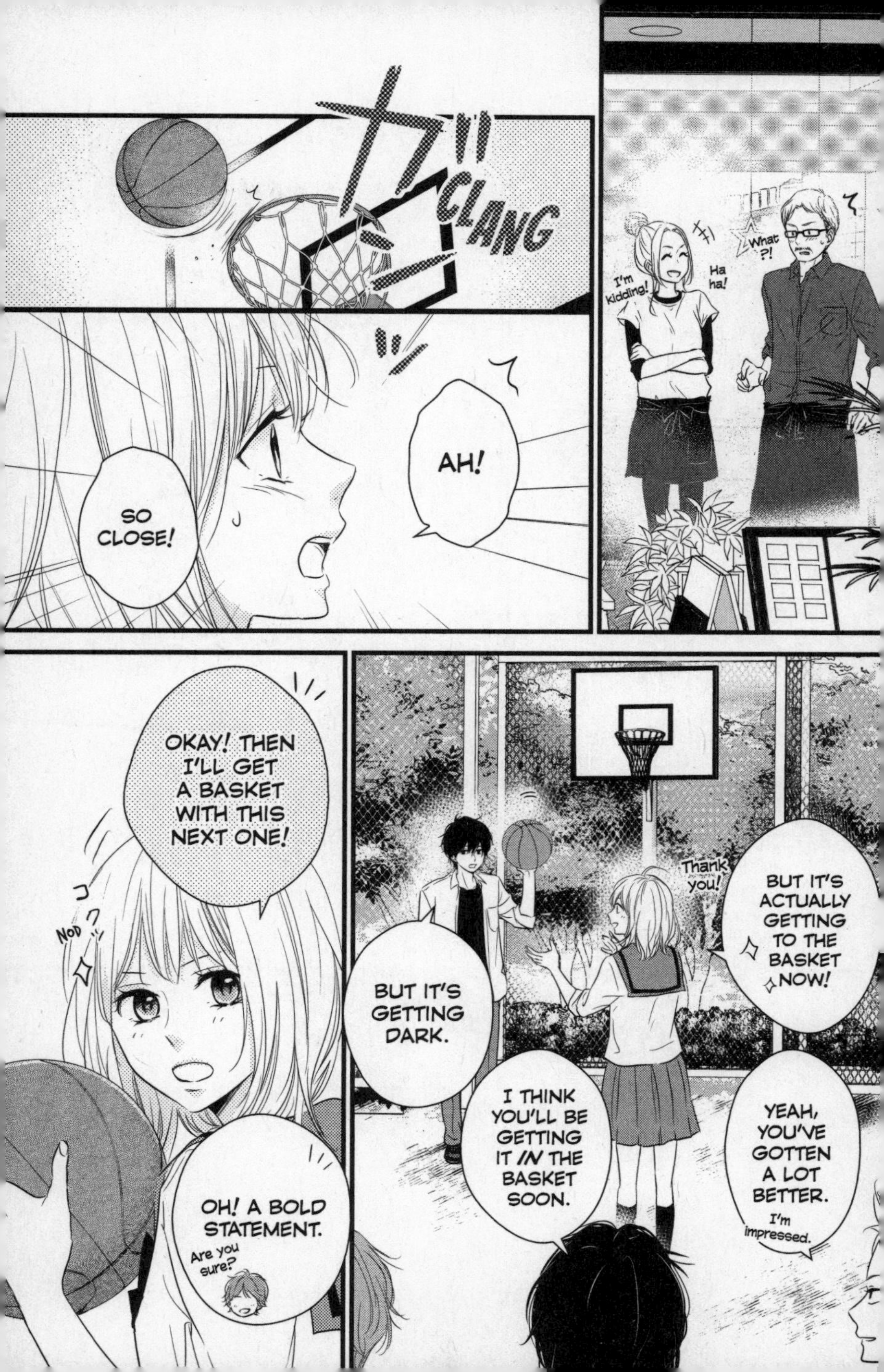
What ?!
Ha ha!
I'm kidding!
CLANG
AH!
SO CLOSE!
BUT IT'S ACTUALLY GETTING TO THE BASKET NOW!
Thank you!
BUT IT'S GETTING DARK.
YEAH, YOU'VE GOTTEN A LOT BETTER.
I'm impressed.
I THINK YOU'LL BE GETTING IT *IN* THE BASKET SOON.
OKAY! THEN I'LL GET A BASKET WITH THIS NEXT ONE!
NOD
OH! A BOLD STATEMENT.
Are you sure?

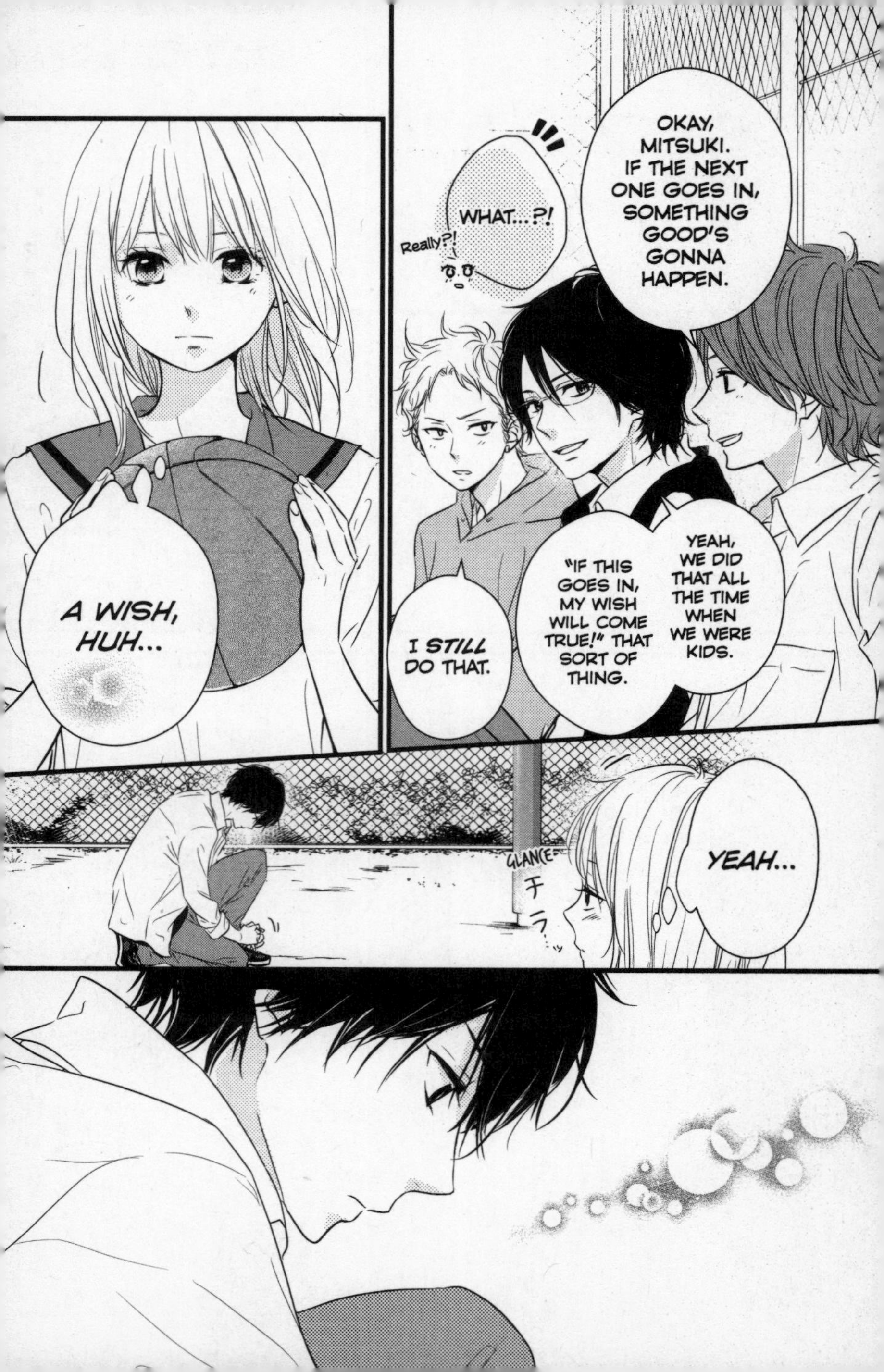
OKAY, MITSUKI. IF THE NEXT ONE GOES IN, SOMETHING GOOD'S GONNA HAPPEN.
WHAT...?!
Really?!
YEAH, WE DID THAT ALL THE TIME WHEN WE WERE KIDS.
"IF THIS GOES IN, MY WISH WILL COME TRUE!" THAT SORT OF THING.
I STILL DO THAT.
A WISH, HUH...
YEAH...
GLANCE
チラ

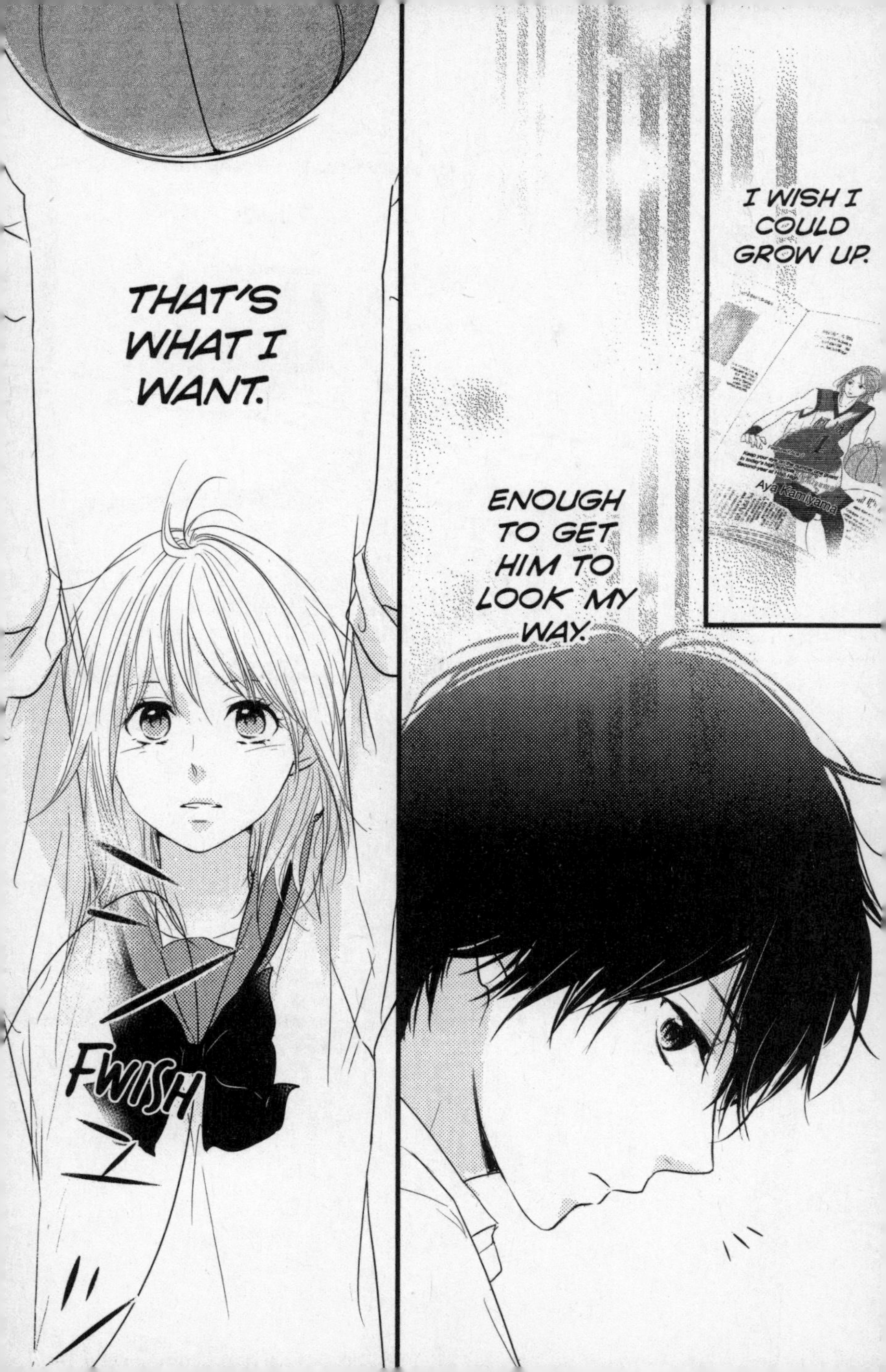
I WISH I COULD GROW UP.
Aya Kamiyama
ENOUGH TO GET HIM TO LOOK MY WAY.
THAT'S WHAT I WANT.
FWISH

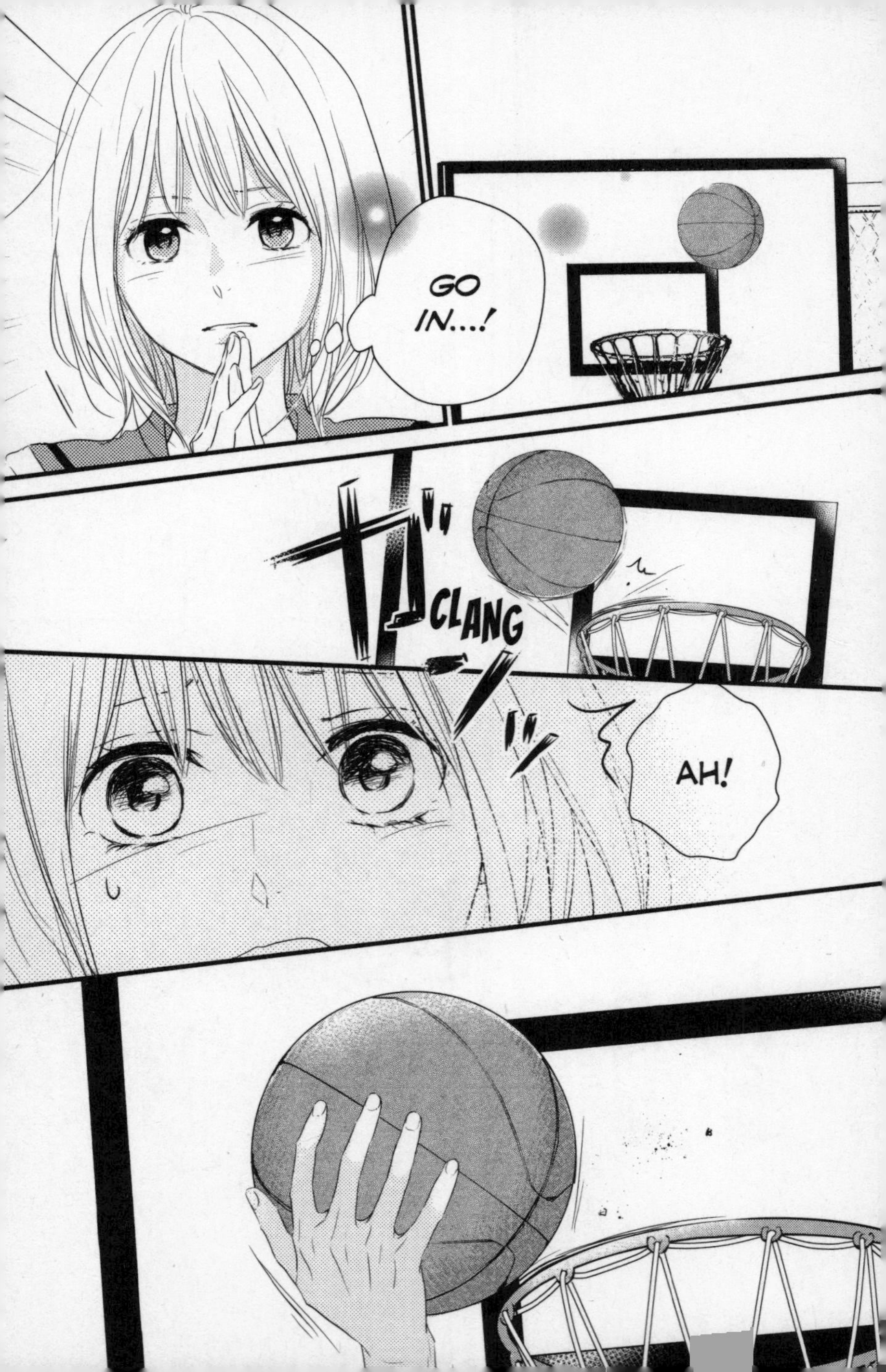
GO IN...!
CLANG
AH!

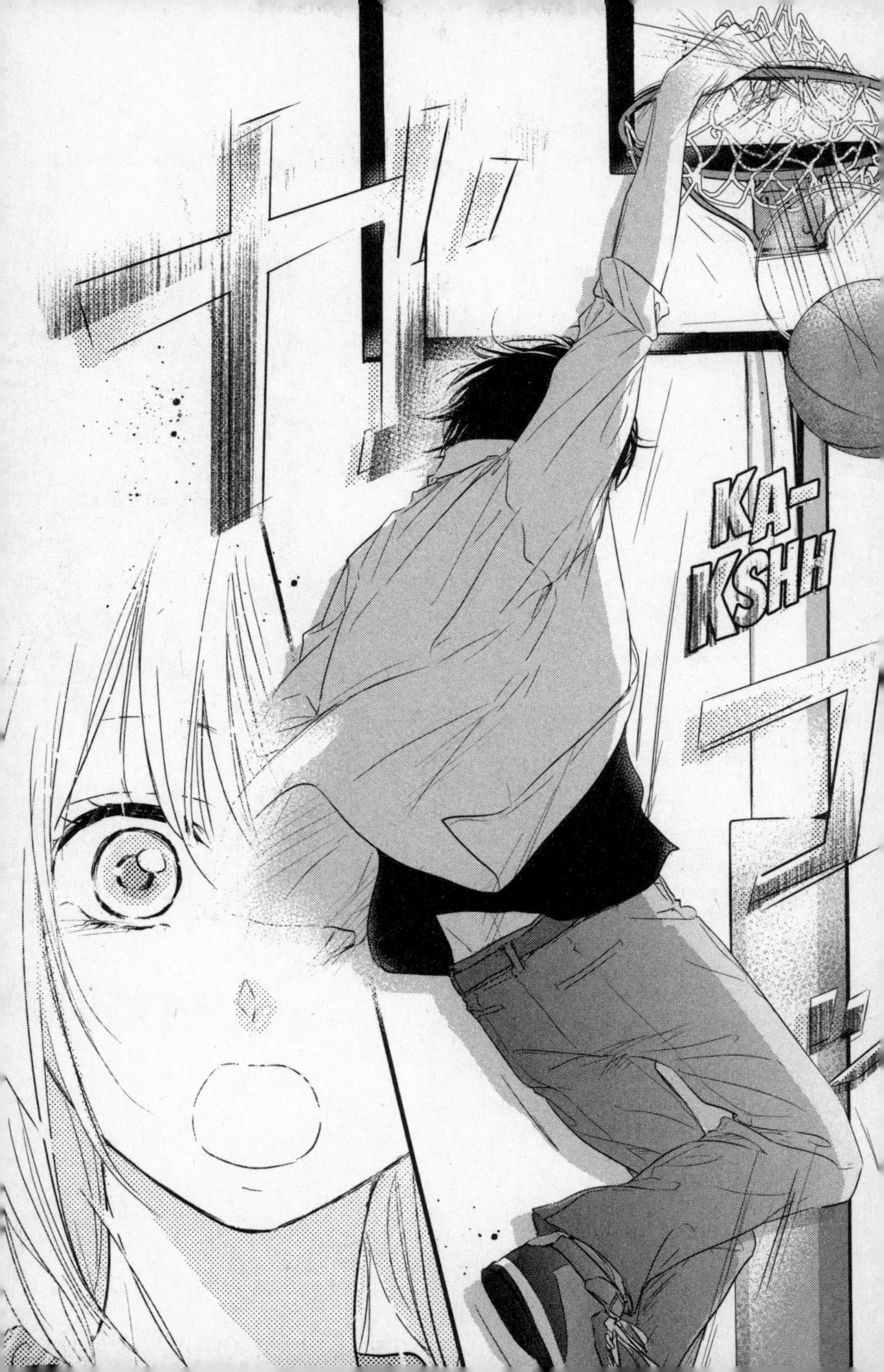
KA-
KSHH

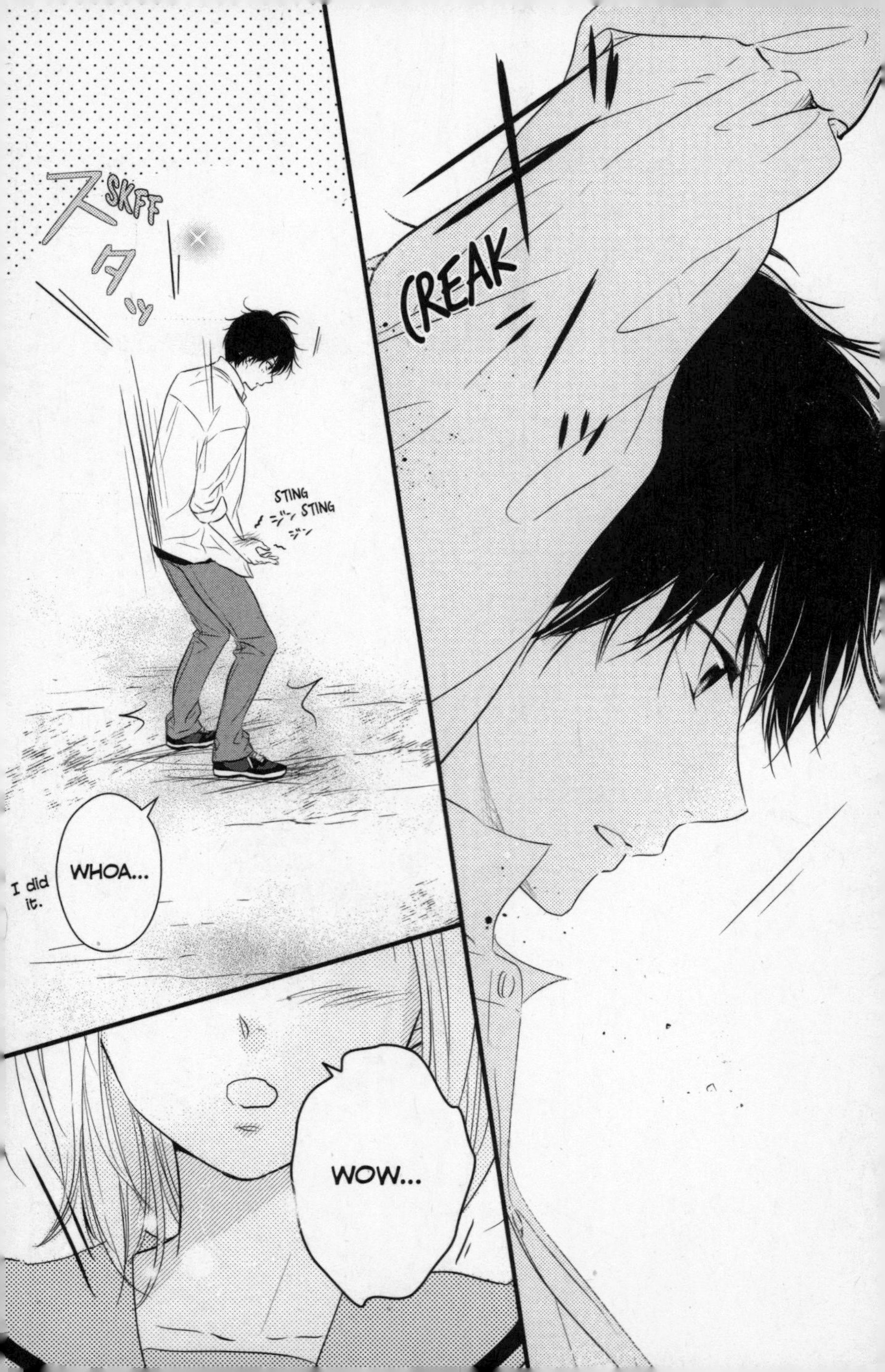
CREAK
SKFF
スタッ
STING STING
ジン ジン
WHOA...
I did it.
WOW...

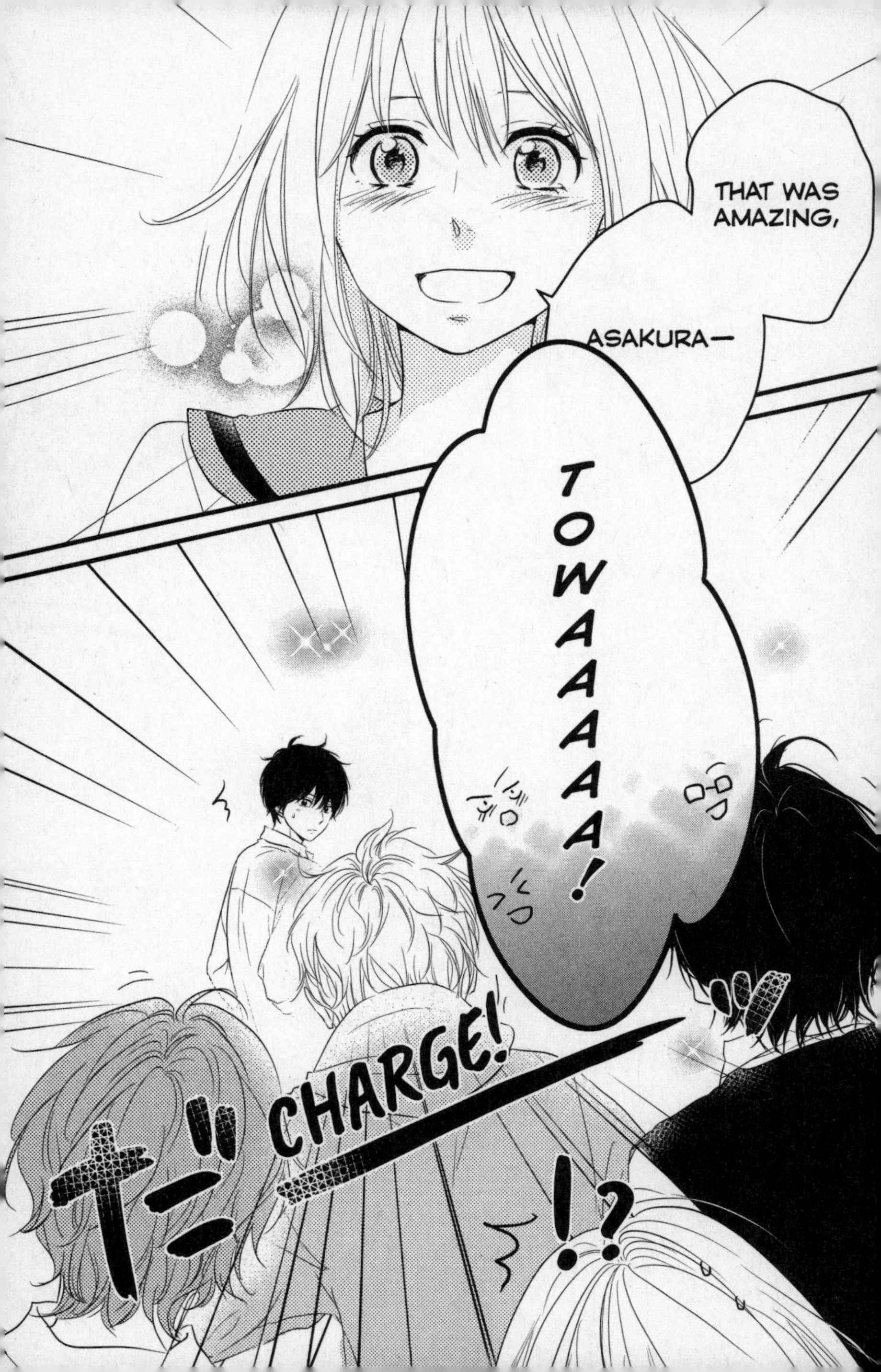
THAT WAS AMAZING,
ASAKURA—
TOWAAAAAA!
CHARGE!
!?

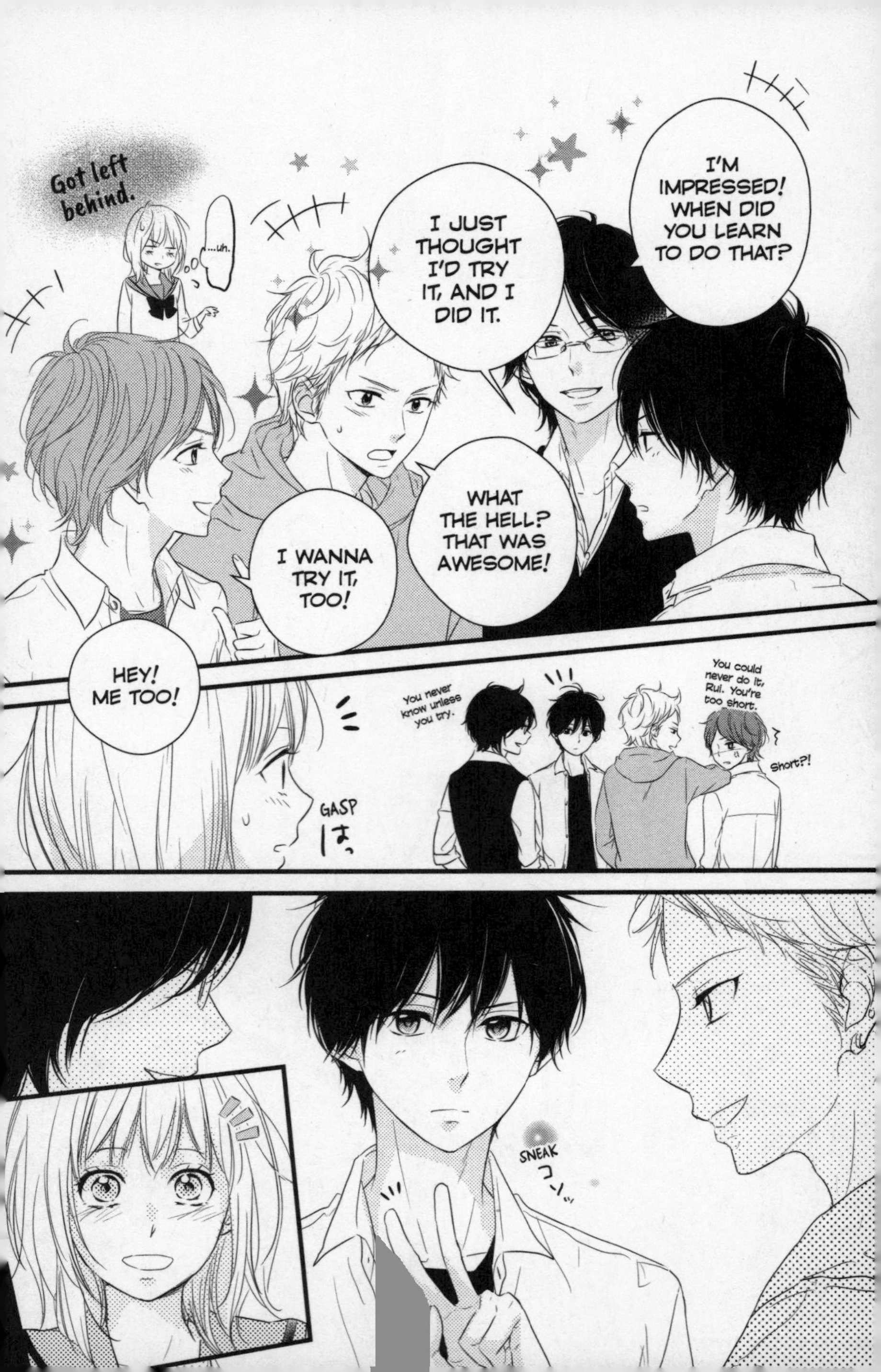
I'M IMPRESSED! WHEN DID YOU LEARN TO DO THAT?
I JUST THOUGHT I'D TRY IT, AND I DID IT.
WHAT THE HELL? THAT WAS AWESOME!
I WANNA TRY IT, TOO!
Got left behind.
...uh.
HEY! ME TOO!
You could never do it, Rui. You're too short.
Short?!
You never know unless you try.
GASP
は、
SNEAK
コソッ

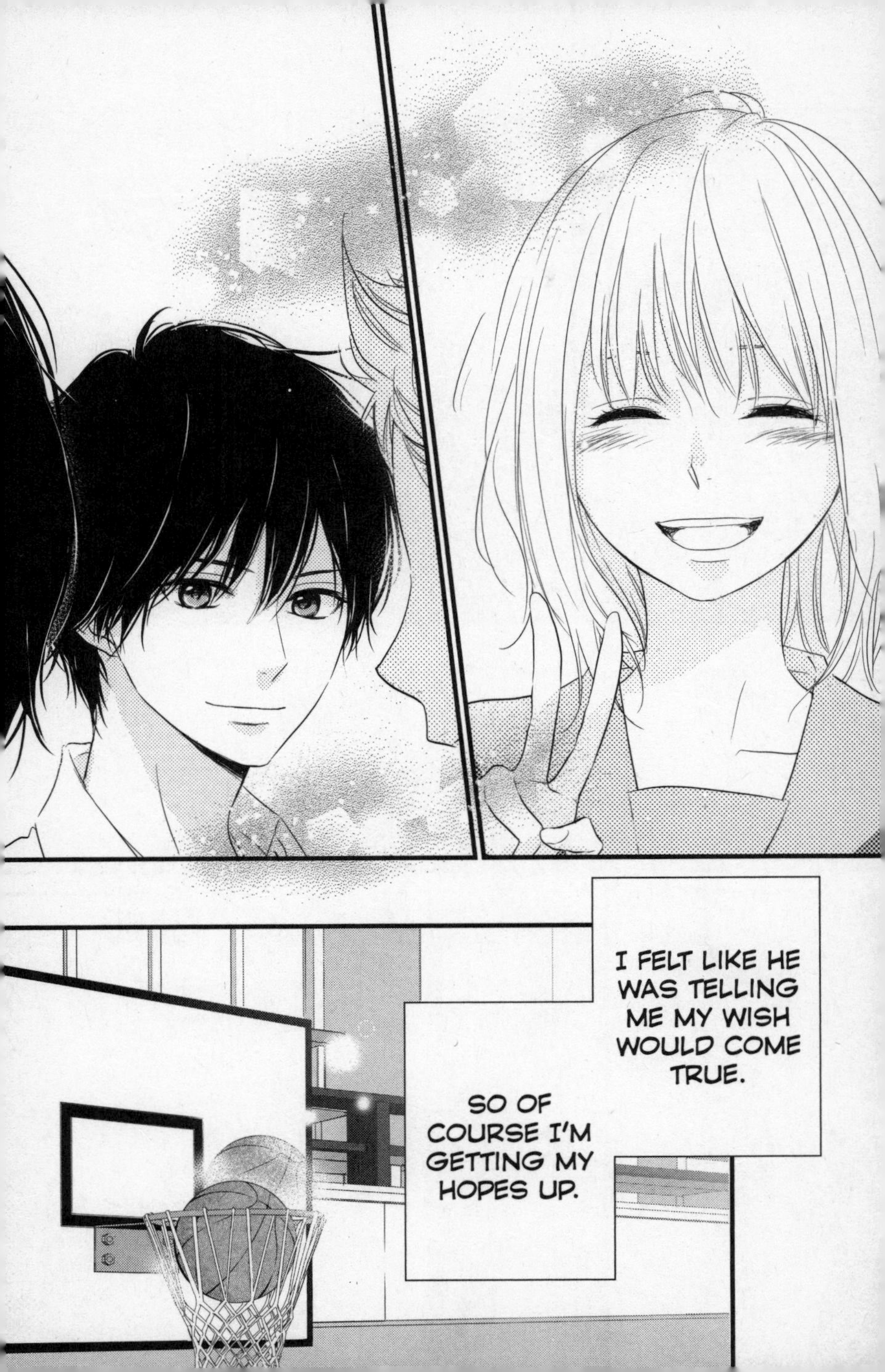
I FELT LIKE HE WAS TELLING ME MY WISH WOULD COME TRUE.
SO OF COURSE I'M GETTING MY HOPES UP.

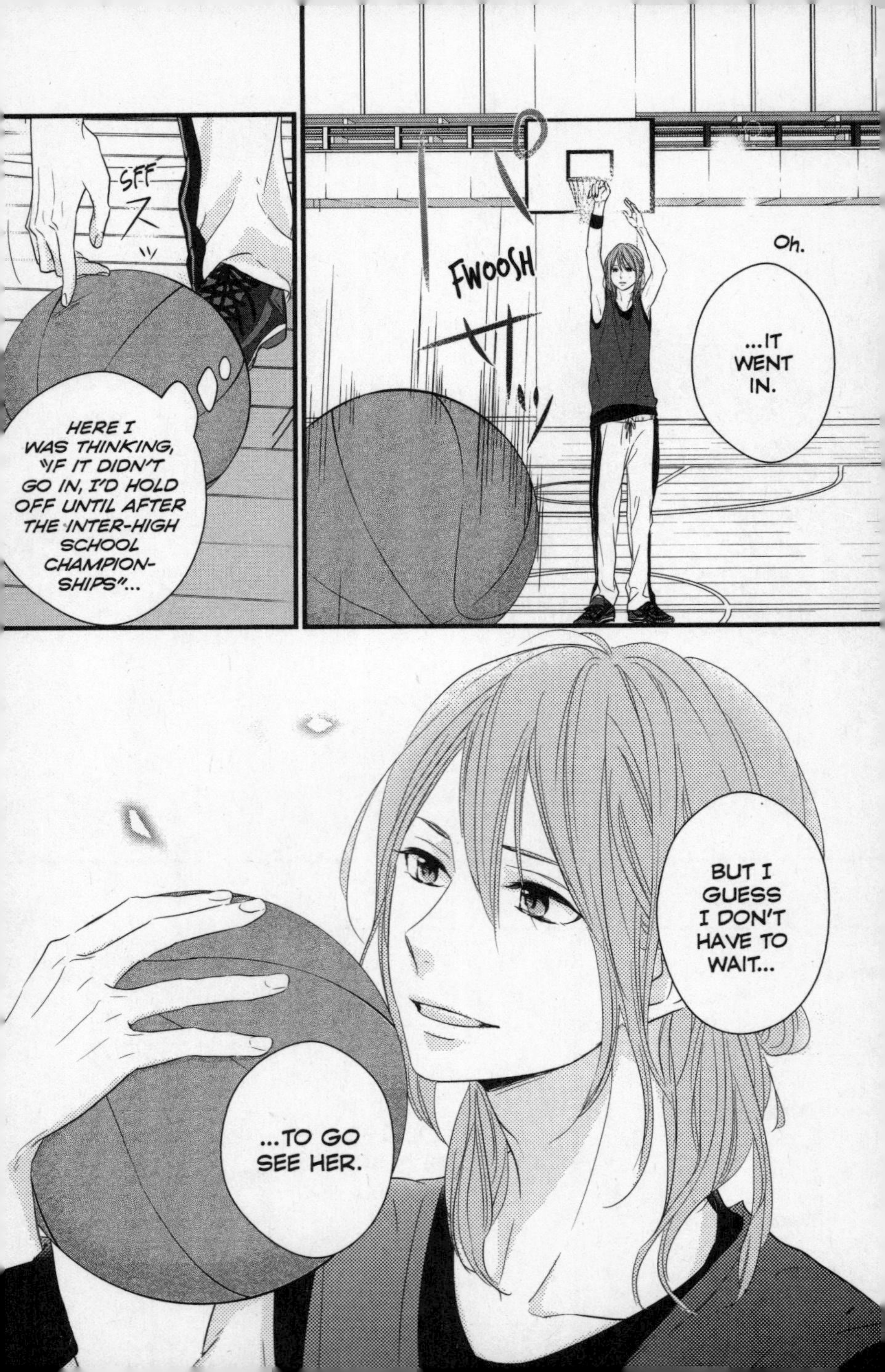
Oh.
...IT WENT IN.
FWOOSH
SFF
HERE I WAS THINKING, "IF IT DIDN'T GO IN, I'D HOLD OFF UNTIL AFTER THE INTER-HIGH SCHOOL CHAMPION-SHIPS"...
BUT I GUESS I DON'T HAVE TO WAIT...
...TO GO SEE HER.

The answer to the silhouette quiz on page 6 is...

What! I don't believe it!!

It was **RUI**!!!

I wonder if anybody got this one...
If you did, please let me know.

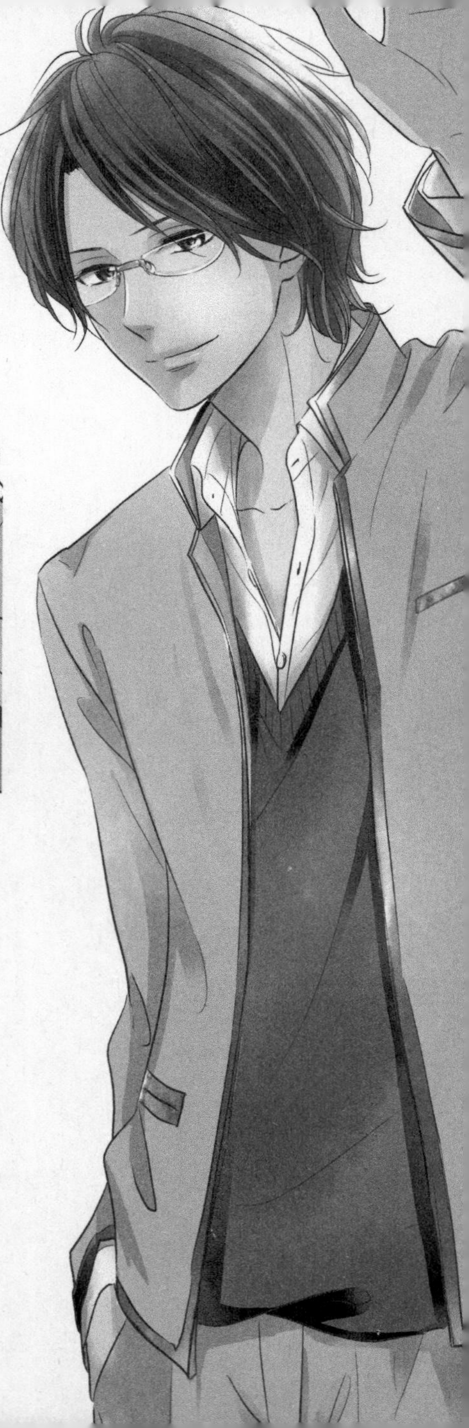
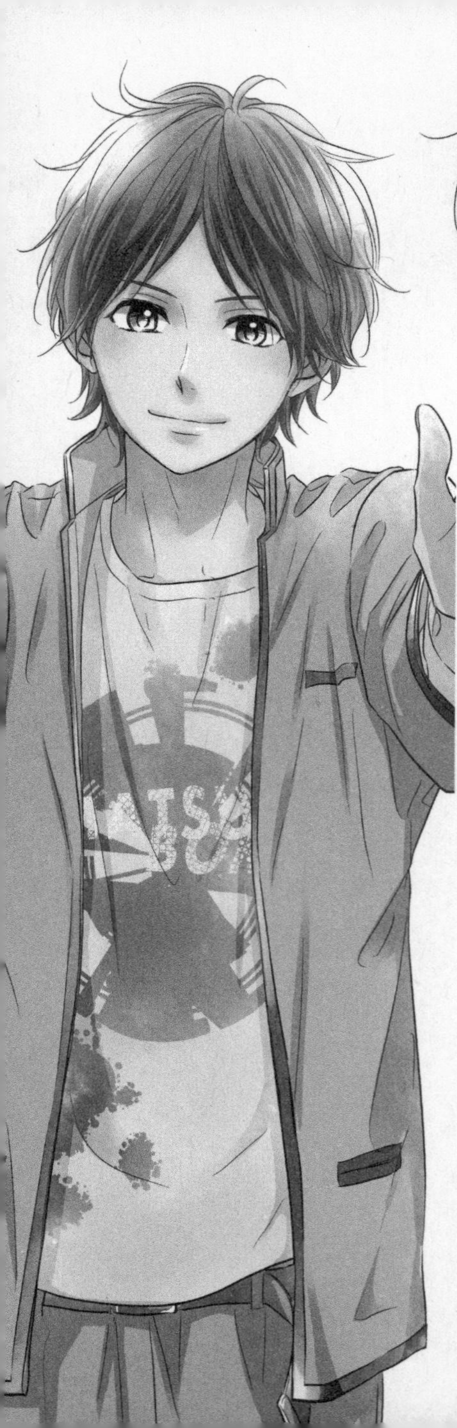

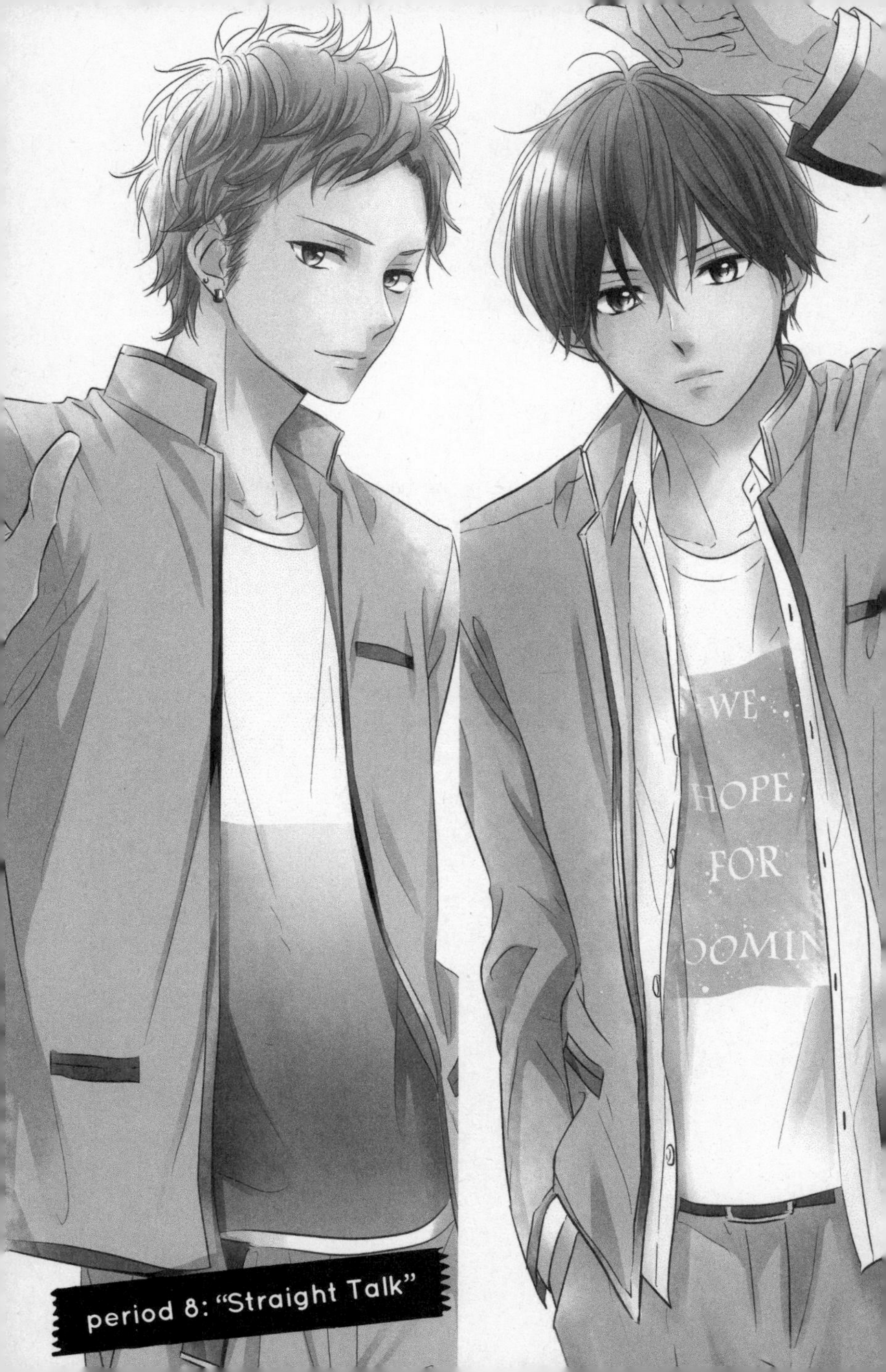
period 8: “Straight Talk”
WE
HOPE
FOR

...Happy Things Report...

When the story that starts on the next page (Chapter 8: "Straight Talk") was published, it was the first time I got to do a cover and opening color pages for an issue of *Dessert Magazine*.

I...I'm so happy...! Oooh!

This is all because of you, the readers who have supported me. Thank you for everything. I mean it.

Dessert December 2014 cover draft 1

(This is one I didn't use.)

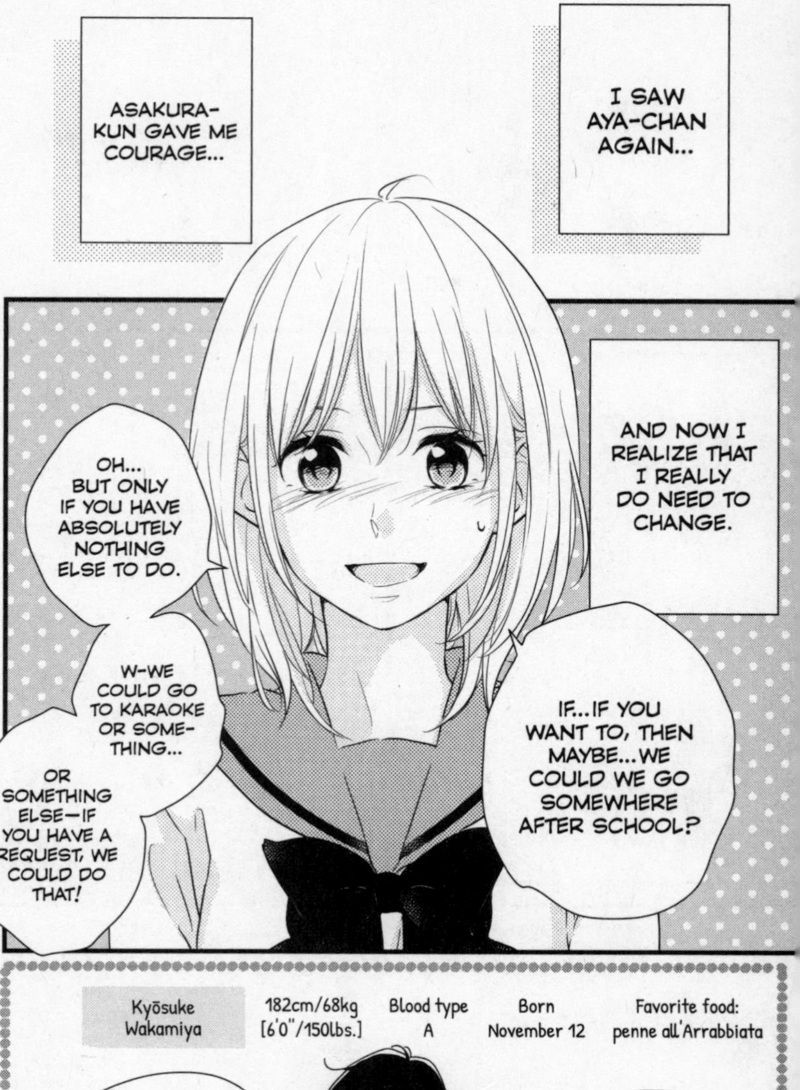
I SAW AYA-CHAN AGAIN...
ASAKURA-KUN GAVE ME COURAGE...
AND NOW I REALIZE THAT I REALLY DO NEED TO CHANGE.
IF...IF YOU WANT TO, THEN MAYBE...WE COULD WE GO SOMEWHERE AFTER SCHOOL?
W-WE COULD GO TO KARAOKE OR SOME-THING...
OR SOMETHING ELSE—IF YOU HAVE A REQUEST, WE COULD DO THAT!
OH... BUT ONLY IF YOU HAVE ABSOLUTELY NOTHING ELSE TO DO.

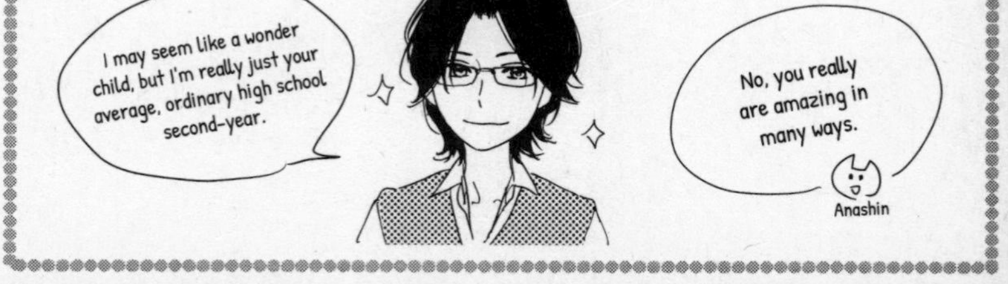
Kyōsuke Wakamiya
182cm/68kg [6'0"/150lbs.]
Blood type A
Born November 12
Favorite food: penne all'Arrabbiata
I may seem like a wonder child, but I'm really just your average, ordinary high school second-year.
No, you really are amazing in many ways.
Anashin

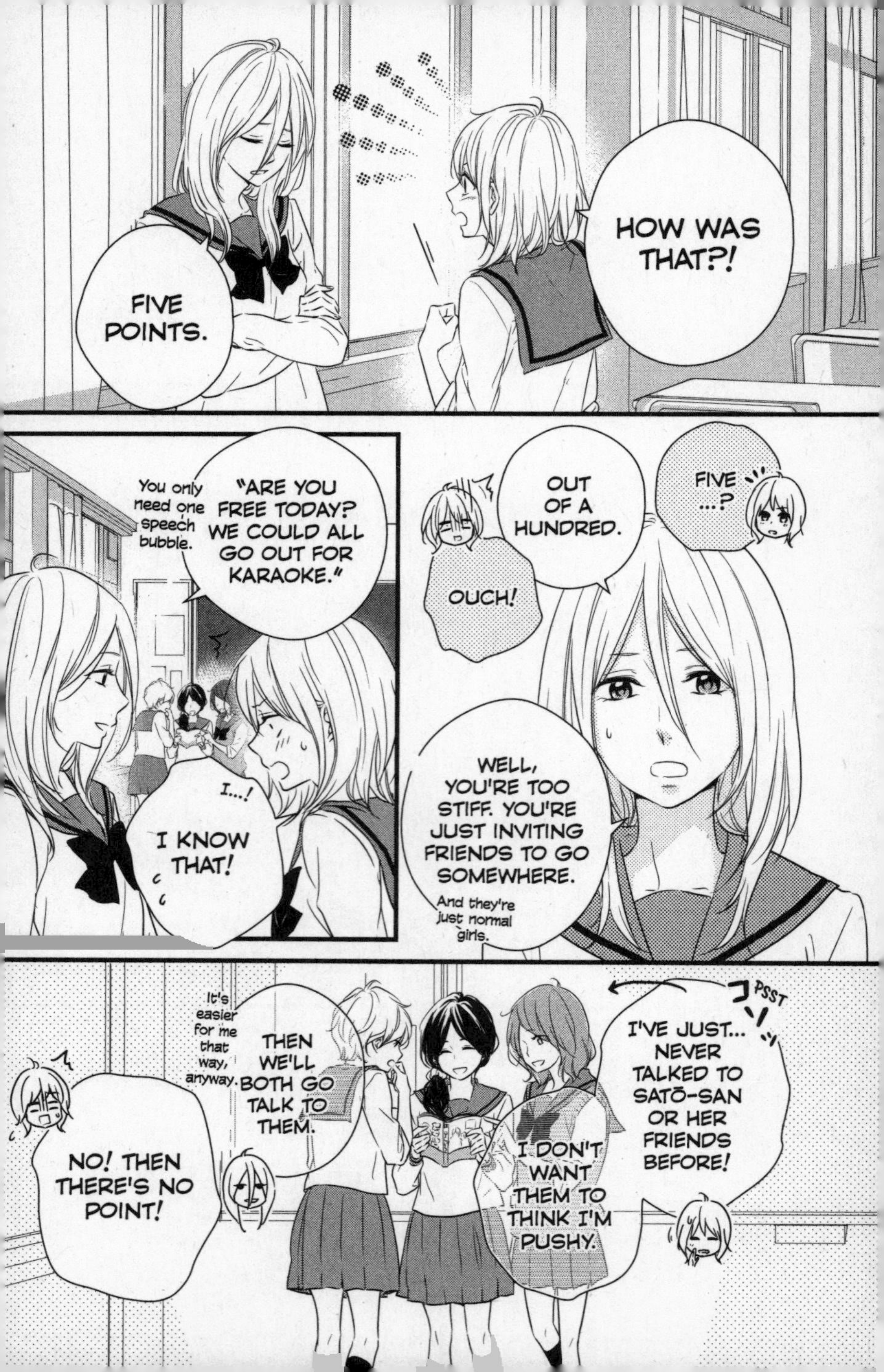
HOW WAS THAT?!
FIVE POINTS.
FIVE ...?
OUT OF A HUNDRED.
OUCH!
WELL, YOU'RE TOO STIFF. YOU'RE JUST INVITING FRIENDS TO GO SOMEWHERE.
And they're just normal girls.
"ARE YOU FREE TODAY? WE COULD ALL GO OUT FOR KARAOKE."
You only need one speech bubble.
I...!
I KNOW THAT!
PSST
I'VE JUST... NEVER TALKED TO SATŌ-SAN OR HER FRIENDS BEFORE!
I DON'T WANT THEM TO THINK I'M PUSHY.
THEN WE'LL BOTH GO TALK TO THEM.
It's easier for me that way, anyway.
NO! THEN THERE'S NO POINT!

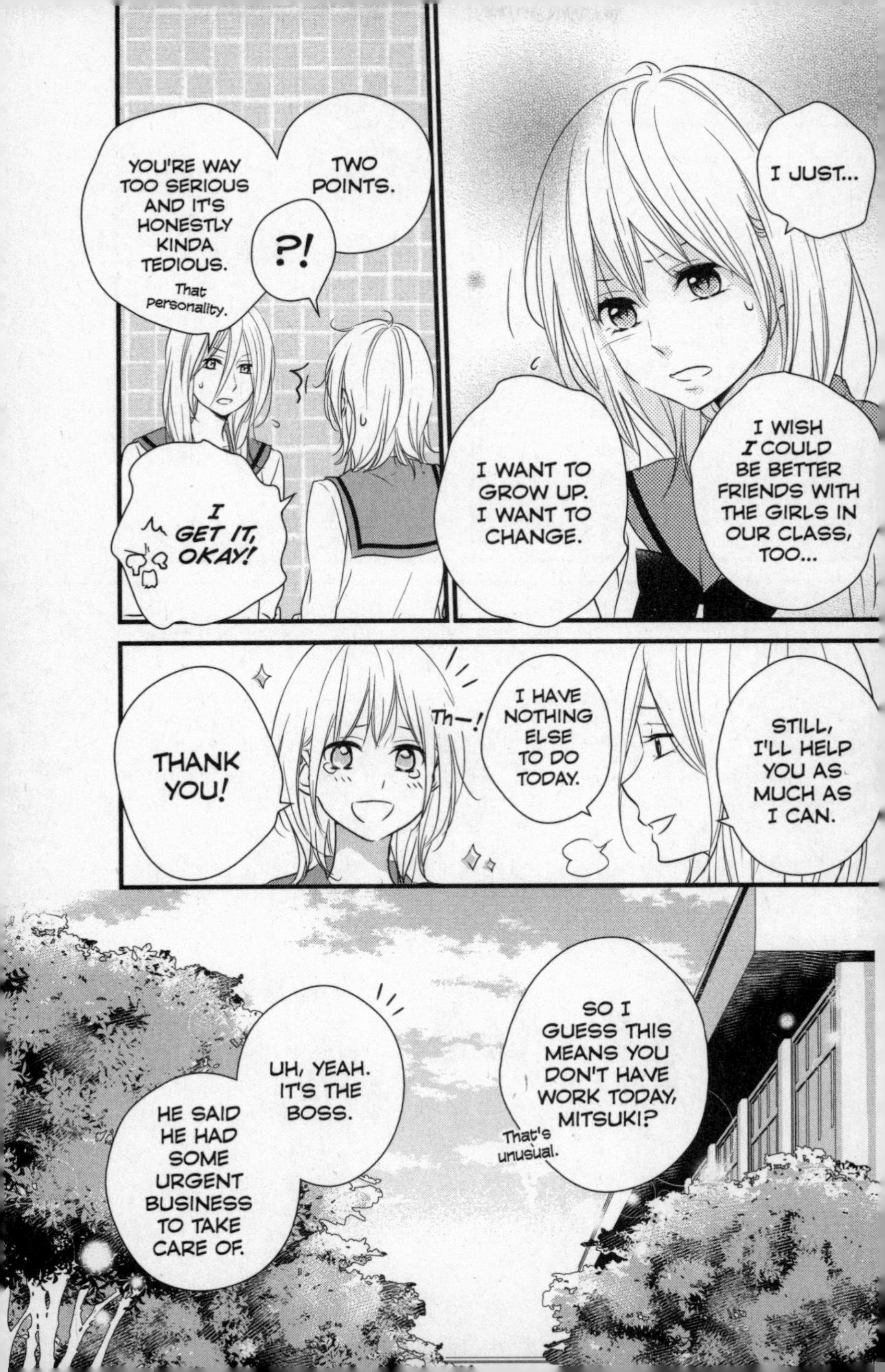
I JUST...
I WISH *I* COULD BE BETTER FRIENDS WITH THE GIRLS IN OUR CLASS, TOO...
I WANT TO GROW UP. I WANT TO CHANGE.
TWO POINTS.
YOU'RE WAY TOO SERIOUS AND IT'S HONESTLY KINDA TEDIOUS.
That personality.
?!
I GET IT, OKAY!
STILL, I'LL HELP YOU AS MUCH AS I CAN.
I HAVE NOTHING ELSE TO DO TODAY.
Th—!
THANK YOU!
SO I GUESS THIS MEANS YOU DON'T HAVE WORK TODAY, MITSUKI?
That's unusual.
UH, YEAH. IT'S THE BOSS.
HE SAID HE HAD SOME URGENT BUSINESS TO TAKE CARE OF.

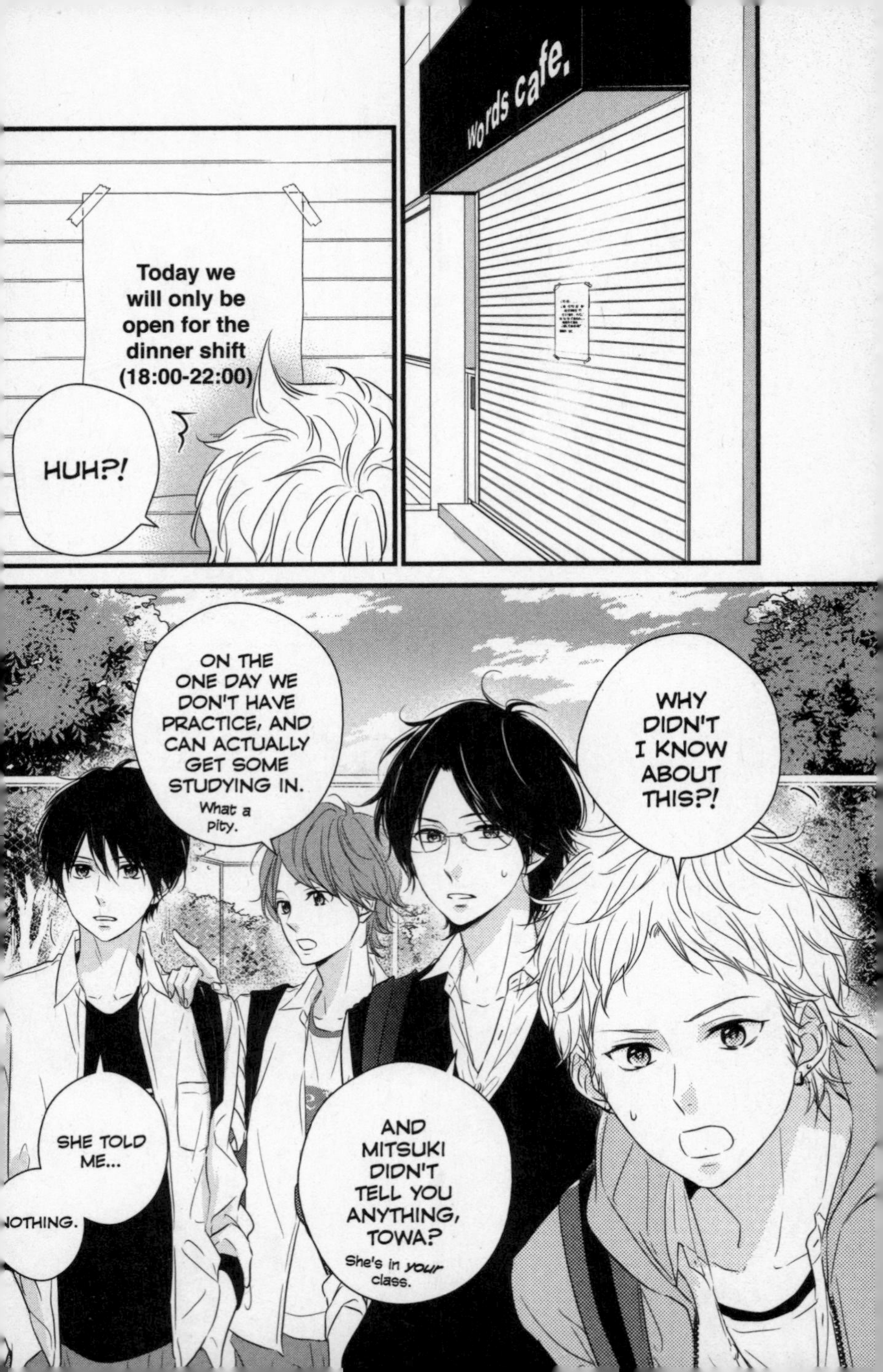
Words cafe.
Today we will only be open for the dinner shift (18:00-22:00)
HUH?!
WHY DIDN'T I KNOW ABOUT THIS?!
ON THE ONE DAY WE DON'T HAVE PRACTICE, AND CAN ACTUALLY GET SOME STUDYING IN.
What a pity.
AND MITSUKI DIDN'T TELL YOU ANYTHING, TOWA?
She's in *your* class.
SHE TOLD ME...
NOTHING.

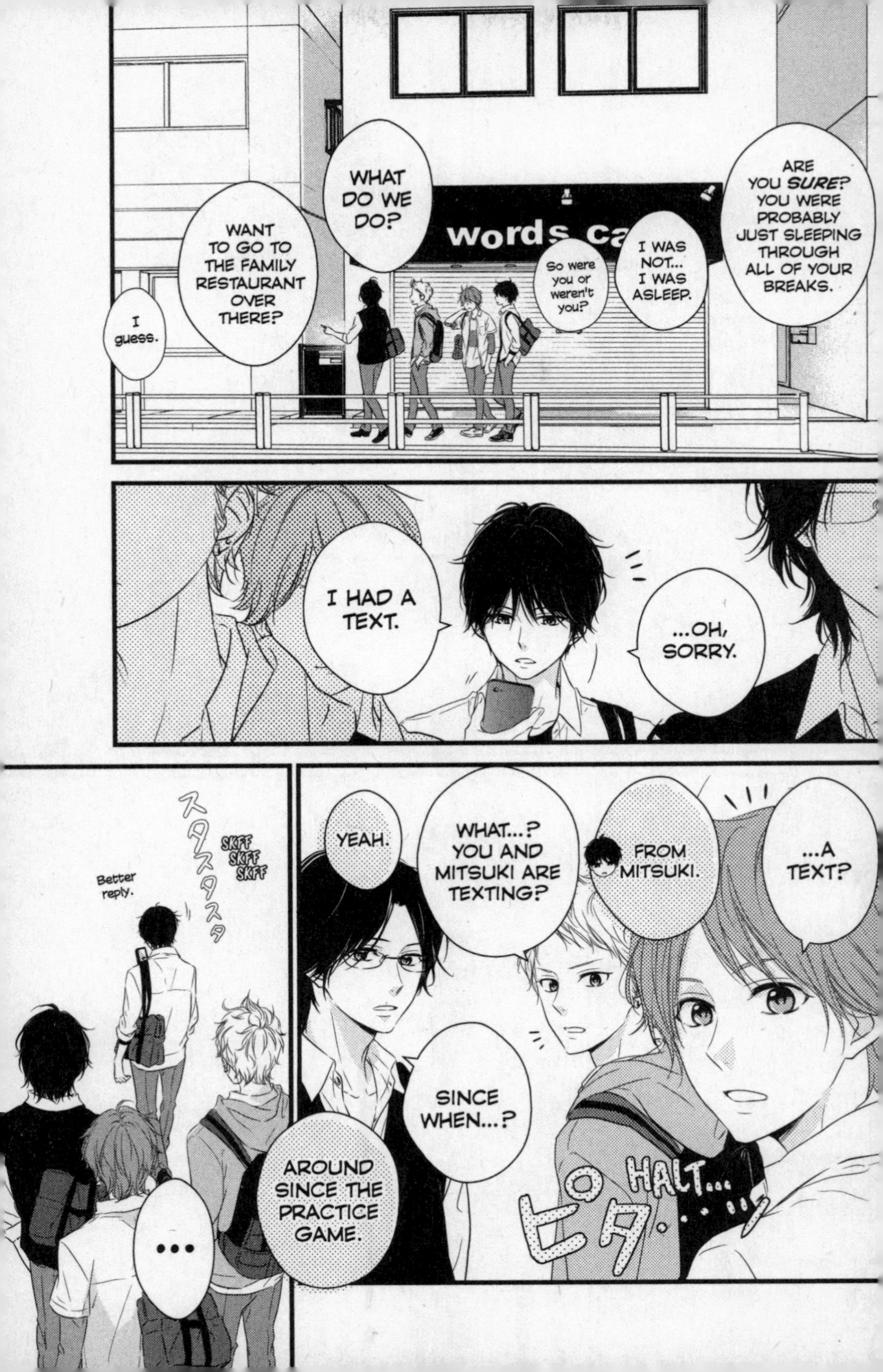
ARE YOU SURE? YOU WERE PROBABLY JUST SLEEPING THROUGH ALL OF YOUR BREAKS.
I WAS NOT... I WAS ASLEEP.
So were you or weren't you?
words ca
WHAT DO WE DO?
WANT TO GO TO THE FAMILY RESTAURANT OVER THERE?
I guess.
...OH, SORRY.
I HAD A TEXT.
...A TEXT?
FROM MITSUKI.
WHAT...? YOU AND MITSUKI ARE TEXTING?
YEAH.
SINCE WHEN...?
AROUND SINCE THE PRACTICE GAME.
HALT...
ピタ
スタスタ
SKFF SKFF SKFF
Better reply.
...

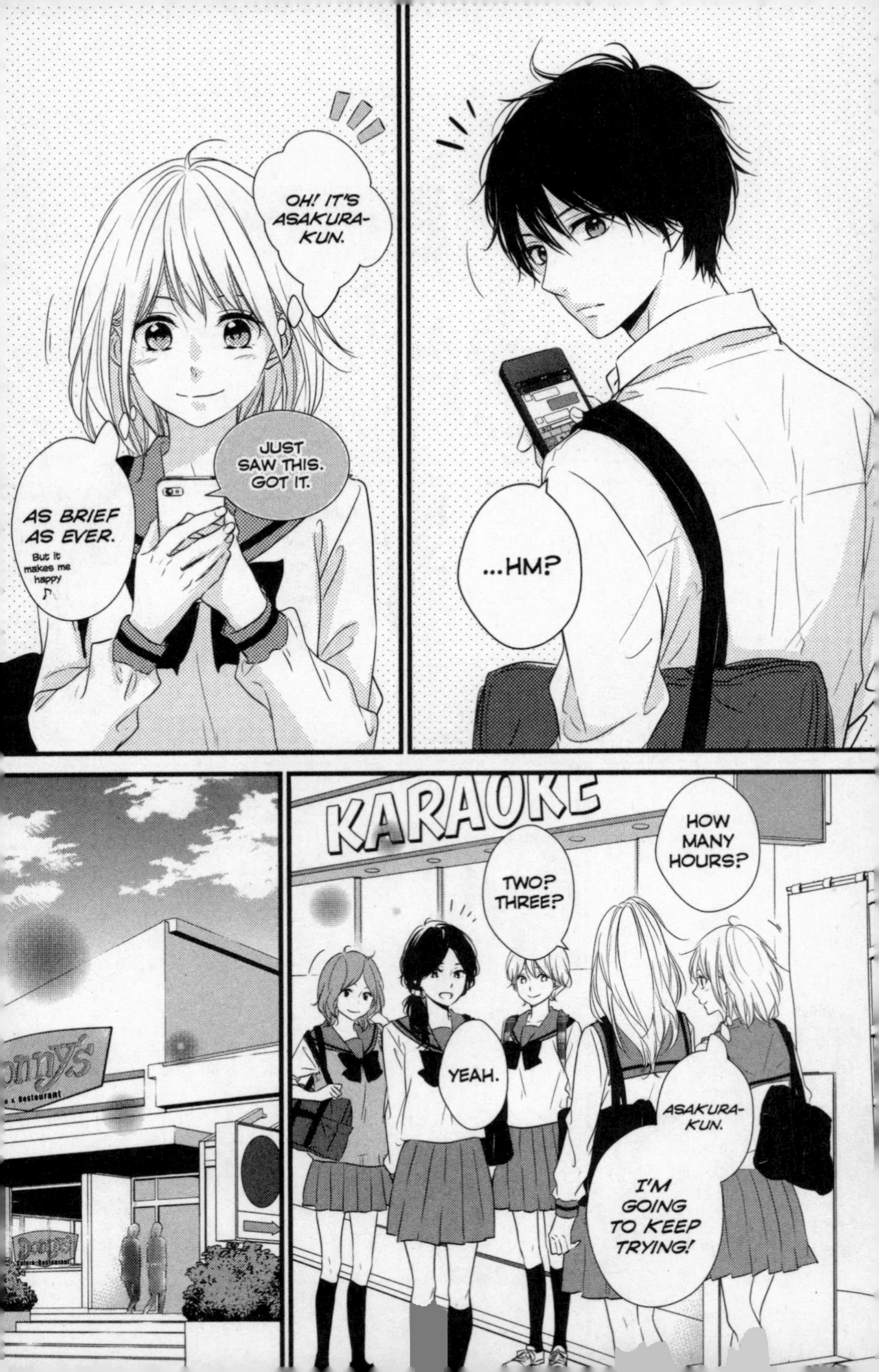
...HM?
OH! IT'S ASAKURA-KUN.
JUST SAW THIS. GOT IT.
AS BRIEF AS EVER.
But it makes me happy ♪
KARAOKE
HOW MANY HOURS?
TWO? THREE?
YEAH.
ASAKURA-KUN.
I'M GOING TO KEEP TRYING!

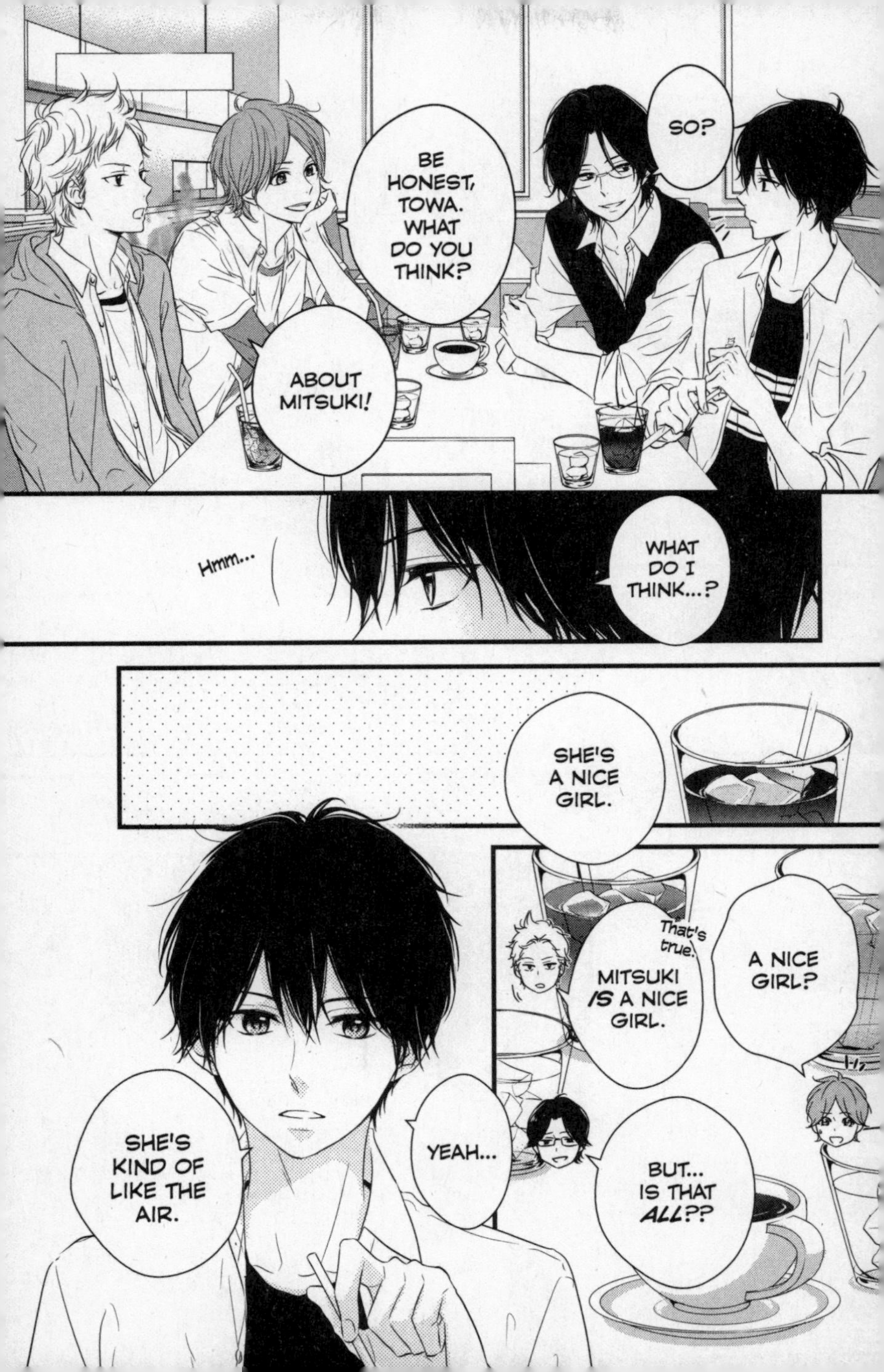

SO?
BE HONEST, TOWA. WHAT DO YOU THINK?
ABOUT MITSUKI!
WHAT DO I THINK...?
Hmm...
SHE'S A NICE GIRL.
A NICE GIRL?
That's true.
MITSUKI *IS* A NICE GIRL.
BUT... IS THAT ***ALL***??
YEAH...
SHE'S KIND OF LIKE THE AIR.

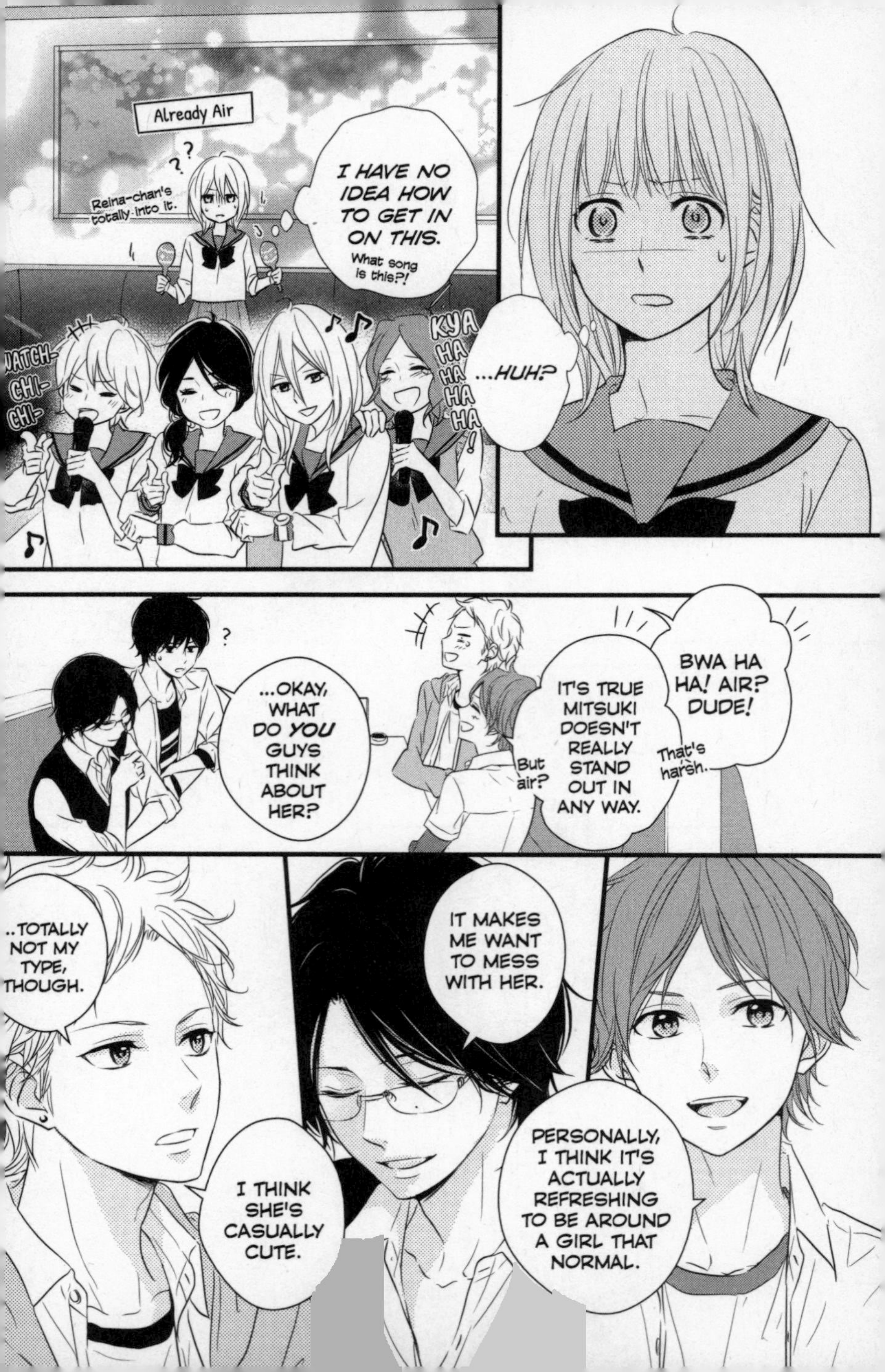
...HUH?
I HAVE NO IDEA HOW TO GET IN ON THIS.
What song is this?!
Already Air
KYA HA HA HA HA!
Reina-chan's totally into it.
WATCH-CHI-CHI-
BWA HA HA! AIR? DUDE!
That's harsh.
IT'S TRUE MITSUKI DOESN'T REALLY STAND OUT IN ANY WAY.
But air?
...OKAY, WHAT DO YOU GUYS THINK ABOUT HER?
PERSONALLY, I THINK IT'S ACTUALLY REFRESHING TO BE AROUND A GIRL THAT NORMAL.
IT MAKES ME WANT TO MESS WITH HER.
I THINK SHE'S CASUALLY CUTE.
...TOTALLY NOT MY TYPE, THOUGH.

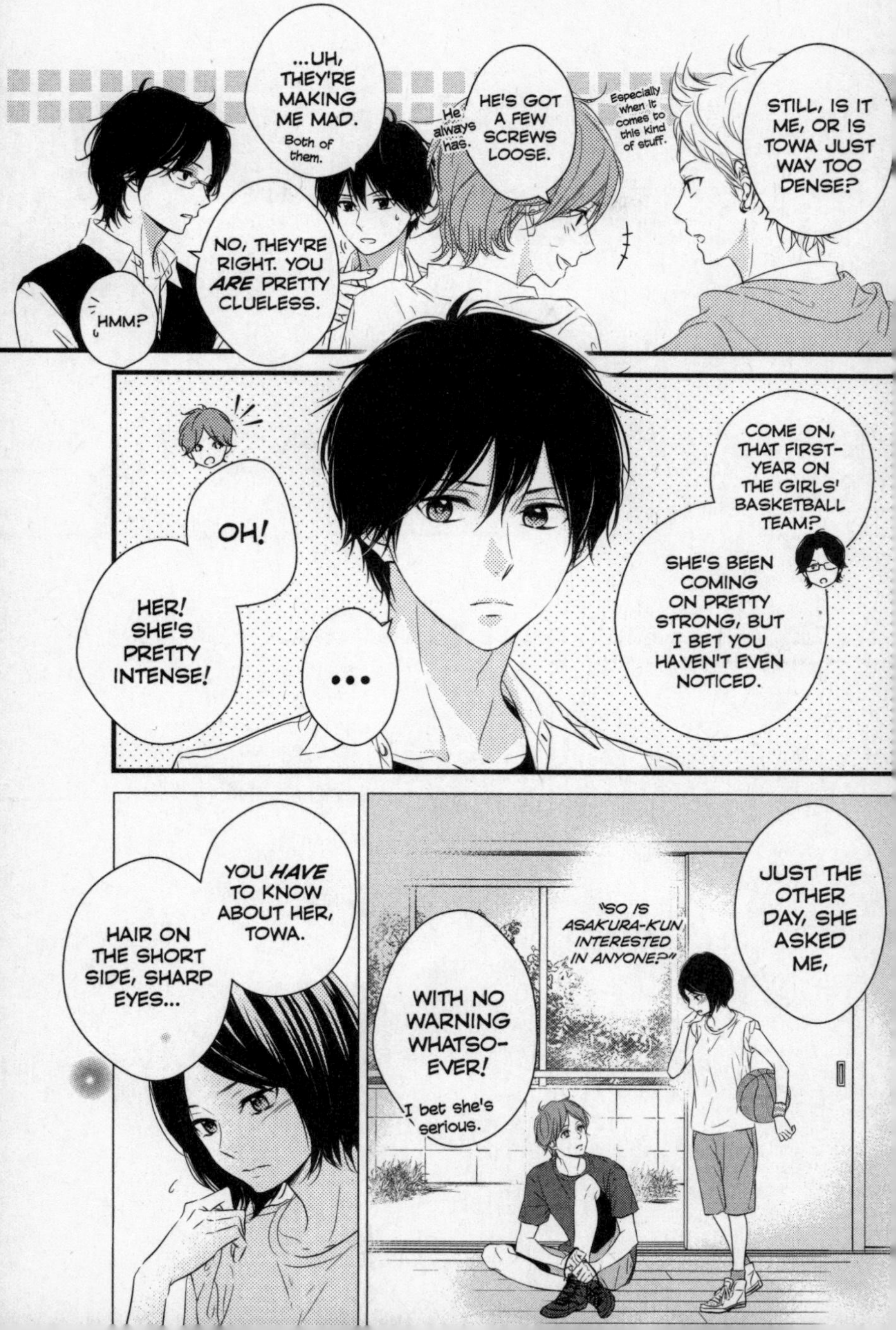
STILL, IS IT ME, OR IS TOWA JUST WAY TOO DENSE?
Especially when it comes to this kind of stuff.
HE'S GOT A FEW SCREWS LOOSE.
He always has.
...UH, THEY'RE MAKING ME MAD.
Both of them.
NO, THEY'RE RIGHT. YOU *ARE* PRETTY CLUELESS.
HMM?
COME ON, THAT FIRST-YEAR ON THE GIRLS' BASKETBALL TEAM?
SHE'S BEEN COMING ON PRETTY STRONG, BUT I BET YOU HAVEN'T EVEN NOTICED.
OH!
HER! SHE'S PRETTY INTENSE!
...
JUST THE OTHER DAY, SHE ASKED ME,
"SO IS ASAKURA-KUN INTERESTED IN ANYONE?"
WITH NO WARNING WHATSO-EVER!
I bet she's serious.
YOU *HAVE* TO KNOW ABOUT HER, TOWA.
HAIR ON THE SHORT SIDE, SHARP EYES...

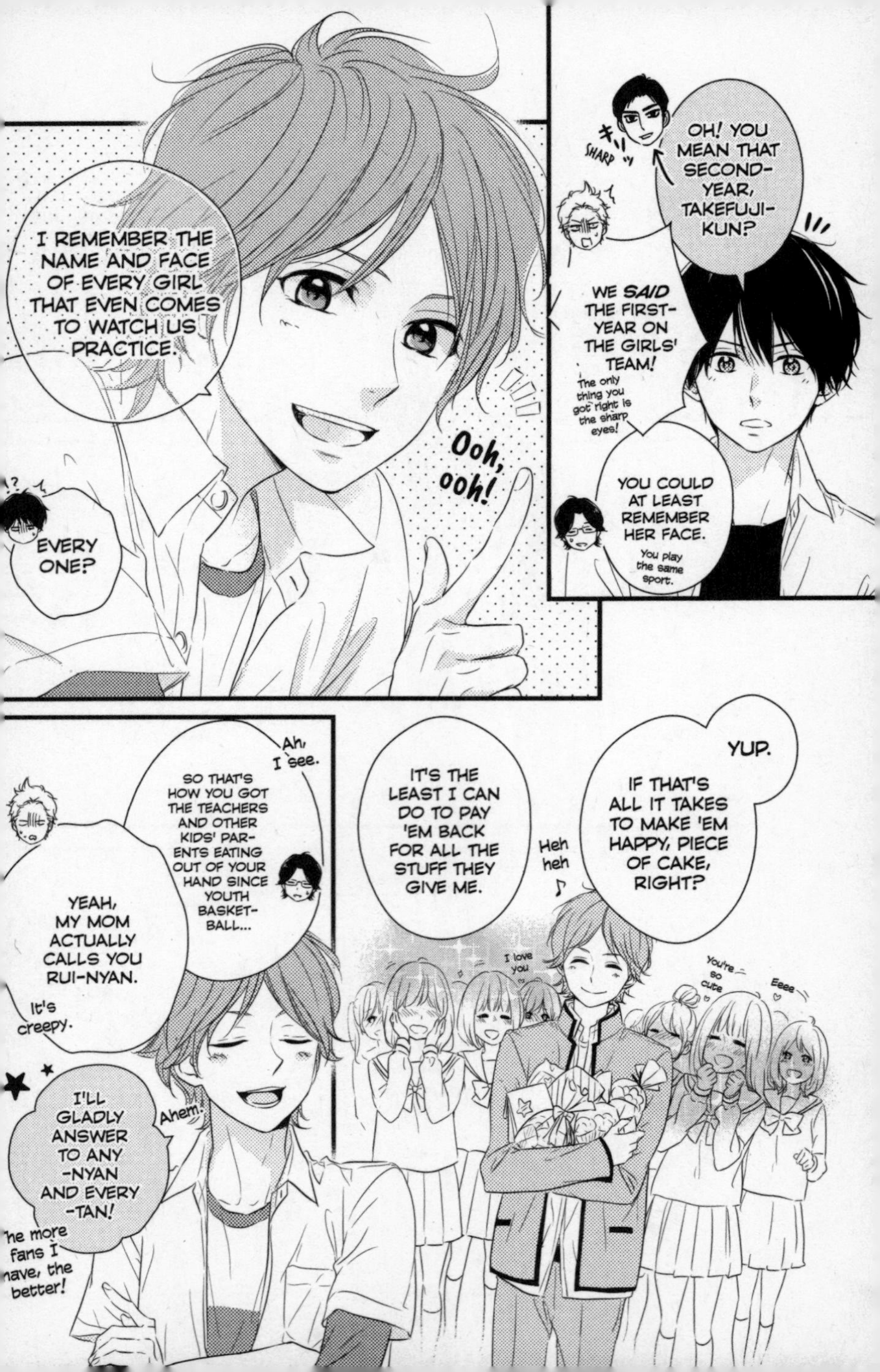

OH! YOU MEAN THAT SECOND-YEAR, TAKEFUJI-KUN?
SHARP
WE SAID THE FIRST-YEAR ON THE GIRLS' TEAM!
The only thing you got right is the sharp eyes!
YOU COULD AT LEAST REMEMBER HER FACE.
You play the same sport.
I REMEMBER THE NAME AND FACE OF EVERY GIRL THAT EVEN COMES TO WATCH US PRACTICE.
Ooh, ooh!
EVERY ONE?
YUP.
IF THAT'S ALL IT TAKES TO MAKE 'EM HAPPY, PIECE OF CAKE, RIGHT?
IT'S THE LEAST I CAN DO TO PAY 'EM BACK FOR ALL THE STUFF THEY GIVE ME.
Heh heh ♪
Eeee
You're so cute
I love you
Ah, I see.
SO THAT'S HOW YOU GOT THE TEACHERS AND OTHER KIDS' PARENTS EATING OUT OF YOUR HAND SINCE YOUTH BASKETBALL...
YEAH, MY MOM ACTUALLY CALLS YOU RUI-NYAN.
It's creepy.
I'LL GLADLY ANSWER TO ANY -NYAN AND EVERY -TAN!
Ahem.
he more fans I nave, the better!

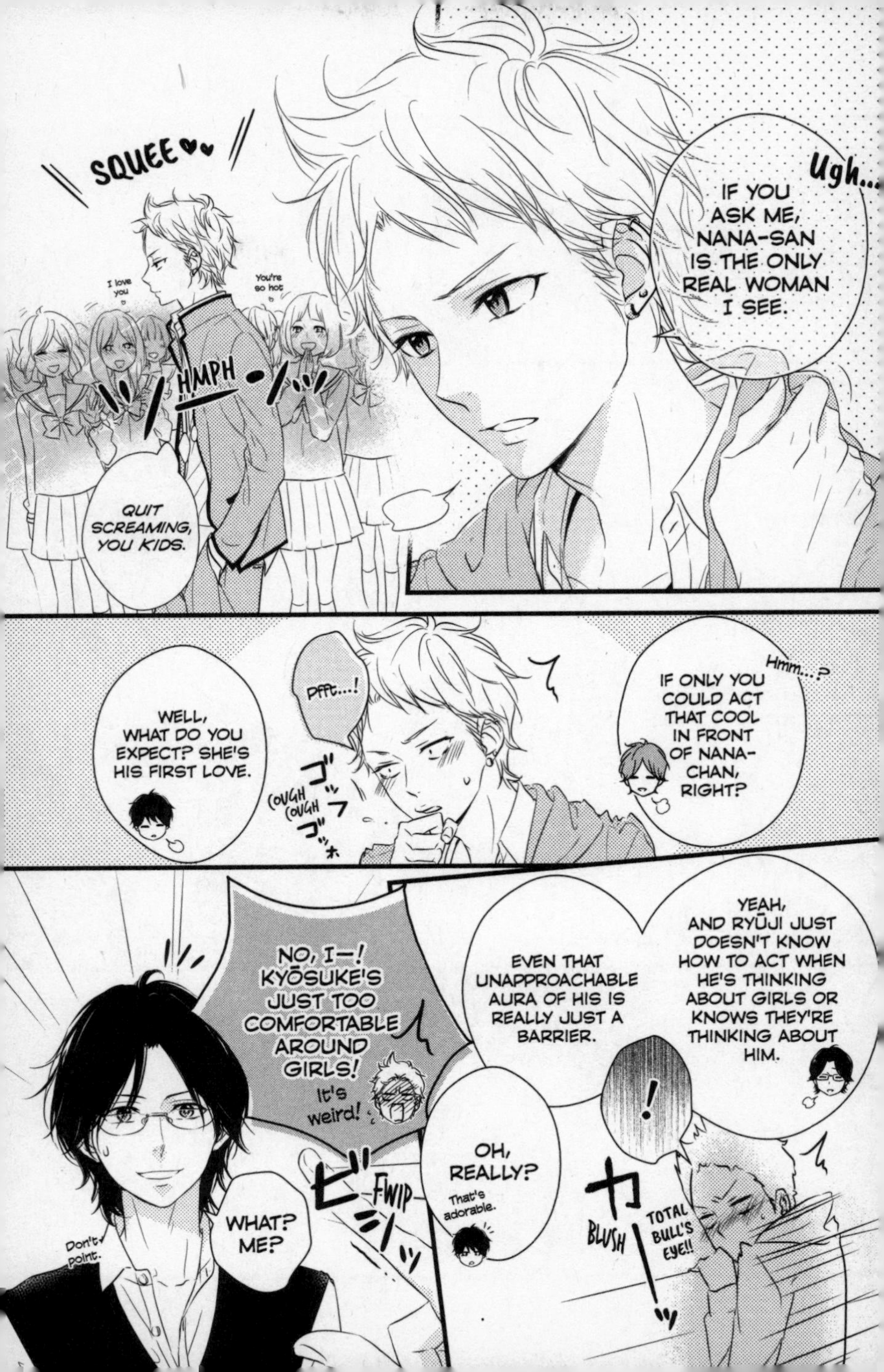
Ugh...
IF YOU ASK ME, NANA-SAN IS THE ONLY REAL WOMAN I SEE.
SQUEE
I love you
You're so hot
HMPH
QUIT SCREAMING, YOU KIDS.
Hmm...?
IF ONLY YOU COULD ACT THAT COOL IN FRONT OF NANA-CHAN, RIGHT?
Pffft...!
COUGH COUGH
WELL, WHAT DO YOU EXPECT? SHE'S HIS FIRST LOVE.
YEAH, AND RYŪJI JUST DOESN'T KNOW HOW TO ACT WHEN HE'S THINKING ABOUT GIRLS OR KNOWS THEY'RE THINKING ABOUT HIM.
EVEN THAT UNAPPROACHABLE AURA OF HIS IS REALLY JUST A BARRIER.
!
TOTAL BULL'S EYE!!
BLUSH
OH, REALLY?
That's adorable.
NO, I—! KYŌSUKE'S JUST TOO COMFORTABLE AROUND GIRLS!
It's weird!
FWIP
WHAT? ME?
Don't point.

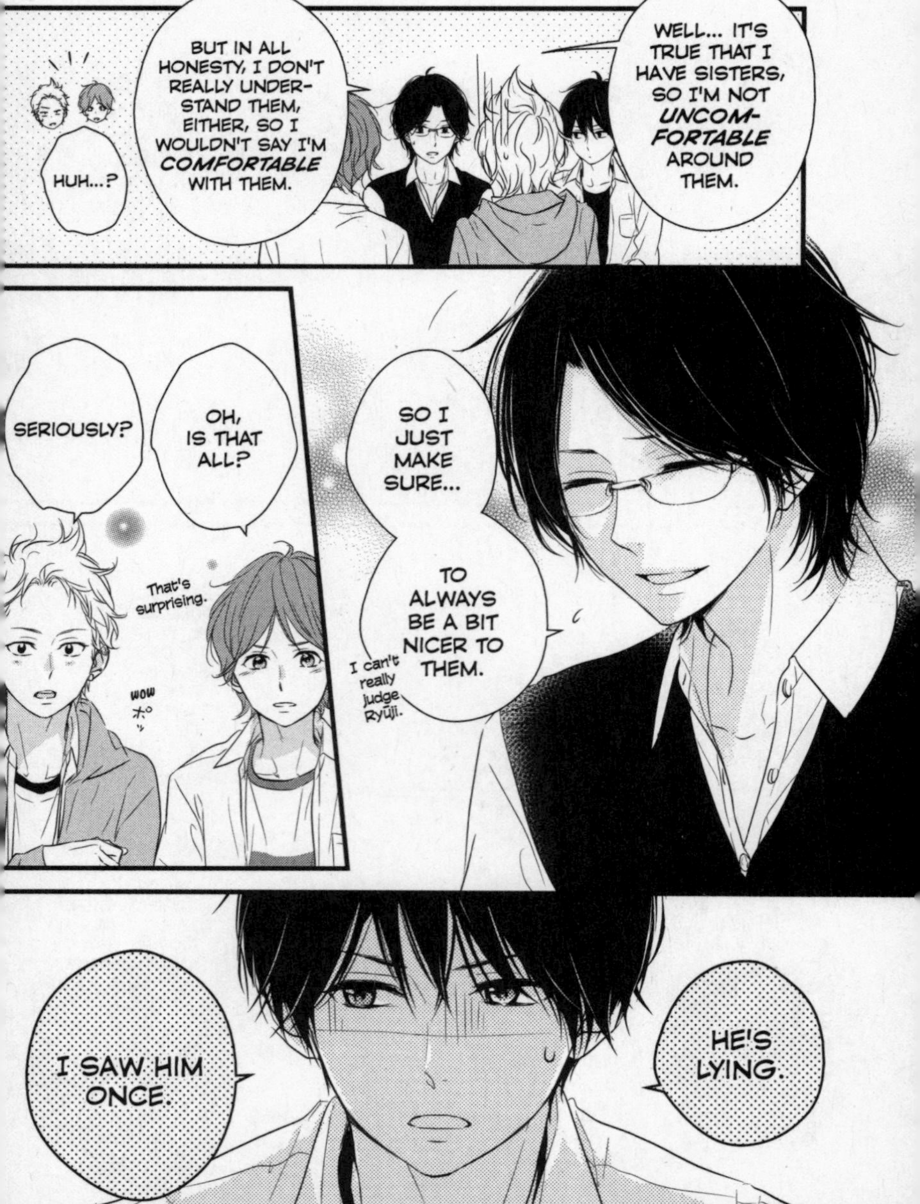
WELL... IT'S TRUE THAT I HAVE SISTERS, SO I'M NOT *UNCOMFORTABLE* AROUND THEM.
BUT IN ALL HONESTY, I DON'T REALLY UNDER-STAND THEM, EITHER, SO I WOULDN'T SAY I'M *COMFORTABLE* WITH THEM.
HUH...?
SO I JUST MAKE SURE...
TO ALWAYS BE A BIT NICER TO THEM.
I can't really judge Ryūji.
OH, IS THAT ALL?
SERIOUSLY?
That's surprising.
WOW
HE'S LYING.
I SAW HIM ONCE.

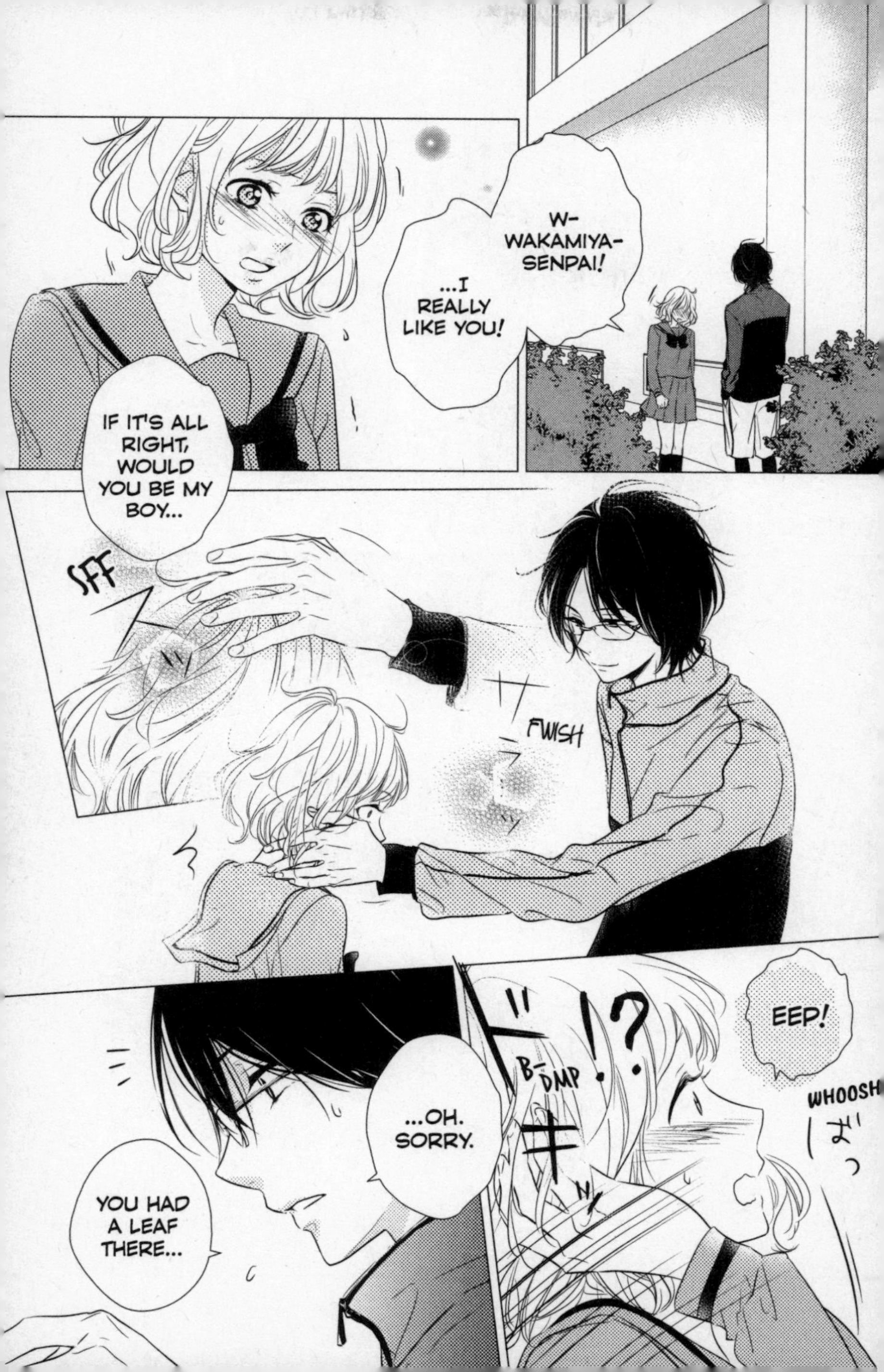
W- WAKAMIYA-SENPAI!
...I REALLY LIKE YOU!
IF IT'S ALL RIGHT, WOULD YOU BE MY BOY...
FWISH
SFF
EEP!
WHOOSH
ばっ
B-DMP
!?
...OH. SORRY.
YOU HAD A LEAF THERE...

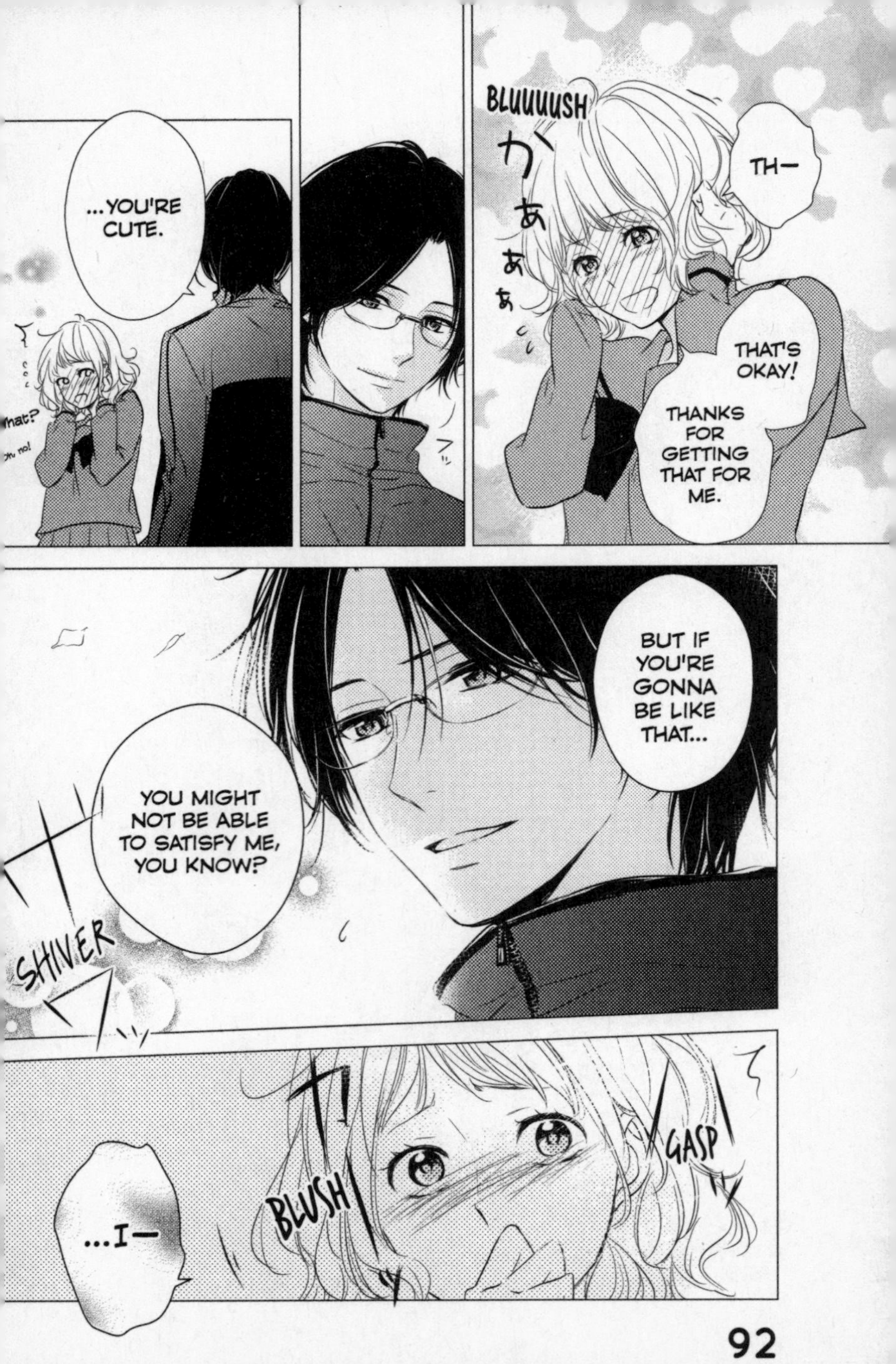
BLUUUUSH
かあああ
TH—
THAT'S OKAY!
THANKS FOR GETTING THAT FOR ME.
...YOU'RE CUTE.
BUT IF YOU'RE GONNA BE LIKE THAT...
YOU MIGHT NOT BE ABLE TO SATISFY ME, YOU KNOW?
SHIVER
GASP
BLUSH
...I—

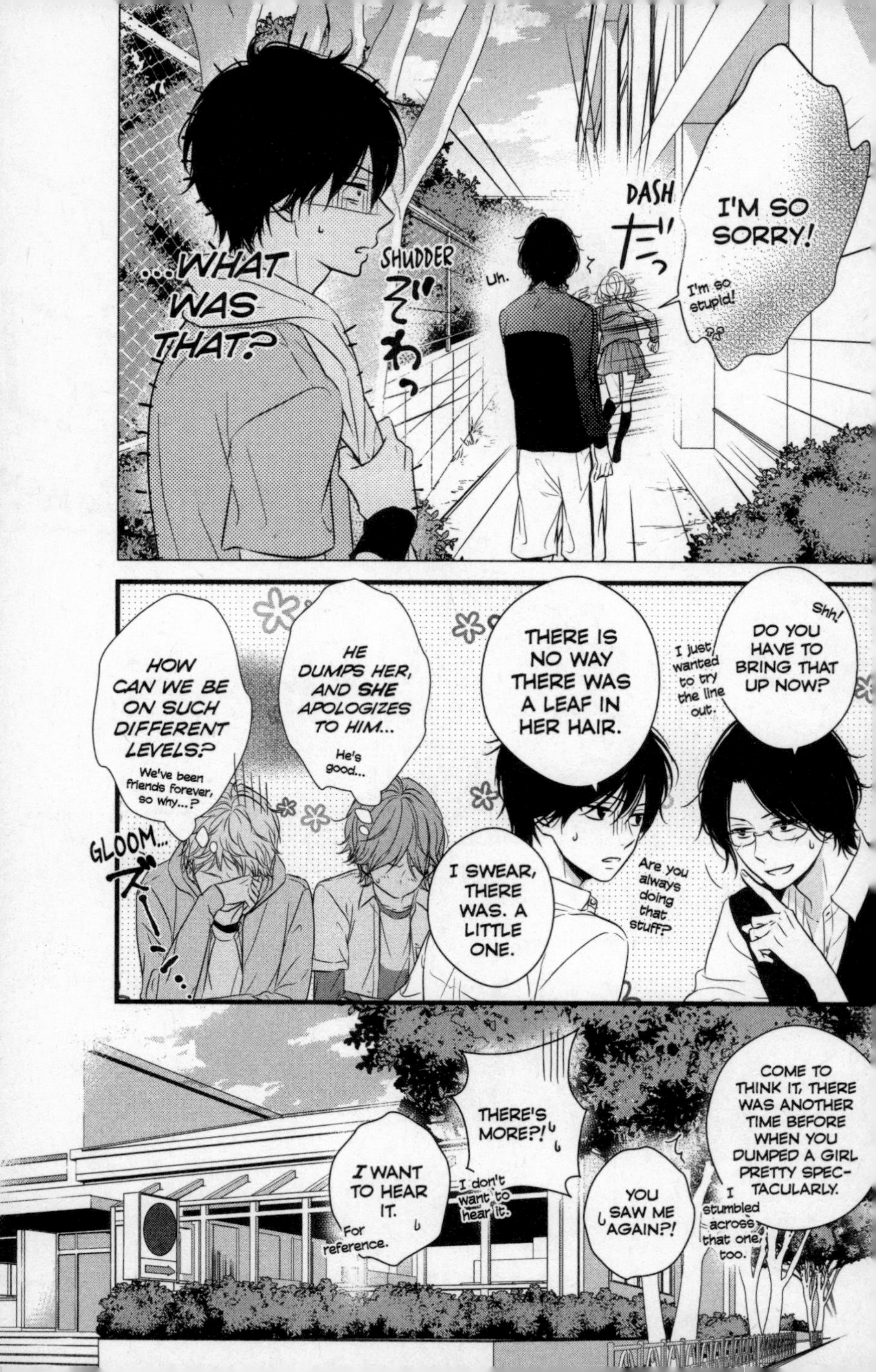
I'M SO SORRY!
I'm so stupid!
DASH
Uh.
SHUDDER
...WHAT WAS THAT?
Shh!
DO YOU HAVE TO BRING THAT UP NOW?
I just wanted to try the line out.
THERE IS NO WAY THERE WAS A LEAF IN HER HAIR.
Are you always doing that stuff?
I SWEAR, THERE WAS. A LITTLE ONE.
HE DUMPS HER, AND SHE APOLOGIZES TO HIM...
He's good...
HOW CAN WE BE ON SUCH DIFFERENT LEVELS?
We've been friends forever, so why...?
GLOOM...
COME TO THINK IT, THERE WAS ANOTHER TIME BEFORE WHEN YOU DUMPED A GIRL PRETTY SPEC-TACULARLY.
I stumbled across that one, too.
YOU SAW ME AGAIN?!
THERE'S MORE?!
I don't want to hear it.
I WANT TO HEAR IT.
For reference.

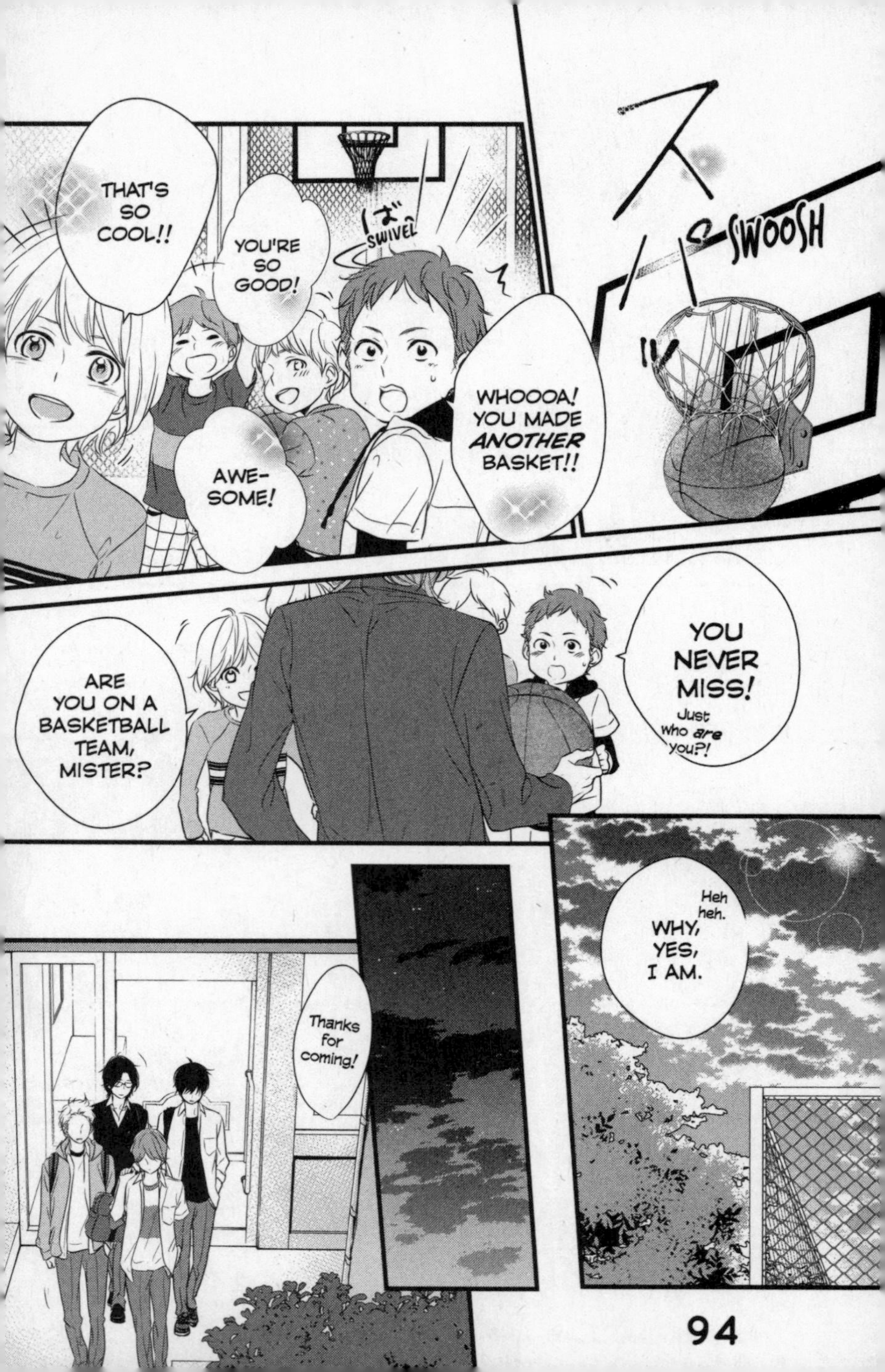
SWOOSH
WHOOOA! YOU MADE ANOTHER BASKET!!
ば SWIVEL
YOU'RE SO GOOD!
THAT'S SO COOL!!
AWE-SOME!
YOU NEVER MISS!
Just who are you?!
ARE YOU ON A BASKETBALL TEAM, MISTER?
Heh heh.
WHY, YES, I AM.
Thanks for coming!

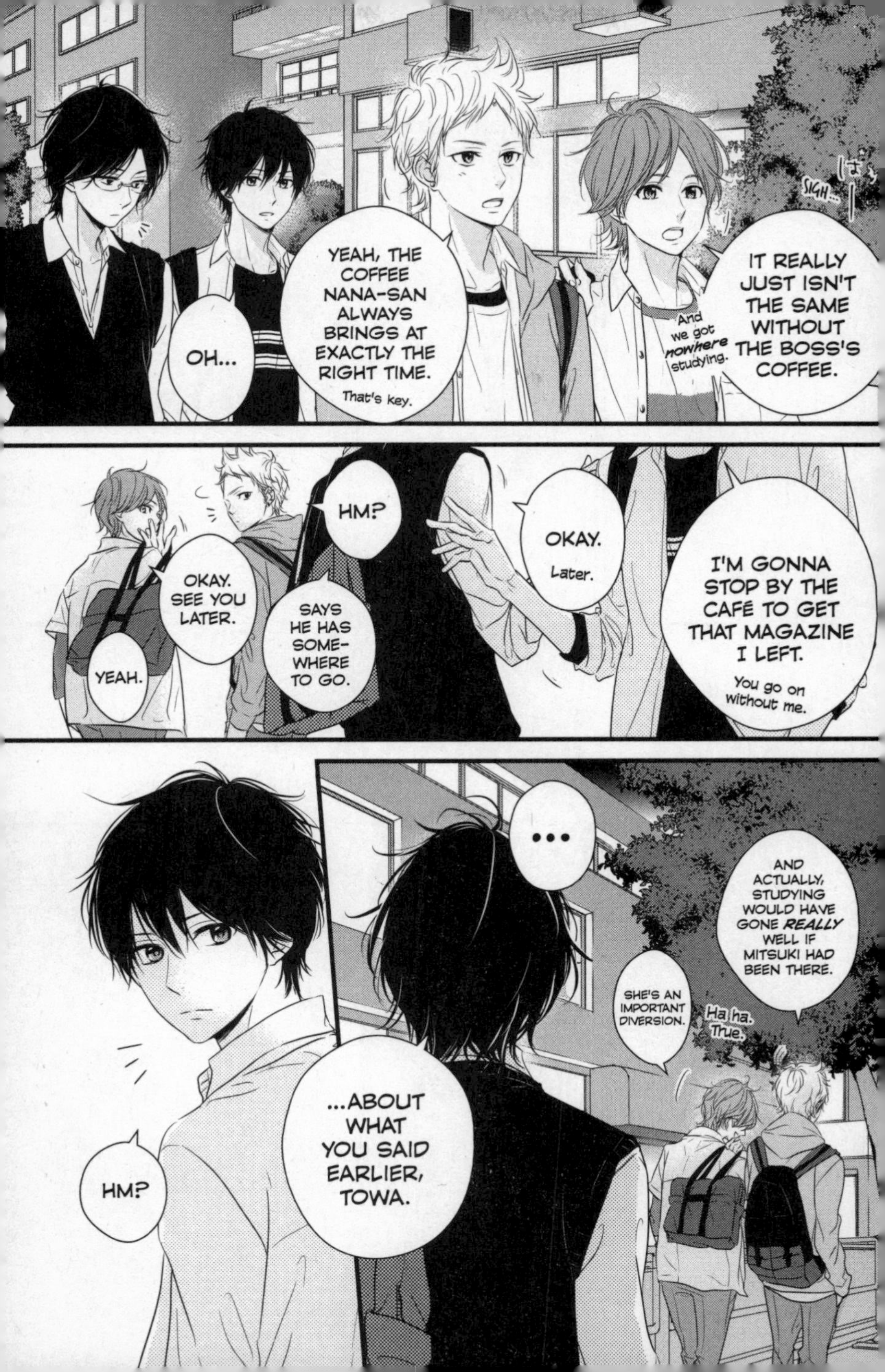
SIGH...
IT REALLY JUST ISN'T THE SAME WITHOUT THE BOSS'S COFFEE.
And we got *nowhere* studying.
YEAH, THE COFFEE NANA-SAN ALWAYS BRINGS AT EXACTLY THE RIGHT TIME.
That's key.
OH...
I'M GONNA STOP BY THE CAFÉ TO GET THAT MAGAZINE I LEFT.
You go on without me.
OKAY.
Later.
HM?
SAYS HE HAS SOME-WHERE TO GO.
OKAY. SEE YOU LATER.
YEAH.
...
AND ACTUALLY, STUDYING WOULD HAVE GONE *REALLY* WELL IF MITSUKI HAD BEEN THERE.
Ha ha. True.
SHE'S AN IMPORTANT DIVERSION.
...ABOUT WHAT YOU SAID EARLIER, TOWA.
HM?

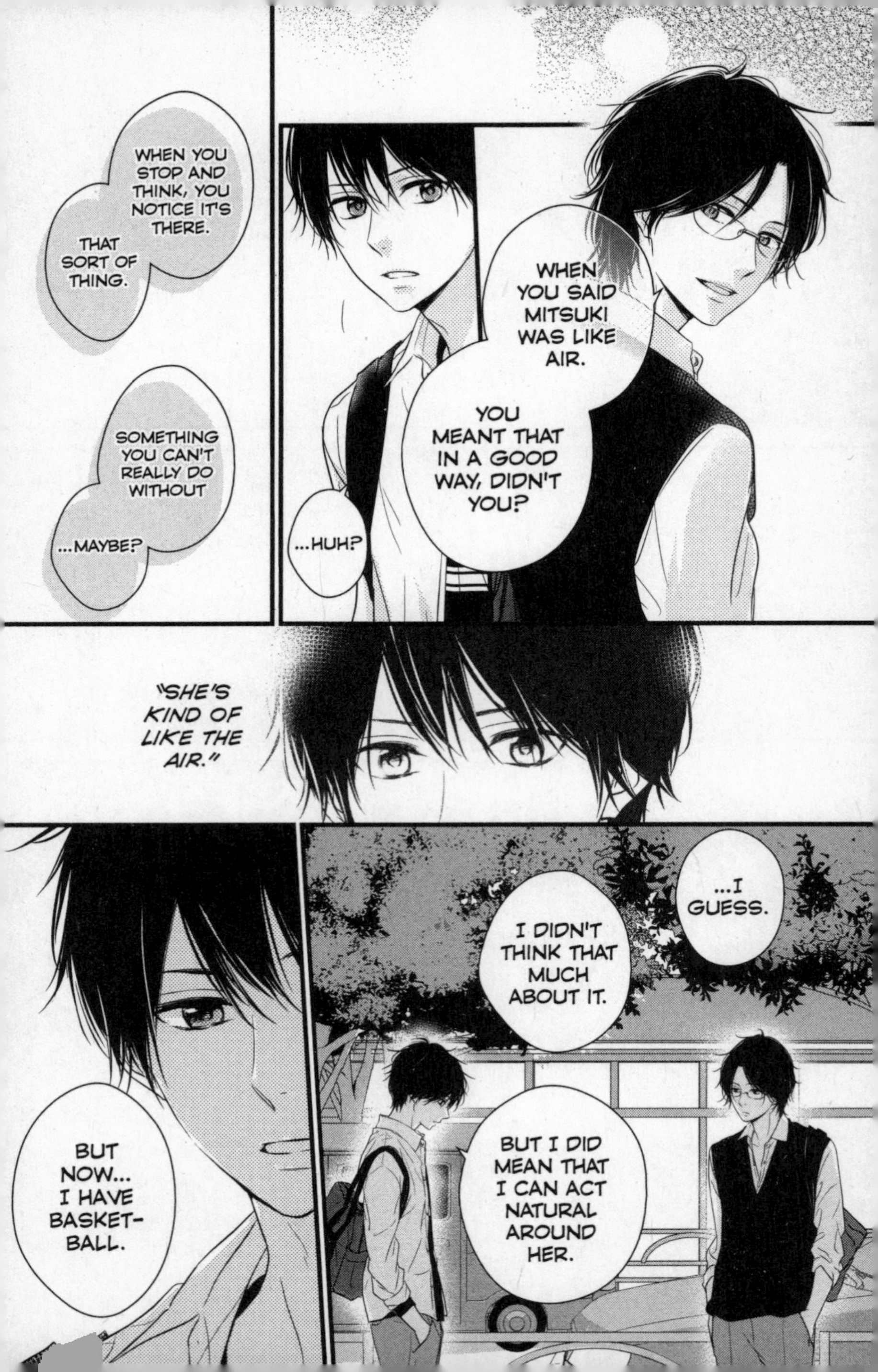
WHEN YOU SAID MITSUKI WAS LIKE AIR.
YOU MEANT THAT IN A GOOD WAY, DIDN'T YOU?
...HUH?
WHEN YOU STOP AND THINK, YOU NOTICE IT'S THERE.
THAT SORT OF THING.
SOMETHING YOU CAN'T REALLY DO WITHOUT
...MAYBE?
"SHE'S KIND OF LIKE THE AIR."
...I GUESS.
I DIDN'T THINK THAT MUCH ABOUT IT.
BUT I DID MEAN THAT I CAN ACT NATURAL AROUND HER.
BUT NOW... I HAVE BASKET-BALL.

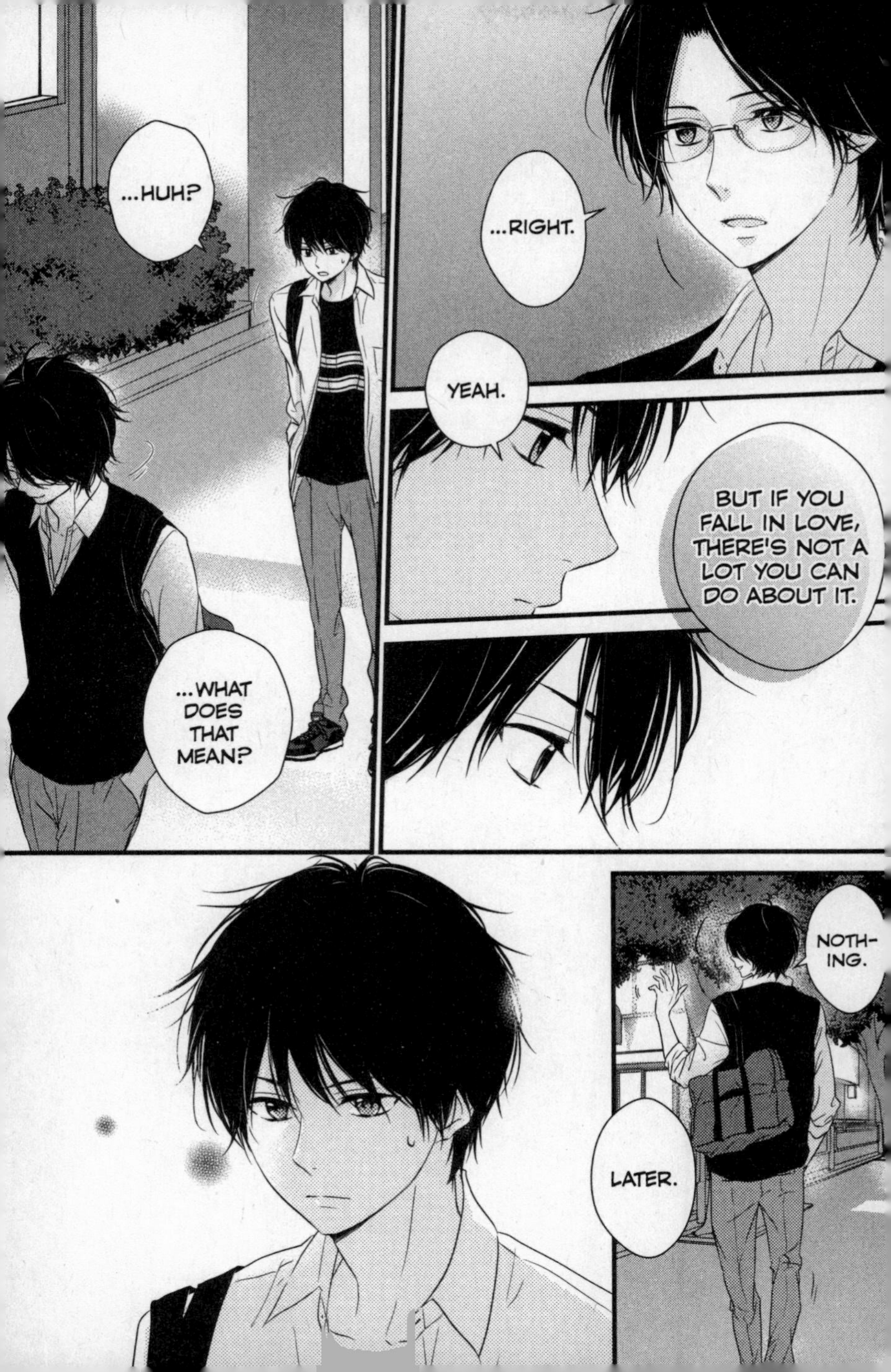
...RIGHT.
YEAH.
BUT IF YOU FALL IN LOVE, THERE'S NOT A LOT YOU CAN DO ABOUT IT.
...HUH?
...WHAT DOES THAT MEAN?
NOTH-ING.
LATER.

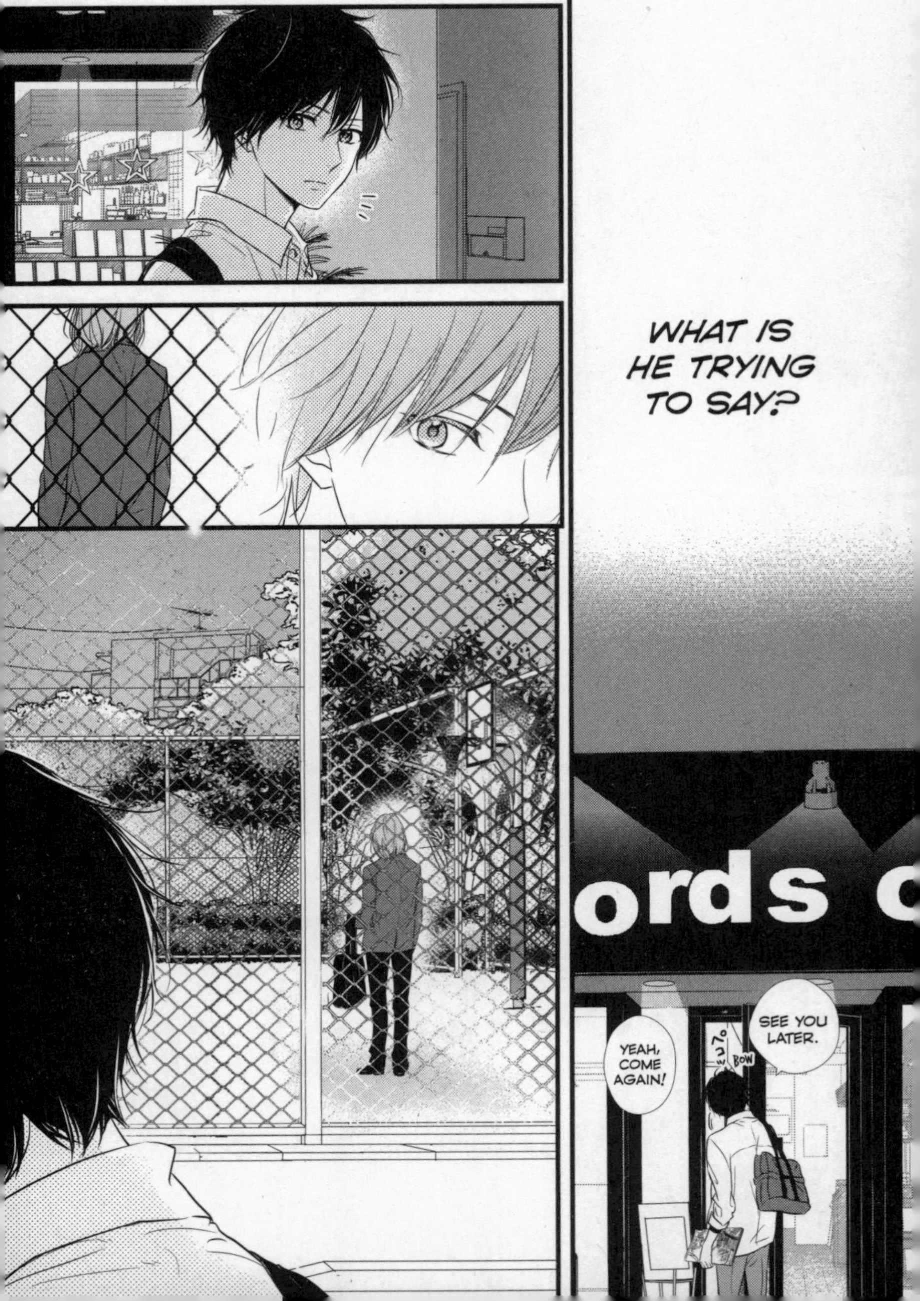
WHAT IS HE TRYING TO SAY?
ords
SEE YOU LATER.
BOW
YEAH, COME AGAIN!

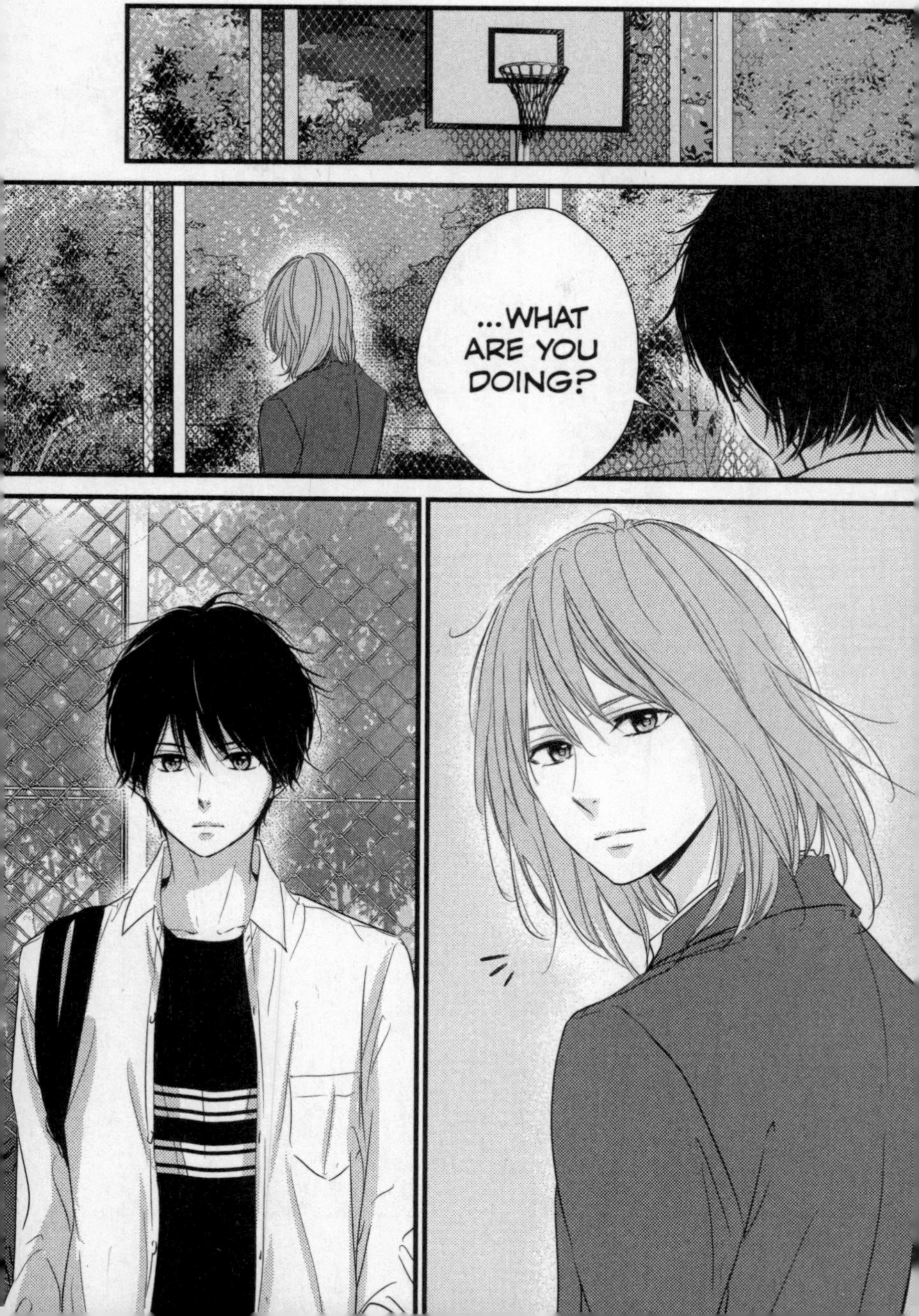
...WHAT
ARE YOU
DOING?

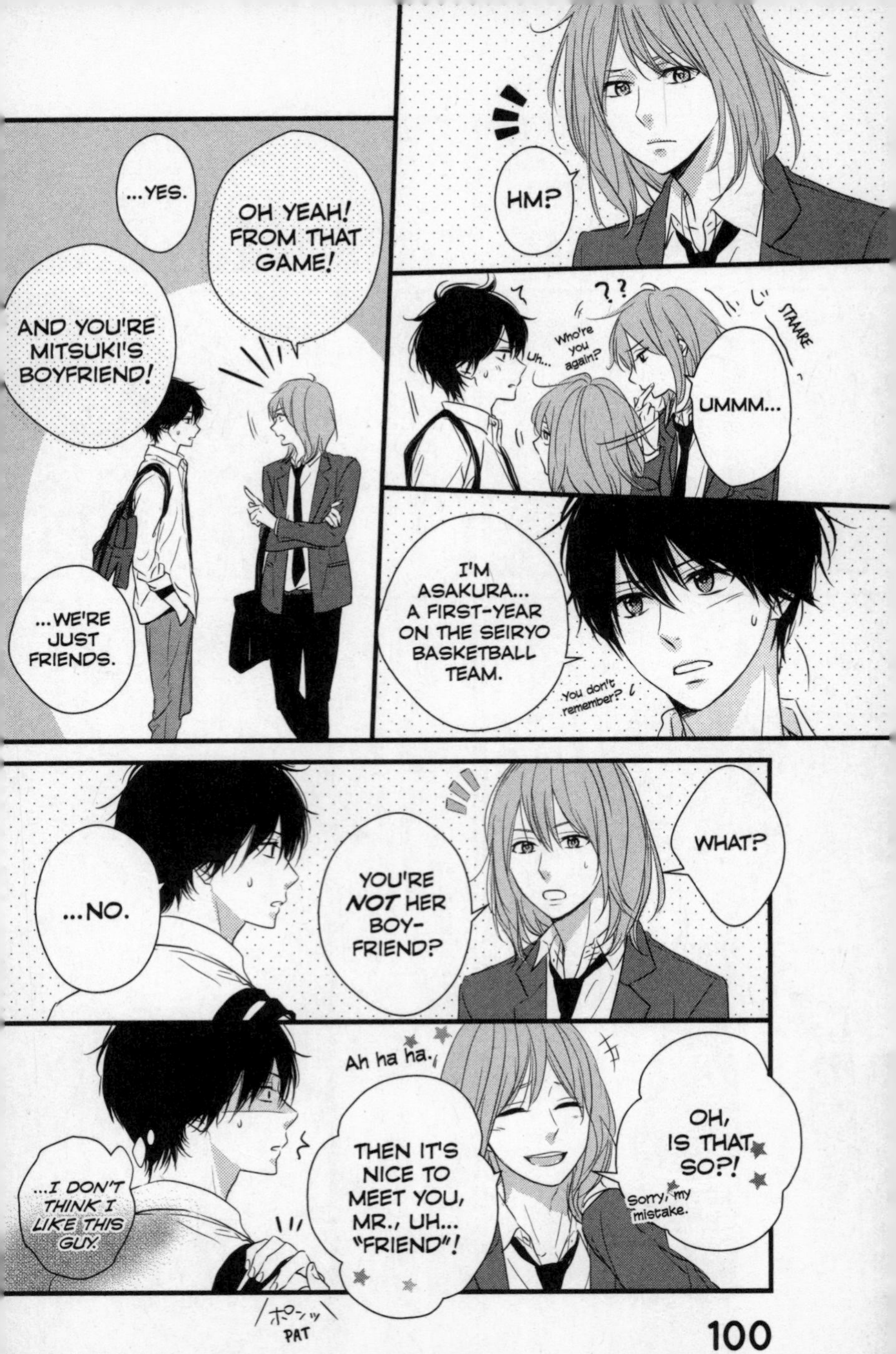
HM?
STAARE
UMMM...
Who're you again?
Uh...
I'M ASAKURA... A FIRST-YEAR ON THE SEIRYO BASKETBALL TEAM.
You don't remember?
OH YEAH! FROM THAT GAME!
...YES.
AND YOU'RE MITSUKI'S BOYFRIEND!
...WE'RE JUST FRIENDS.
WHAT?
YOU'RE *NOT* HER BOY-FRIEND?
...NO.
OH, IS THAT SO?!
Sorry, my mistake.
Ah ha ha.
THEN IT'S NICE TO MEET YOU, MR., UH... "FRIEND"!
...I DON'T THINK I LIKE THIS GUY.
ポーンッ
PAT

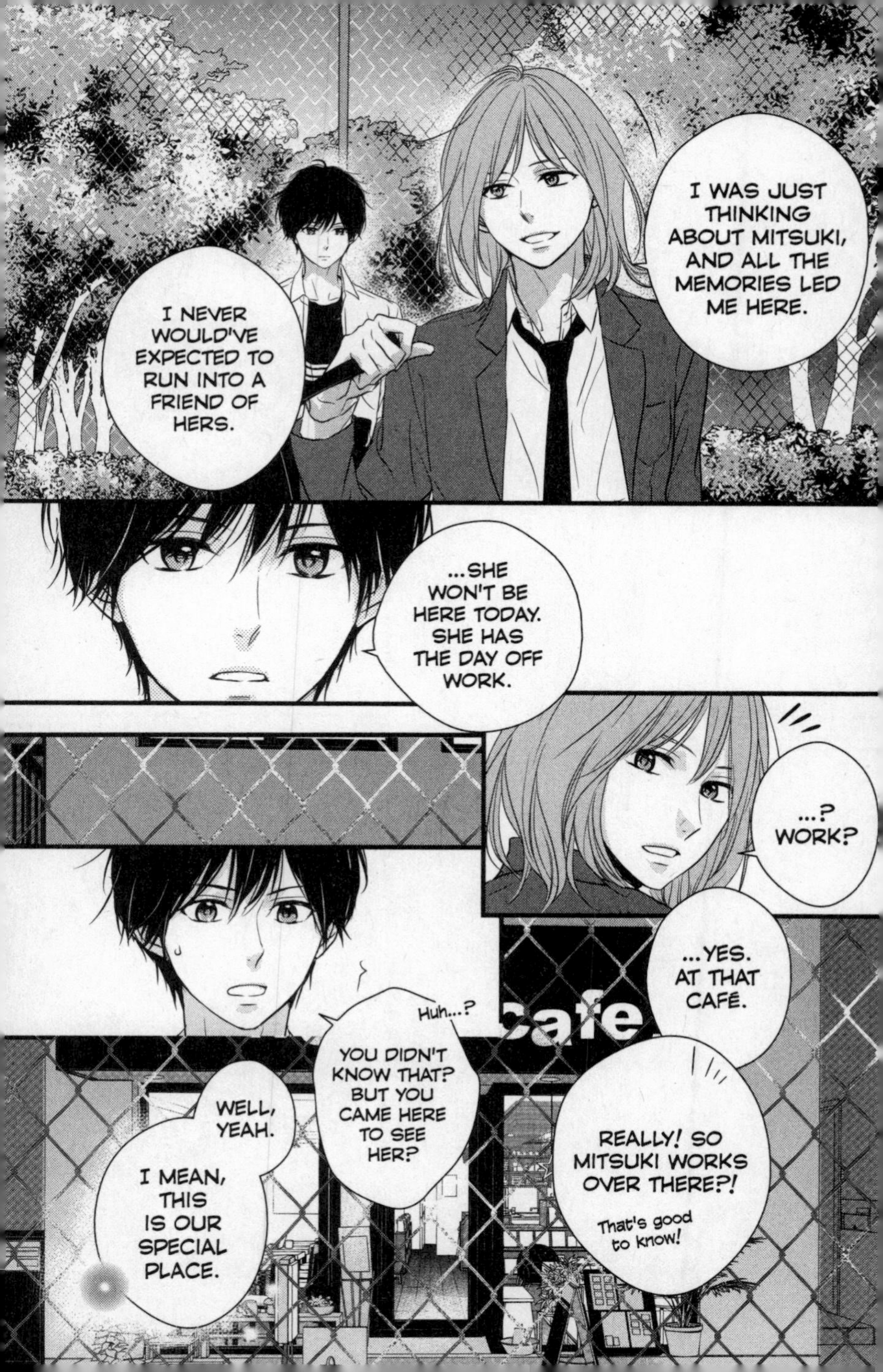
I WAS JUST THINKING ABOUT MITSUKI, AND ALL THE MEMORIES LED ME HERE.
I NEVER WOULD'VE EXPECTED TO RUN INTO A FRIEND OF HERS.
...SHE WON'T BE HERE TODAY. SHE HAS THE DAY OFF WORK.
...? WORK?
...YES. AT THAT CAFÉ.
cafe
REALLY! SO MITSUKI WORKS OVER THERE?!
That's good to know!
Huh...?
YOU DIDN'T KNOW THAT? BUT YOU CAME HERE TO SEE HER?
WELL, YEAH.
I MEAN, THIS IS OUR SPECIAL PLACE.

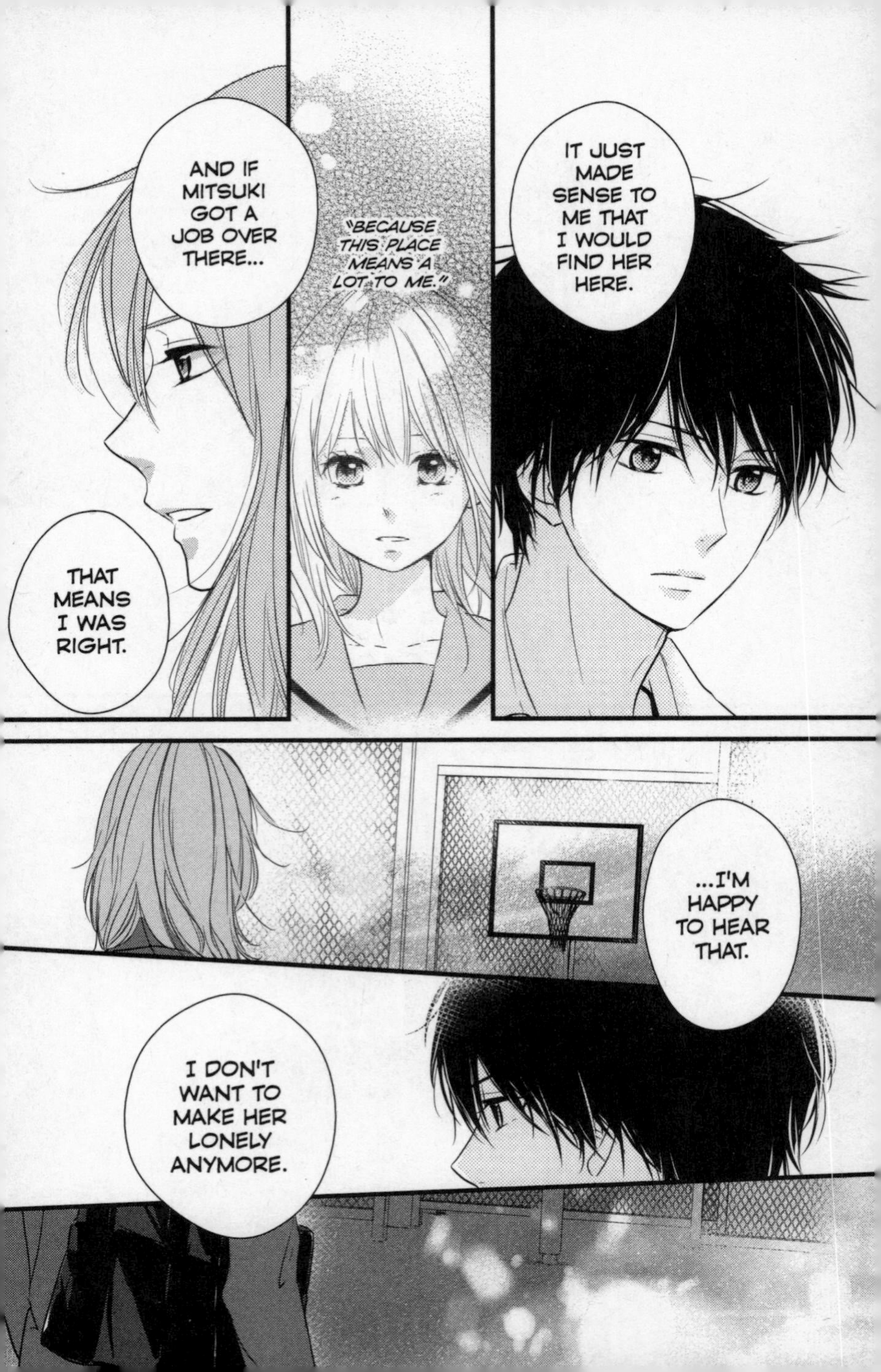
IT JUST MADE SENSE TO ME THAT I WOULD FIND HER HERE.
"BECAUSE THIS PLACE MEANS A LOT TO ME."
AND IF MITSUKI GOT A JOB OVER THERE...
THAT MEANS I WAS RIGHT.
...I'M HAPPY TO HEAR THAT.
I DON'T WANT TO MAKE HER LONELY ANYMORE.

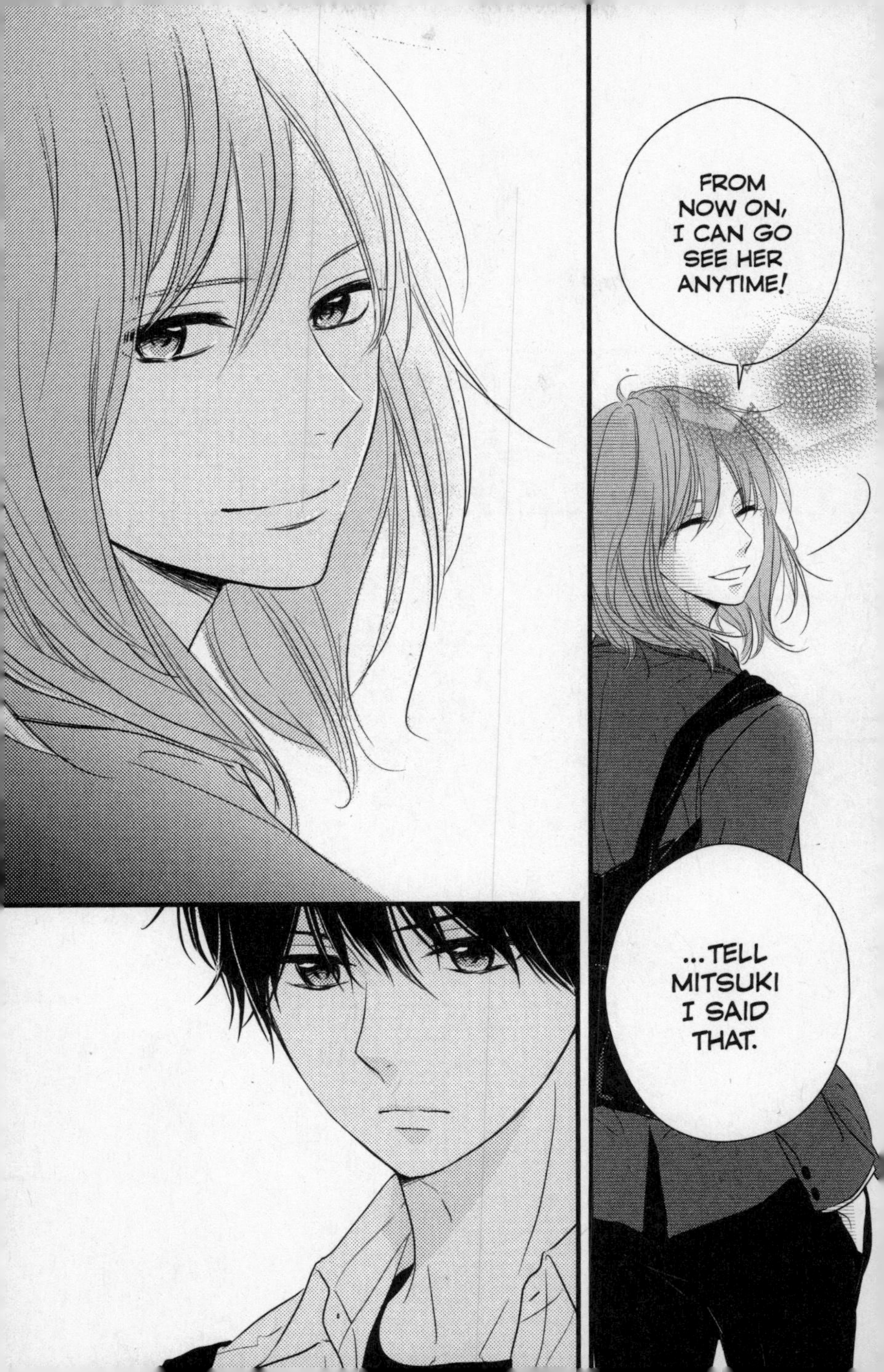
FROM NOW ON, I CAN GO SEE HER ANYTIME!
...TELL MITSUKI I SAID THAT.

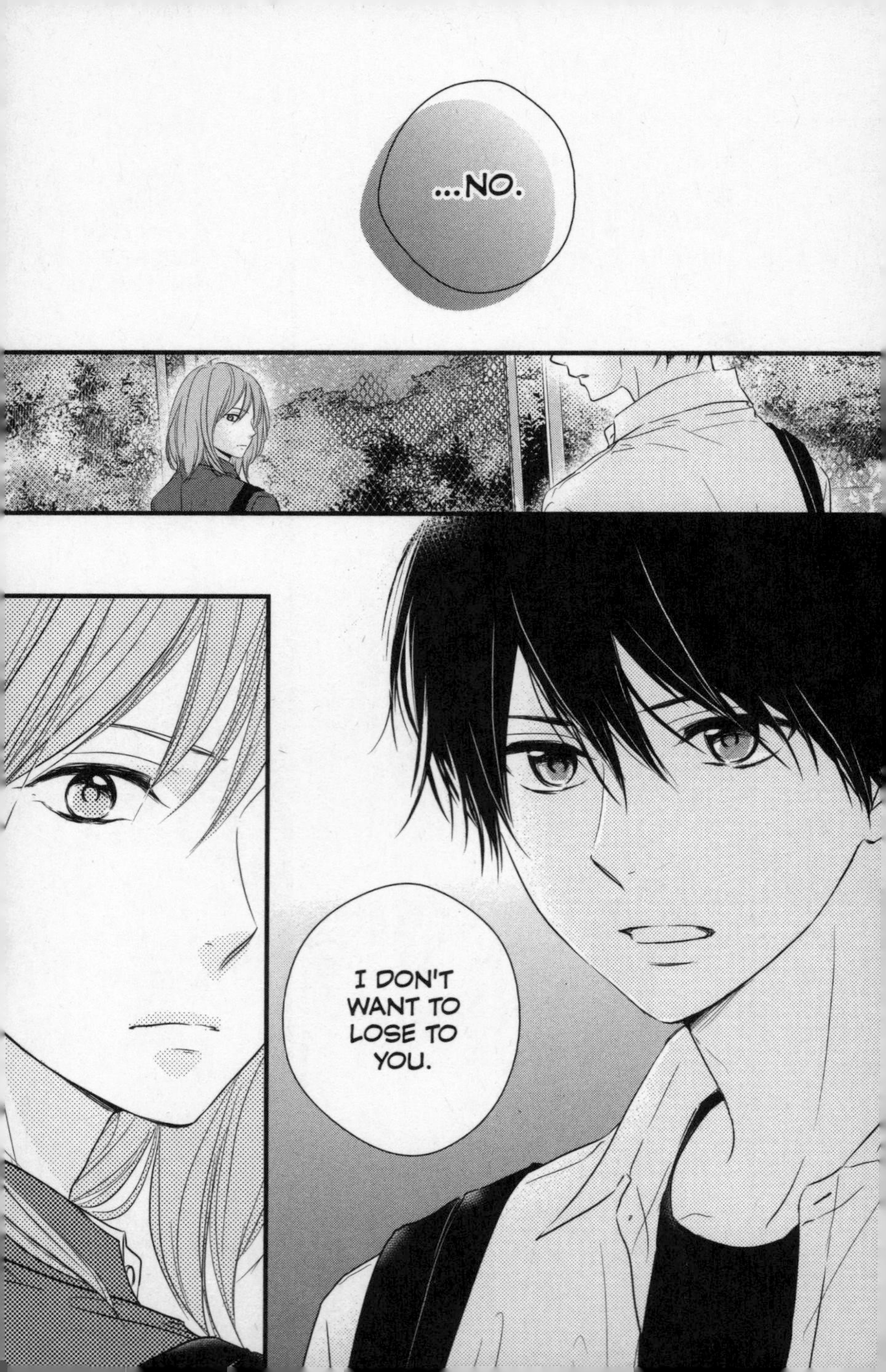
...NO.
I DON'T WANT TO LOSE TO YOU.

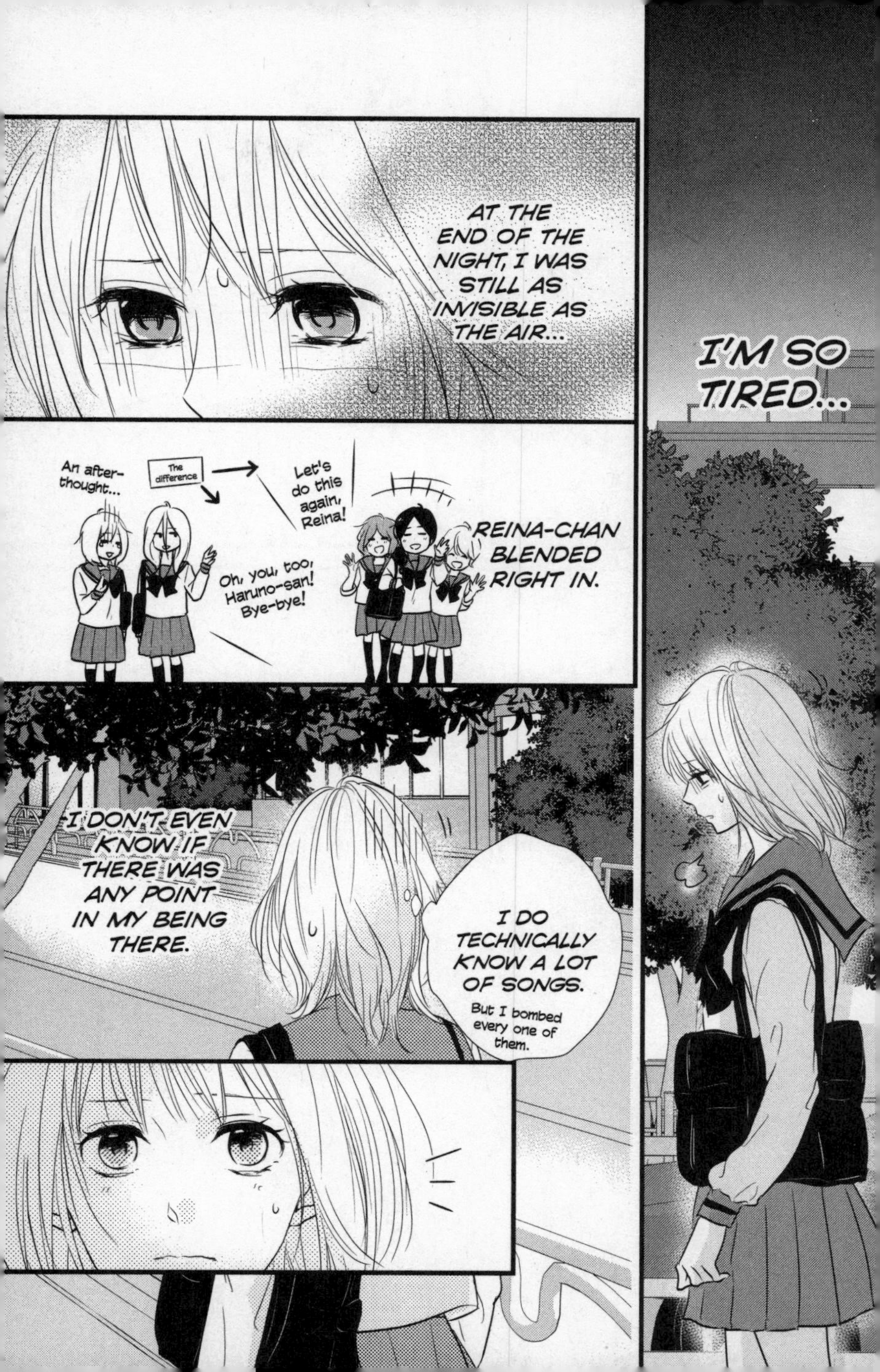
I'M SO TIRED...
AT THE END OF THE NIGHT, I WAS STILL AS INVISIBLE AS THE AIR...
REINA-CHAN BLENDED RIGHT IN.
Let's do this again, Reina!
Oh, you, too, Haruno-san! Bye-bye!
The difference
An after-thought...
I DO TECHNICALLY KNOW A LOT OF SONGS.
But I bombed every one of them.
I DON'T EVEN KNOW IF THERE WAS ANY POINT IN MY BEING THERE.

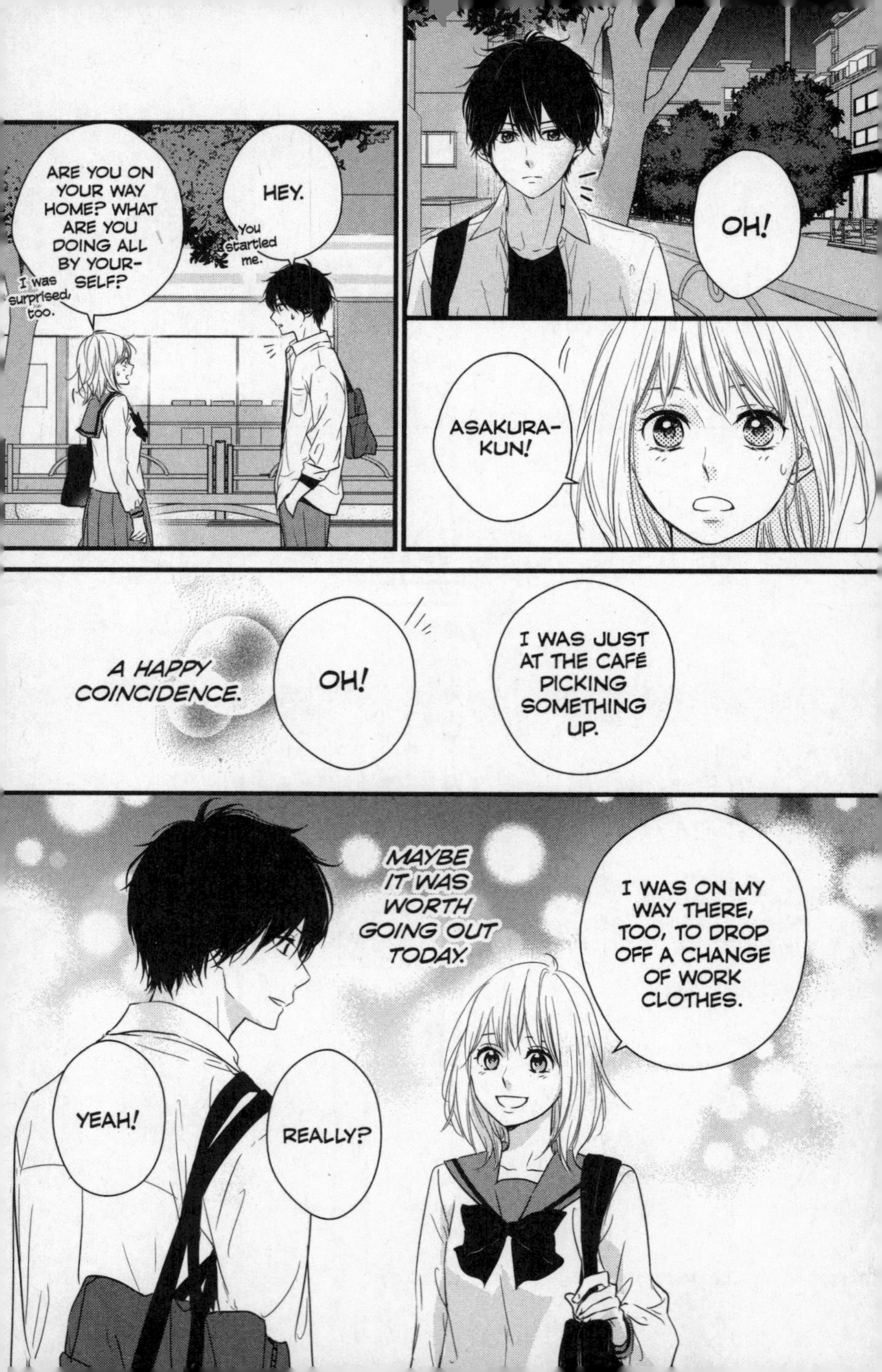
OH!
ASAKURA-KUN!
HEY.
You startled me.
ARE YOU ON YOUR WAY HOME? WHAT ARE YOU DOING ALL BY YOUR-SELF?
I was surprised, too.
I WAS JUST AT THE CAFÉ PICKING SOMETHING UP.
OH!
A HAPPY COINCIDENCE.
I WAS ON MY WAY THERE, TOO, TO DROP OFF A CHANGE OF WORK CLOTHES.
MAYBE IT WAS WORTH GOING OUT TODAY.
REALLY?
YEAH!

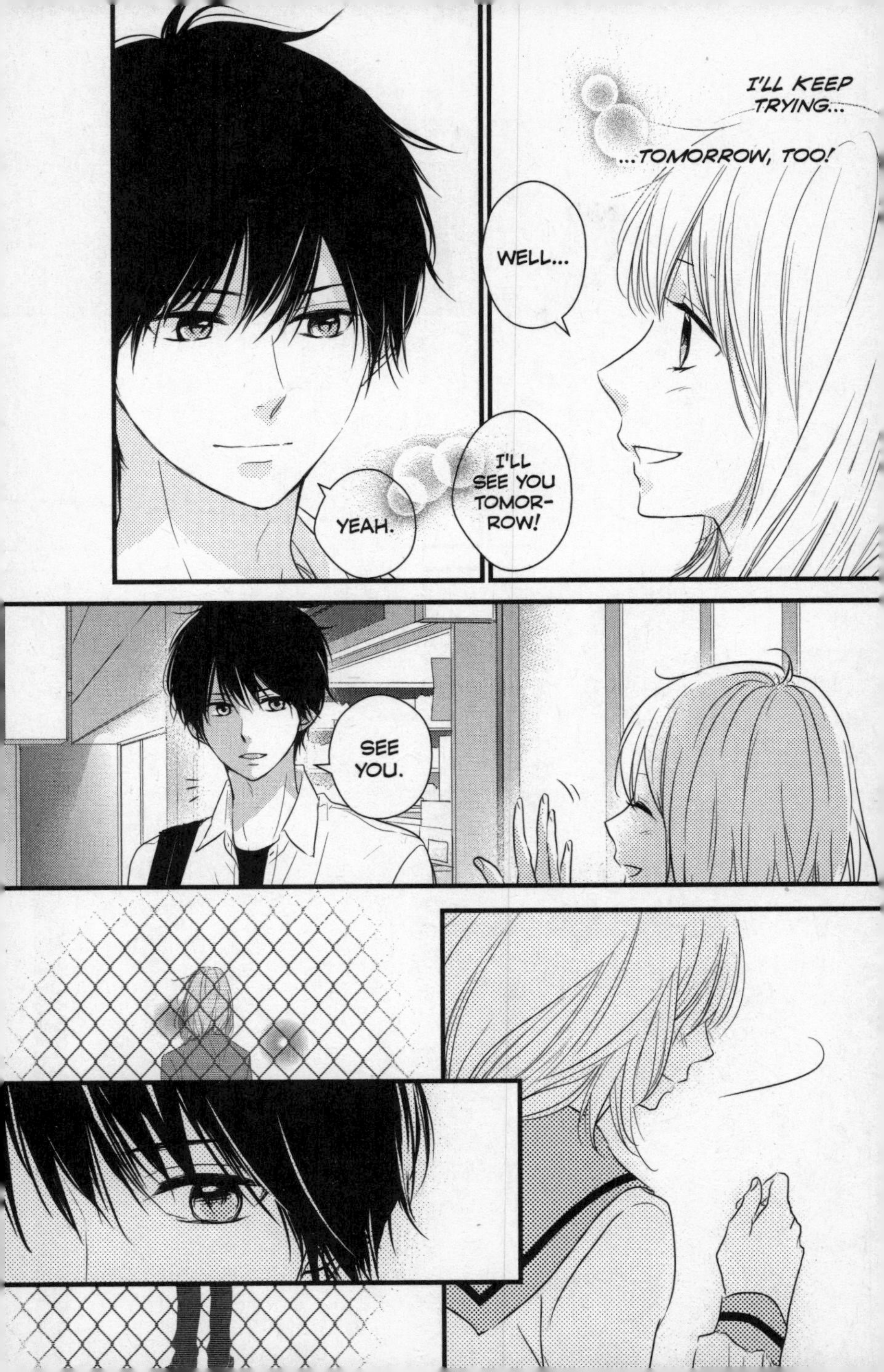
I'LL KEEP TRYING...
...TOMORROW, TOO!
WELL...
I'LL SEE YOU TOMORROW!
YEAH.
SEE YOU.

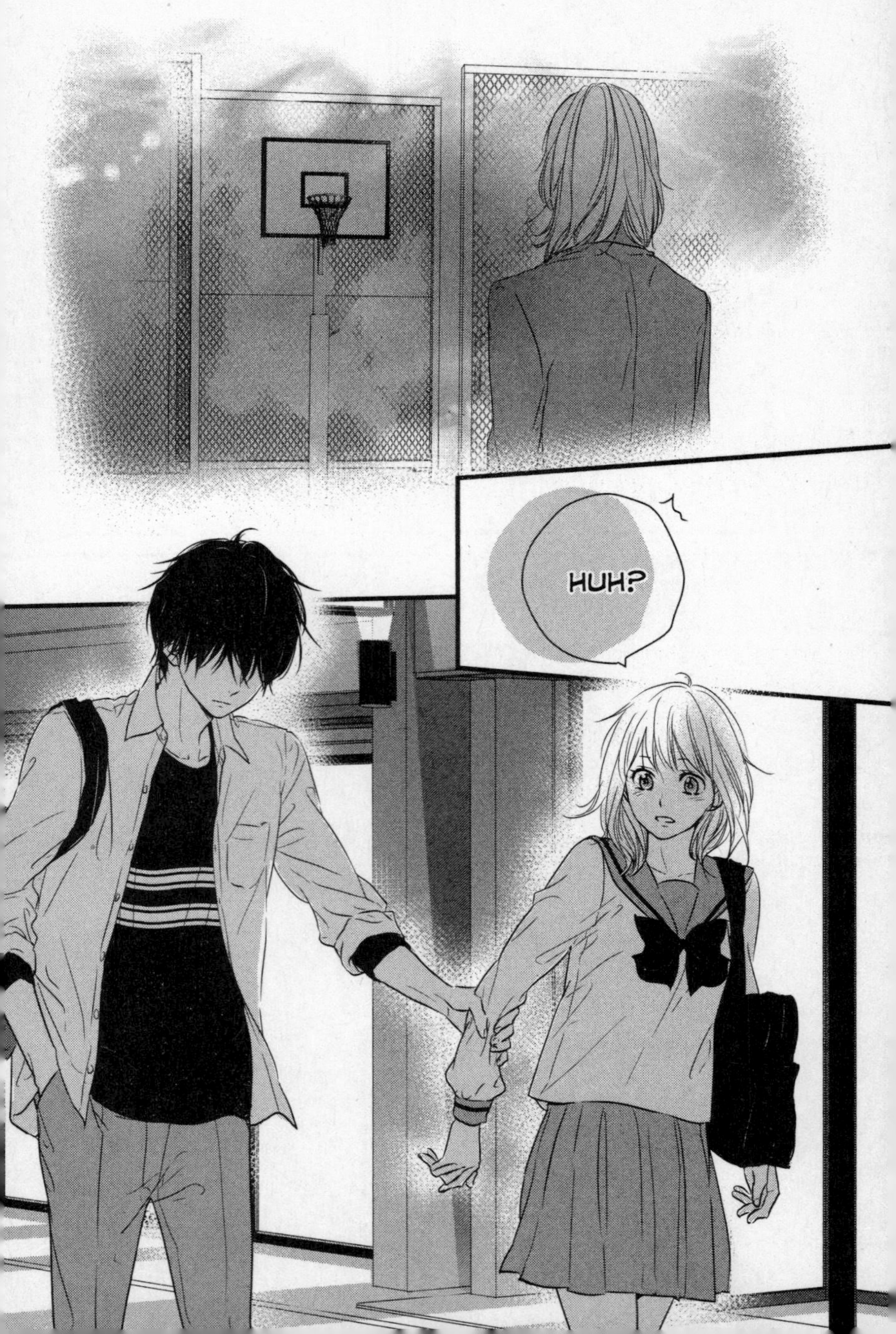
HUH?

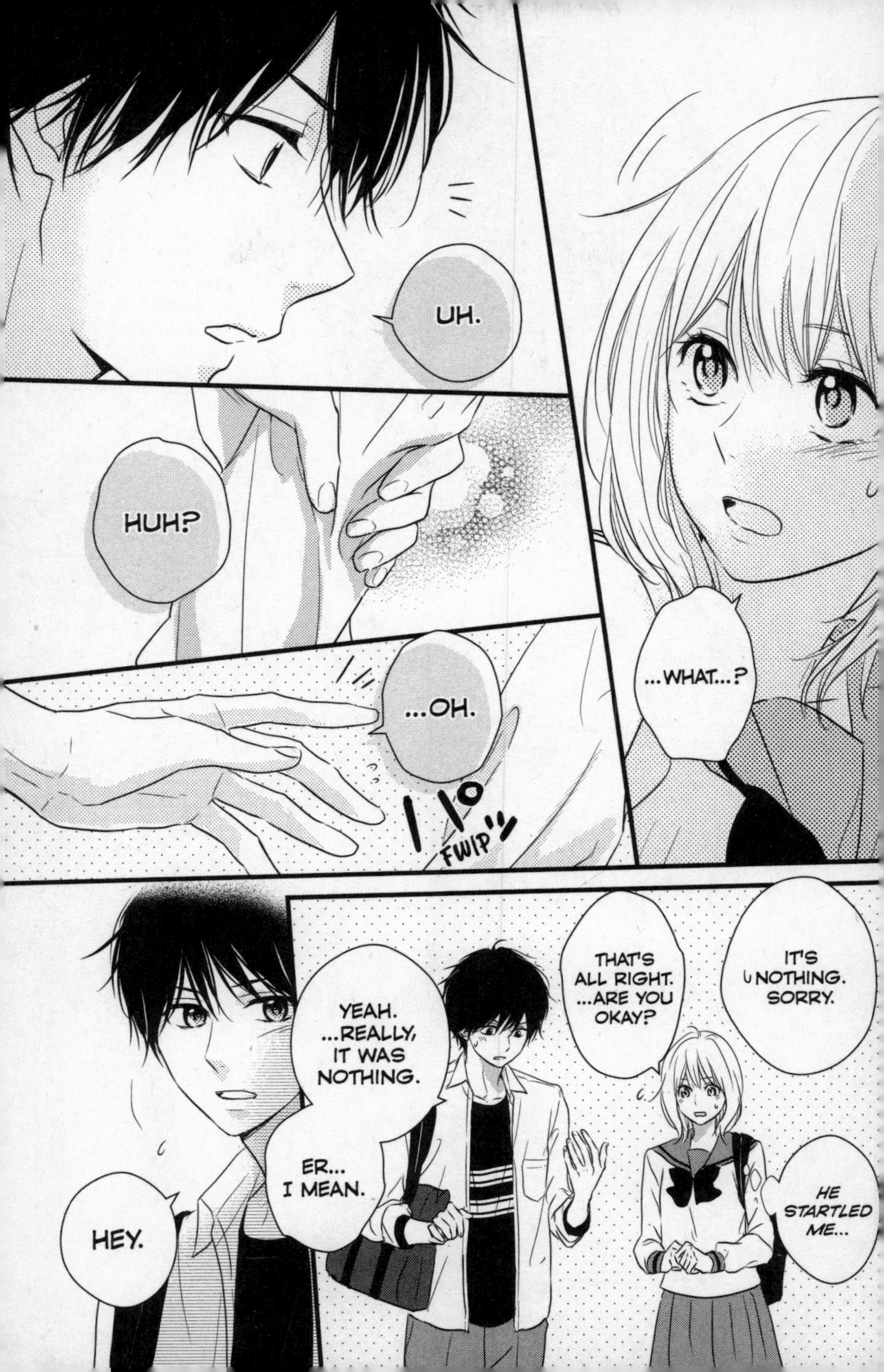
UH.
HUH?
...OH.
FWIP
...WHAT...?
IT'S NOTHING. SORRY.
THAT'S ALL RIGHT. ...ARE YOU OKAY?
HE STARTLED ME...
YEAH. ...REALLY, IT WAS NOTHING.
ER... I MEAN.
HEY.

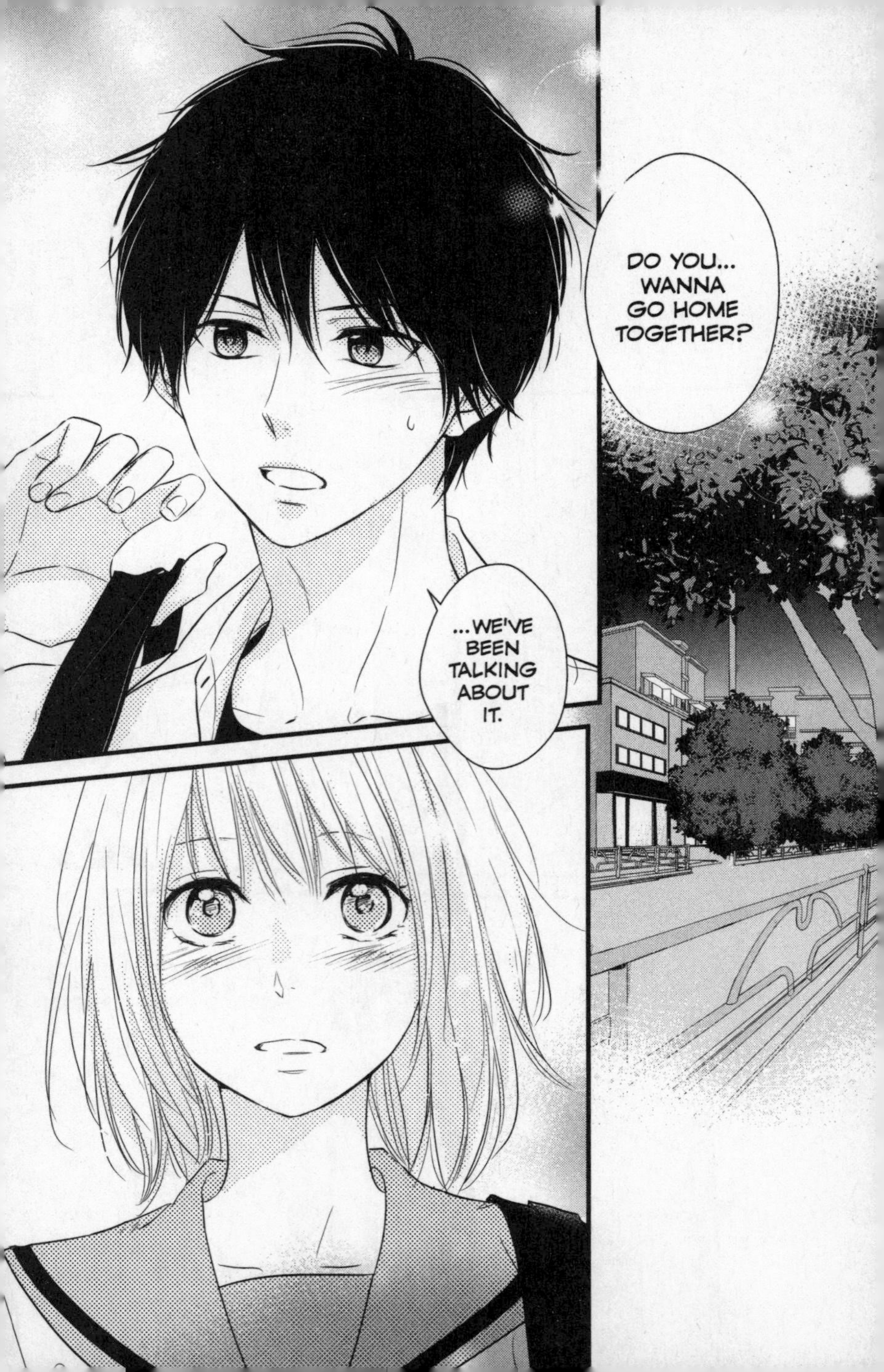
DO YOU... WANNA GO HOME TOGETHER?
...WE'VE BEEN TALKING ABOUT IT.

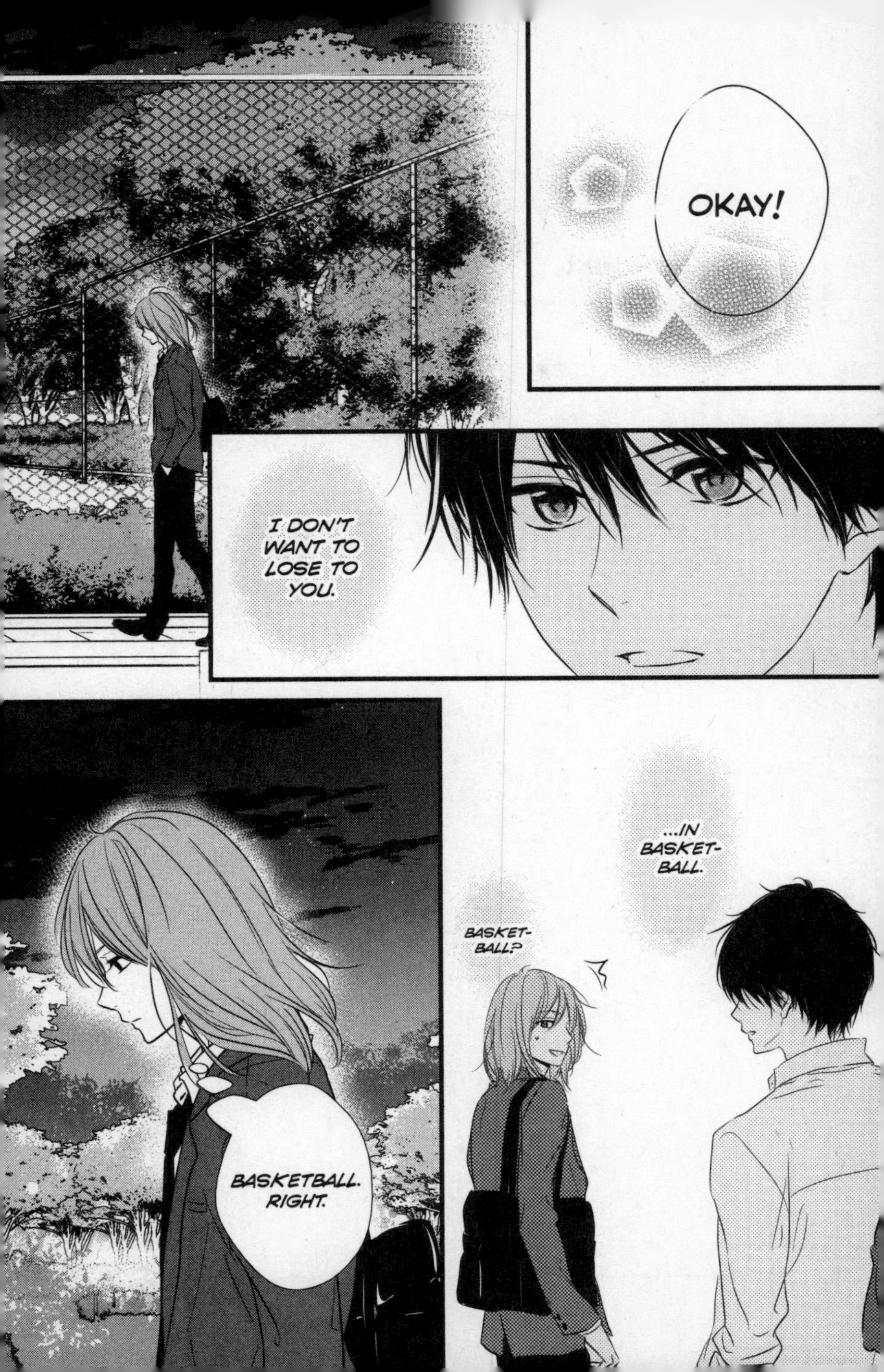
OKAY!
I DON'T WANT TO LOSE TO YOU.
...IN BASKET-BALL.
BASKET-BALL?
BASKETBALL. RIGHT.

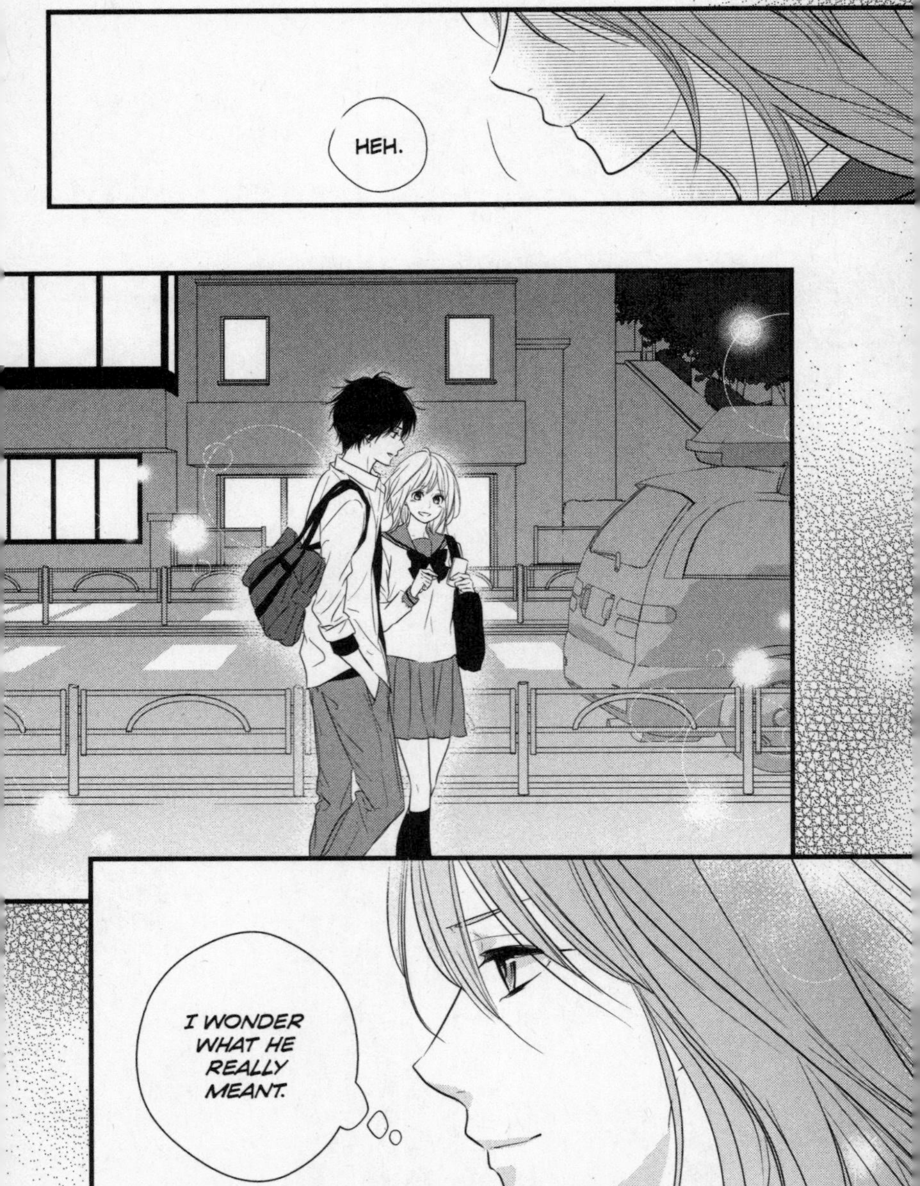
HEH.
I WONDER WHAT HE REALLY MEANT.

period 9: “Heart-Pounding Time”

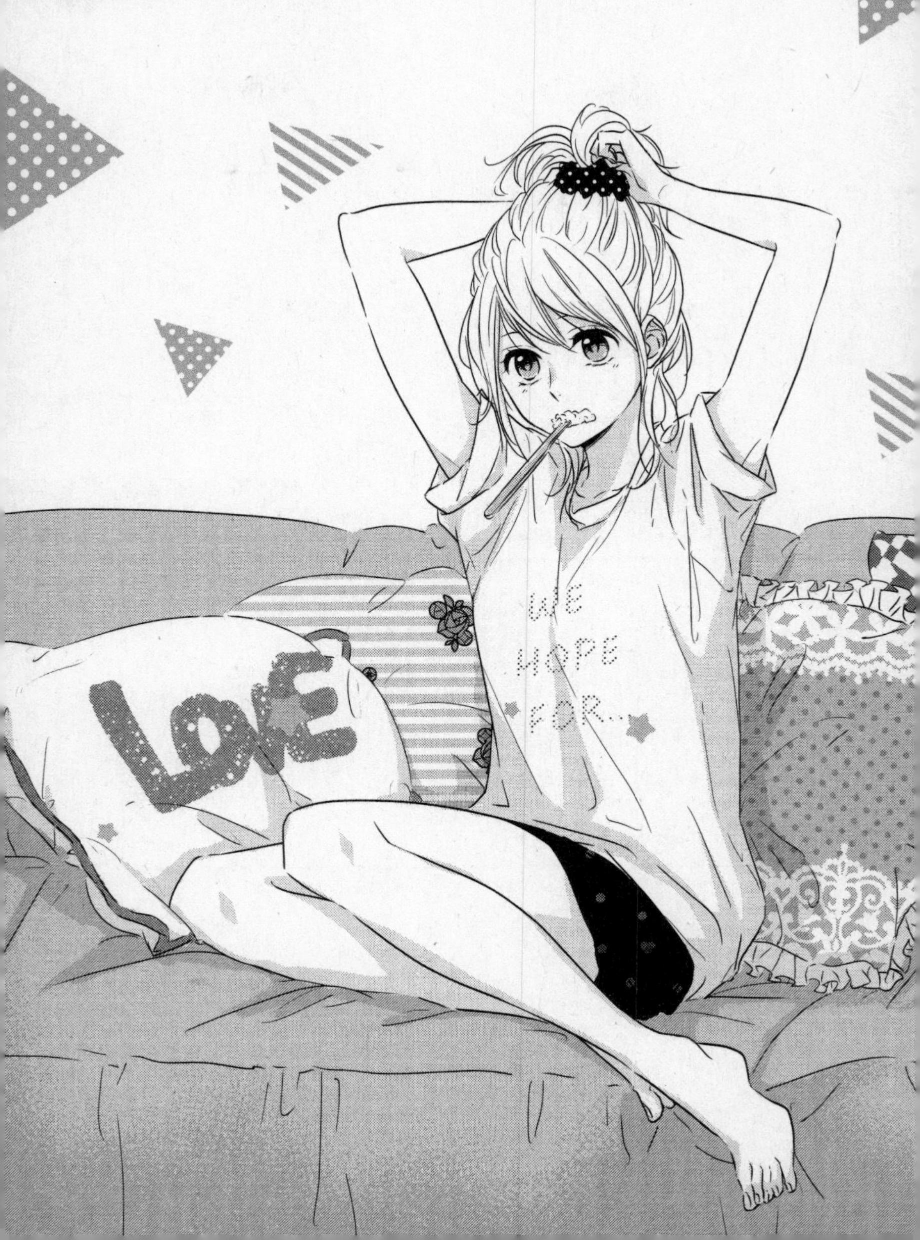
WE HOPE FOR...
LOVE

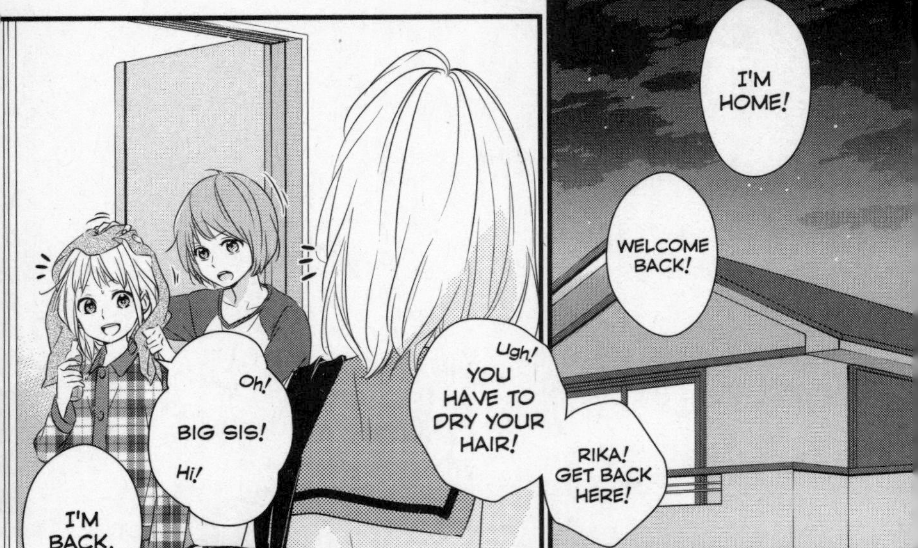
I'M HOME!
WELCOME BACK!
RIKA! GET BACK HERE!
Ugh! YOU HAVE TO DRY YOUR HAIR!
Oh! BIG SIS! Hi!
I'M BACK.
WELCOME HOME...?
BIG SIS, WHAT'S WRONG?

Ryūji Tada	180cm/67kg [5'11"/148lbs.]	Blood type O	Born August 21	Favorite food: Hamburg steak

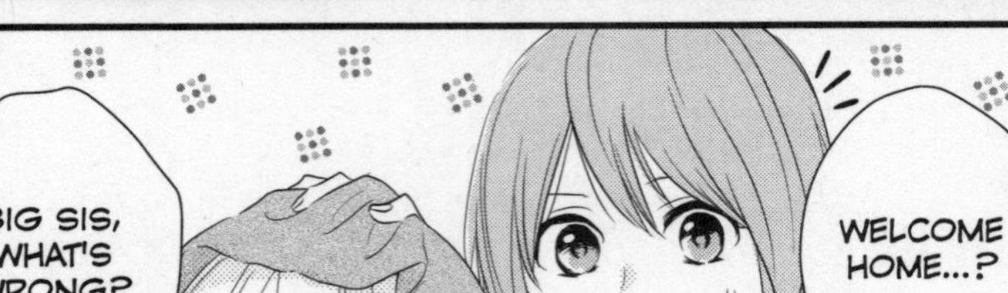
I have two piercings in my left ear and three in my right, but they're a pain in the butt, so I usually just use three.
One
Two
Three
Just like me. But I still mix them up sometimes...
Anashin

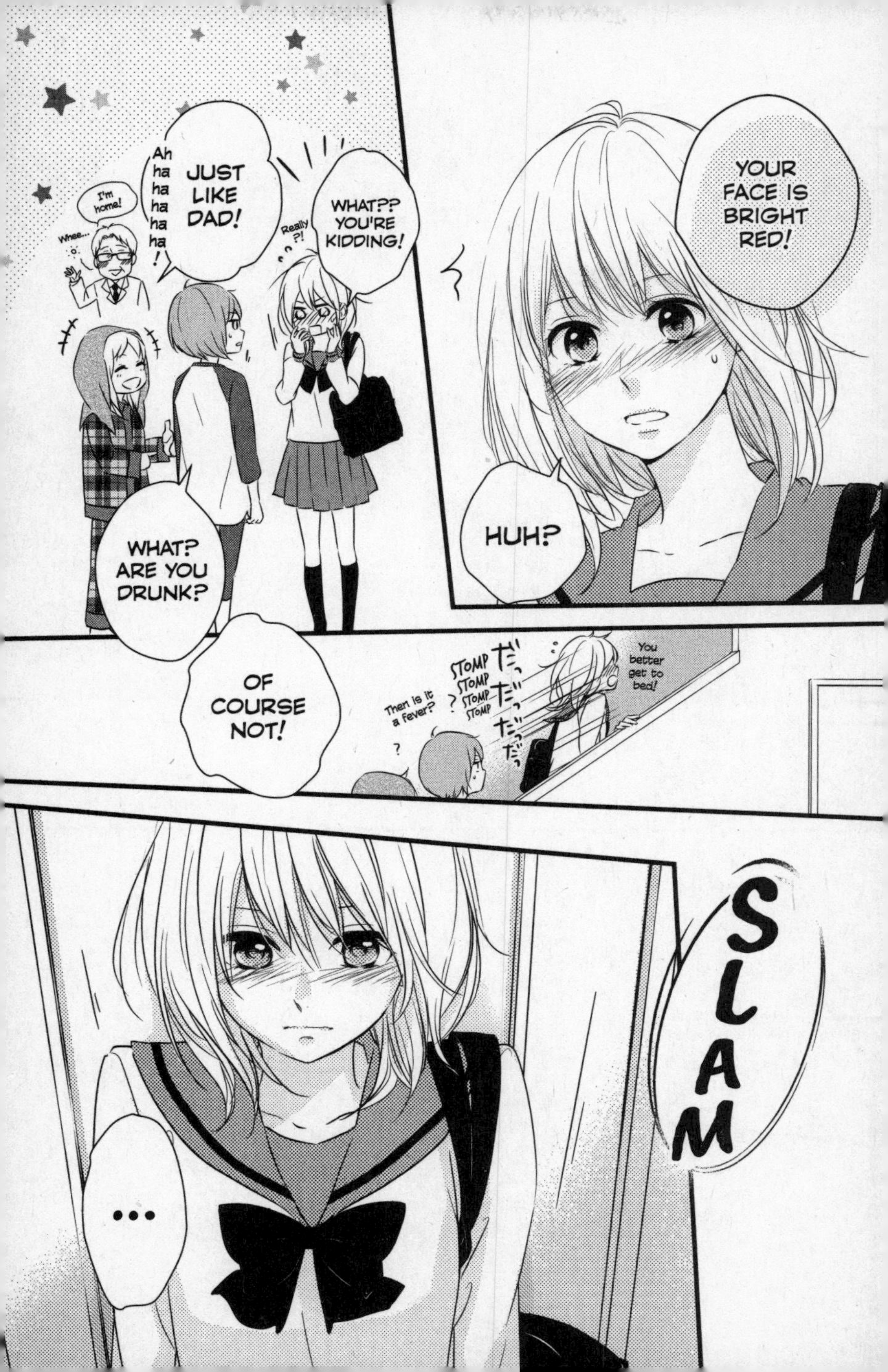
YOUR FACE IS BRIGHT RED!
HUH?
WHAT?? YOU'RE KIDDING!
Really?!
JUST LIKE DAD!
Ah ha ha ha ha ha!
I'm home!
Whee...
WHAT? ARE YOU DRUNK?
You better get to bed!
STOMP STOMP STOMP STOMP
Then is it a fever?
OF COURSE NOT!
SLAM
...

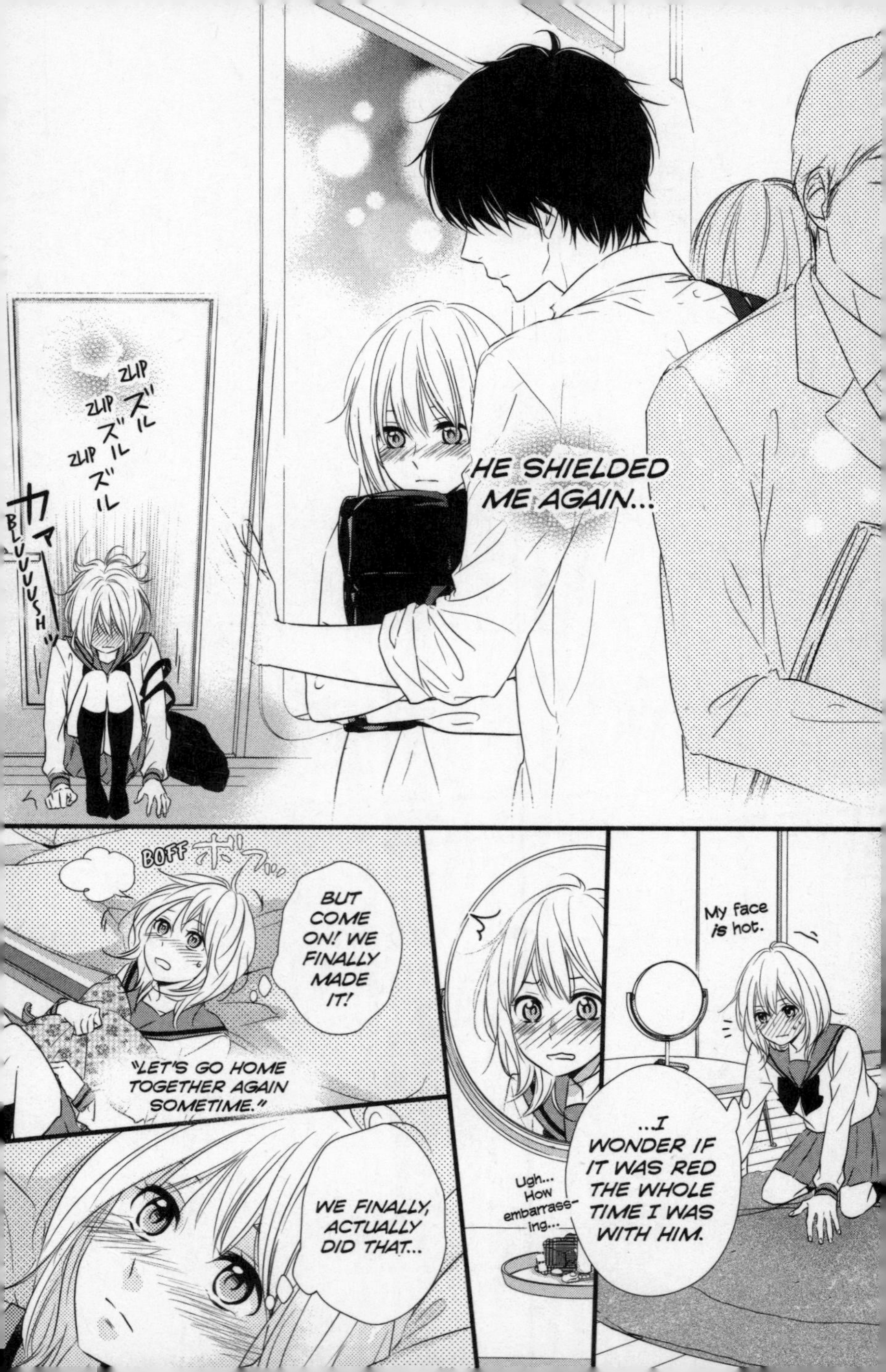
HE SHIELDED ME AGAIN...
ZLIP ズル
ZLIP ズル
ZLIP ズル
カァ BLUUUUSH
My face is hot.
...I WONDER IF IT WAS RED THE WHOLE TIME I WAS WITH HIM.
Ugh... How embarrass-ing...
BOFF ボフ
BUT COME ON! WE FINALLY MADE IT!
"LET'S GO HOME TOGETHER AGAIN SOMETIME."
WE FINALLY, ACTUALLY DID THAT...

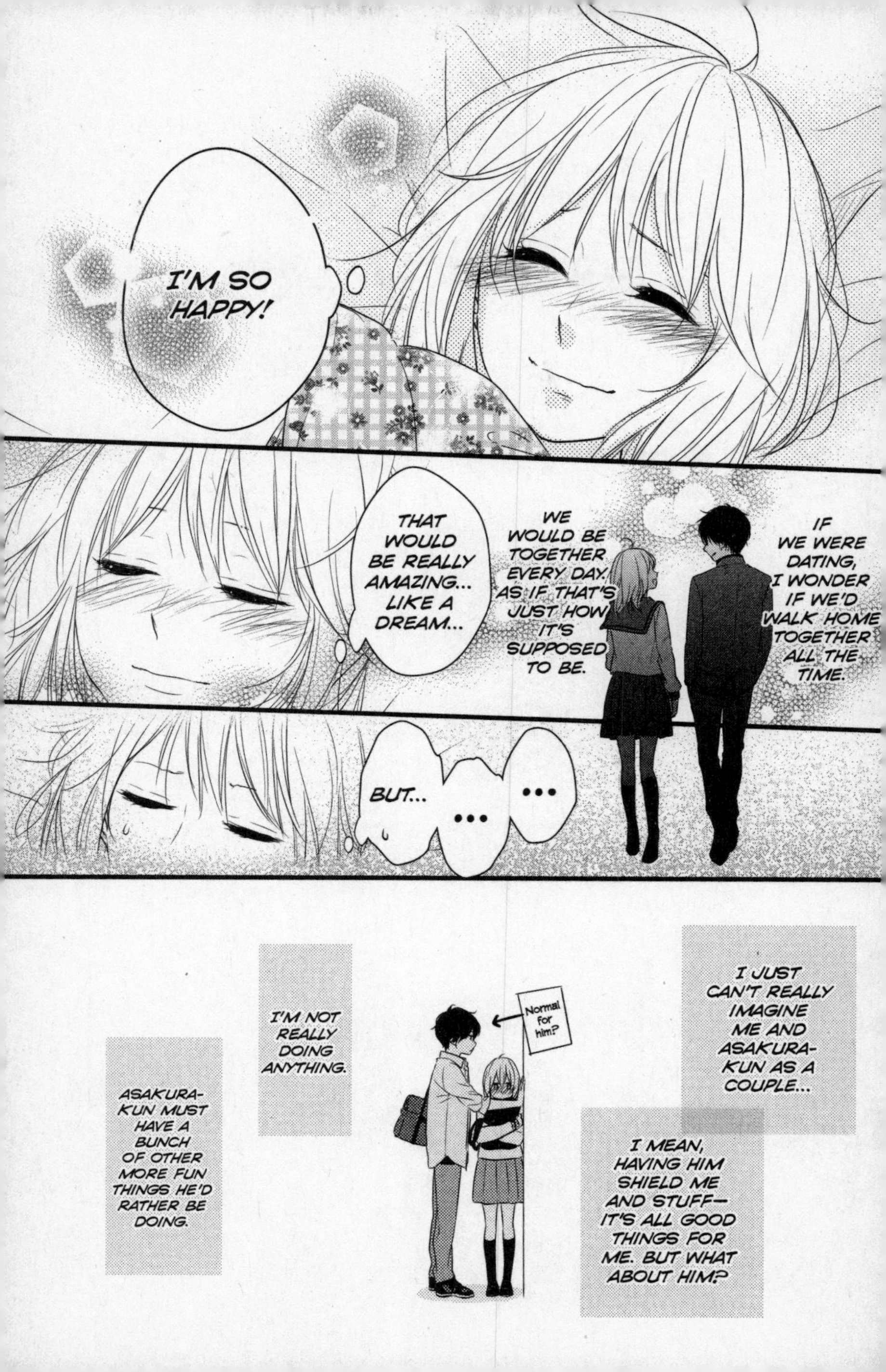
I'M SO HAPPY!
IF WE WERE DATING, I WONDER IF WE'D WALK HOME TOGETHER ALL THE TIME.
WE WOULD BE TOGETHER EVERY DAY. AS IF THAT'S JUST HOW IT'S SUPPOSED TO BE.
THAT WOULD BE REALLY AMAZING... LIKE A DREAM...
...
...
BUT...
I JUST CAN'T REALLY IMAGINE ME AND ASAKURA-KUN AS A COUPLE...
I MEAN, HAVING HIM SHIELD ME AND STUFF— IT'S ALL GOOD THINGS FOR ME. BUT WHAT ABOUT HIM?
Normal for him?
I'M NOT REALLY DOING ANYTHING.
ASAKURA-KUN MUST HAVE A BUNCH OF OTHER MORE FUN THINGS HE'D RATHER BE DOING.

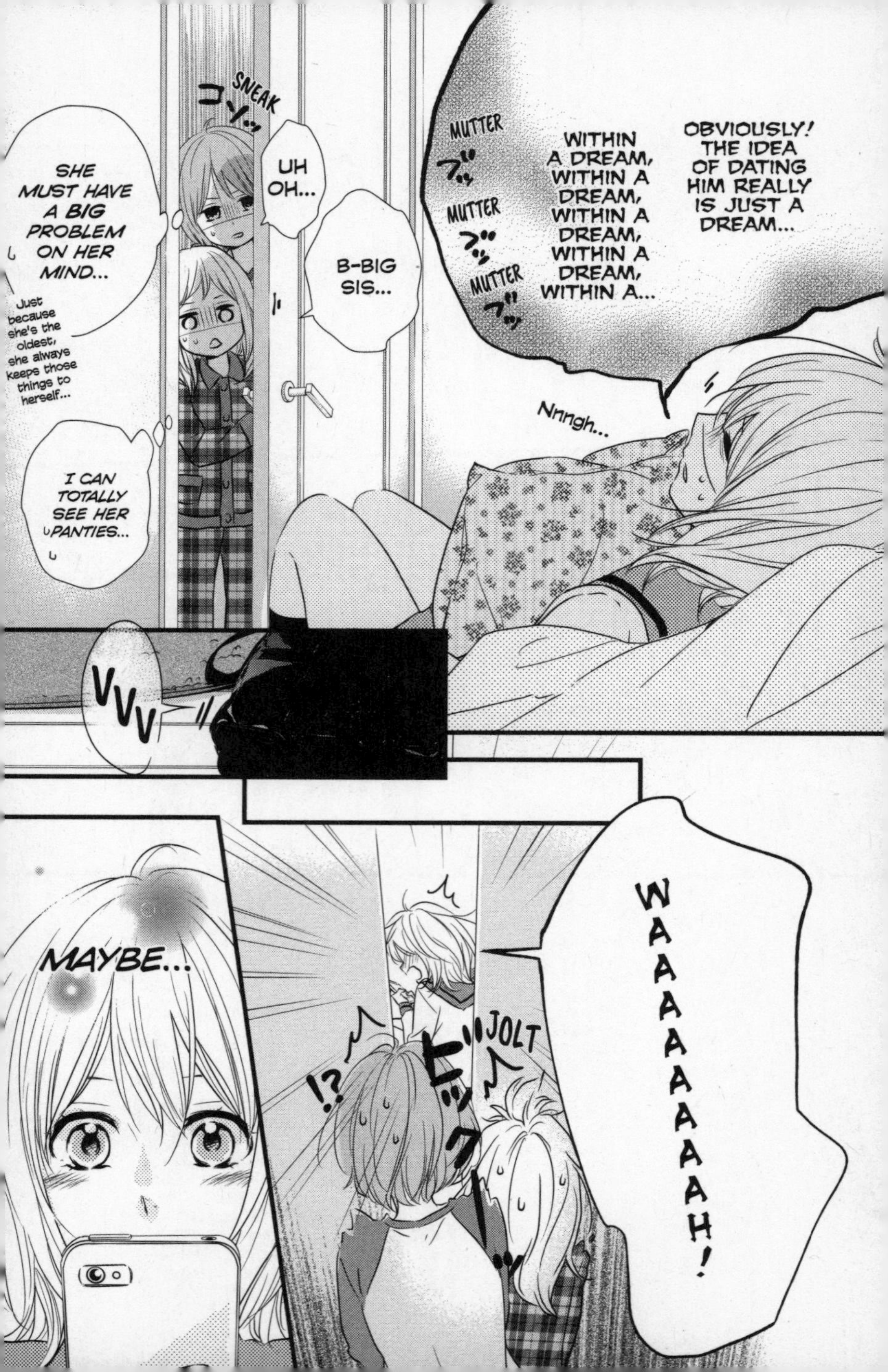
OBVIOUSLY! THE IDEA OF DATING HIM REALLY IS JUST A DREAM...
WITHIN A DREAM, WITHIN A DREAM, WITHIN A DREAM, WITHIN A DREAM, WITHIN A...
MUTTER
MUTTER
MUTTER
Nnngh...
SNEAK
UH OH...
B-BIG SIS...
SHE MUST HAVE A BIG PROBLEM ON HER MIND...
Just because she's the oldest, she always keeps those things to herself...
I CAN TOTALLY SEE HER PANTIES...
VVV
WAAAAAAAAAH!
JOLT
!?
MAYBE...

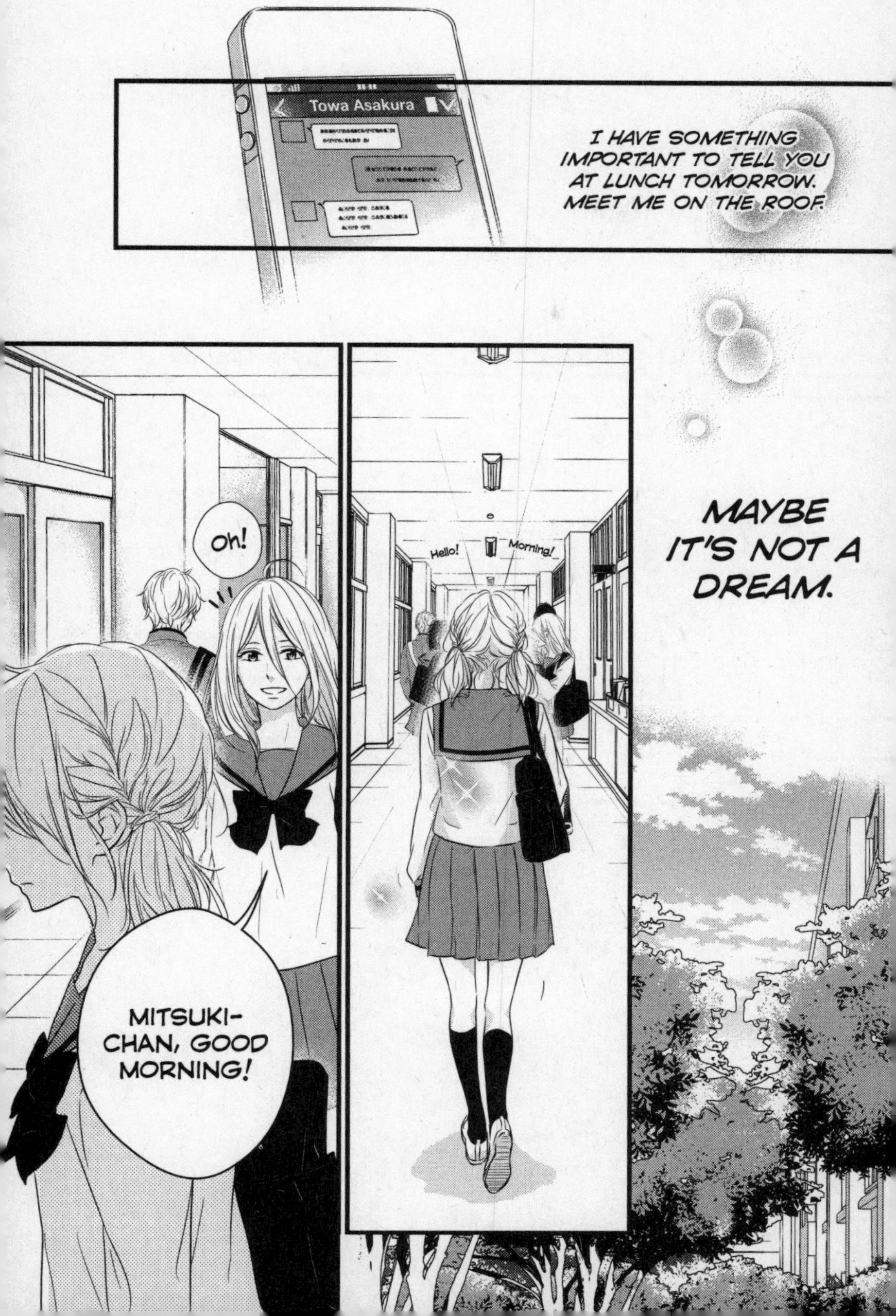
Towa Asakura
I HAVE SOMETHING IMPORTANT TO TELL YOU AT LUNCH TOMORROW. MEET ME ON THE ROOF.
MAYBE IT'S NOT A DREAM.
Morning!
Hello!
Oh!
MITSUKI-CHAN, GOOD MORNING!

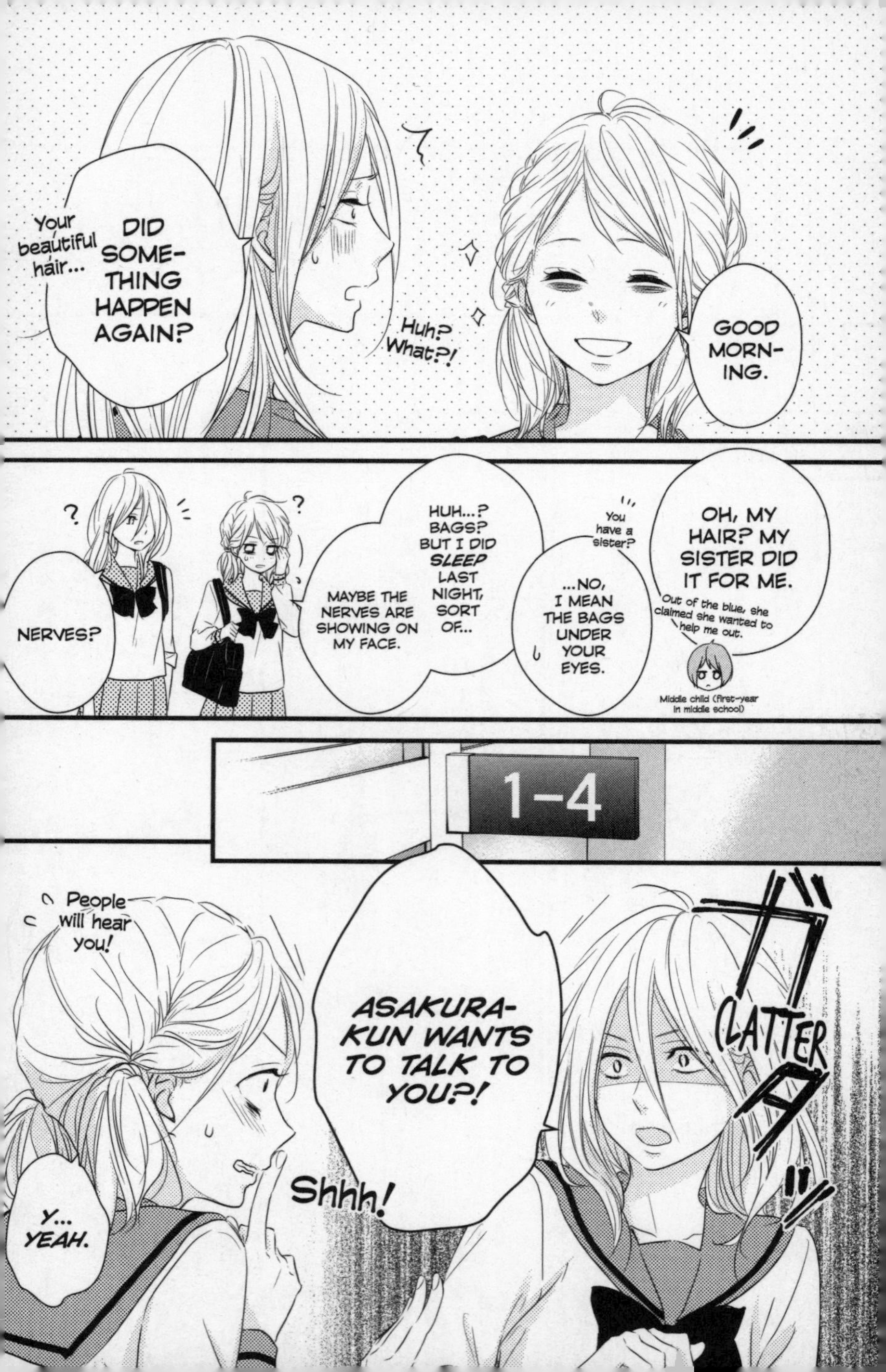
GOOD MORNING.
Huh? What?!
DID SOMETHING HAPPEN AGAIN?
Your beautiful hair...
OH, MY HAIR? MY SISTER DID IT FOR ME.
Out of the blue, she claimed she wanted to help me out.
Middle child (first-year in middle school)
You have a sister?
...NO, I MEAN THE BAGS UNDER YOUR EYES.
HUH...? BAGS? BUT I DID SLEEP LAST NIGHT, SORT OF...
MAYBE THE NERVES ARE SHOWING ON MY FACE.
NERVES?
1-4
CLATTER
ASAKURA-KUN WANTS TO TALK TO YOU?!
Shhh!
People will hear you!
Y... YEAH.

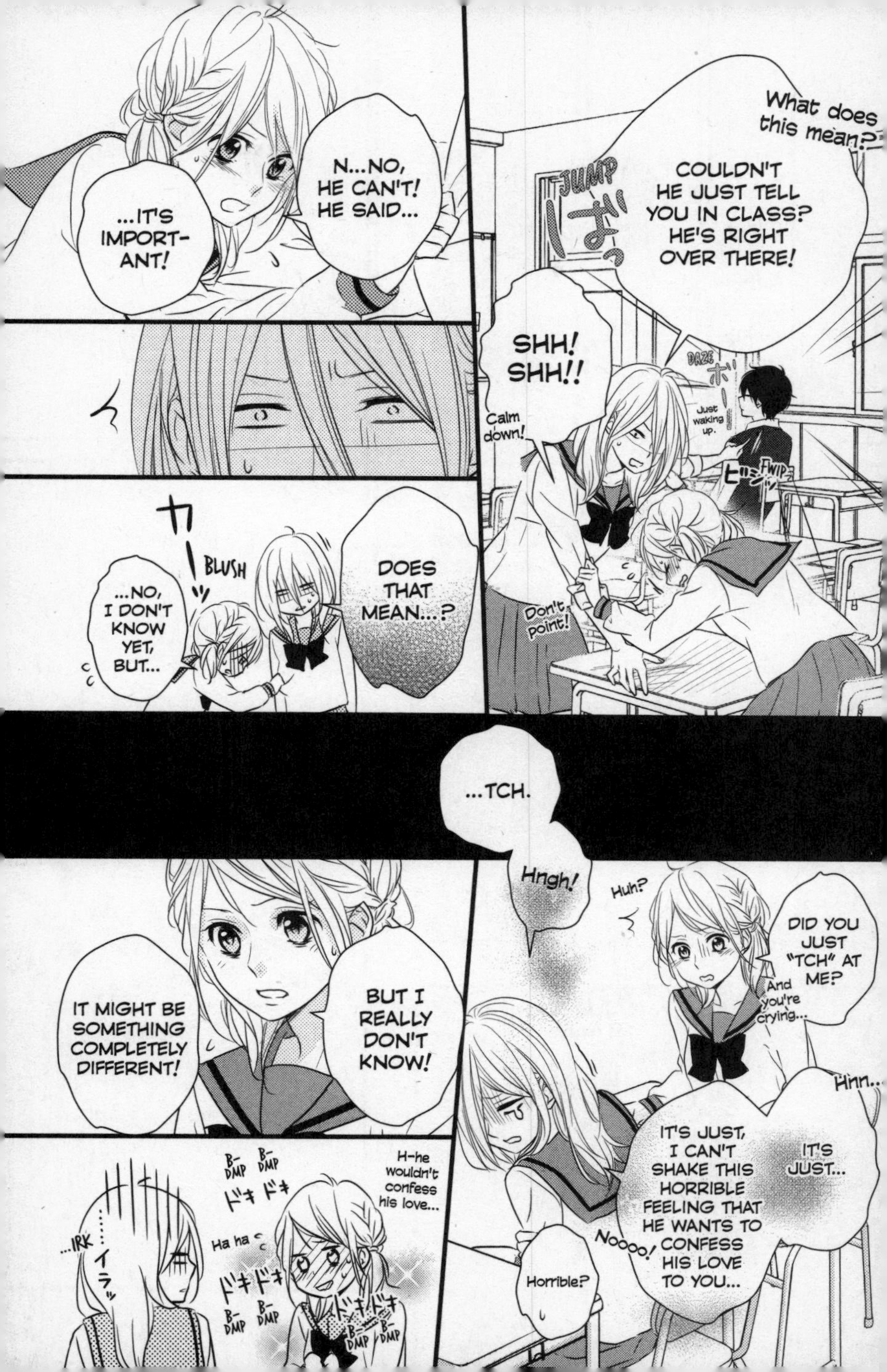
What does this mean?
JUMP
COULDN'T HE JUST TELL YOU IN CLASS? HE'S RIGHT OVER THERE!
SHH! SHH!!
Calm down!
DAZE
Just waking up.
FWIP
Don't point!
N...NO, HE CAN'T! HE SAID...
...IT'S IMPORT-ANT!
DOES THAT MEAN...?
BLUSH
...NO, I DON'T KNOW YET, BUT...
...TCH.
DID YOU JUST "TCH" AT ME?
And you're crying...
Huh?
Hngh!
Hnn...
IT'S JUST...
IT'S JUST, I CAN'T SHAKE THIS HORRIBLE FEELING THAT HE WANTS TO CONFESS HIS LOVE TO YOU...
Noooo!
Horrible?
BUT I REALLY DON'T KNOW!
IT MIGHT BE SOMETHING COMPLETELY DIFFERENT!
H-he wouldn't confess his love...
B-DMP B-DMP
Ha ha
B-DMP B-DMP
B-DMP B-DMP
...IRK

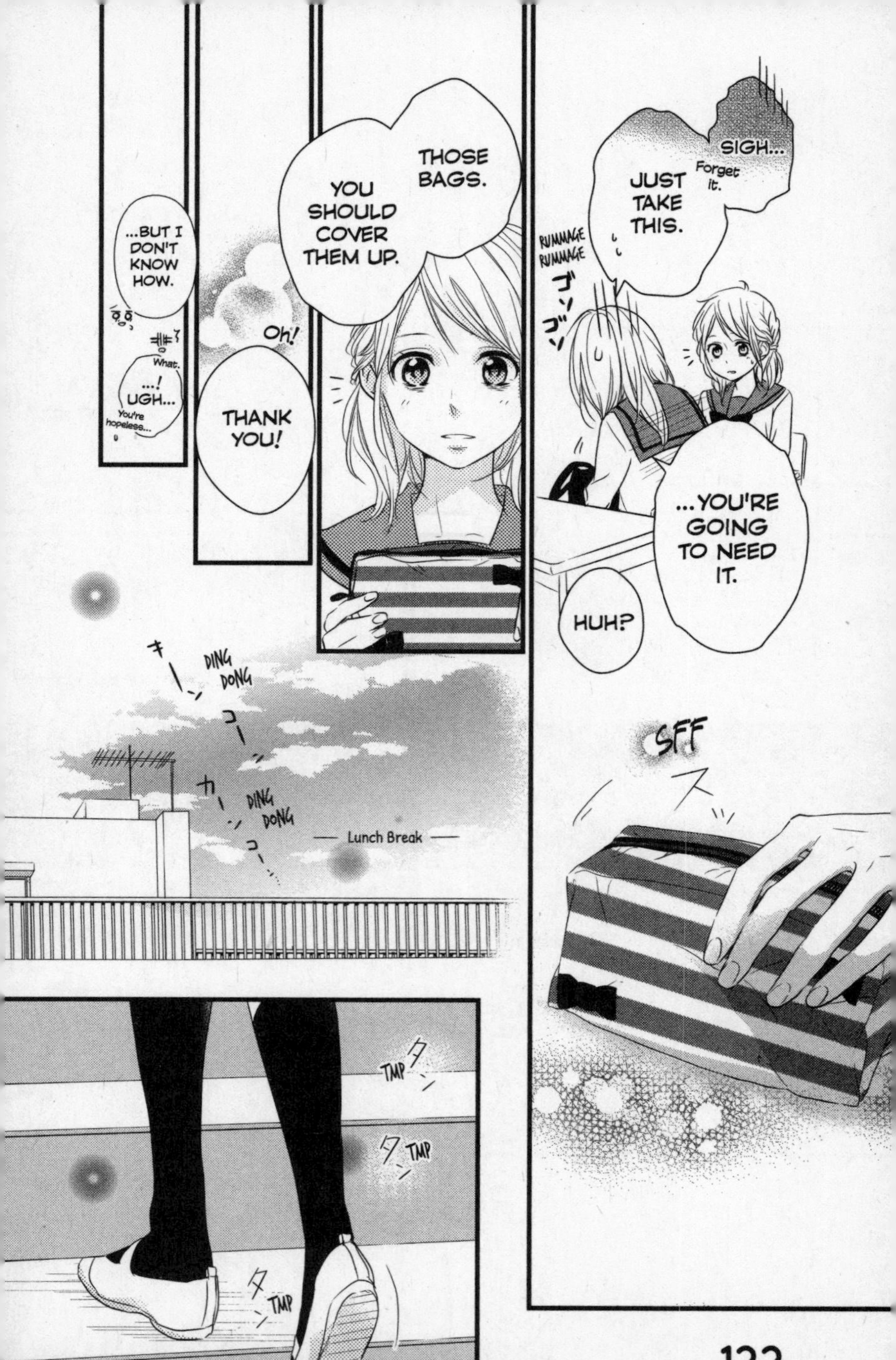
SIGH...
Forget it.
JUST TAKE THIS.
RUMMAGE RUMMAGE
...YOU'RE GOING TO NEED IT.
HUH?
SFF
THOSE BAGS.
YOU SHOULD COVER THEM UP.
Oh!
THANK YOU!
...BUT I DON'T KNOW HOW.
What.
...! UGH...
You're hopeless...
DING DONG
DING DONG
— Lunch Break —
TMP
TMP
TMP

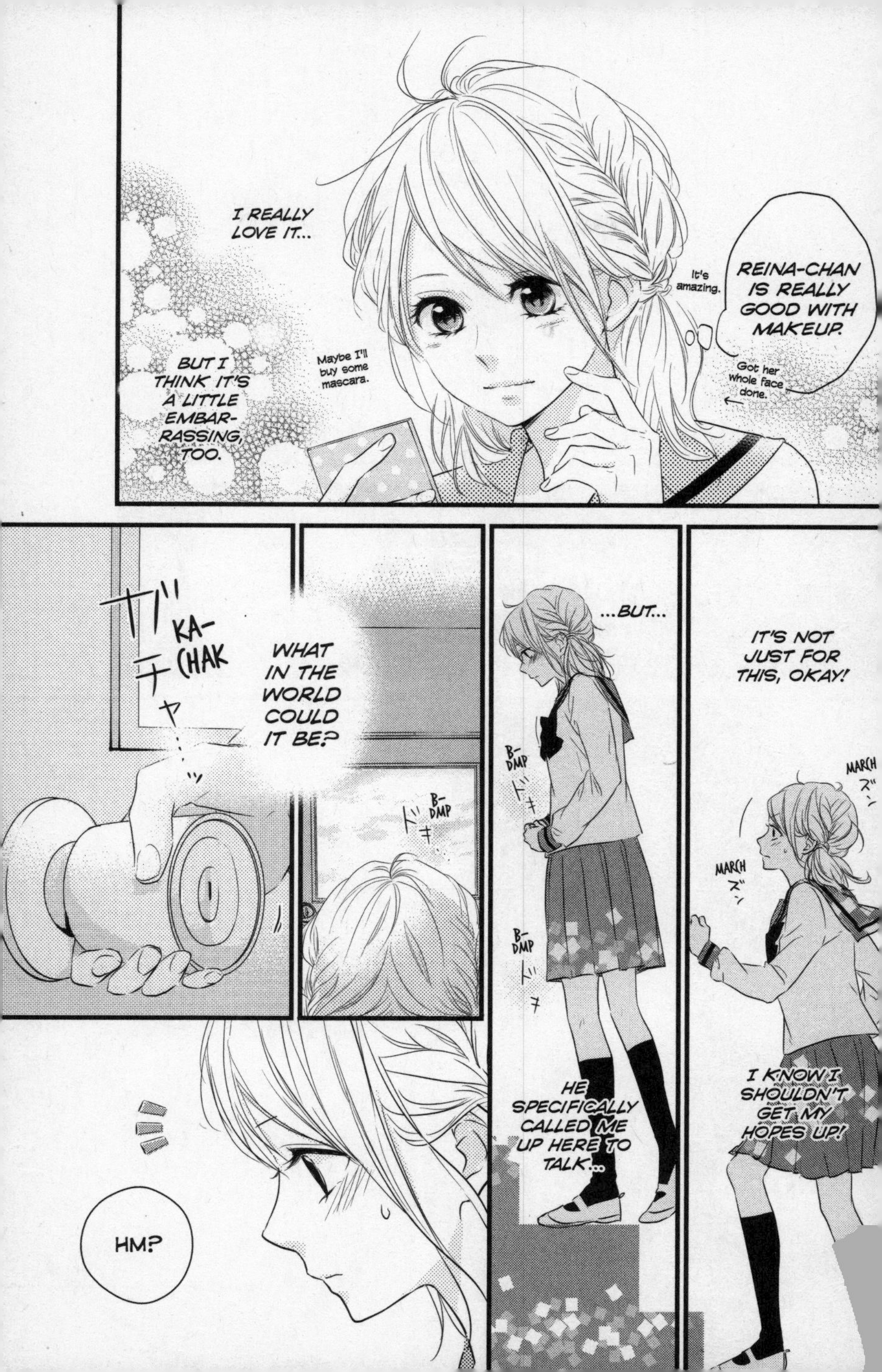
REINA-CHAN IS REALLY GOOD WITH MAKEUP.
It's amazing.
Got her whole face done.
I REALLY LOVE IT...
Maybe I'll buy some mascara.
BUT I THINK IT'S A LITTLE EMBARRASSING, TOO.
IT'S NOT JUST FOR THIS, OKAY!
MARCH
MARCH
I KNOW I SHOULDN'T GET MY HOPES UP!
...BUT...
B-DMP
B-DMP
HE SPECIFICALLY CALLED ME UP HERE TO TALK...
B-DMP
WHAT IN THE WORLD COULD IT BE?
KA-CHAK
HM?

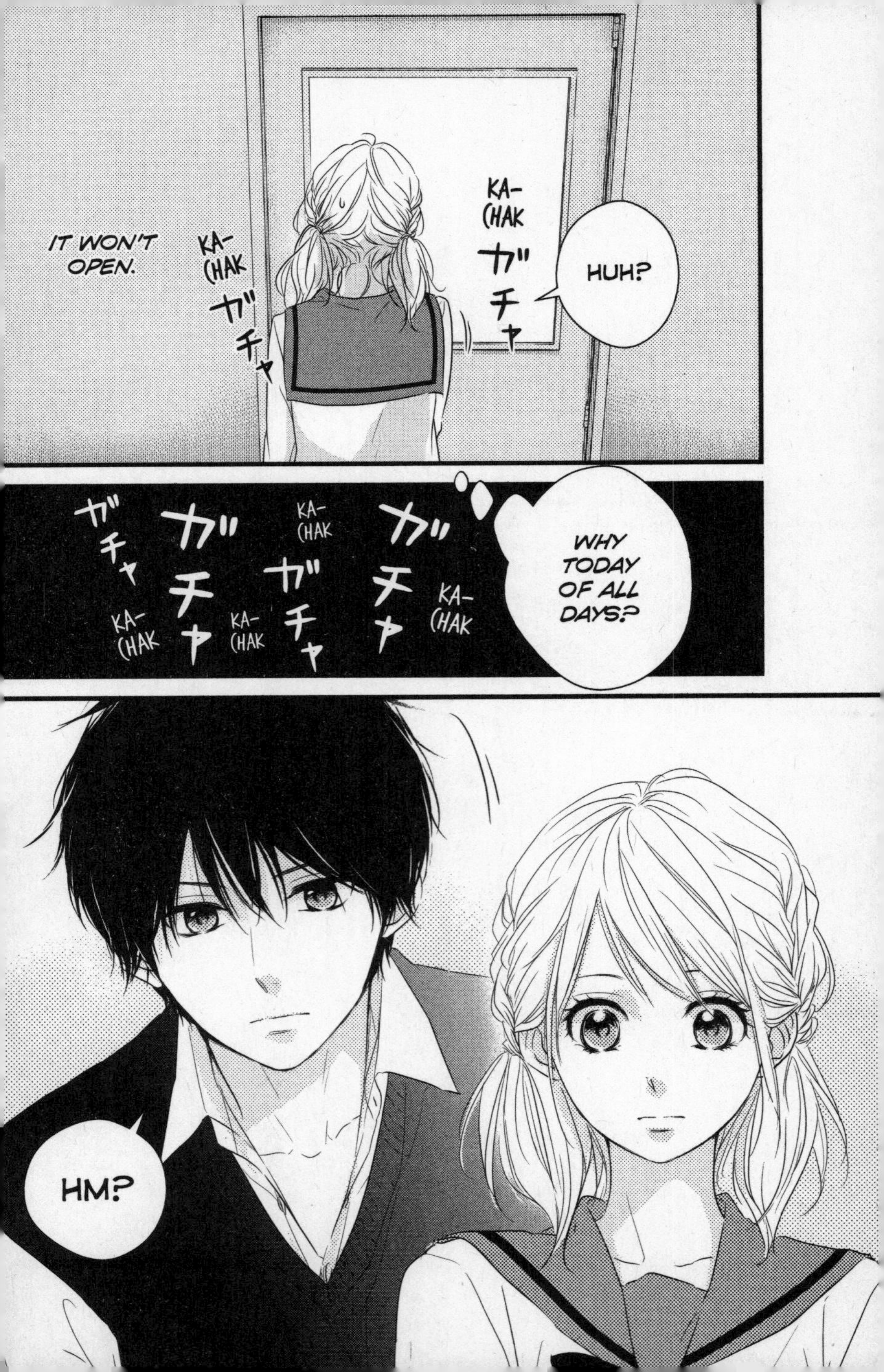
HUH?
KA-CHAK
ガチャ
KA-CHAK
ガチャ
IT WON'T OPEN.
WHY TODAY OF ALL DAYS?
KA-CHAK
ガチャ
KA-CHAK
ガチャ
KA-CHAK
ガチャ
KA-CHAK
ガチャ
HM?

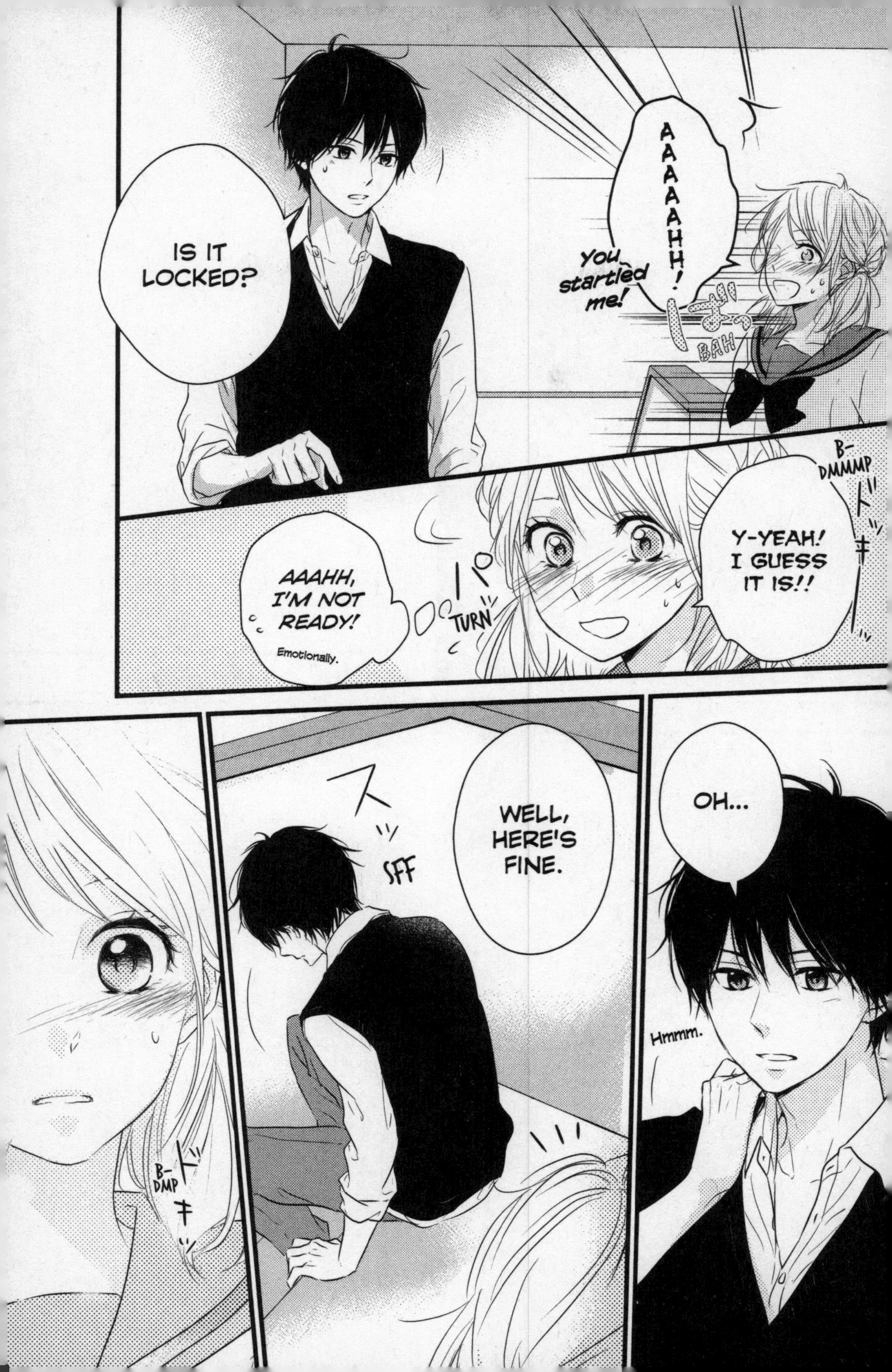

AAAAAAHH!
You startled me!
BAH
IS IT LOCKED?
B-DMMMP
Y-YEAH! I GUESS IT IS!!
TURN
AAAHH, I'M NOT READY!
Emotionally.
OH...
Hmmm.
WELL, HERE'S FINE.
SFF
B-DMP

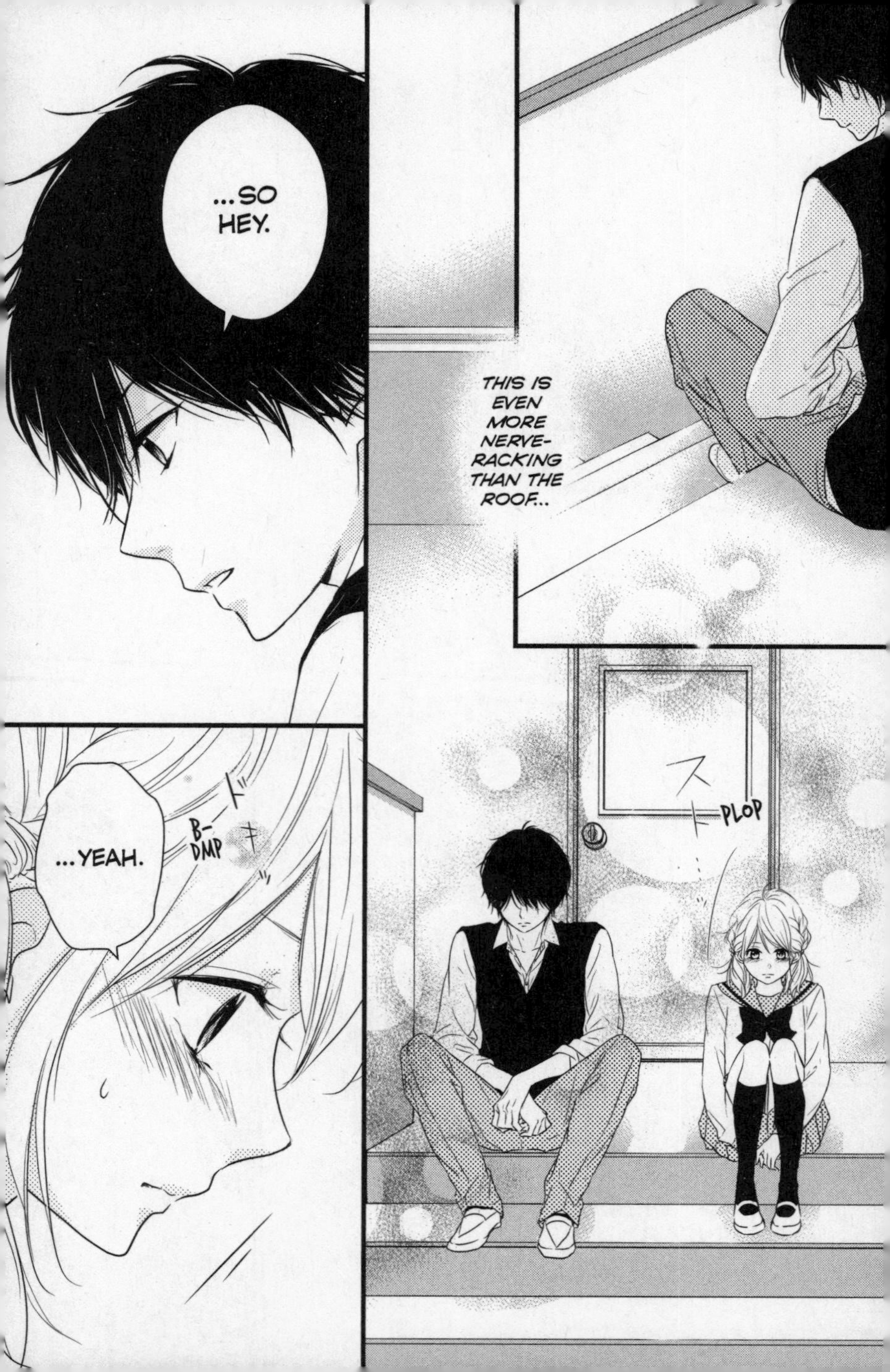
THIS IS EVEN MORE NERVE-RACKING THAN THE ROOF...
...SO HEY.
PLOP
...YEAH.
B-DMP

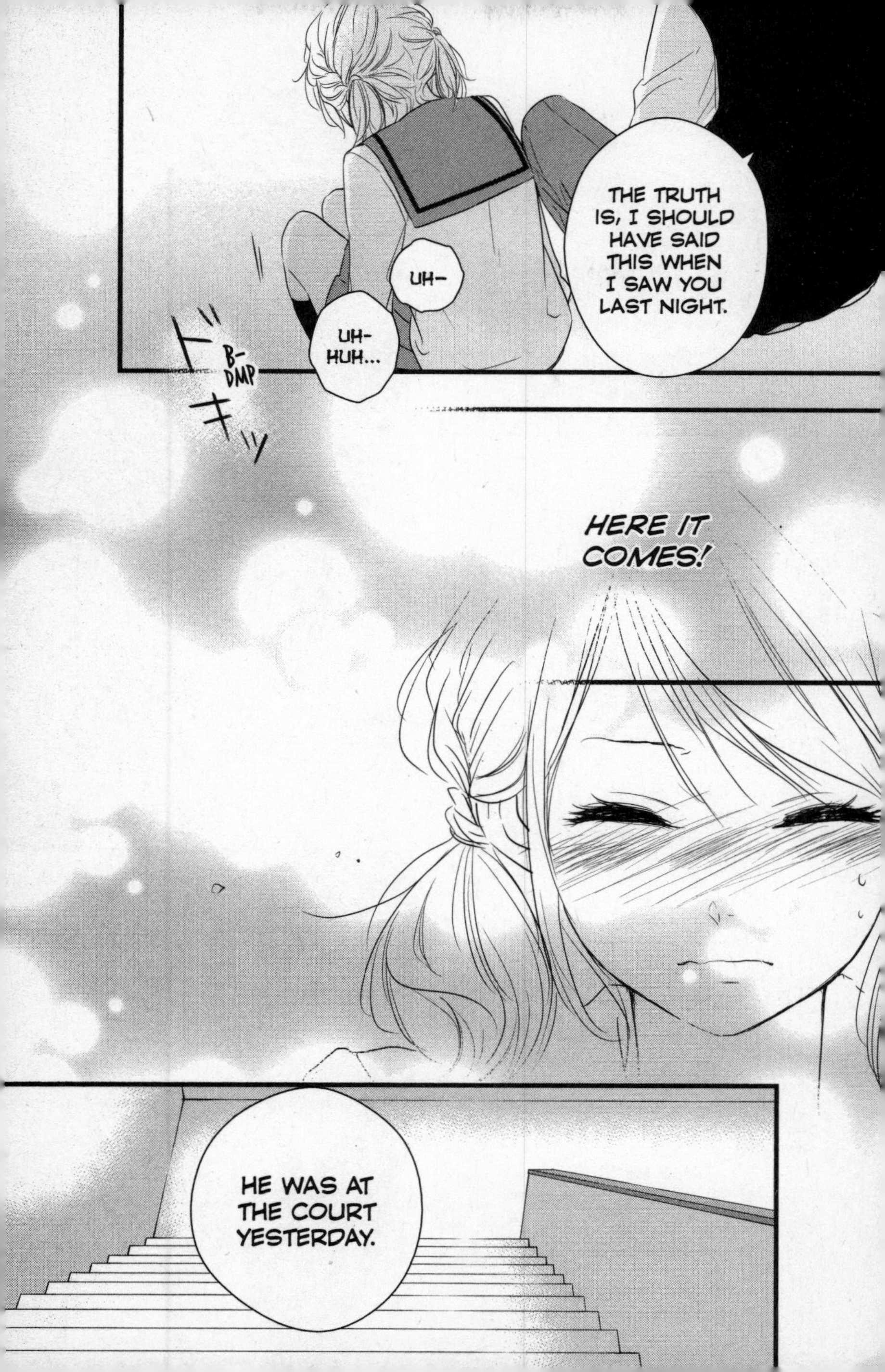
THE TRUTH IS, I SHOULD HAVE SAID THIS WHEN I SAW YOU LAST NIGHT.
UH-
UH-HUH...
B-DMP
HERE IT COMES!
HE WAS AT THE COURT YESTERDAY.

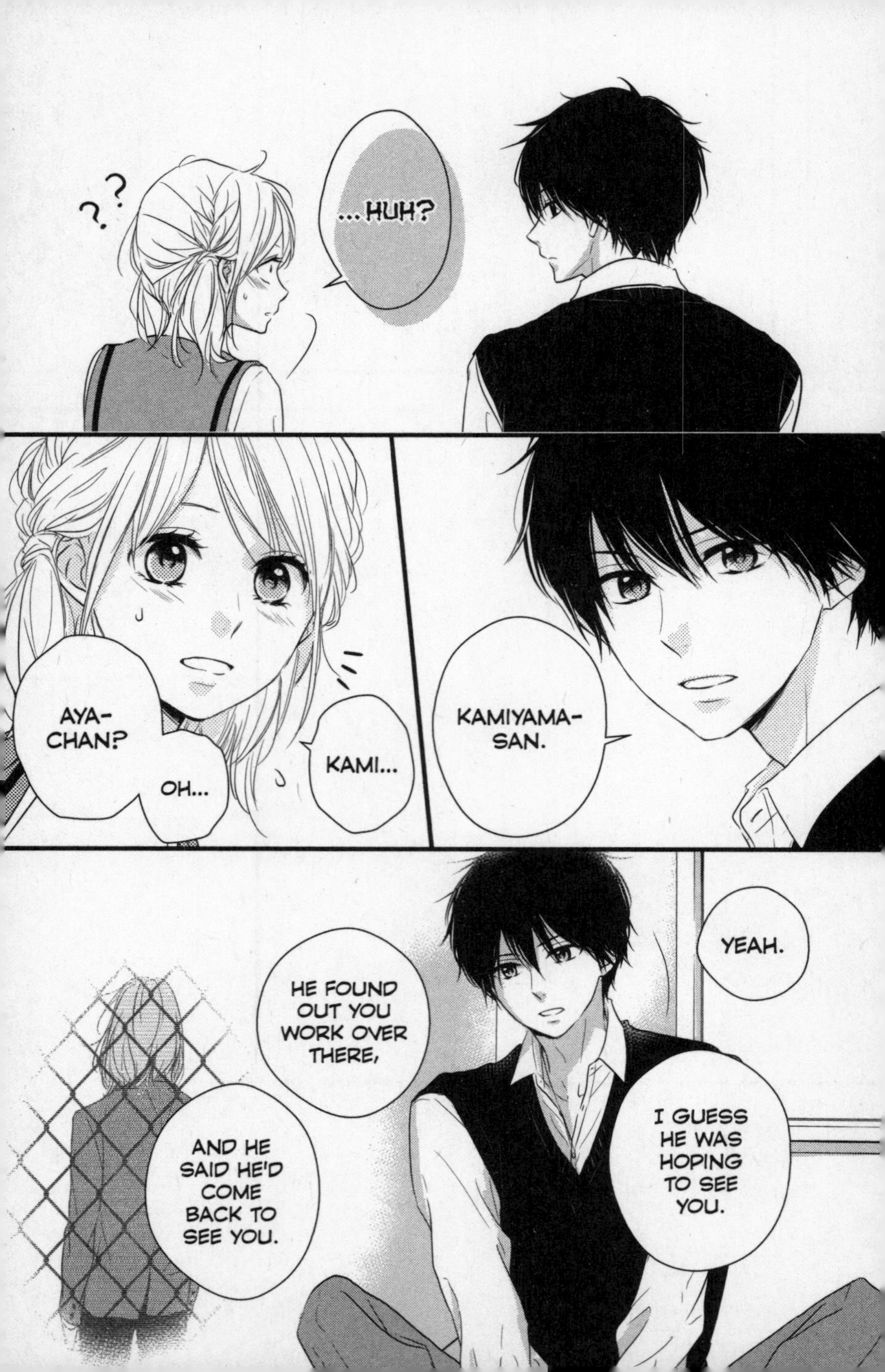
... HUH?
KAMIYAMA-SAN.
AYA-CHAN?
OH...
KAMI...
YEAH.
HE FOUND OUT YOU WORK OVER THERE,
AND HE SAID HE'D COME BACK TO SEE YOU.
I GUESS HE WAS HOPING TO SEE YOU.

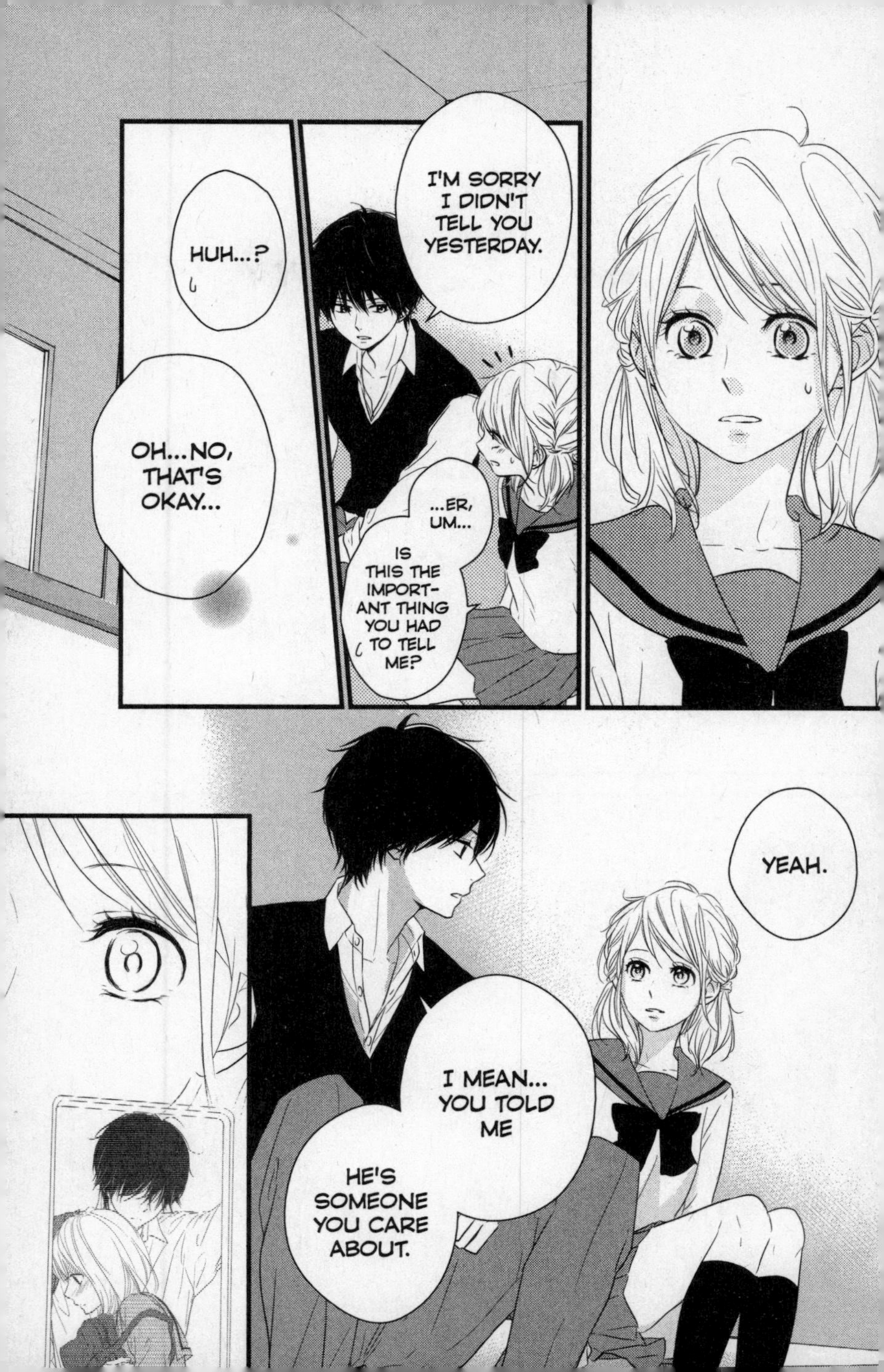
I'M SORRY I DIDN'T TELL YOU YESTERDAY.
...ER, UM...
IS THIS THE IMPORT-ANT THING YOU HAD TO TELL ME?
HUH...?
OH...NO, THAT'S OKAY...
YEAH.
I MEAN... YOU TOLD ME
HE'S SOMEONE YOU CARE ABOUT.

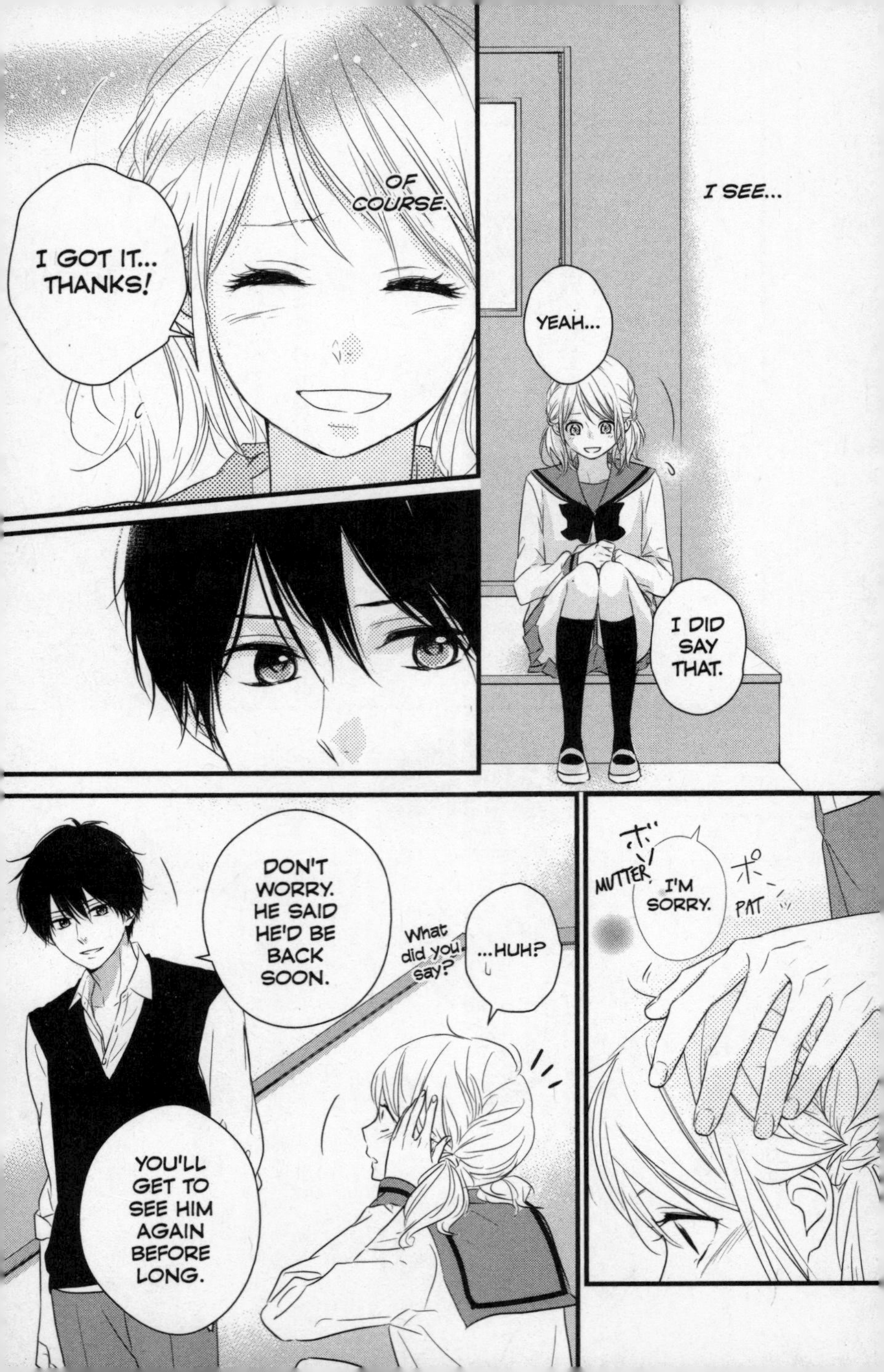
I SEE...
YEAH...
I DID SAY THAT.
OF COURSE.
I GOT IT... THANKS!
I'M SORRY.
ポ
MUTTER
ポ
PAT
...HUH?
What did you say?
DON'T WORRY. HE SAID HE'D BE BACK SOON.
YOU'LL GET TO SEE HIM AGAIN BEFORE LONG.

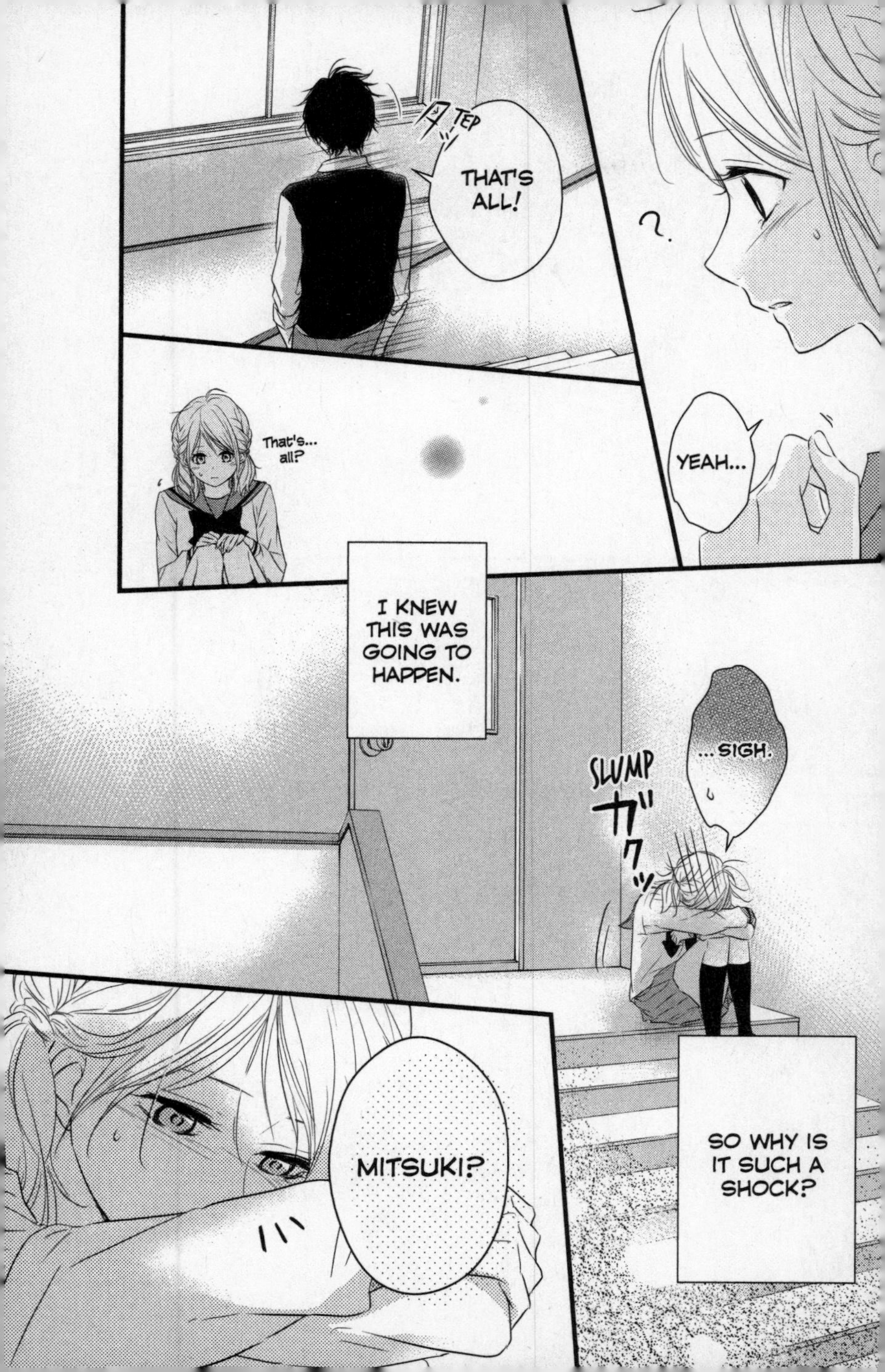
?
YEAH...
TEP
THAT'S ALL!
That's... all?
I KNEW THIS WAS GOING TO HAPPEN.
...SIGH.
SLUMP
SO WHY IS IT SUCH A SHOCK?
MITSUKI?

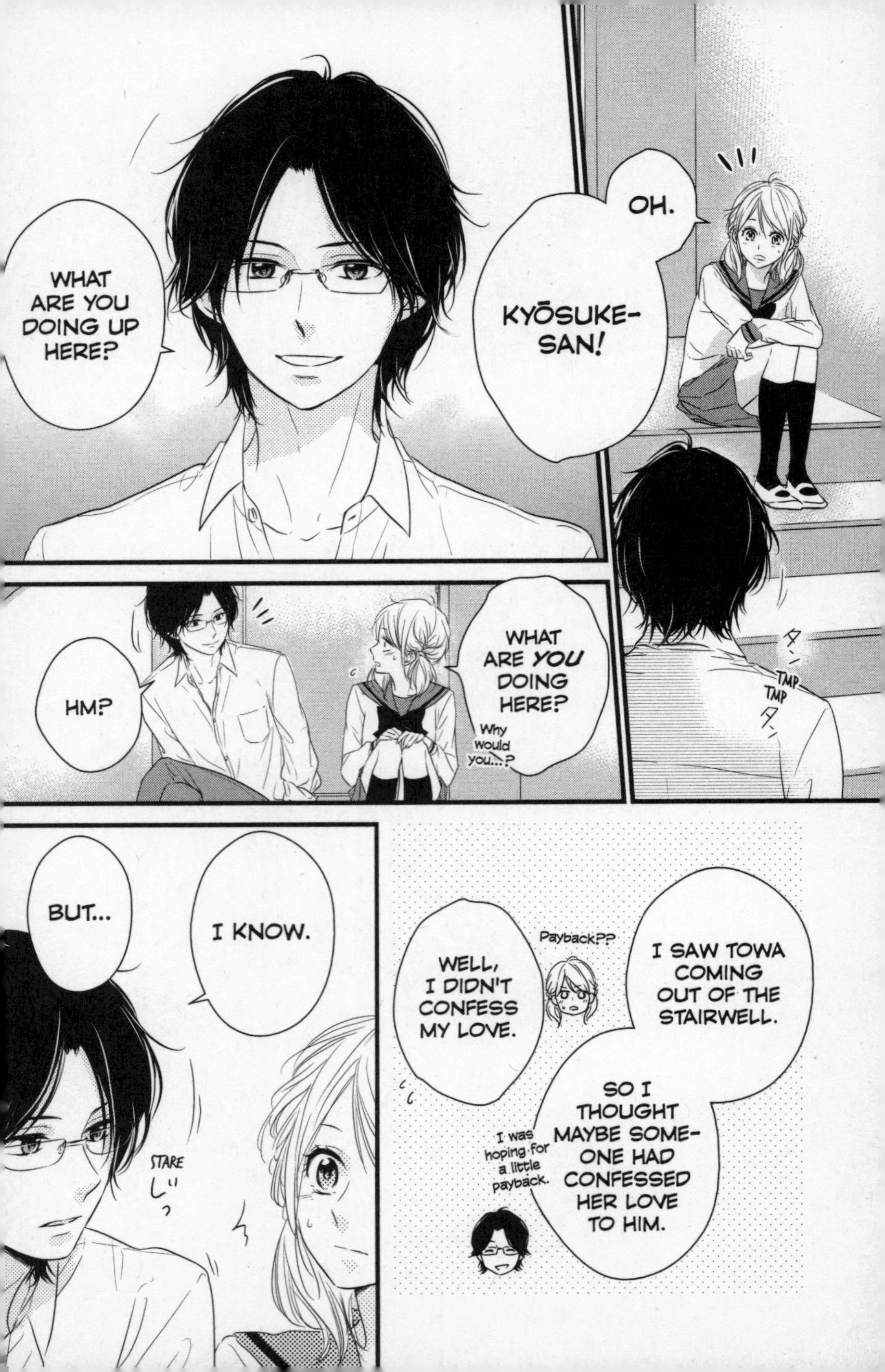
OH.
KYŌSUKE-SAN!
TMP TMP
WHAT ARE YOU DOING UP HERE?
WHAT ARE *YOU* DOING HERE?
Why would you...?
HM?
I SAW TOWA COMING OUT OF THE STAIRWELL.
SO I THOUGHT MAYBE SOME-ONE HAD CONFESSED HER LOVE TO HIM.
I was hoping for a little payback.
Payback??
WELL, I DIDN'T CONFESS MY LOVE.
I KNOW.
BUT...
STARE

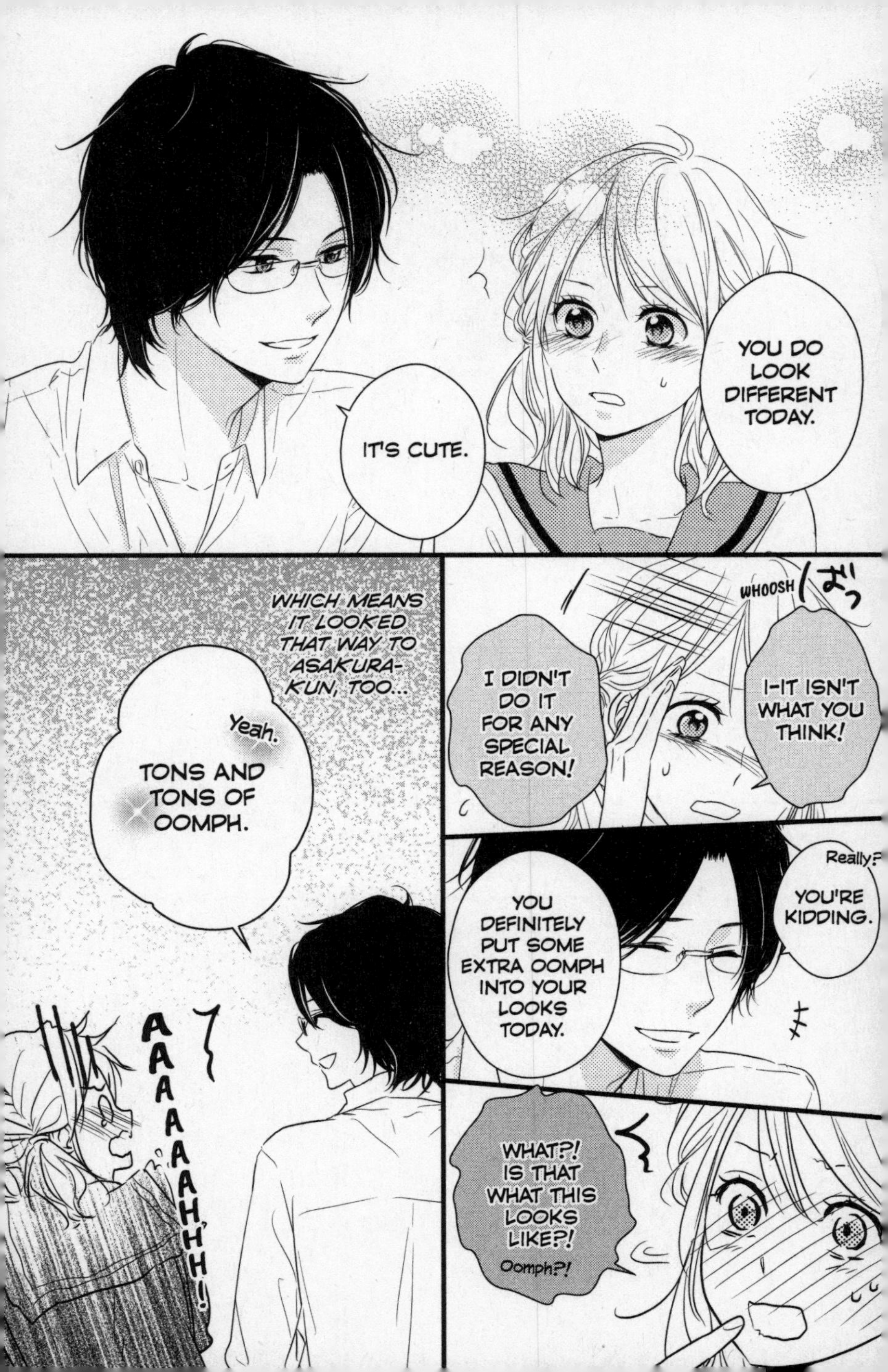
YOU DO LOOK DIFFERENT TODAY.
IT'S CUTE.
WHOOSH ばっ
I-IT ISN'T WHAT YOU THINK!
I DIDN'T DO IT FOR ANY SPECIAL REASON!
Really?
YOU'RE KIDDING.
YOU DEFINITELY PUT SOME EXTRA OOMPH INTO YOUR LOOKS TODAY.
WHAT?! IS THAT WHAT THIS LOOKS LIKE?!
Oomph?!
WHICH MEANS IT LOOKED THAT WAY TO ASAKURA-KUN, TOO...
Yeah.
TONS AND TONS OF OOMPH.
AAAAAAHHH!

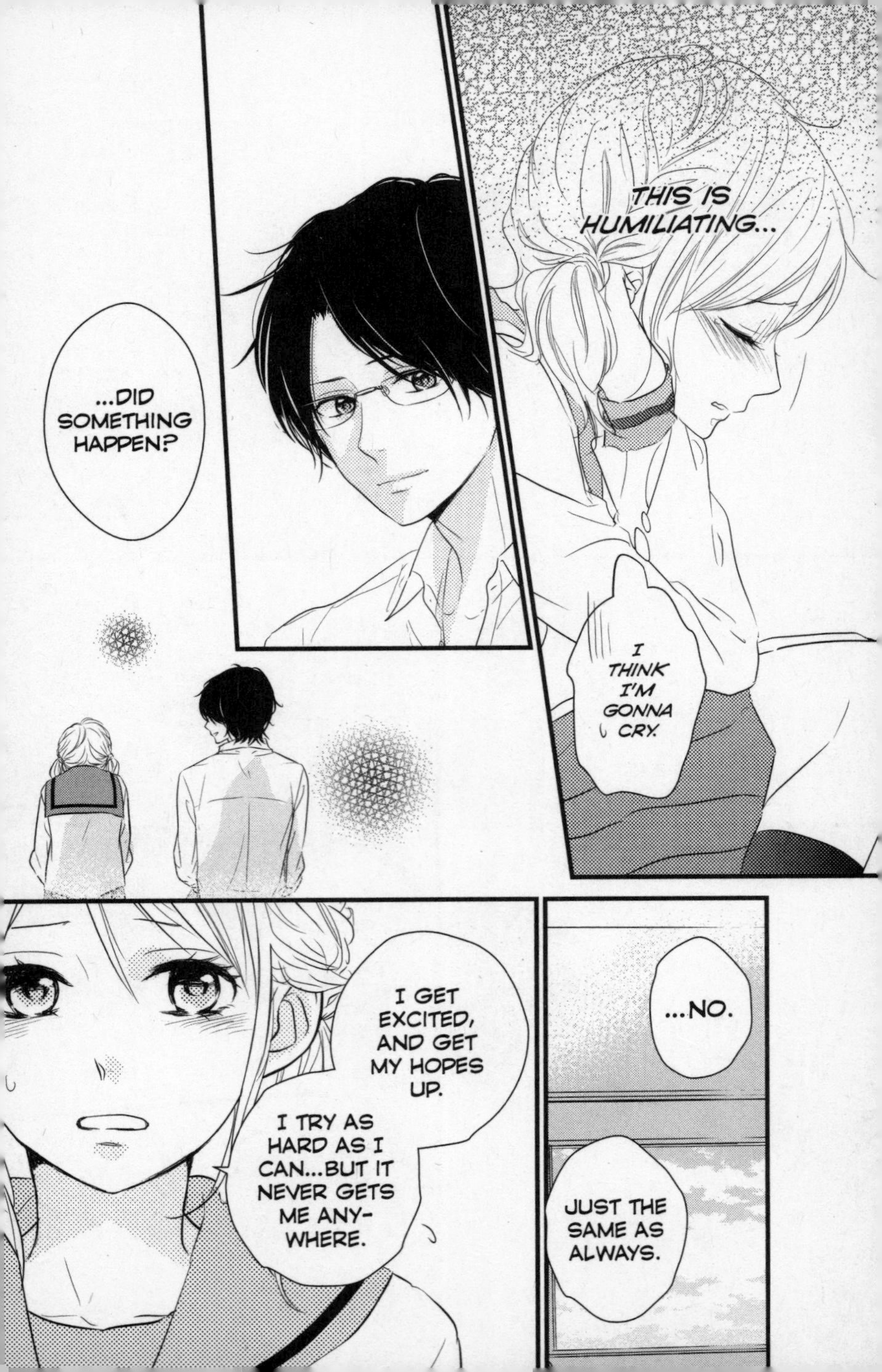
THIS IS HUMILIATING...
I THINK I'M GONNA CRY.
...DID SOMETHING HAPPEN?
...NO.
JUST THE SAME AS ALWAYS.
I GET EXCITED, AND GET MY HOPES UP.
I TRY AS HARD AS I CAN...BUT IT NEVER GETS ME ANY-WHERE.

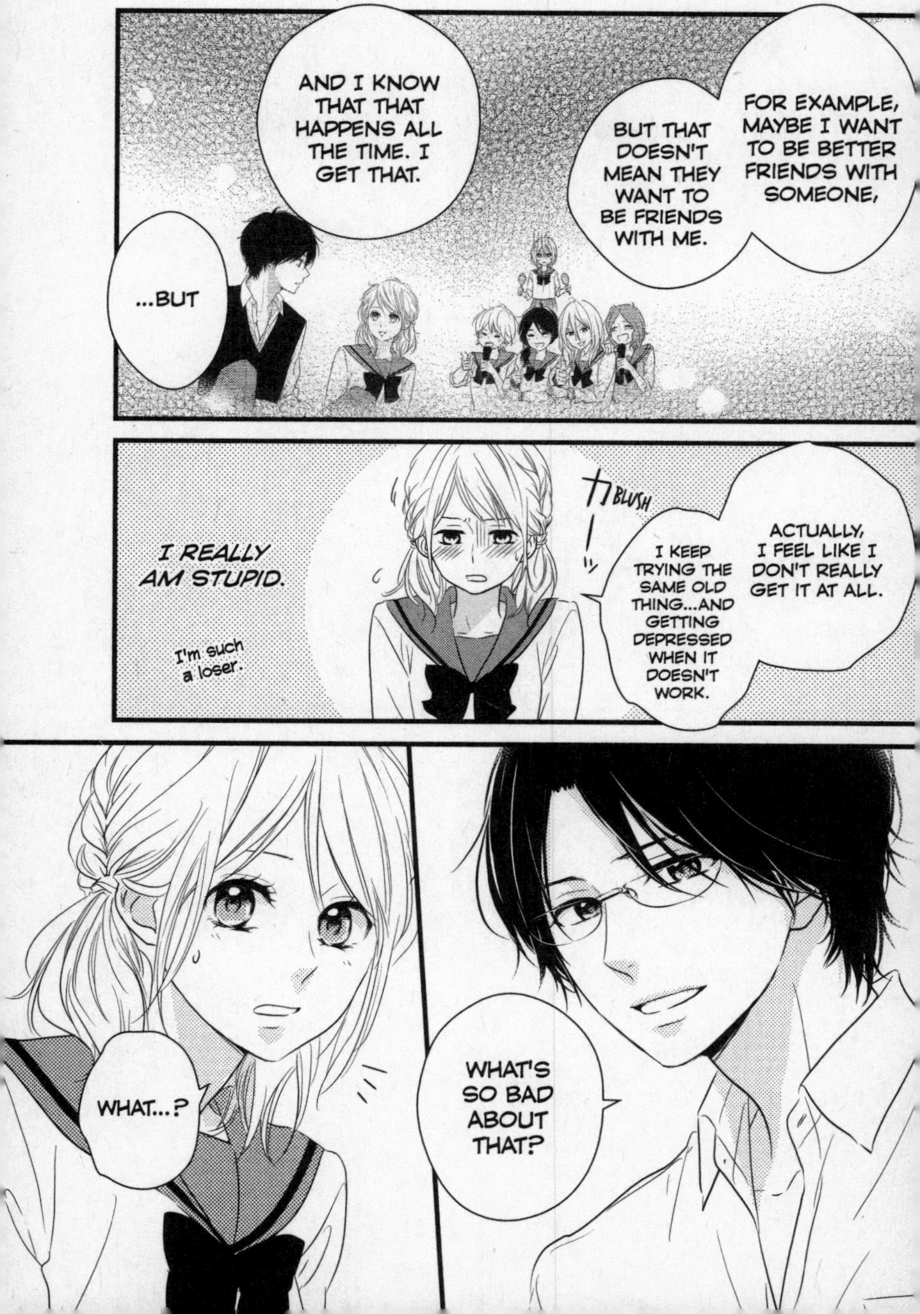
FOR EXAMPLE, MAYBE I WANT TO BE BETTER FRIENDS WITH SOMEONE,
BUT THAT DOESN'T MEAN THEY WANT TO BE FRIENDS WITH ME.
AND I KNOW THAT THAT HAPPENS ALL THE TIME. I GET THAT.
...BUT
ACTUALLY, I FEEL LIKE I DON'T REALLY GET IT AT ALL.
I KEEP TRYING THE SAME OLD THING...AND GETTING DEPRESSED WHEN IT DOESN'T WORK.
BLUSH
I REALLY AM STUPID.
I'm such a loser.
WHAT'S SO BAD ABOUT THAT?
WHAT...?

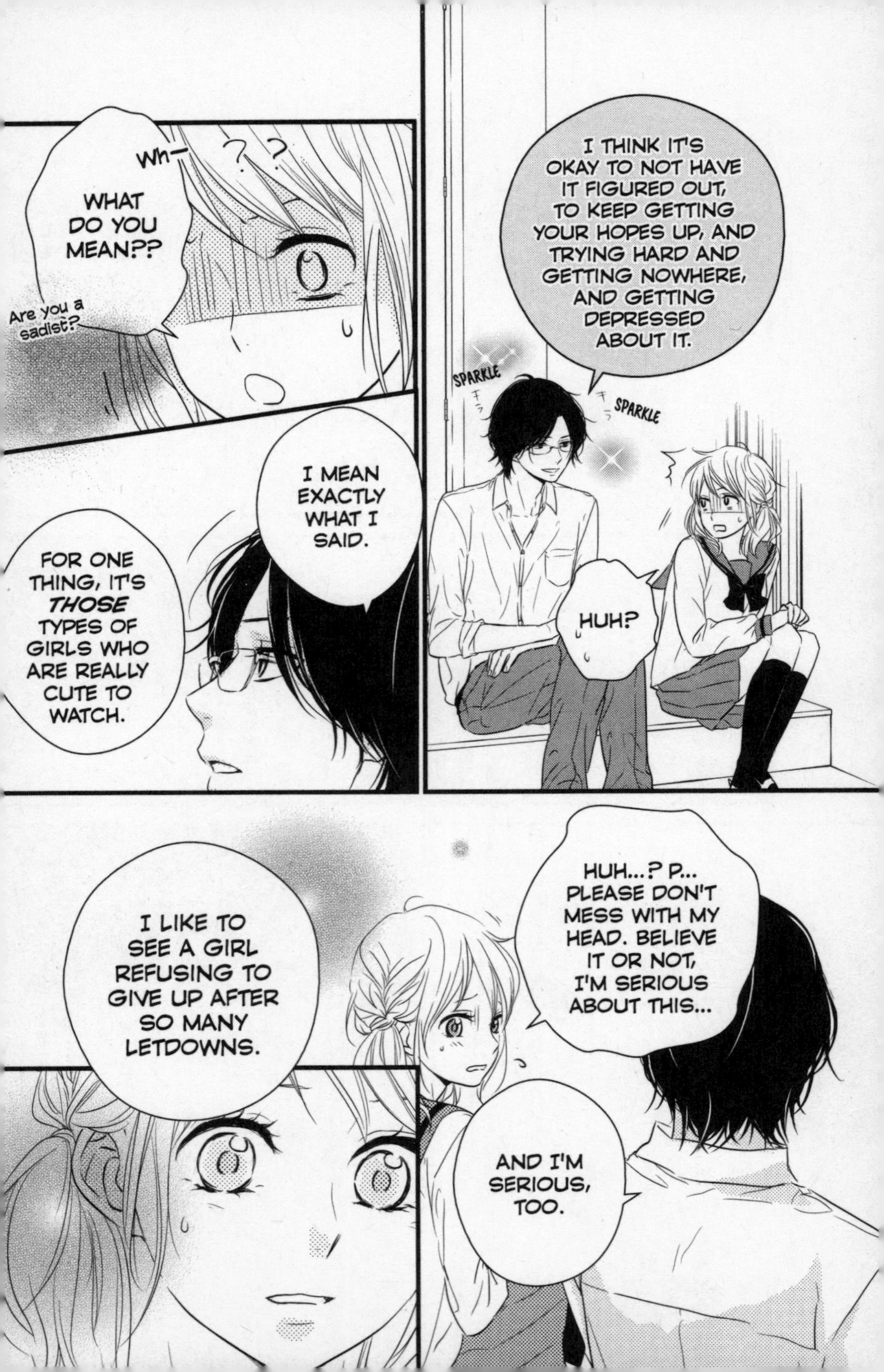
I THINK IT'S OKAY TO NOT HAVE IT FIGURED OUT, TO KEEP GETTING YOUR HOPES UP, AND TRYING HARD AND GETTING NOWHERE, AND GETTING DEPRESSED ABOUT IT.
SPARKLE
SPARKLE
HUH?
Wh—
??
WHAT DO YOU MEAN??
Are you a sadist?
I MEAN EXACTLY WHAT I SAID.
FOR ONE THING, IT'S *THOSE* TYPES OF GIRLS WHO ARE REALLY CUTE TO WATCH.
I LIKE TO SEE A GIRL REFUSING TO GIVE UP AFTER SO MANY LETDOWNS.
HUH...? P... PLEASE DON'T MESS WITH MY HEAD. BELIEVE IT OR NOT, I'M SERIOUS ABOUT THIS...
AND I'M SERIOUS, TOO.

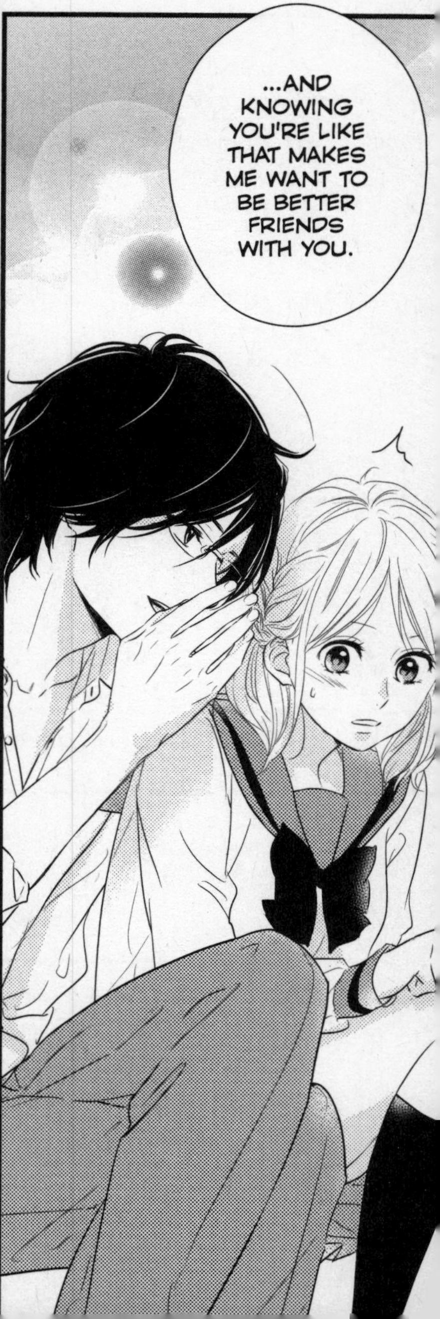
...AND KNOWING YOU'RE LIKE THAT MAKES ME WANT TO BE BETTER FRIENDS WITH YOU.

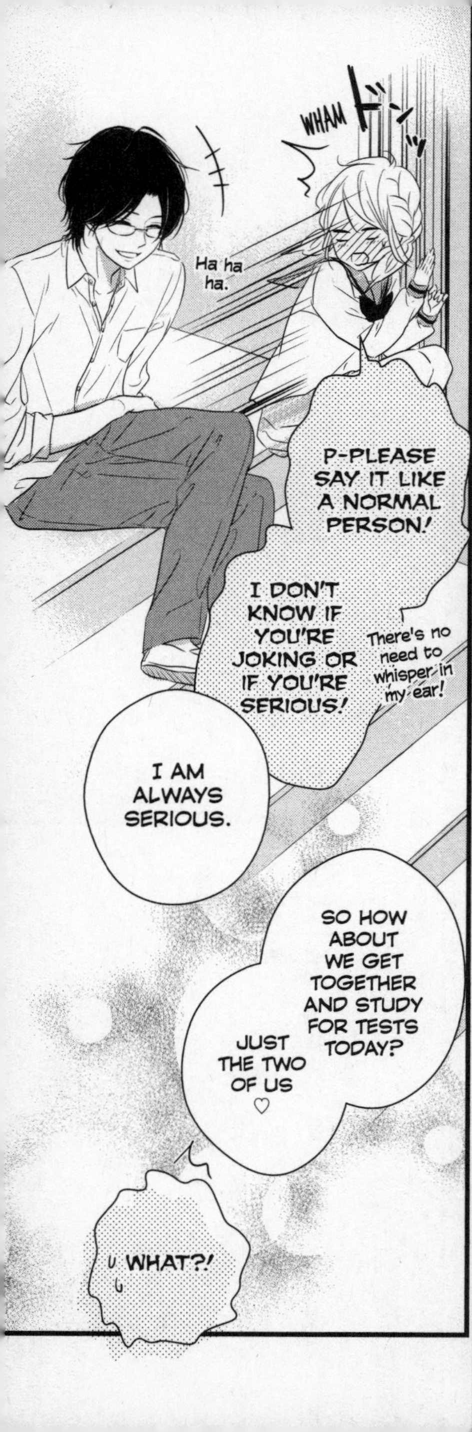
WHAM
Ha ha ha.
P-PLEASE SAY IT LIKE A NORMAL PERSON!
I DON'T KNOW IF YOU'RE JOKING OR IF YOU'RE SERIOUS!
There's no need to whisper in my ear!
I AM ALWAYS SERIOUS.
SO HOW ABOUT WE GET TOGETHER AND STUDY FOR TESTS TODAY?
JUST THE TWO OF US ♡
WHAT?!

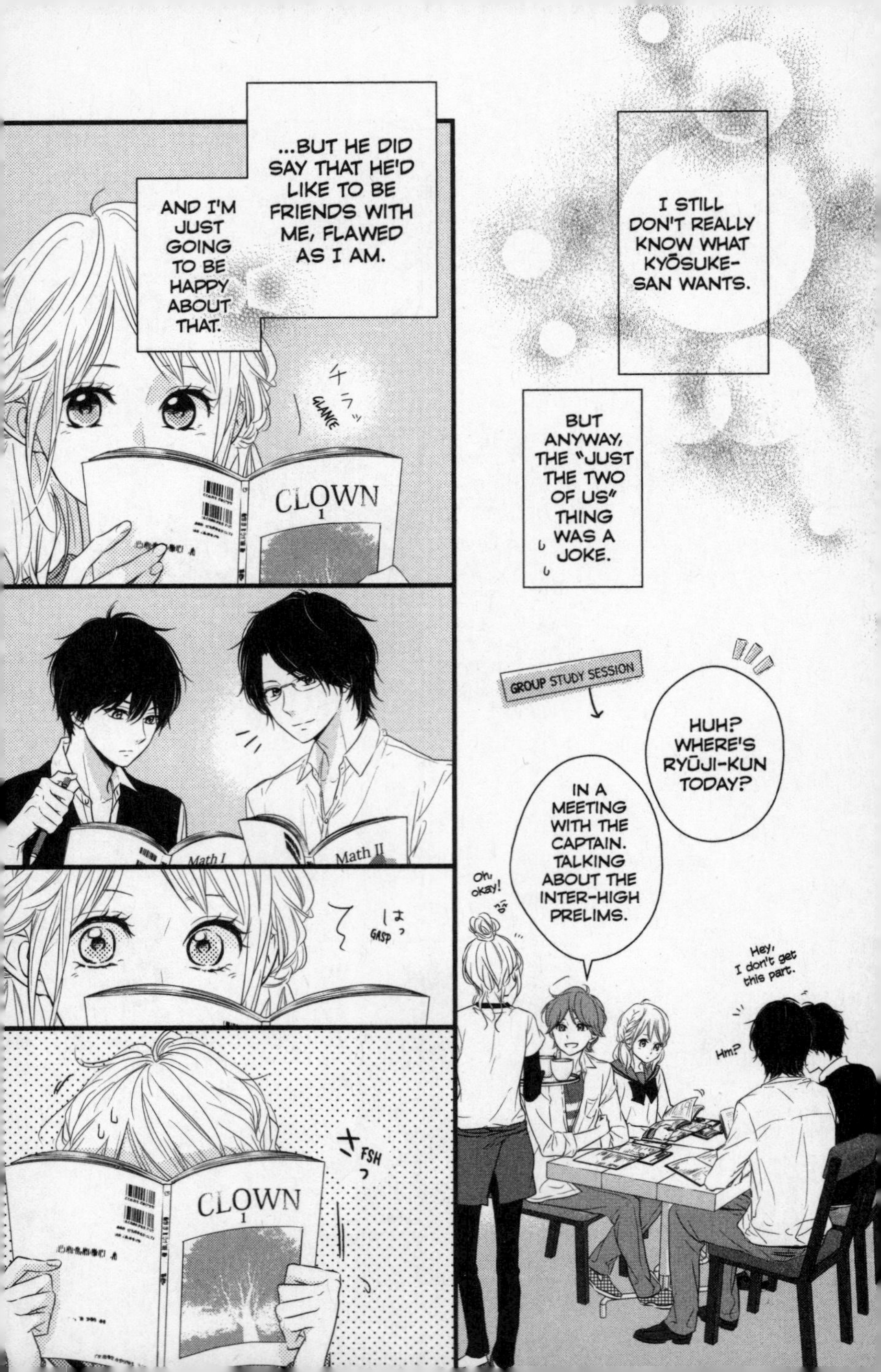
I STILL DON'T REALLY KNOW WHAT KYŌSUKE-SAN WANTS.
BUT ANYWAY, THE "JUST THE TWO OF US" THING WAS A JOKE.
GROUP STUDY SESSION
HUH? WHERE'S RYŪJI-KUN TODAY?
IN A MEETING WITH THE CAPTAIN. TALKING ABOUT THE INTER-HIGH PRELIMS.
Oh, okay!
Hey, I don't get this part.
Hm?
...BUT HE DID SAY THAT HE'D LIKE TO BE FRIENDS WITH ME, FLAWED AS I AM.
AND I'M JUST GOING TO BE HAPPY ABOUT THAT.
チラッ
GLANCE
CLOWN
Math I
Math II
はっ
GASP
FSH
CLOWN

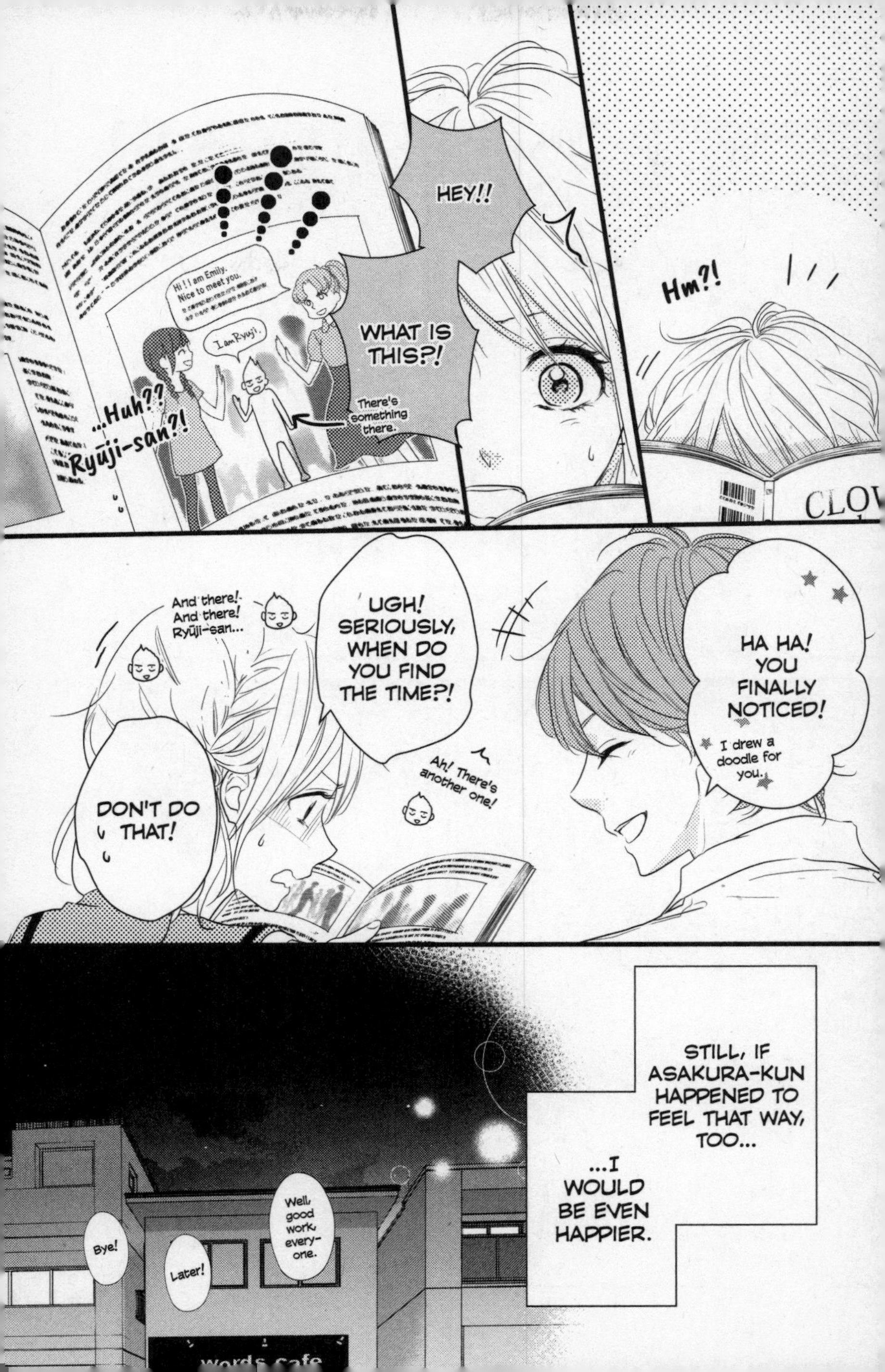
Hm?!
HEY!!
WHAT IS THIS?!
There's something there.
Hi! I am Emily. Nice to meet you.
I am Ryuji.
...Huh?? Ryūji-san?!
HA HA! YOU FINALLY NOTICED!
I drew a doodle for you.
UGH! SERIOUSLY, WHEN DO YOU FIND THE TIME?!
Ah! There's another one!
And there! And there! Ryūji-san...
DON'T DO THAT!
STILL, IF ASAKURA-KUN HAPPENED TO FEEL THAT WAY, TOO...
...I WOULD BE EVEN HAPPIER.
Well, good work, every-one.
Later!
Bye!
words cafe

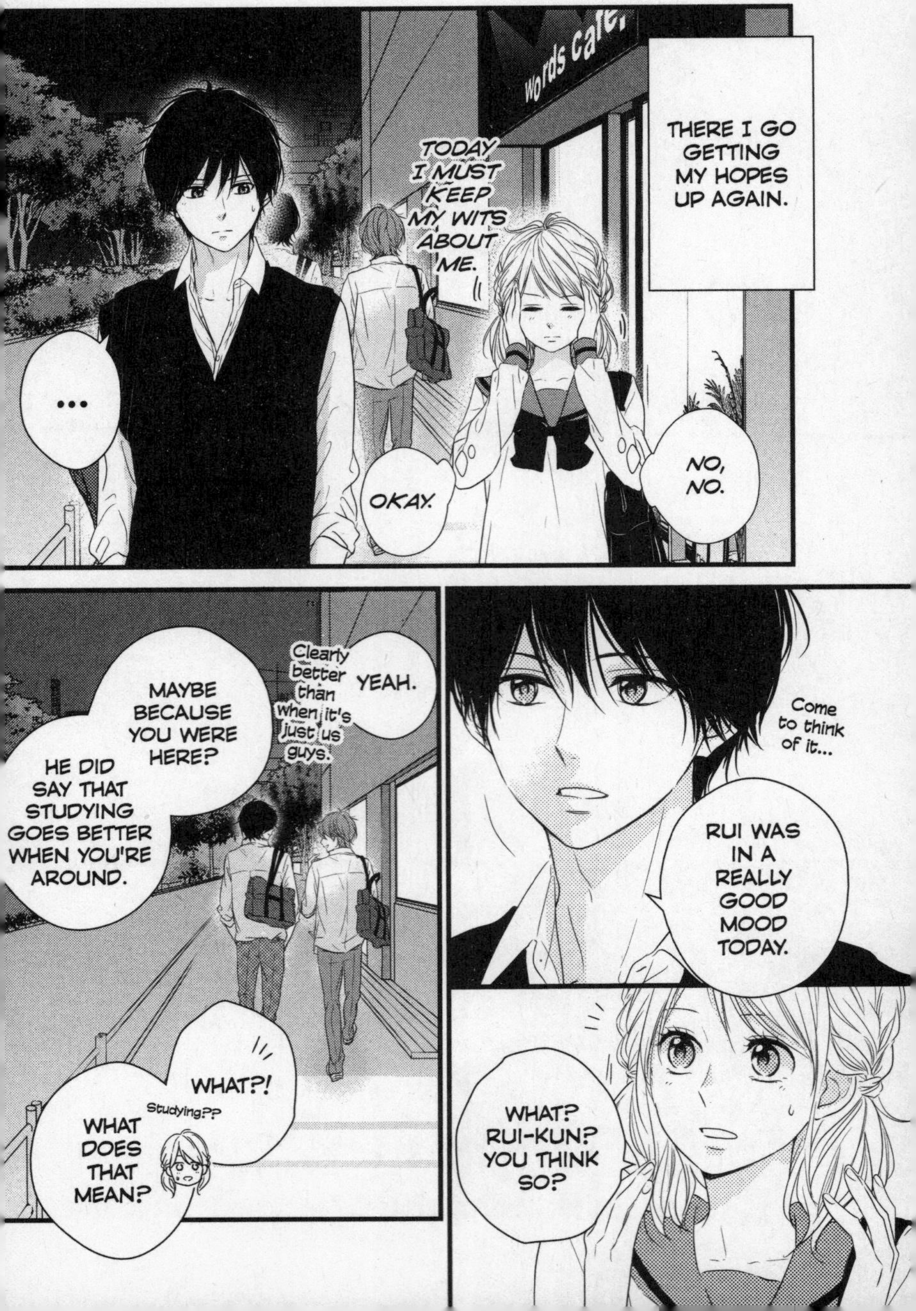
THERE I GO GETTING MY HOPES UP AGAIN.
words cafe
TODAY I MUST KEEP MY WITS ABOUT ME.
NO, NO.
OKAY.
...
Come to think of it...
RUI WAS IN A REALLY GOOD MOOD TODAY.
WHAT? RUI-KUN? YOU THINK SO?
YEAH.
Clearly better than when it's just us guys.
MAYBE BECAUSE YOU WERE HERE?
HE DID SAY THAT STUDYING GOES BETTER WHEN YOU'RE AROUND.
WHAT?!
Studying??
WHAT DOES THAT MEAN?

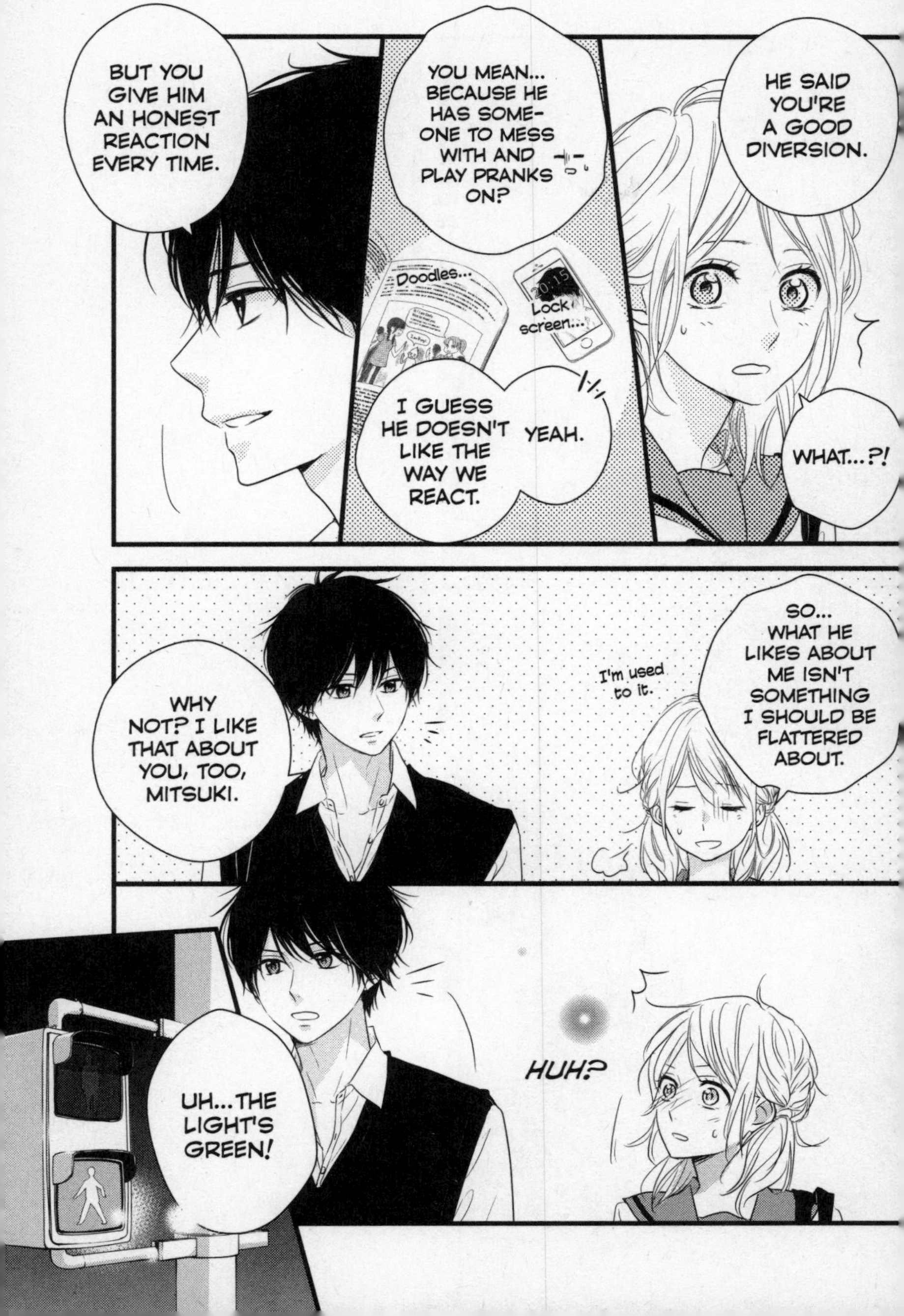
HE SAID YOU'RE A GOOD DIVERSION.
WHAT...?!
YOU MEAN... BECAUSE HE HAS SOME-ONE TO MESS WITH AND PLAY PRANKS ON?
20:15
Lock screen...
Doodles...
YEAH.
I GUESS HE DOESN'T LIKE THE WAY WE REACT.
BUT YOU GIVE HIM AN HONEST REACTION EVERY TIME.
SO... WHAT HE LIKES ABOUT ME ISN'T SOMETHING I SHOULD BE FLATTERED ABOUT.
I'm used to it.
WHY NOT? I LIKE THAT ABOUT YOU, TOO, MITSUKI.
HUH?
UH...THE LIGHT'S GREEN!

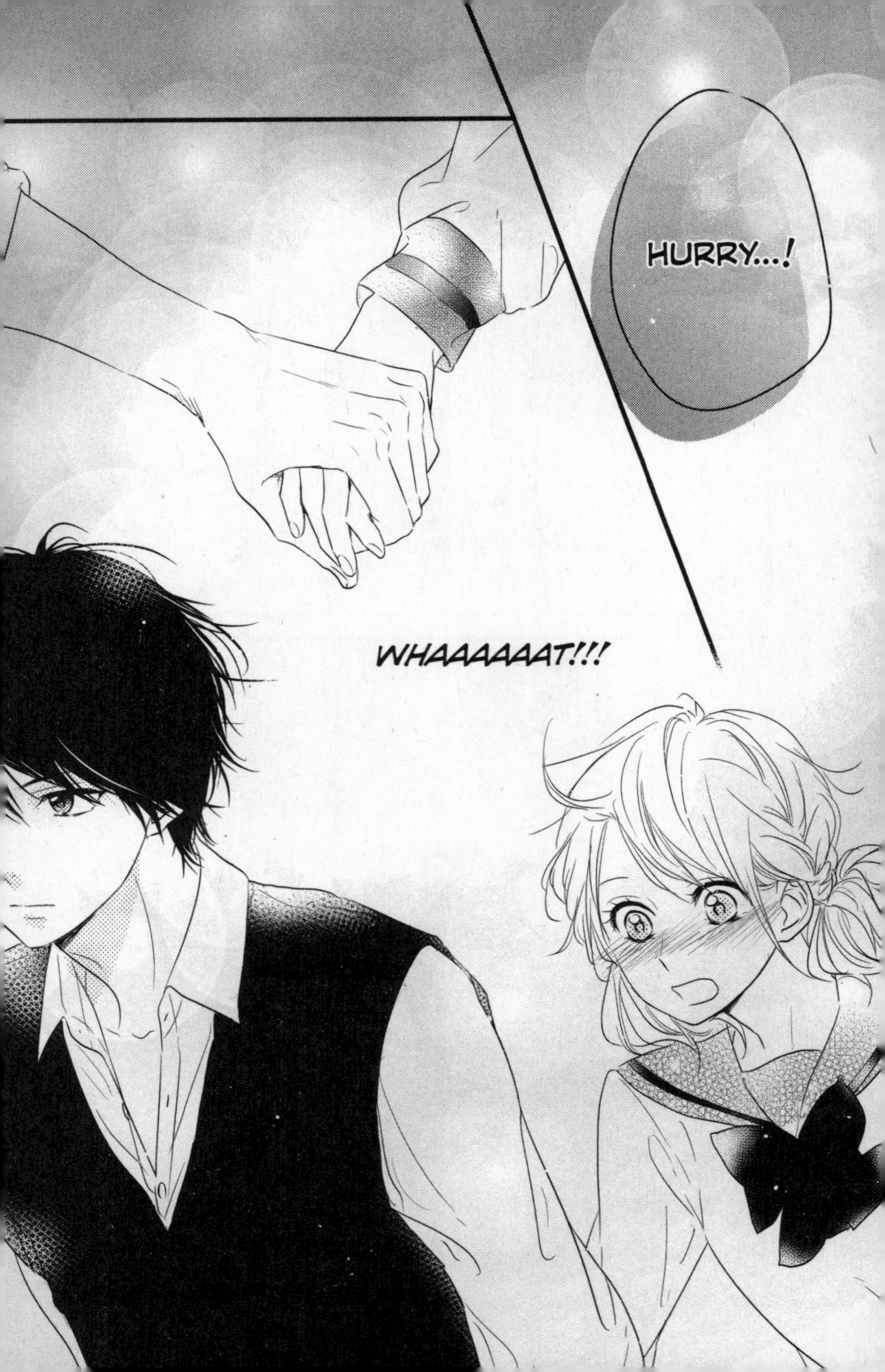
HURRY...!
WHAAAAAAAT!!!

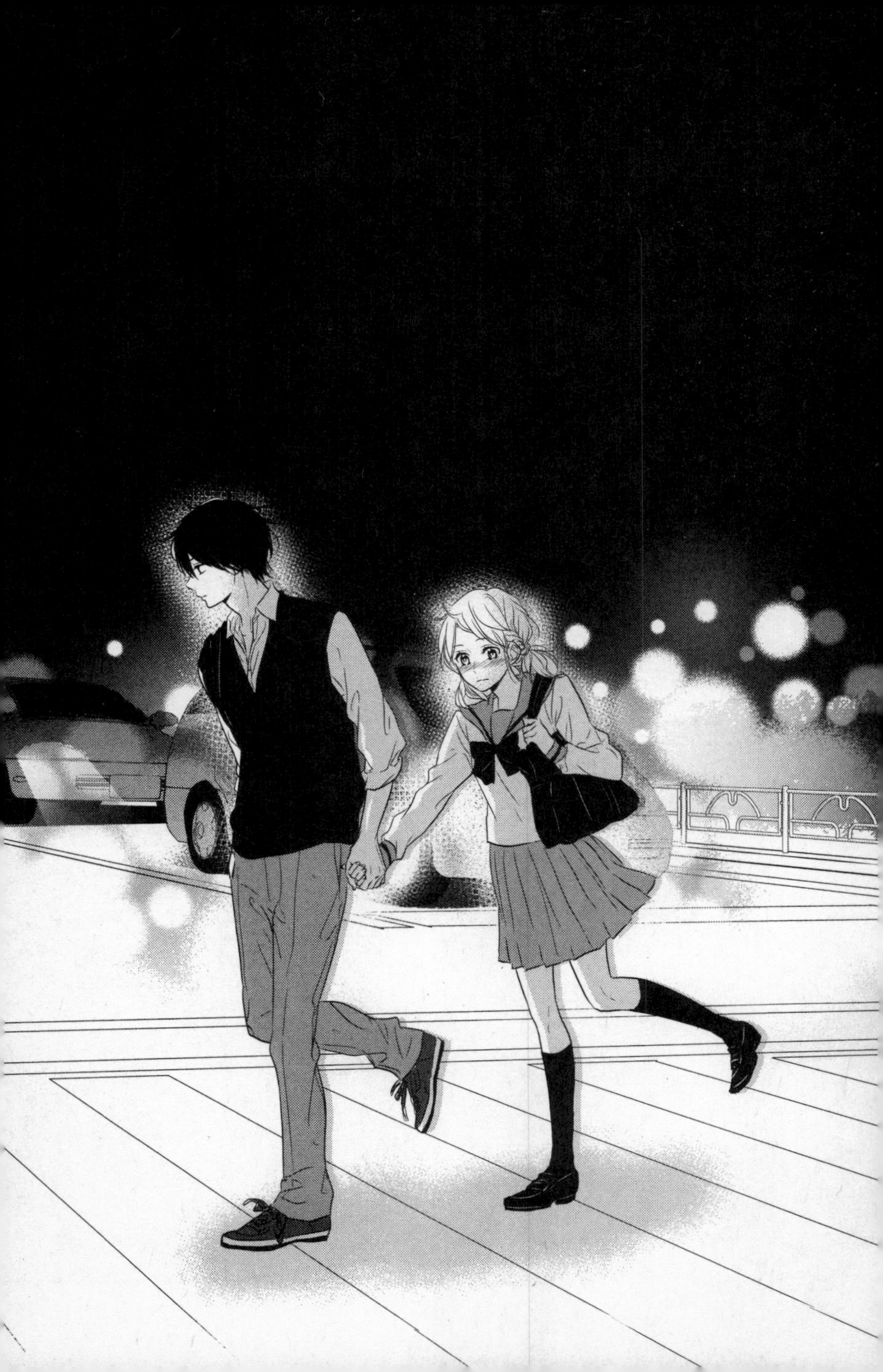

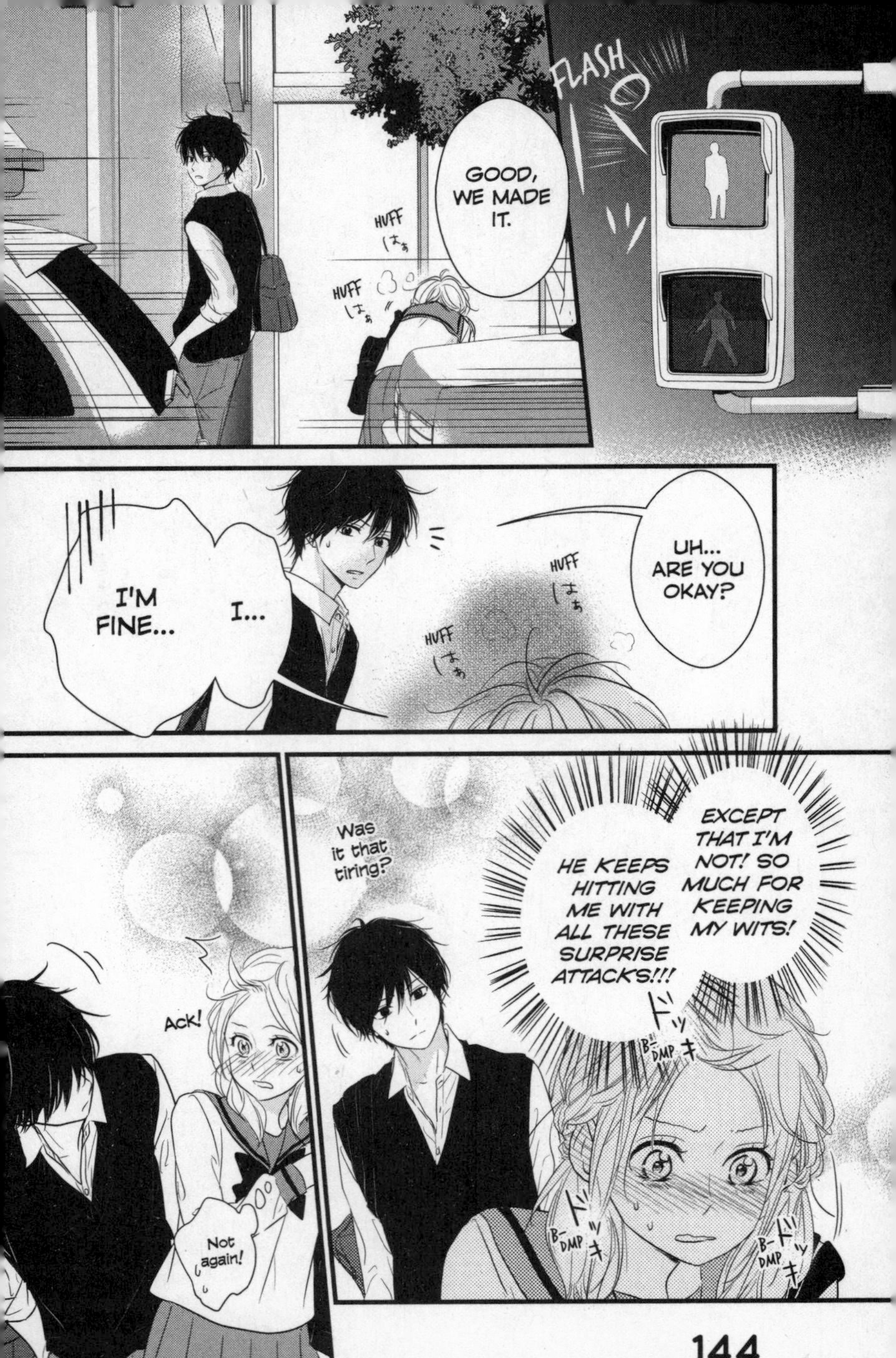
FLASH
GOOD, WE MADE IT.
HUFF はぁ
HUFF はぁ
UH... ARE YOU OKAY?
HUFF はぁ
HUFF はぁ
I'M FINE... I...
EXCEPT THAT I'M NOT! SO MUCH FOR KEEPING MY WITS!
HE KEEPS HITTING ME WITH ALL THESE SURPRISE ATTACKS!!!
Was it that tiring?
ドッキ B-DMP
ドッキ B-DMP
ドッキ B-DMP
Ack!
Not again!

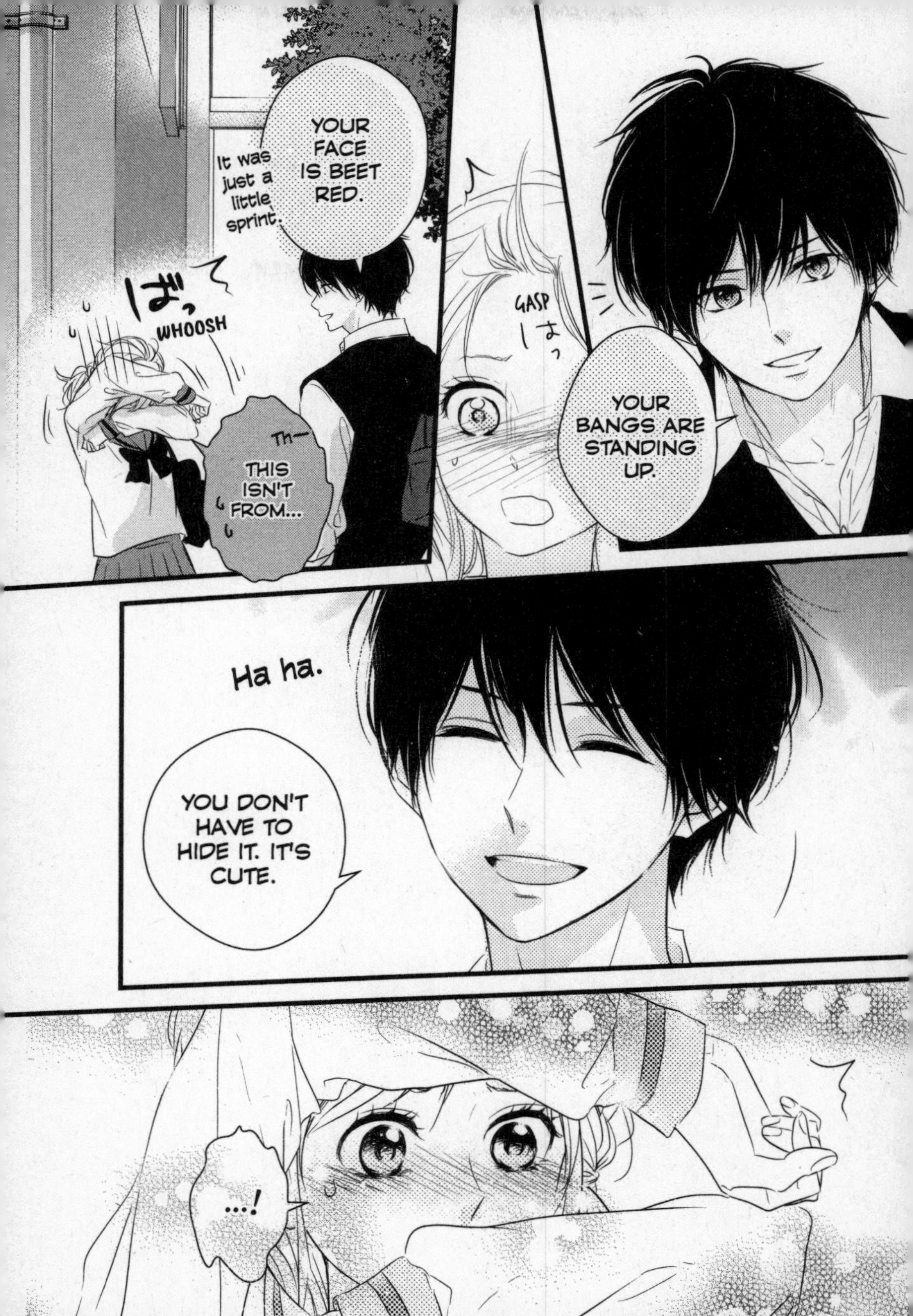
YOUR BANGS ARE STANDING UP.
GASP
はっ
YOUR FACE IS BEET RED.
It was just a little sprint.
ばっ
WHOOSH
Th—
THIS ISN'T FROM...
Ha ha.
YOU DON'T HAVE TO HIDE IT. IT'S CUTE.
...!

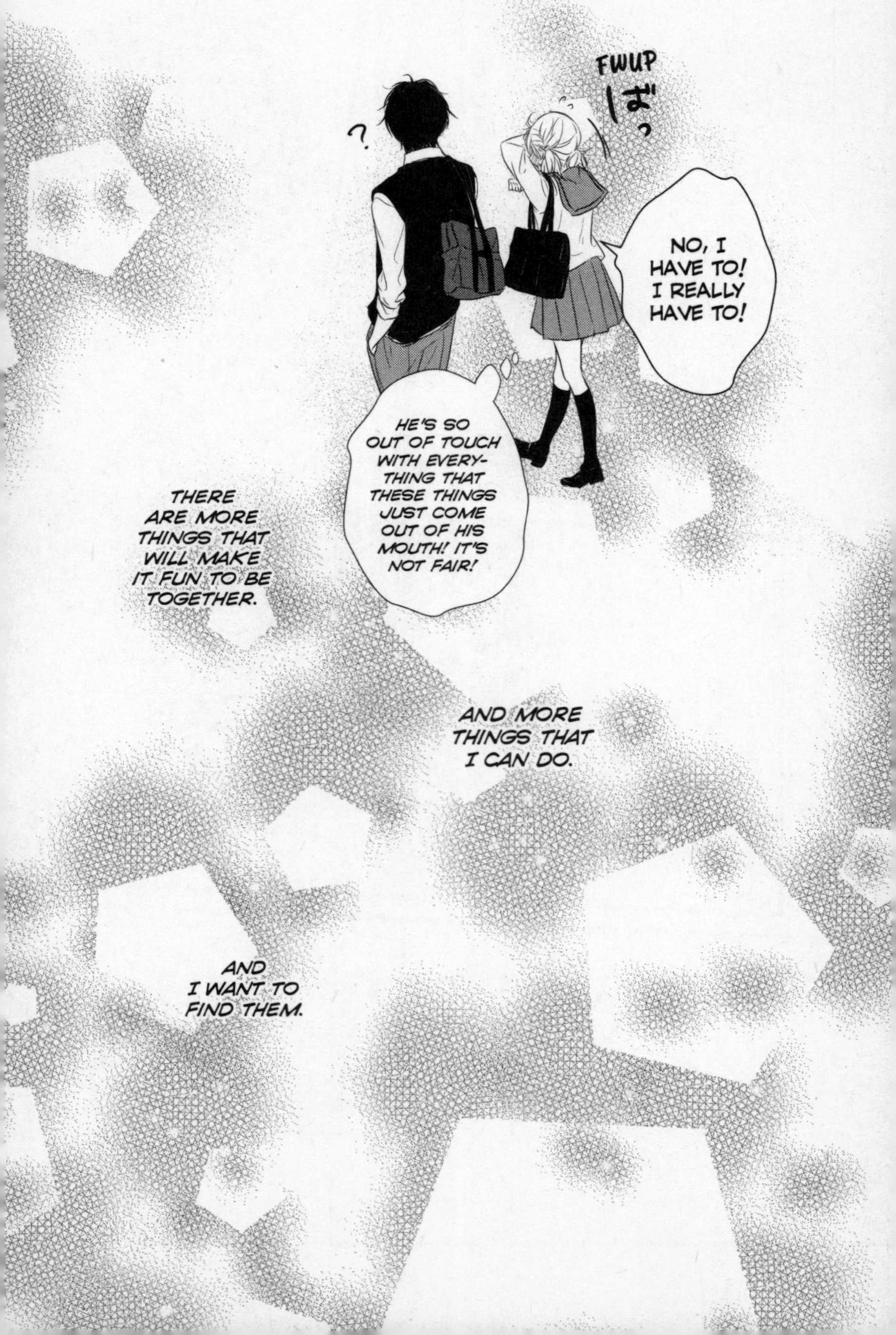
FWUP
ばっ
?
NO, I HAVE TO! I REALLY HAVE TO!
HE'S SO OUT OF TOUCH WITH EVERY-THING THAT THESE THINGS JUST COME OUT OF HIS MOUTH! IT'S NOT FAIR!
THERE ARE MORE THINGS THAT WILL MAKE IT FUN TO BE TOGETHER.
AND MORE THINGS THAT I CAN DO.
AND I WANT TO FIND THEM.

period 10: "Aya-chan Attack"

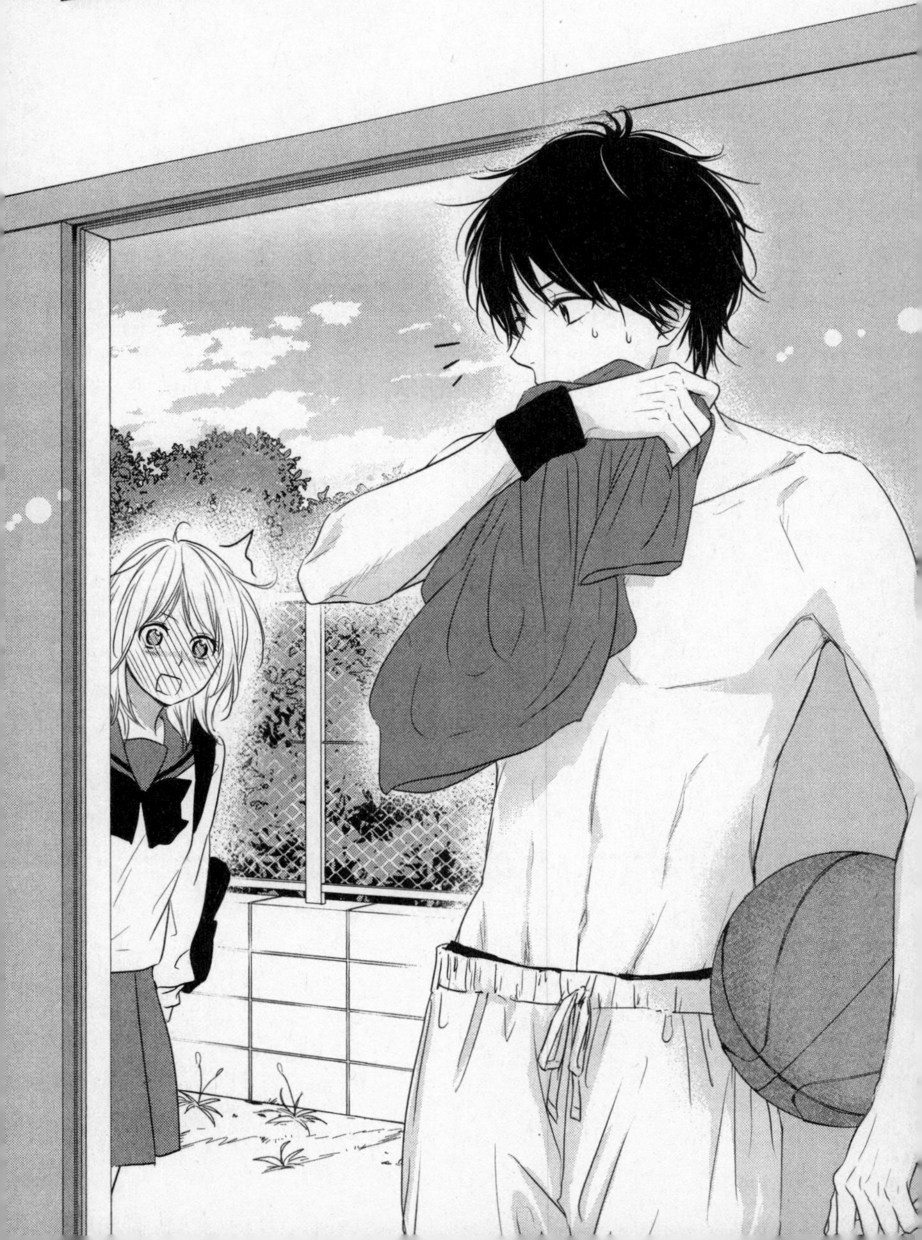

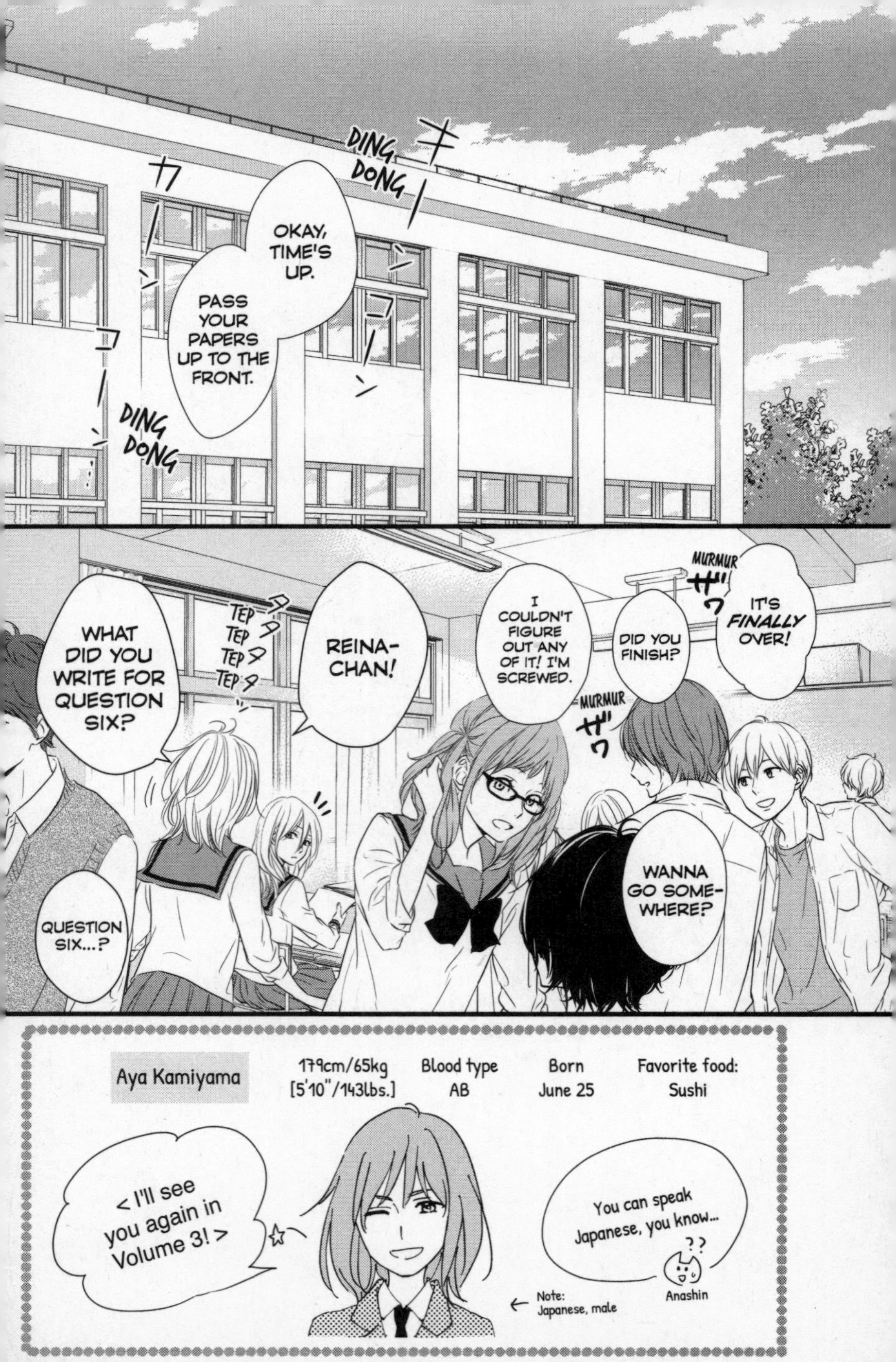
DING DONG
OKAY, TIME'S UP.
PASS YOUR PAPERS UP TO THE FRONT.
DING DONG
MURMUR
IT'S *FINALLY* OVER!
DID YOU FINISH?
I COULDN'T FIGURE OUT ANY OF IT! I'M SCREWED.
MURMUR
WANNA GO SOME-WHERE?
REINA-CHAN!
TEP TEP TEP TEP
WHAT DID YOU WRITE FOR QUESTION SIX?
QUESTION SIX...?
Aya Kamiyama
179cm/65kg [5'10"/143lbs.]
Blood type AB
Born June 25
Favorite food: Sushi
< I'll see you again in Volume 3! >
You can speak Japanese, you know...
Anashin
Note: Japanese, male

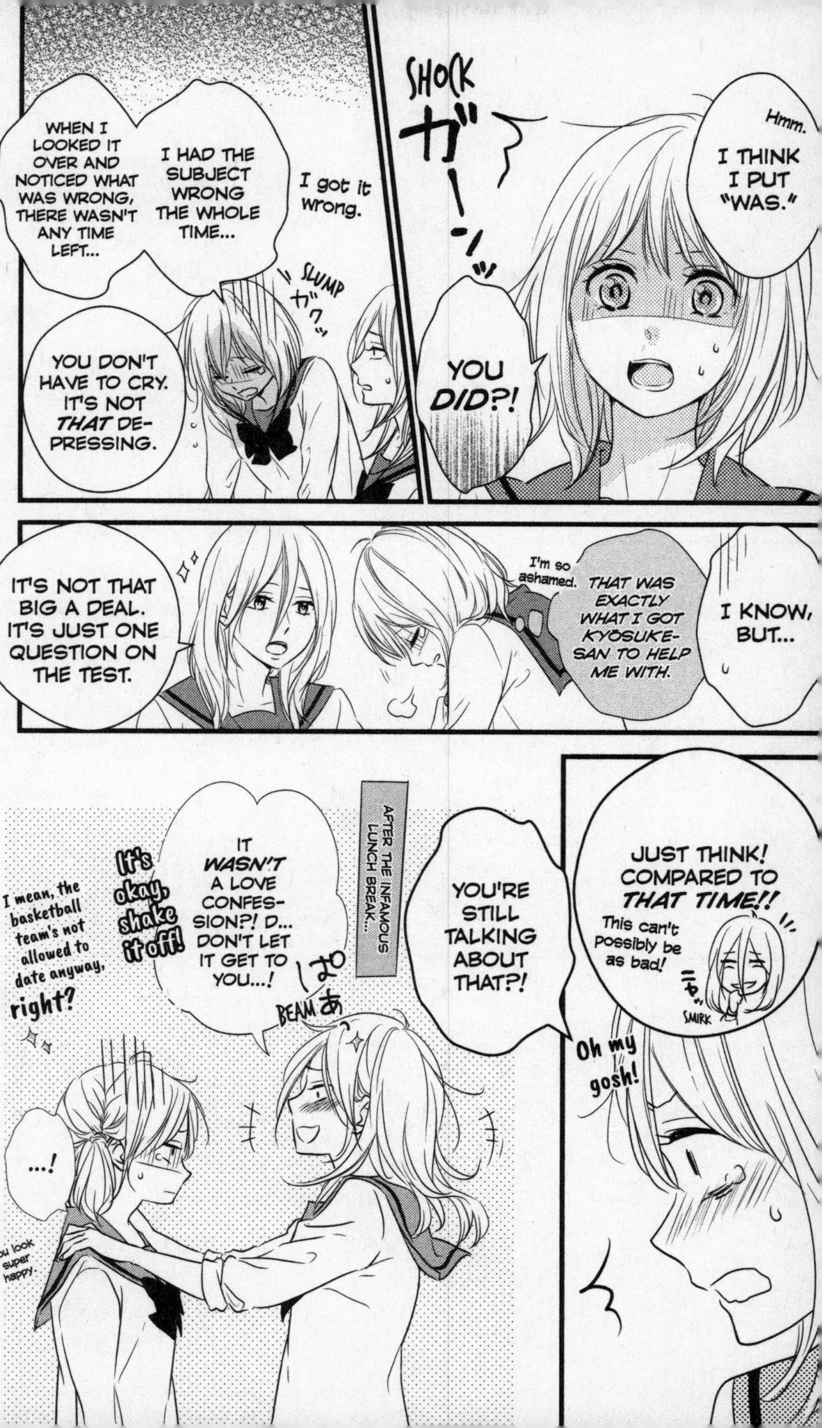
Hmm.
I THINK I PUT "WAS."
SHOCK
ガーン
YOU DID?!
I got it wrong.
I HAD THE SUBJECT WRONG THE WHOLE TIME...
WHEN I LOOKED IT OVER AND NOTICED WHAT WAS WRONG, THERE WASN'T ANY TIME LEFT...
SLUMP
ガクッ
YOU DON'T HAVE TO CRY. IT'S NOT THAT DE-PRESSING.
I KNOW, BUT...
THAT WAS EXACTLY WHAT I GOT KYŌSUKE-SAN TO HELP ME WITH.
I'm so ashamed.
IT'S NOT THAT BIG A DEAL. IT'S JUST ONE QUESTION ON THE TEST.
JUST THINK! COMPARED TO THAT TIME!!
This can't possibly be as bad!
SMIRK
ニヤッ
YOU'RE STILL TALKING ABOUT THAT?!
Oh my gosh!
AFTER THE INFAMOUS LUNCH BREAK...
IT WASN'T A LOVE CONFESSION?! D... DON'T LET IT GET TO YOU...!
BEAM
ぱあ
It's okay, shake it off!
I mean, the basketball team's not allowed to date anyway, right?
...!
You look super happy.

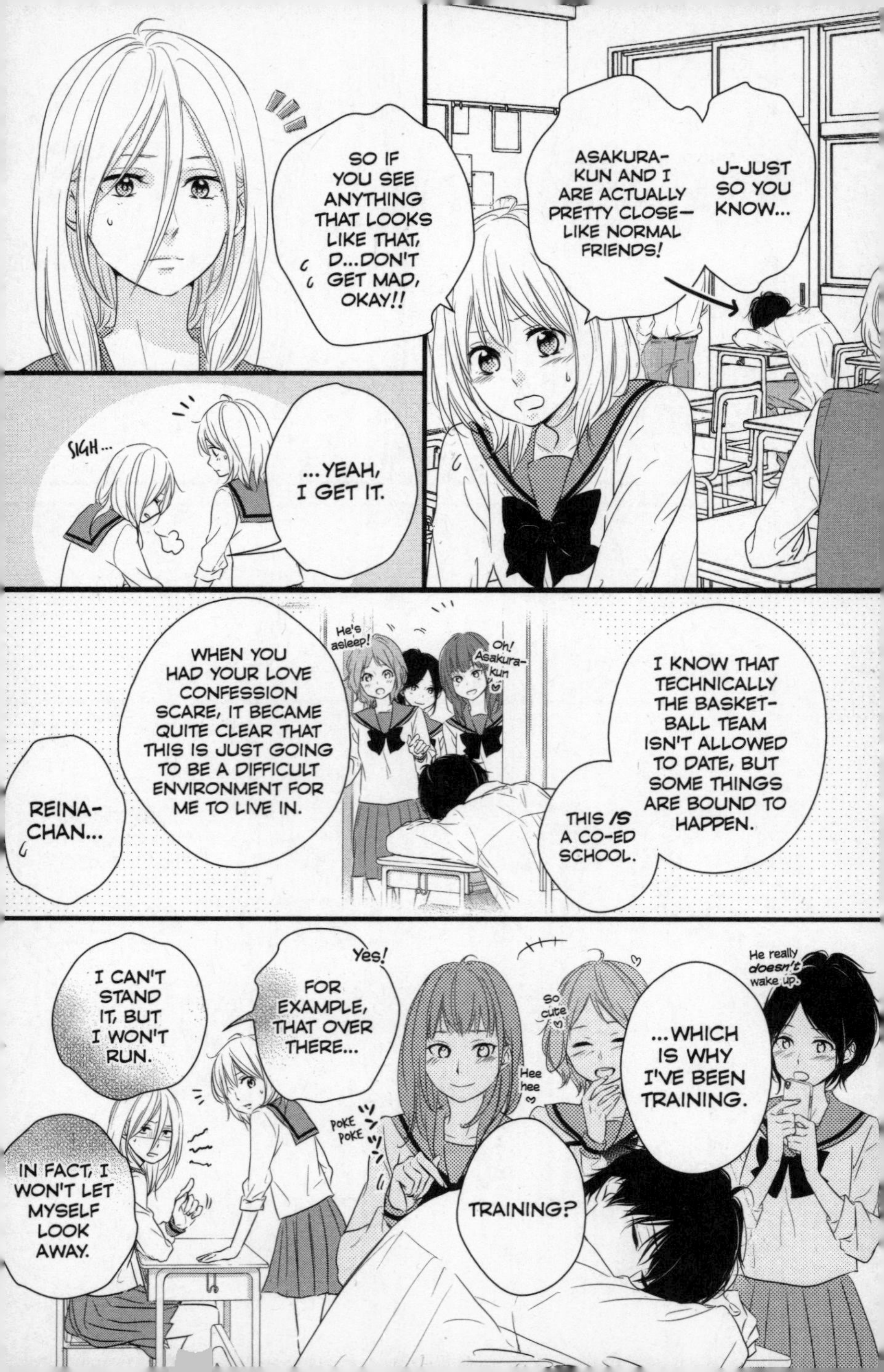
J-JUST SO YOU KNOW...
ASAKURA-KUN AND I ARE ACTUALLY PRETTY CLOSE—LIKE NORMAL FRIENDS!
SO IF YOU SEE ANYTHING THAT LOOKS LIKE THAT, D...DON'T GET MAD, OKAY!!
...YEAH, I GET IT.
SIGH...
I KNOW THAT TECHNICALLY THE BASKET-BALL TEAM ISN'T ALLOWED TO DATE, BUT SOME THINGS ARE BOUND TO HAPPEN.
THIS IS A CO-ED SCHOOL.
Oh! Asakura-kun
He's asleep!
WHEN YOU HAD YOUR LOVE CONFESSION SCARE, IT BECAME QUITE CLEAR THAT THIS IS JUST GOING TO BE A DIFFICULT ENVIRONMENT FOR ME TO LIVE IN.
REINA-CHAN...
He really doesn't wake up.
...WHICH IS WHY I'VE BEEN TRAINING.
So cute
Hee hee
TRAINING?
POKE POKE
Yes!
FOR EXAMPLE, THAT OVER THERE...
I CAN'T STAND IT, BUT I WON'T RUN.
IN FACT, I WON'T LET MYSELF LOOK AWAY.

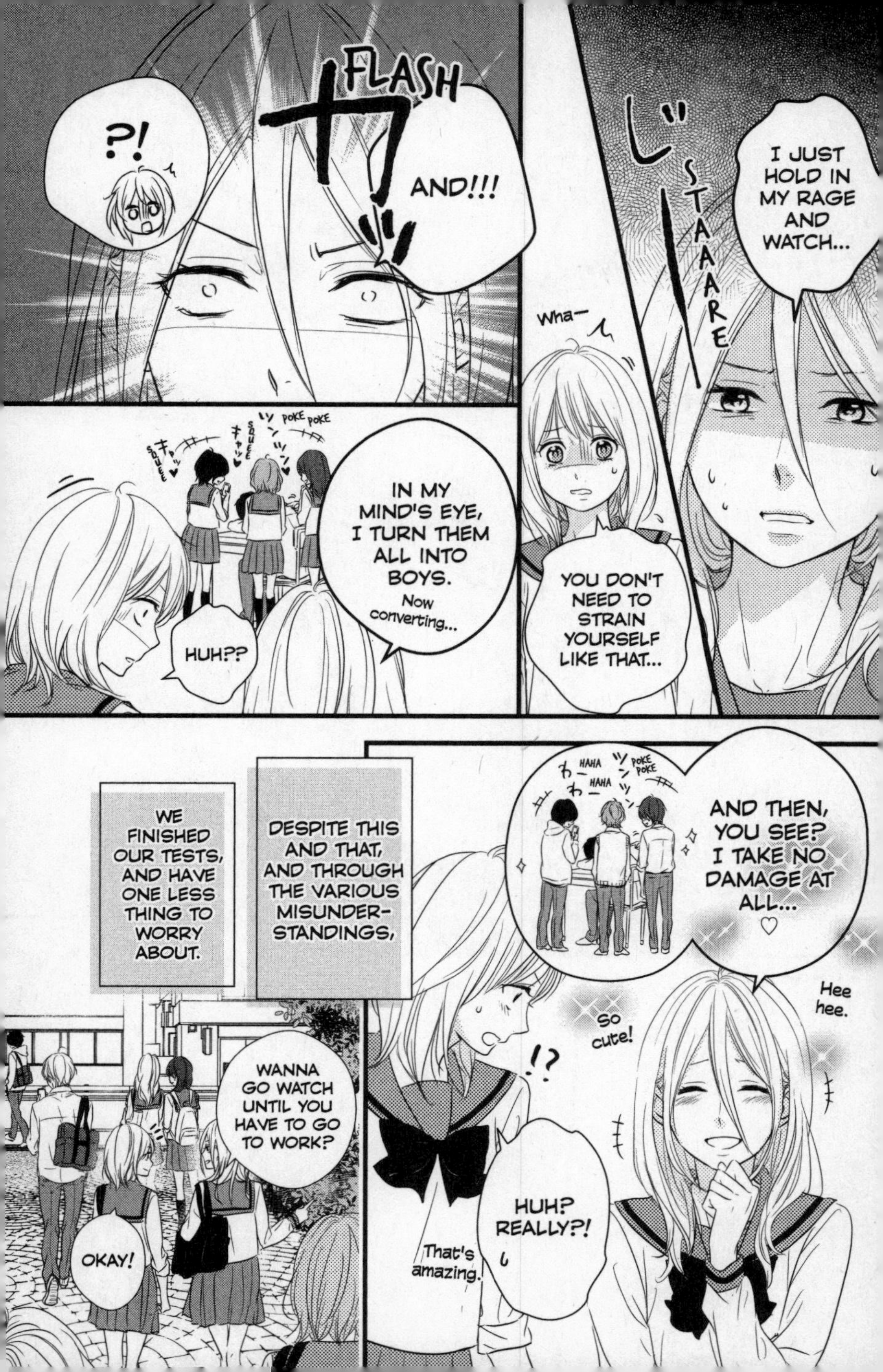
I JUST HOLD IN MY RAGE AND WATCH...
STAAARE
Wha—
YOU DON'T NEED TO STRAIN YOURSELF LIKE THAT...
FLASH
AND!!!
?!
POKE POKE
SQUEE
SQUEE
IN MY MIND'S EYE, I TURN THEM ALL INTO BOYS. Now converting...
HUH??
AND THEN, YOU SEE? I TAKE NO DAMAGE AT ALL... ♡
POKE POKE
HAHA
HAHA
Hee hee.
So cute!
!?
HUH? REALLY?!
That's amazing.
DESPITE THIS AND THAT, AND THROUGH THE VARIOUS MISUNDER-STANDINGS,
WE FINISHED OUR TESTS, AND HAVE ONE LESS THING TO WORRY ABOUT.
WANNA GO WATCH UNTIL YOU HAVE TO GO TO WORK?
OKAY!

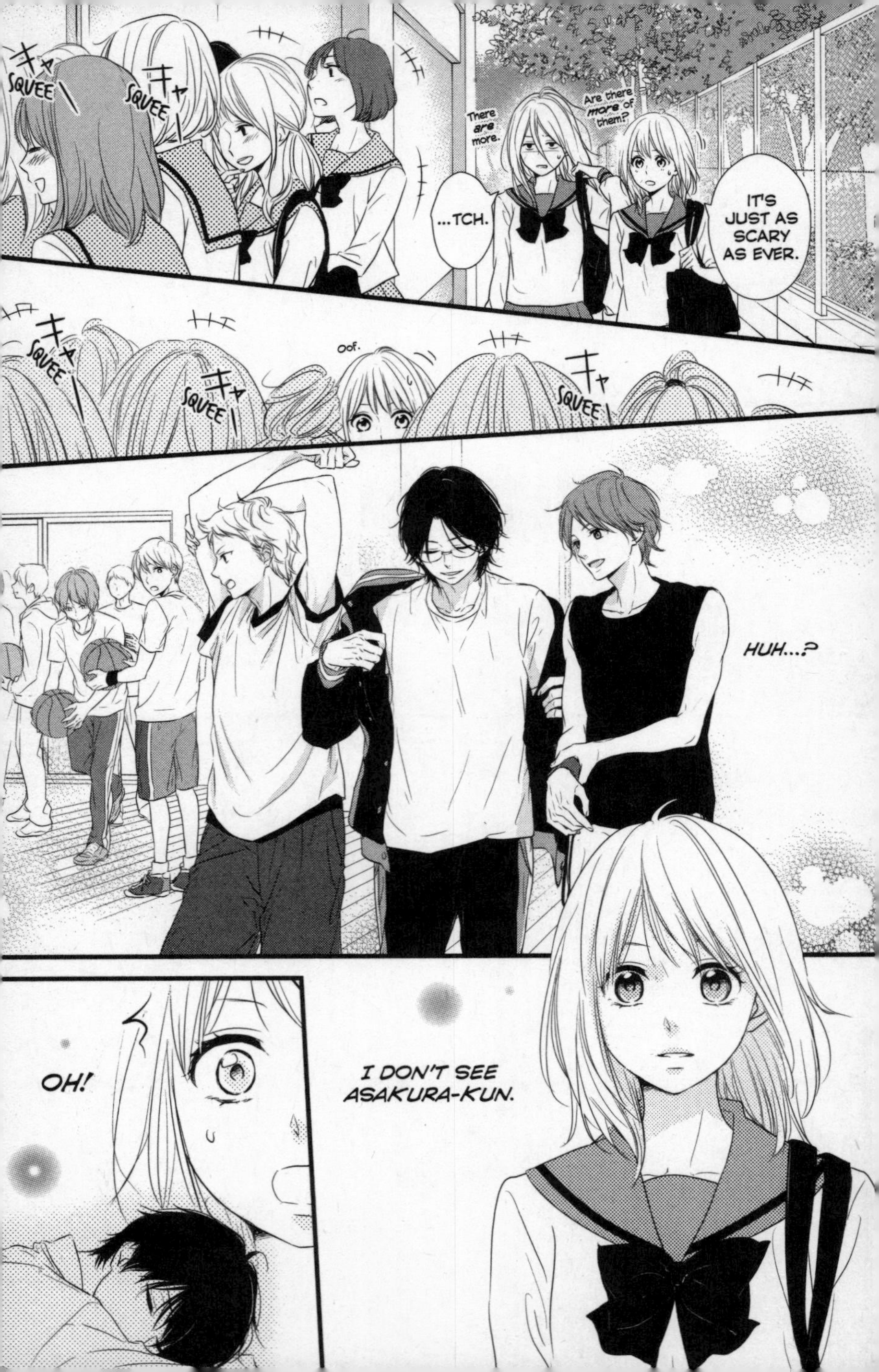
Are there more of them?
There are more.
IT'S JUST AS SCARY AS EVER.
...TCH.
キャー SQUEE
キャー SQUEE
キャー SQUEE
キャー SQUEE
Oof.
キャー SQUEE
HUH...?
I DON'T SEE ASAKURA-KUN.
OH!

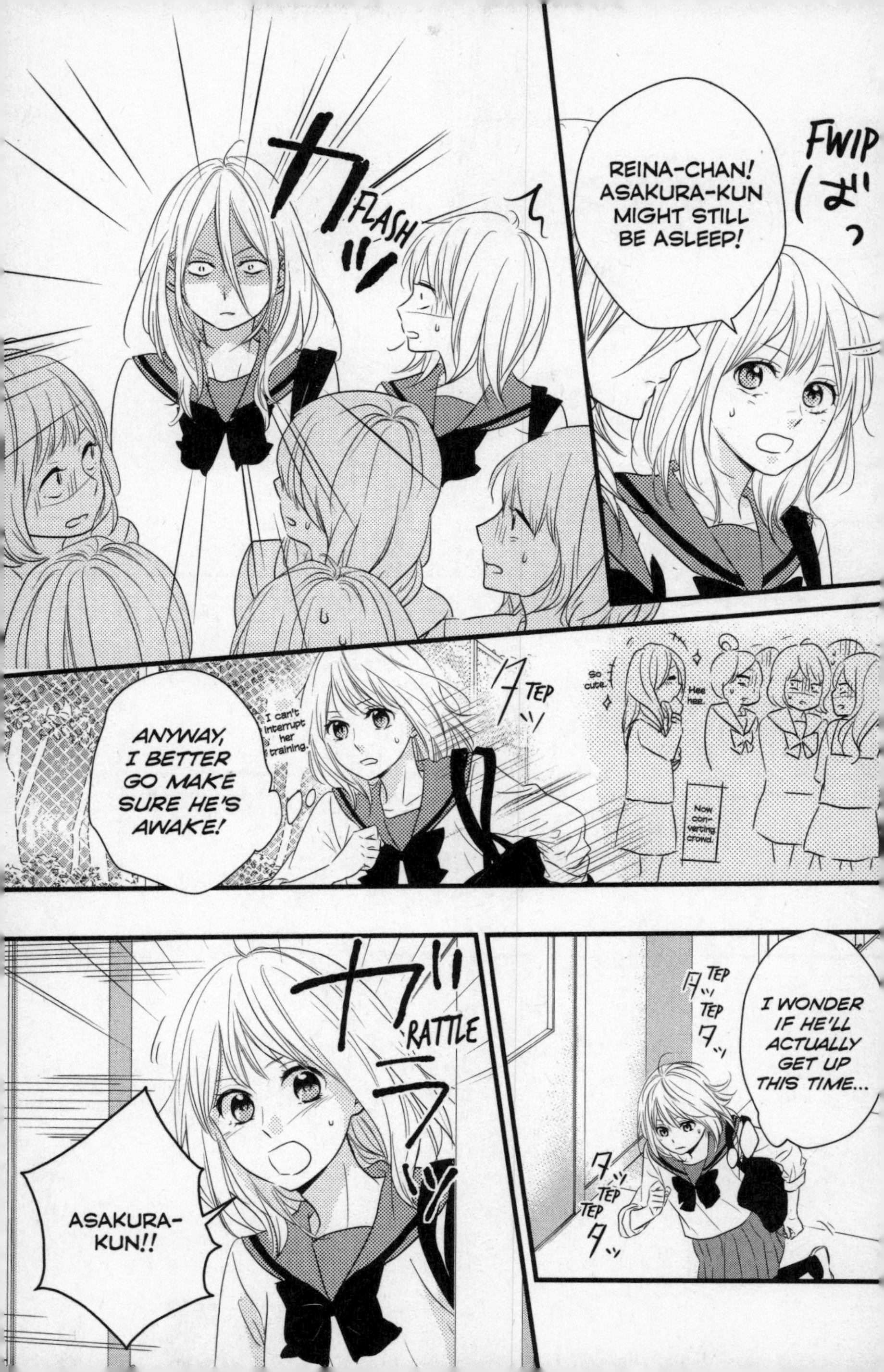
FWIP
ぱっ
REINA-CHAN! ASAKURA-KUN MIGHT STILL BE ASLEEP!
カッ
FLASH
So cute.
Hee hee.
Now converting crowd.
タッ
TEP
I can't interrupt her training.
ANYWAY, I BETTER GO MAKE SURE HE'S AWAKE!
I WONDER IF HE'LL ACTUALLY GET UP THIS TIME...
タッ
TEP
タッ
TEP
タッ
TEP
タッ
TEP
ガラッ
RATTLE
ASAKURA-KUN!!

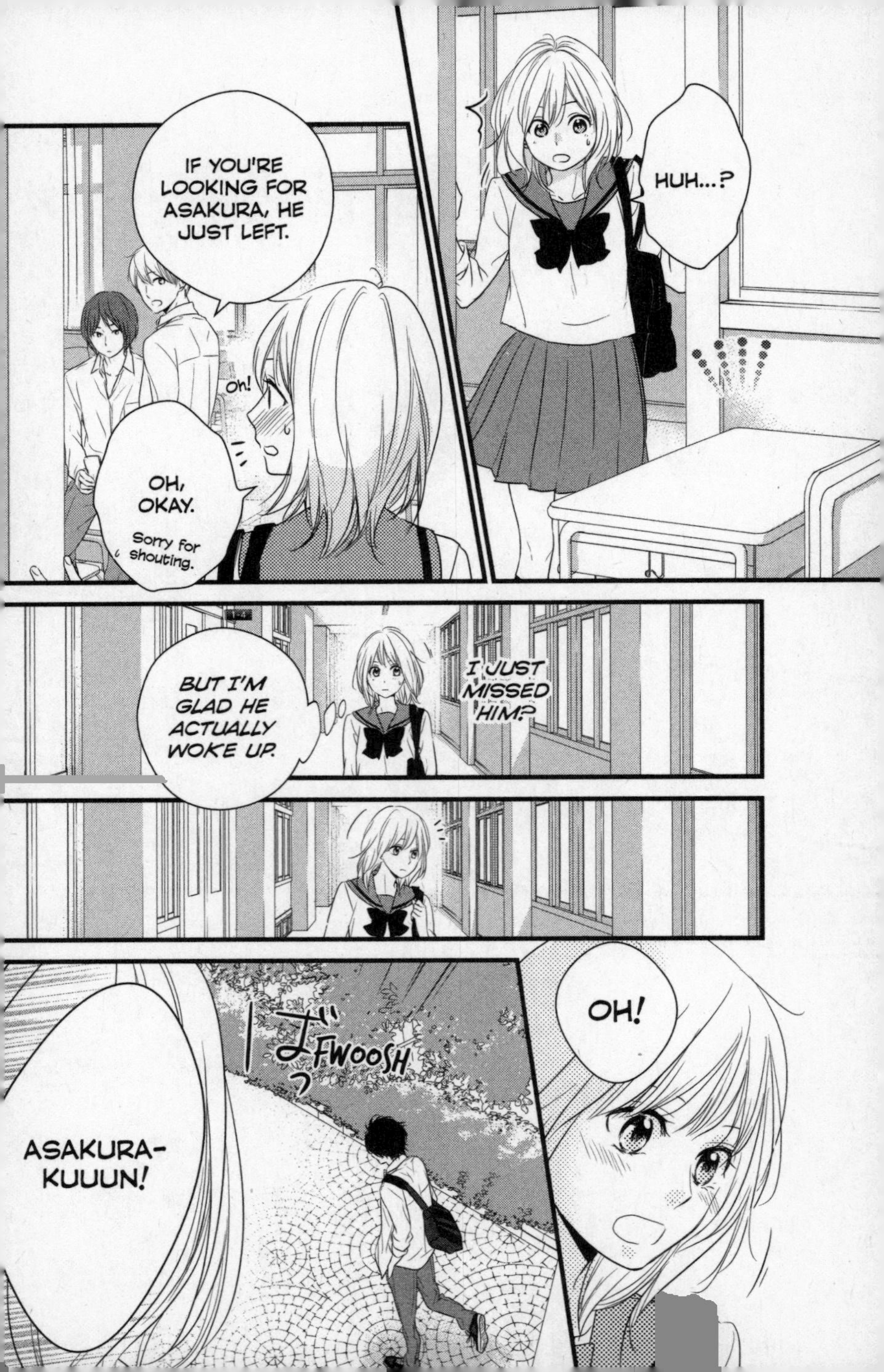
HUH...?
IF YOU'RE LOOKING FOR ASAKURA, HE JUST LEFT.
Oh!
OH, OKAY.
Sorry for shouting.
I JUST MISSED HIM?
BUT I'M GLAD HE ACTUALLY WOKE UP.
OH!
FWOOSH
ASAKURA-KUUUN!

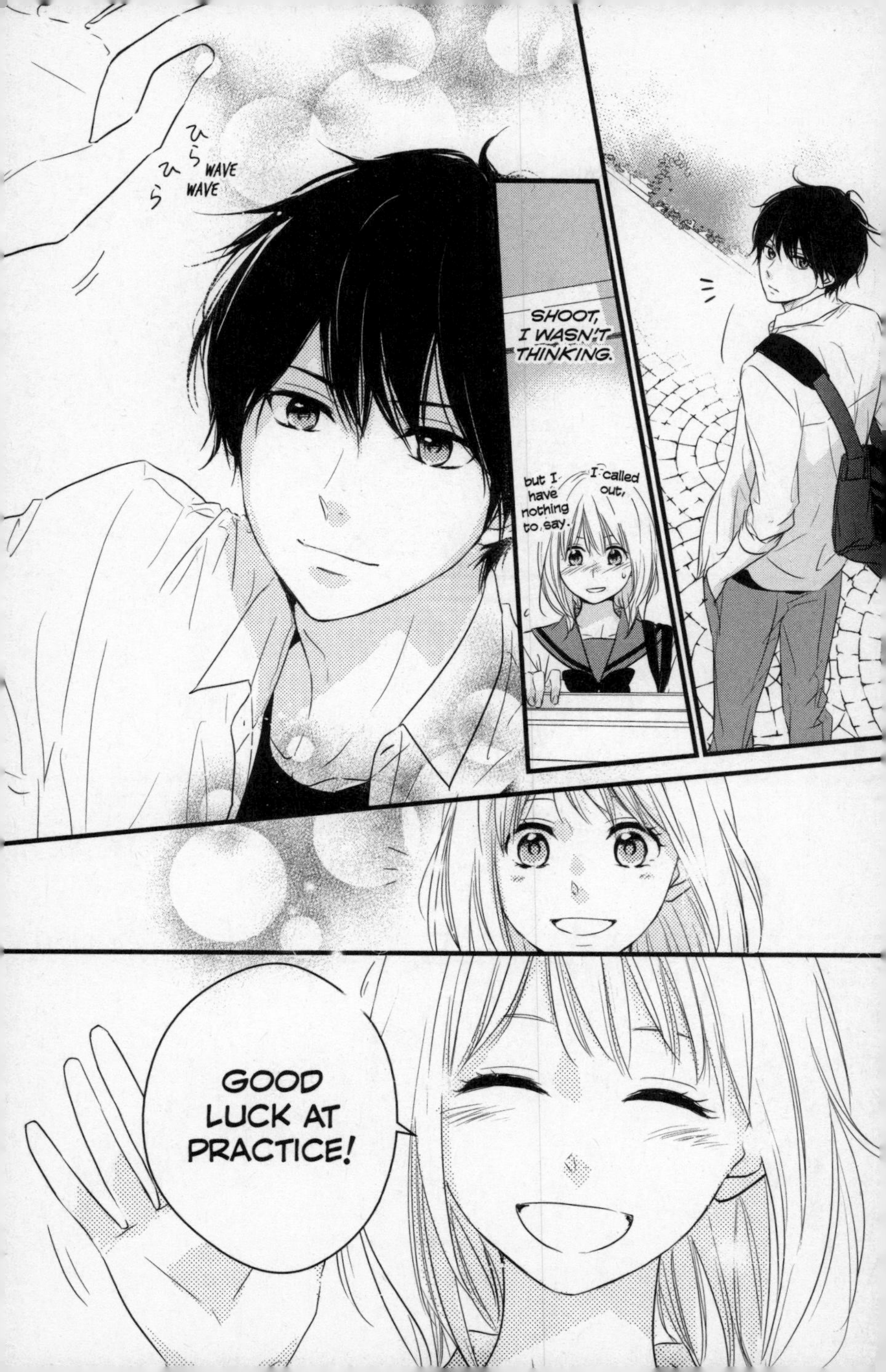

SHOOT, I WASN'T THINKING.
I called out,
but I have nothing to say.
ひらひら
WAVE WAVE
GOOD LUCK AT PRACTICE!

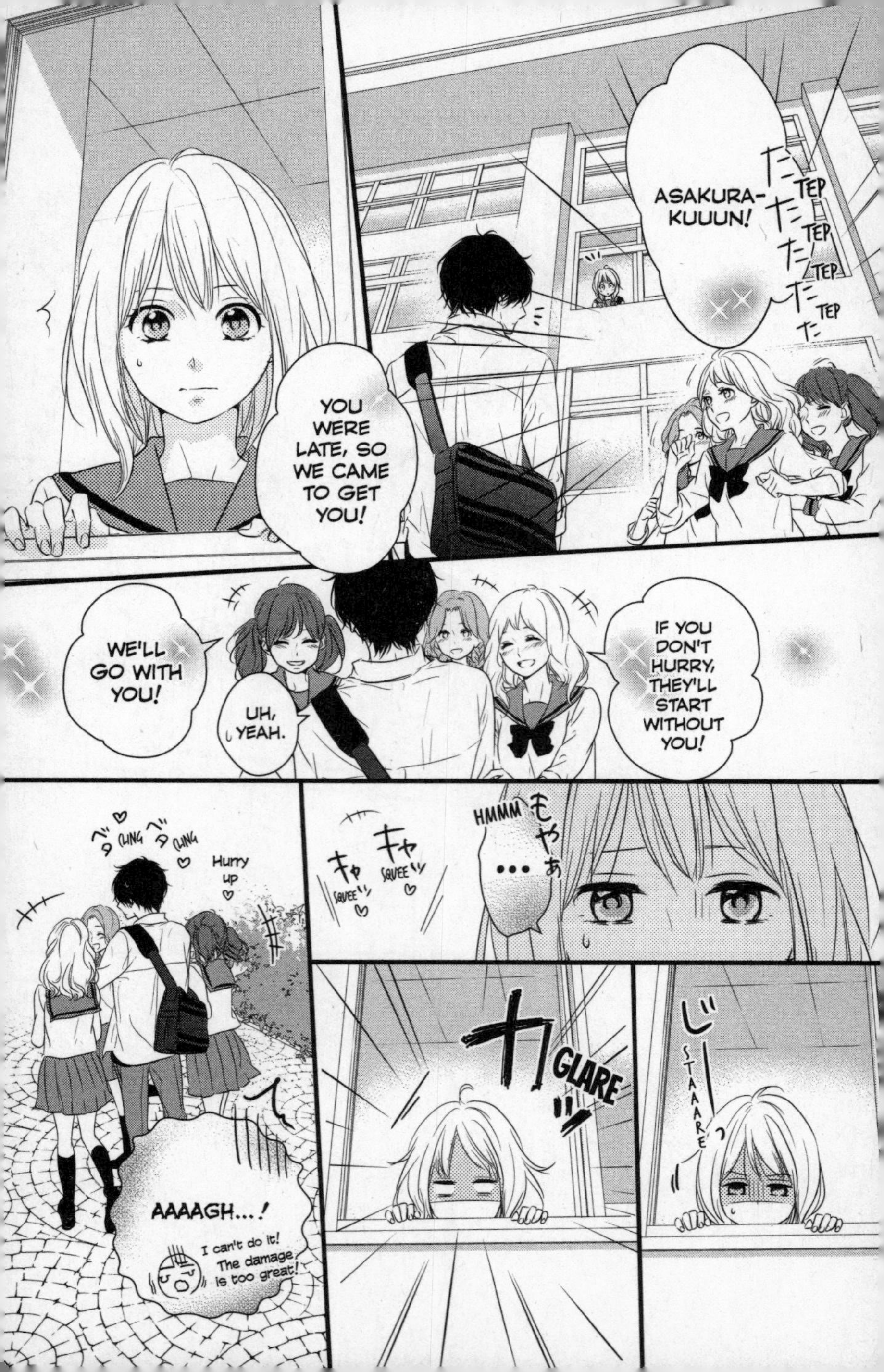
ASAKURA-KUUUN!
たっ TEP たっ TEP たっ TEP たっ TEP たっ
YOU WERE LATE, SO WE CAME TO GET YOU!
IF YOU DON'T HURRY, THEY'LL START WITHOUT YOU!
WE'LL GO WITH YOU!
UH, YEAH.
HMMM もやぁ
...
キャ SQUEE
キャ SQUEE
じー STAAARE
カッ GLARE
ベタ CLING ベタ CLING
Hurry up
AAAAGH...!
I can't do it! The damage is too great!

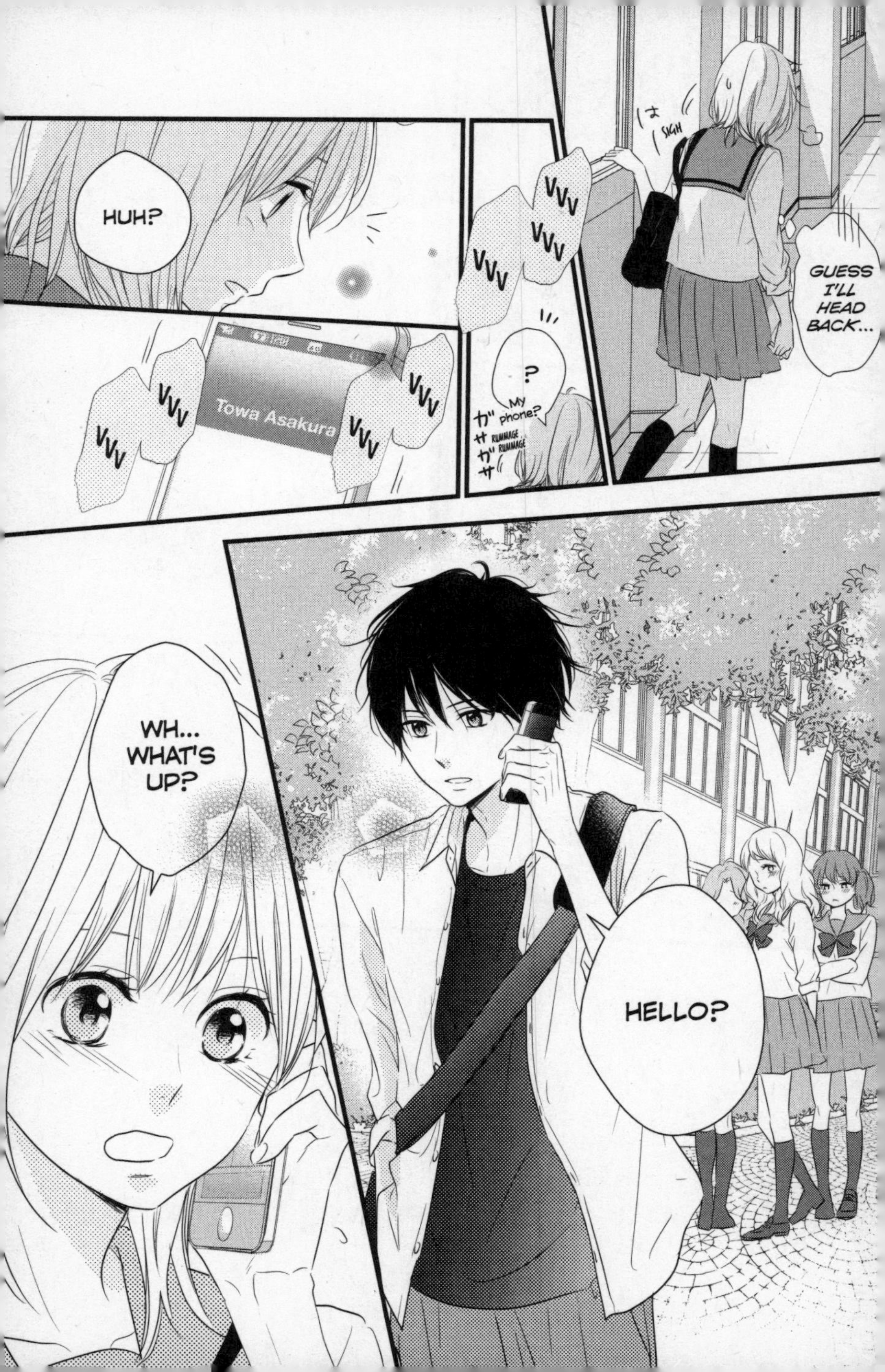
は
SIGH
GUESS I'LL HEAD BACK...
VVV
VVV
VVV
?
My phone?
ガサ
RUMMAGE
ガサ
RUMMAGE
HUH?
VVV
VVV
Towa Asakura
VVV
VVV
HELLO?
WH... WHAT'S UP?

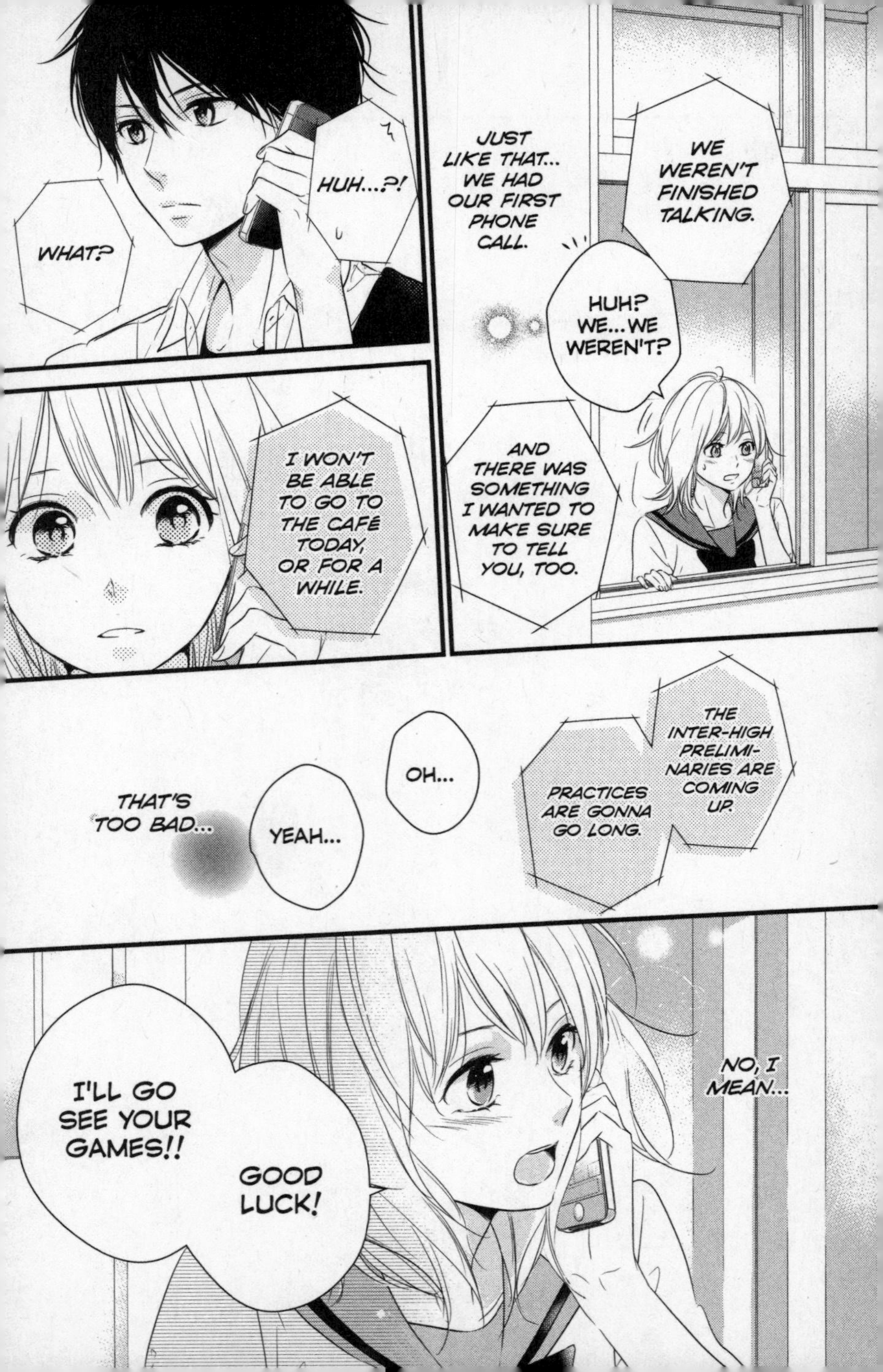
WE WEREN'T FINISHED TALKING.
JUST LIKE THAT... WE HAD OUR FIRST PHONE CALL.
HUH? WE...WE WEREN'T?
AND THERE WAS SOMETHING I WANTED TO MAKE SURE TO TELL YOU, TOO.
HUH...?!
WHAT?
I WON'T BE ABLE TO GO TO THE CAFÉ TODAY, OR FOR A WHILE.
THE INTER-HIGH PRELIMI-NARIES ARE COMING UP.
PRACTICES ARE GONNA GO LONG.
OH...
YEAH...
THAT'S TOO BAD...
NO, I MEAN...
I'LL GO SEE YOUR GAMES!!
GOOD LUCK!

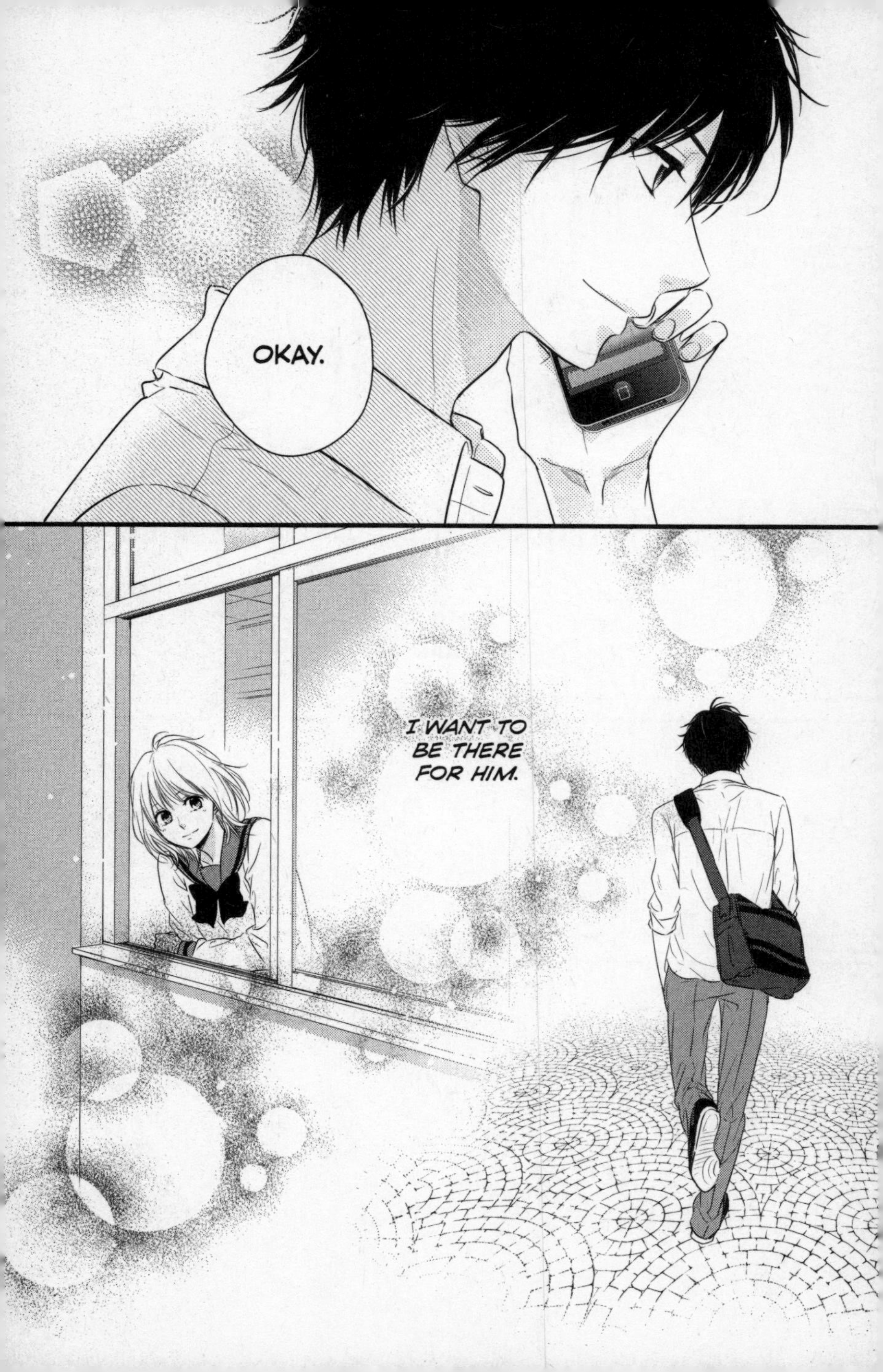
OKAY.
I WANT TO BE THERE FOR HIM.

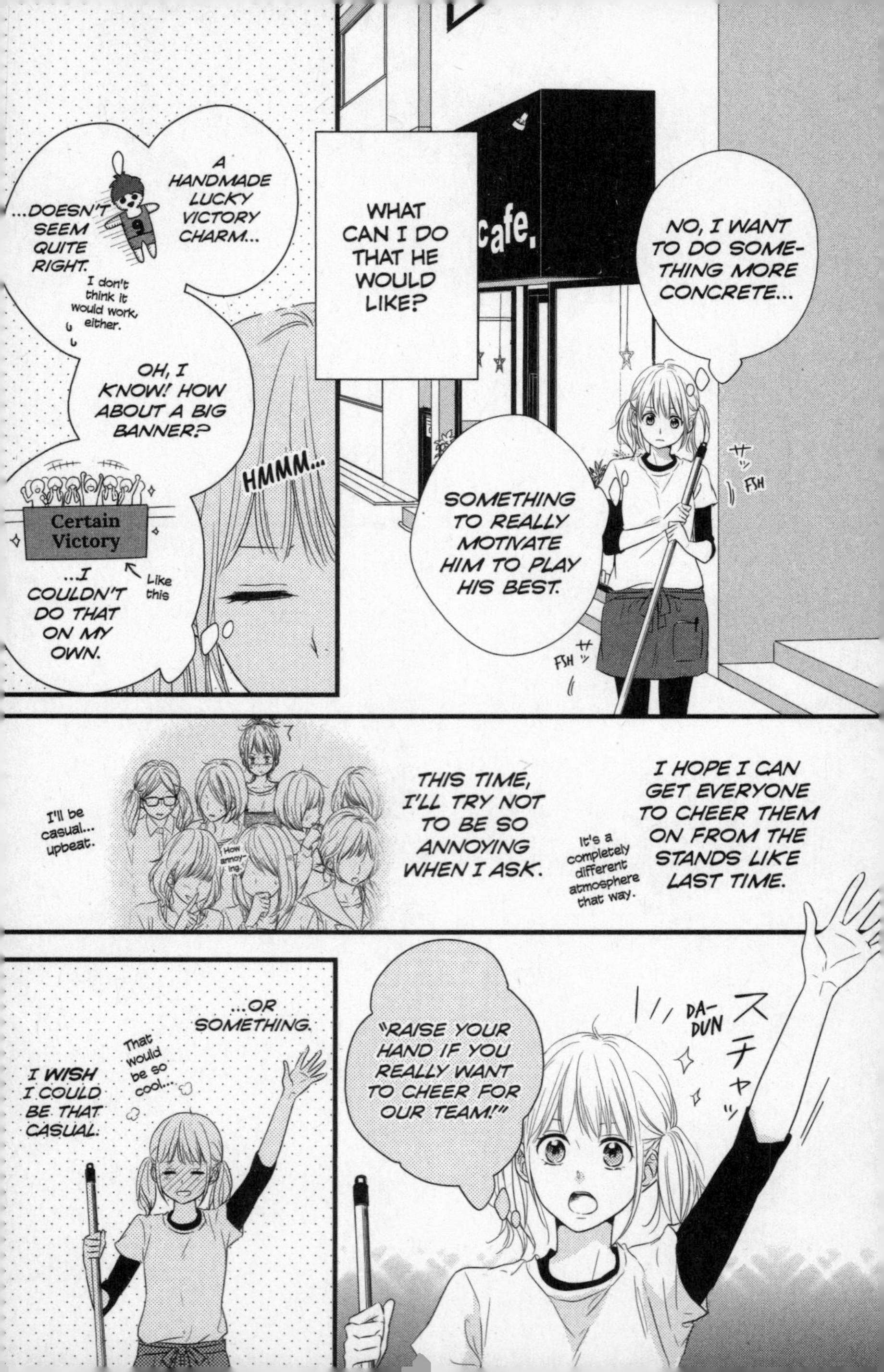
WHAT CAN I DO THAT HE WOULD LIKE?
NO, I WANT TO DO SOME-THING MORE CONCRETE...
SOMETHING TO REALLY MOTIVATE HIM TO PLAY HIS BEST.
サッ FSH
サッ FSH
cafe.
A HANDMADE LUCKY VICTORY CHARM...
...DOESN'T SEEM QUITE RIGHT.
I don't think it would work, either.
OH, I KNOW! HOW ABOUT A BIG BANNER?
HMMM...
Certain Victory
Like this
...I COULDN'T DO THAT ON MY OWN.
I HOPE I CAN GET EVERYONE TO CHEER THEM ON FROM THE STANDS LIKE LAST TIME.
It's a completely different atmosphere that way.
THIS TIME, I'LL TRY NOT TO BE SO ANNOYING WHEN I ASK.
How annoy-ing.
I'll be casual... upbeat.
スチャッ DA-DUN
"RAISE YOUR HAND IF YOU REALLY WANT TO CHEER FOR OUR TEAM!"
...OR SOMETHING.
That would be so cool...
I WISH I COULD BE THAT CASUAL.

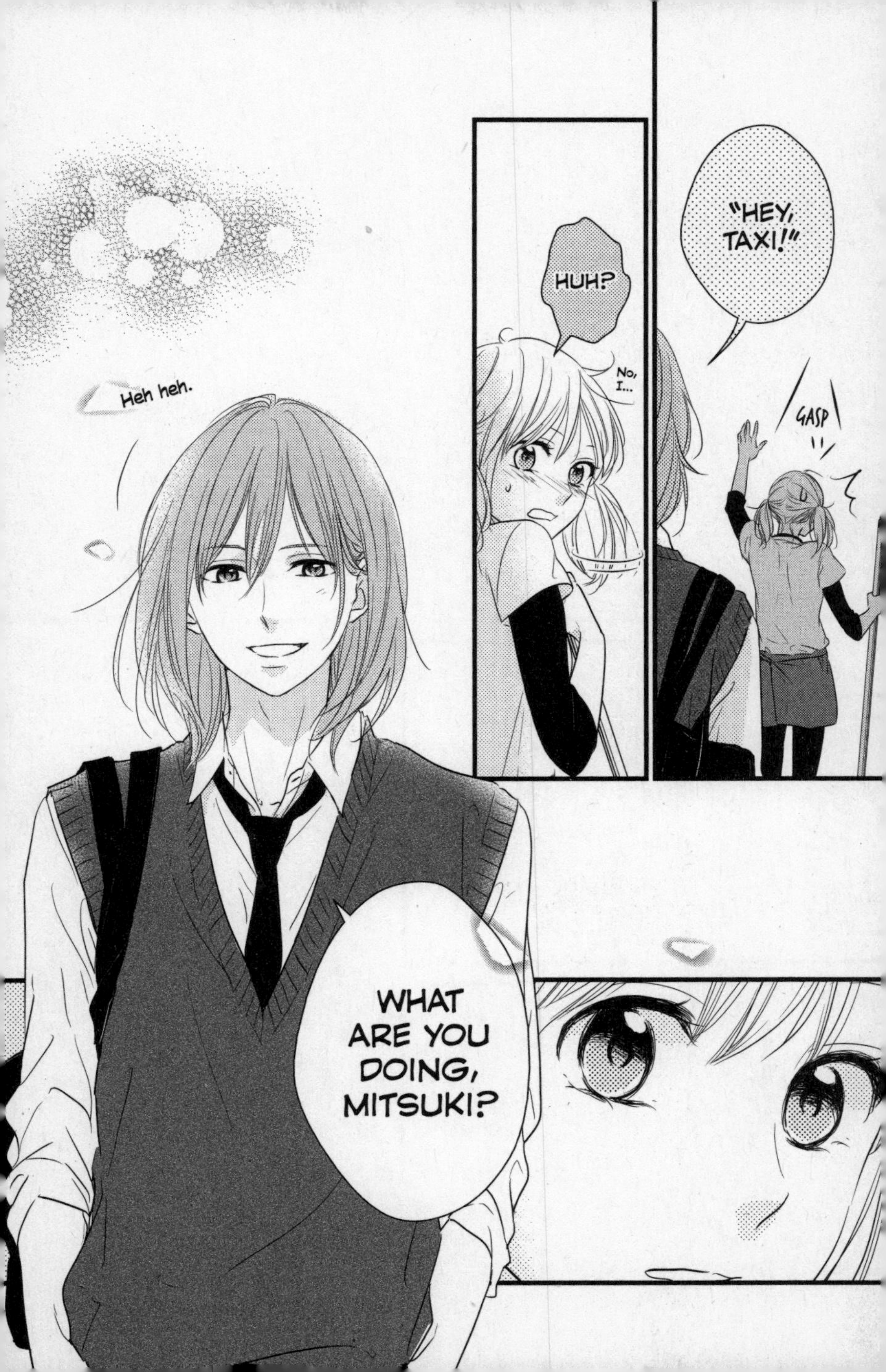
"HEY, TAXI!"
GASP
HUH?
No, I...
Heh heh.
WHAT ARE YOU DOING, MITSUKI?

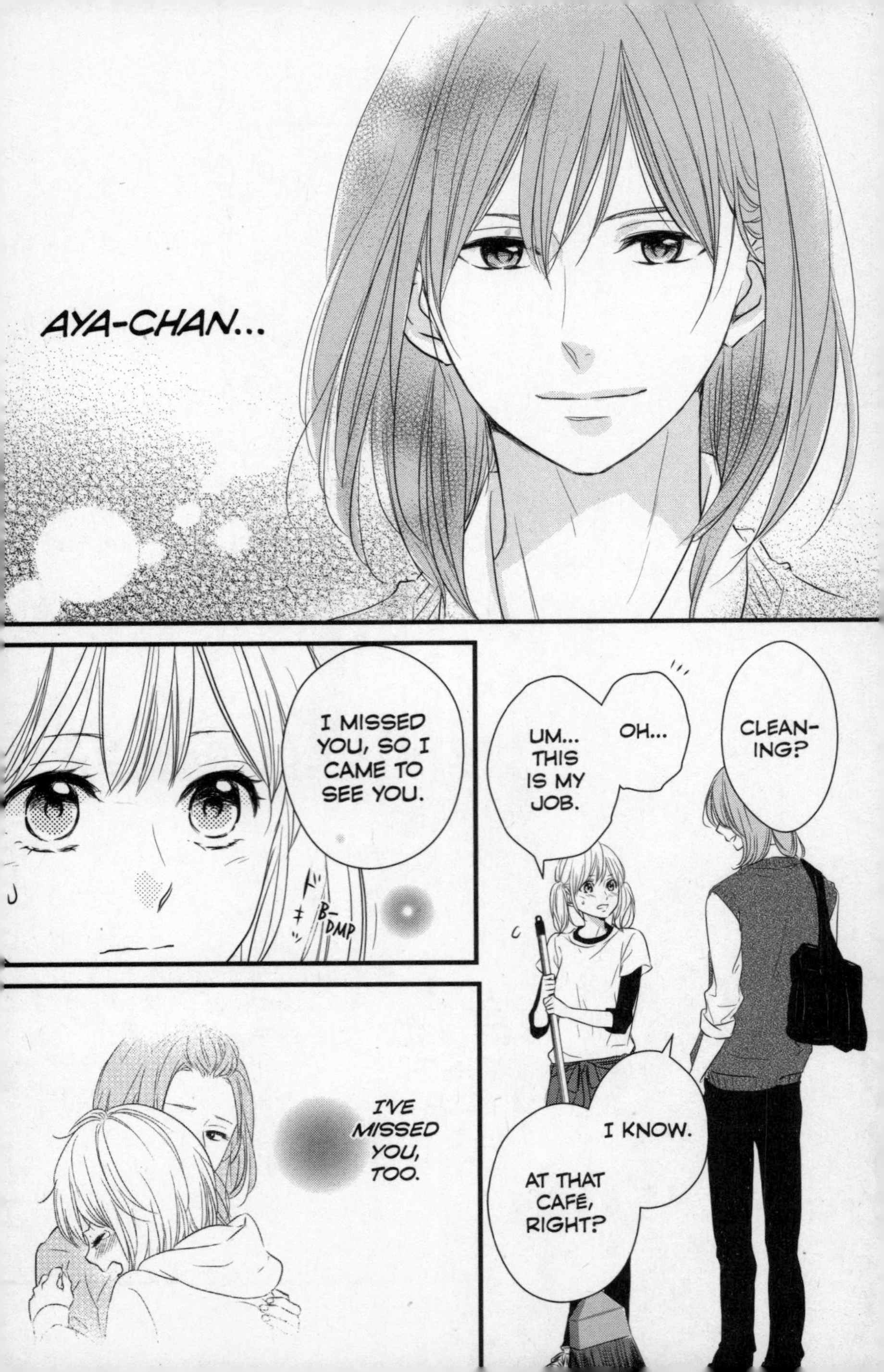
AYA-CHAN...
CLEANING?
OH...
UM... THIS IS MY JOB.
I KNOW.
AT THAT CAFÉ, RIGHT?
I MISSED YOU, SO I CAME TO SEE YOU.
B-DMP
I'VE MISSED YOU, TOO.

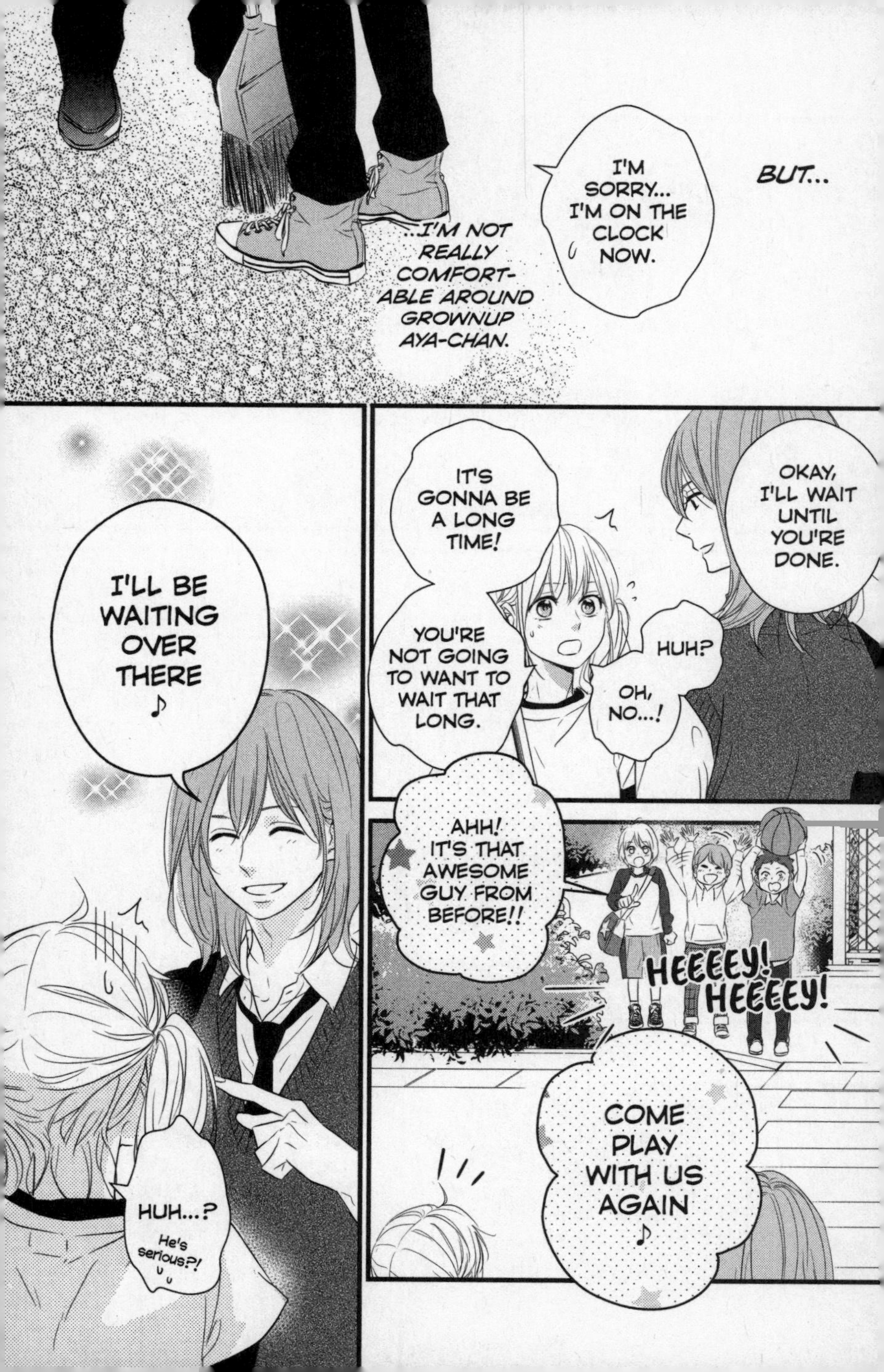
BUT...
I'M SORRY... I'M ON THE CLOCK NOW.
...I'M NOT REALLY COMFORT-ABLE AROUND GROWNUP AYA-CHAN.
OKAY, I'LL WAIT UNTIL YOU'RE DONE.
HUH?
OH, NO...!
IT'S GONNA BE A LONG TIME!
YOU'RE NOT GOING TO WANT TO WAIT THAT LONG.
AHH! IT'S THAT AWESOME GUY FROM BEFORE!!
HEEEEY! HEEEEY!
COME PLAY WITH US AGAIN ♪
I'LL BE WAITING OVER THERE ♪
HUH...?
He's serious?!

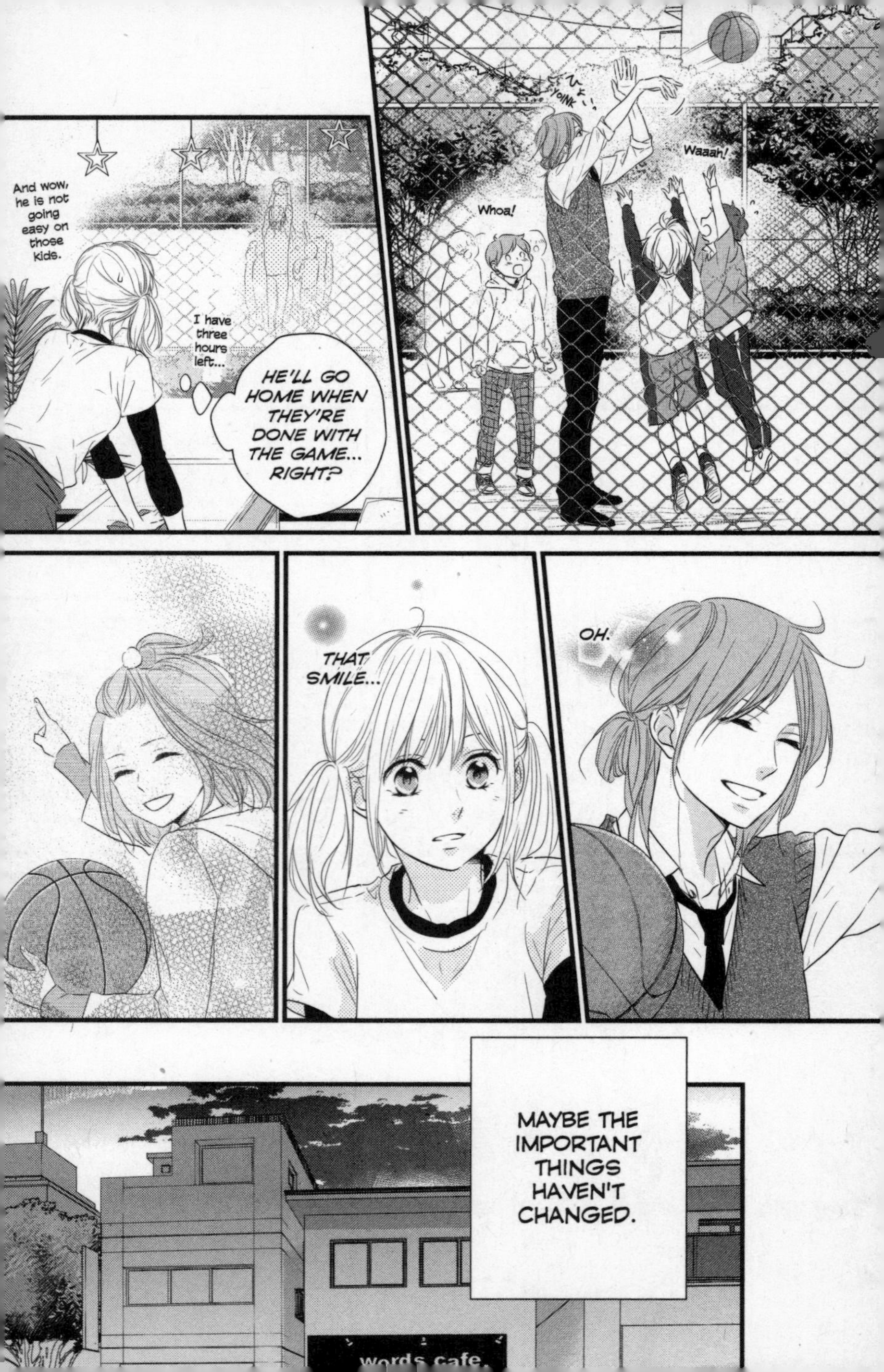
YOINK
Waaah!
Whoa!
I have three hours left...
HE'LL GO HOME WHEN THEY'RE DONE WITH THE GAME... RIGHT?
And wow, he is not going easy on those kids.
OH.
THAT SMILE...
MAYBE THE IMPORTANT THINGS HAVEN'T CHANGED.
words cafe

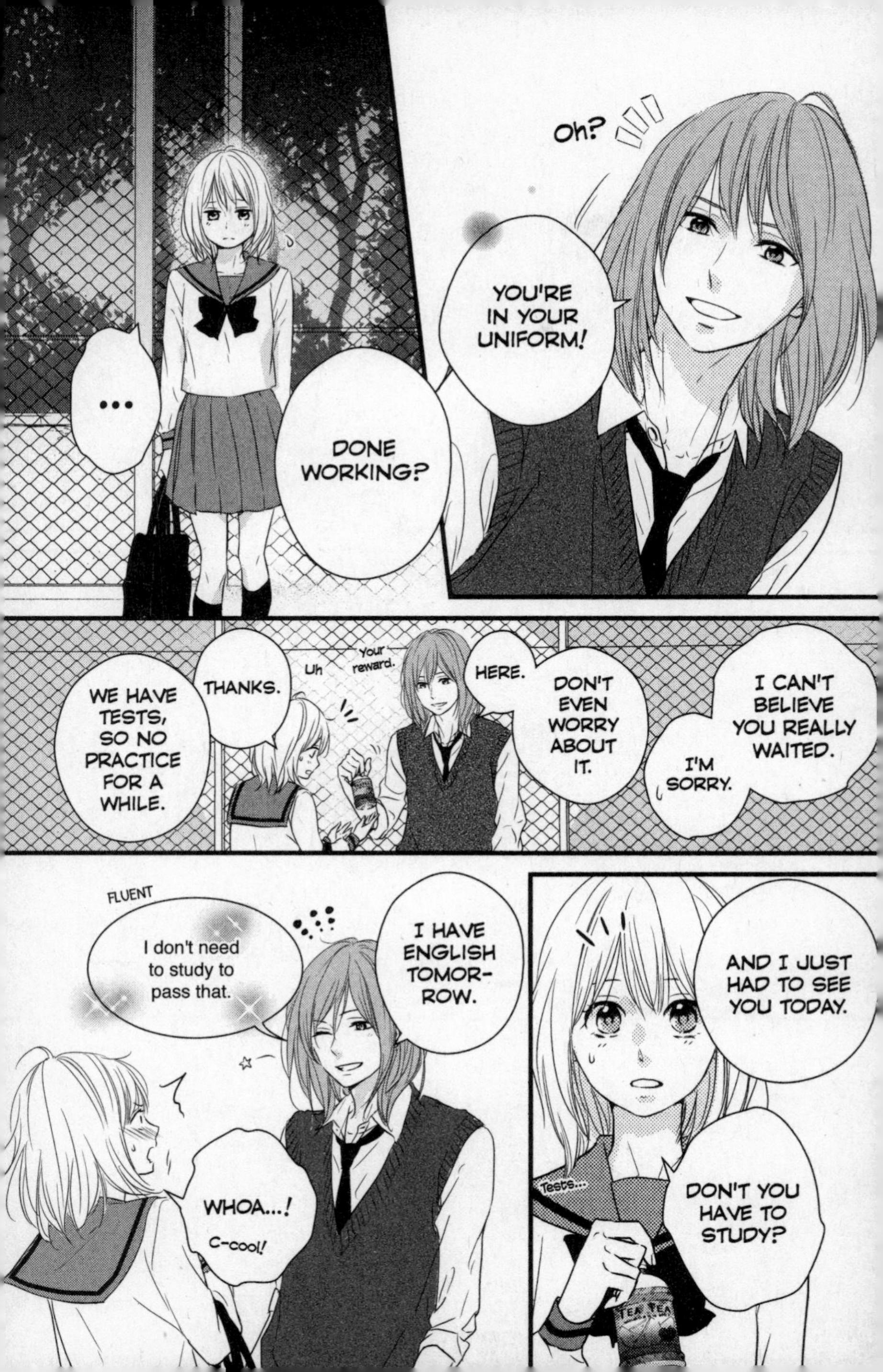
Oh?
YOU'RE IN YOUR UNIFORM!
DONE WORKING?
...
I CAN'T BELIEVE YOU REALLY WAITED.
I'M SORRY.
DON'T EVEN WORRY ABOUT IT.
HERE.
Your reward.
Uh
THANKS.
WE HAVE TESTS, SO NO PRACTICE FOR A WHILE.
AND I JUST HAD TO SEE YOU TODAY.
Tests...
DON'T YOU HAVE TO STUDY?
I HAVE ENGLISH TOMOR-ROW.
FLUENT
I don't need to study to pass that.
WHOA...!
C-cool!

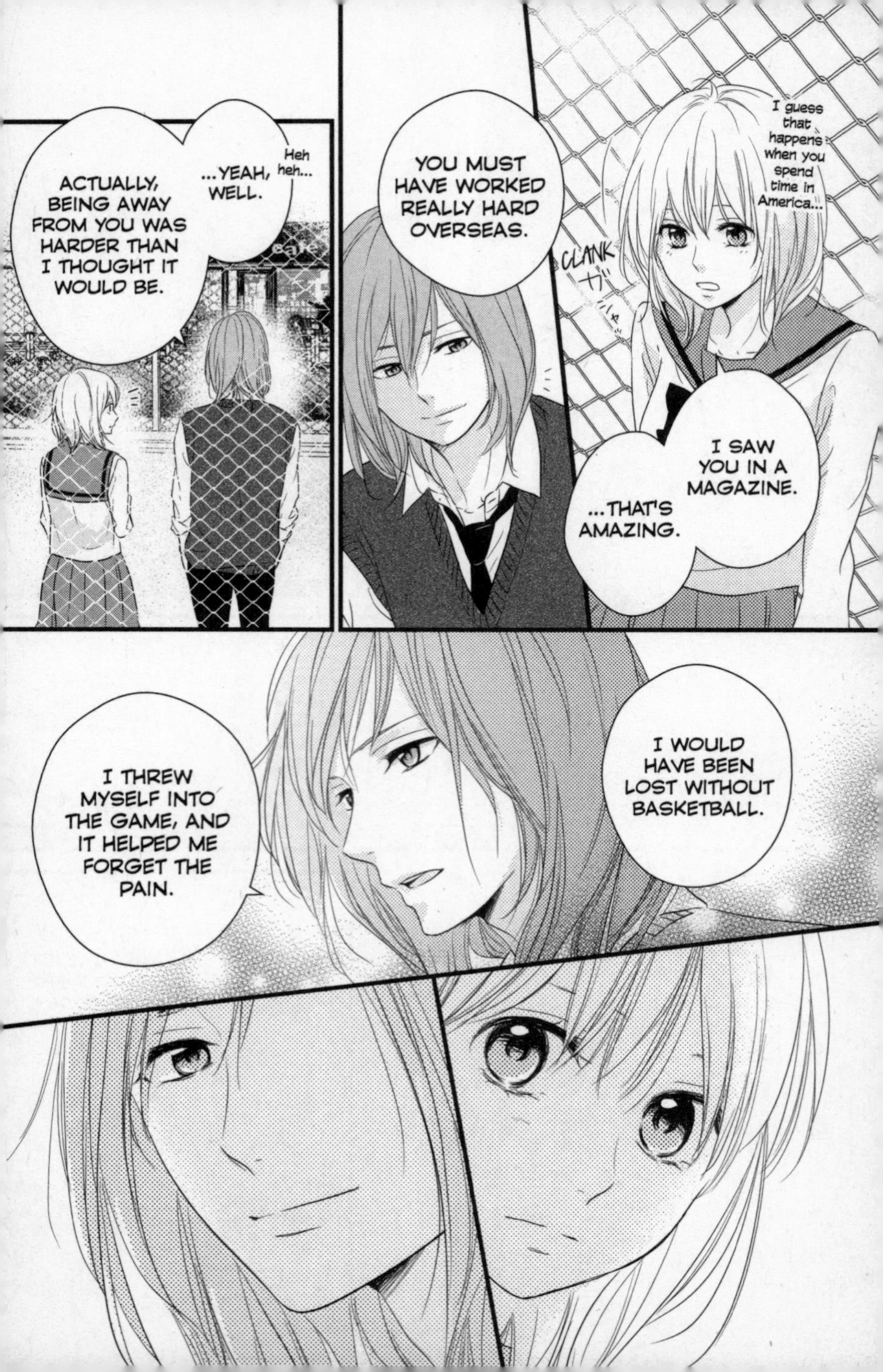
I guess that happens when you spend time in America...
CLANK
I SAW YOU IN A MAGAZINE.
...THAT'S AMAZING.
YOU MUST HAVE WORKED REALLY HARD OVERSEAS.
Heh heh...
...YEAH, WELL.
ACTUALLY, BEING AWAY FROM YOU WAS HARDER THAN I THOUGHT IT WOULD BE.
I WOULD HAVE BEEN LOST WITHOUT BASKETBALL.
I THREW MYSELF INTO THE GAME, AND IT HELPED ME FORGET THE PAIN.

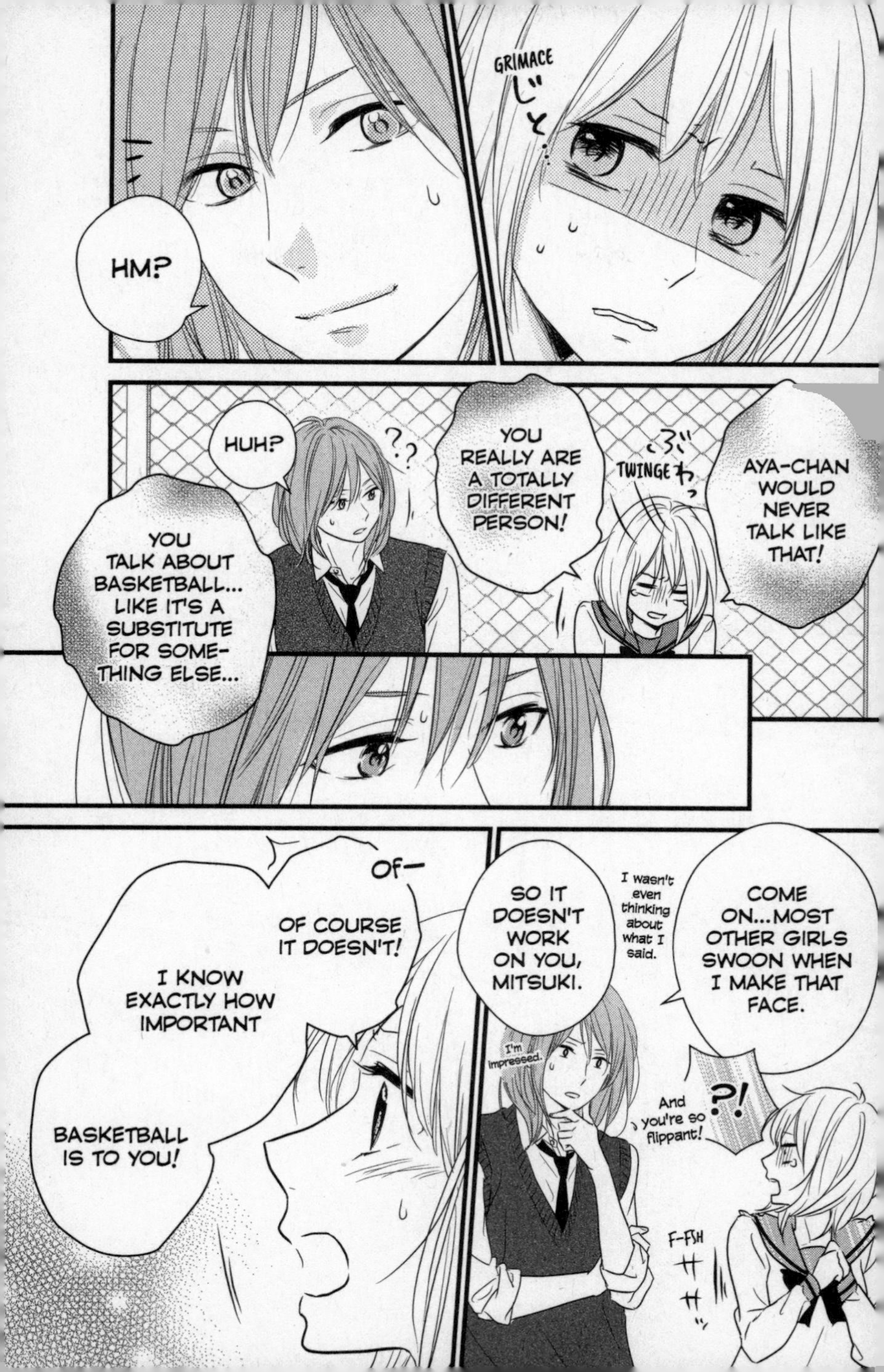
GRIMACE
じと
HM?
AYA-CHAN WOULD NEVER TALK LIKE THAT!
TWINGE
YOU REALLY ARE A TOTALLY DIFFERENT PERSON!
HUH?
YOU TALK ABOUT BASKETBALL... LIKE IT'S A SUBSTITUTE FOR SOME-THING ELSE...
COME ON...MOST OTHER GIRLS SWOON WHEN I MAKE THAT FACE.
I wasn't even thinking about what I said.
SO IT DOESN'T WORK ON YOU, MITSUKI.
I'm impressed.
?!
And you're so flippant!
F-FSH
OF—
OF COURSE IT DOESN'T!
I KNOW EXACTLY HOW IMPORTANT
BASKETBALL IS TO YOU!

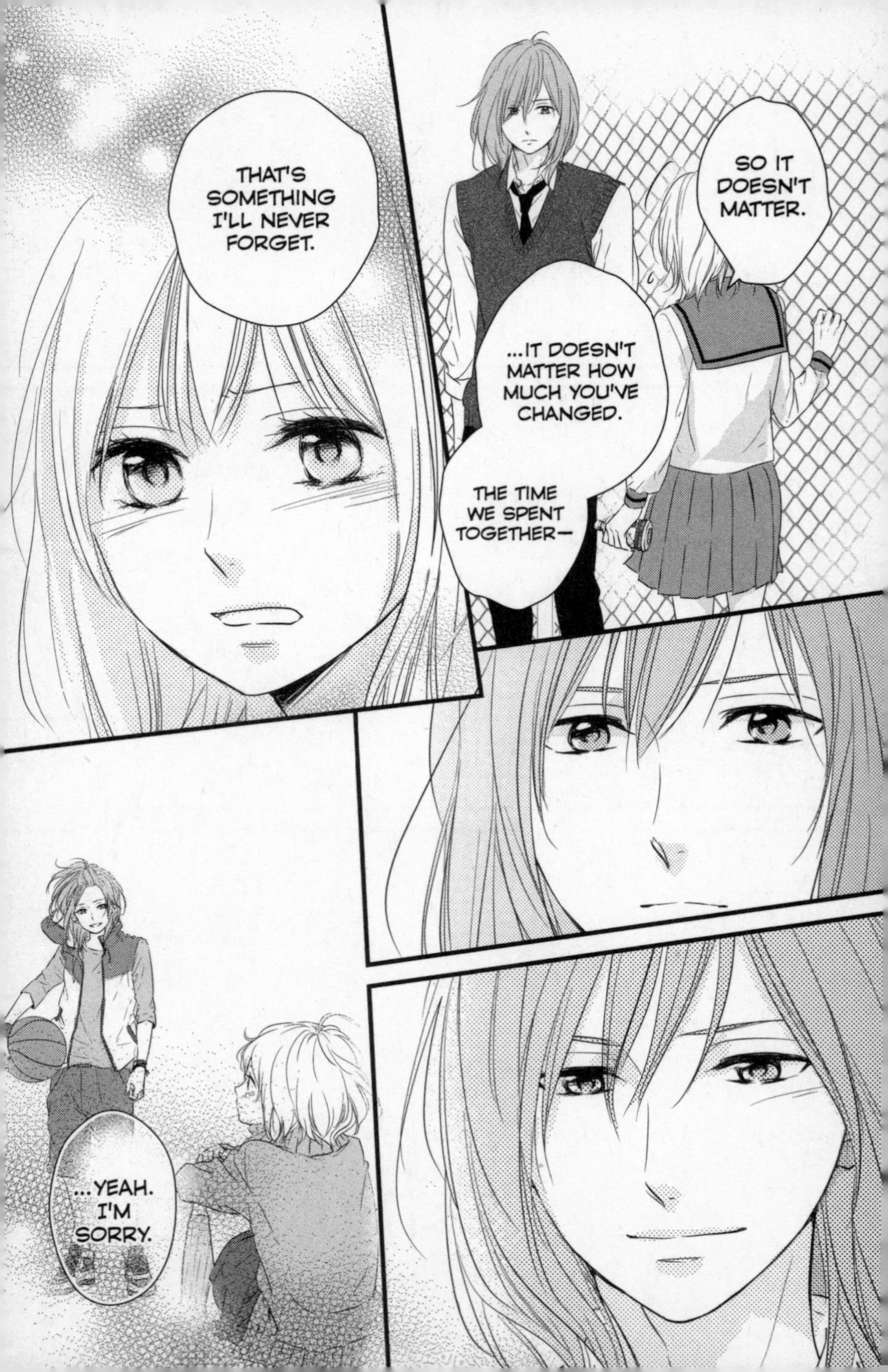
SO IT DOESN'T MATTER.
...IT DOESN'T MATTER HOW MUCH YOU'VE CHANGED.
THE TIME WE SPENT TOGETHER—
THAT'S SOMETHING I'LL NEVER FORGET.
...YEAH. I'M SORRY.

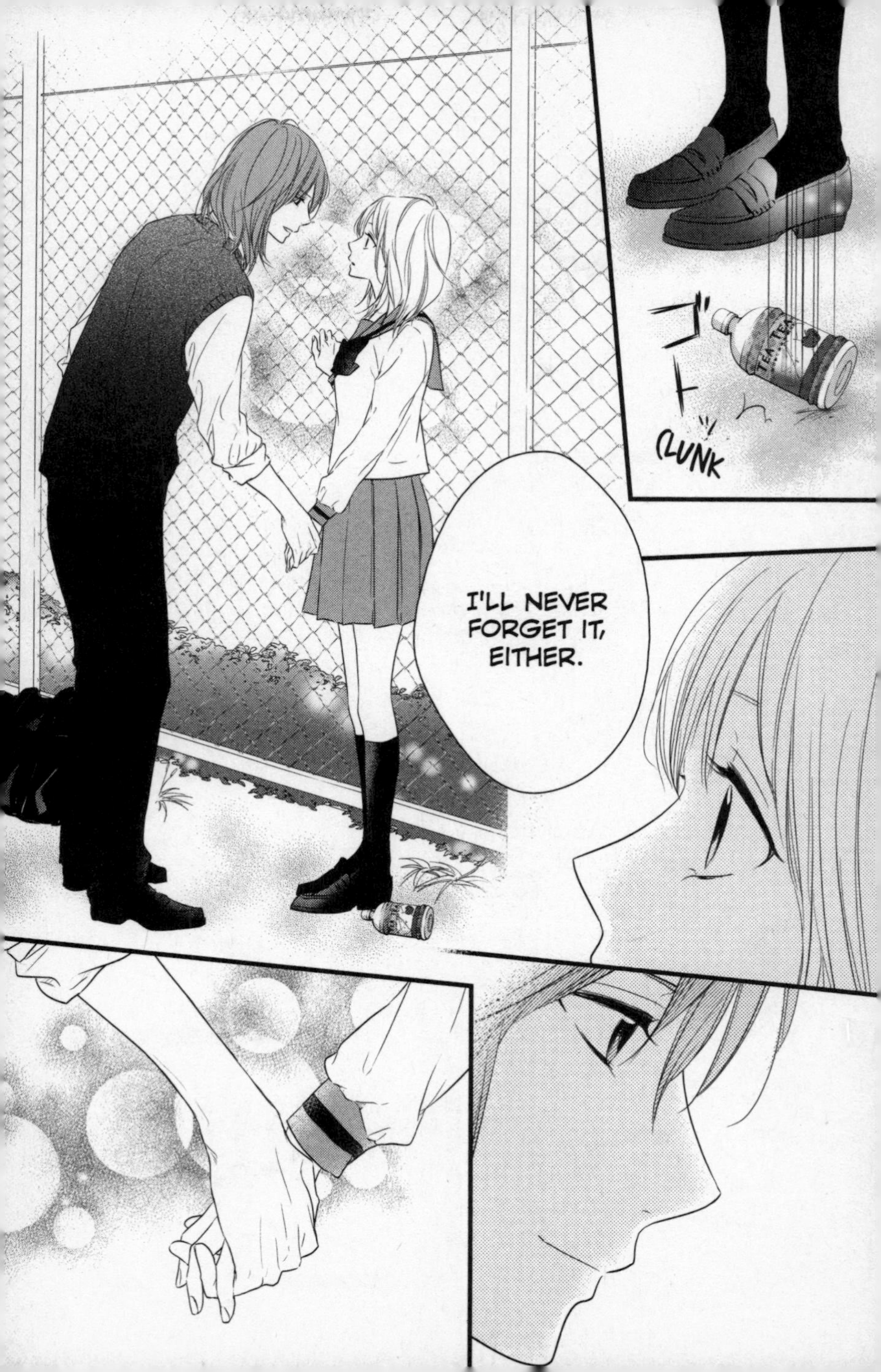
ゴト
CLUNK
I'LL NEVER FORGET IT, EITHER.

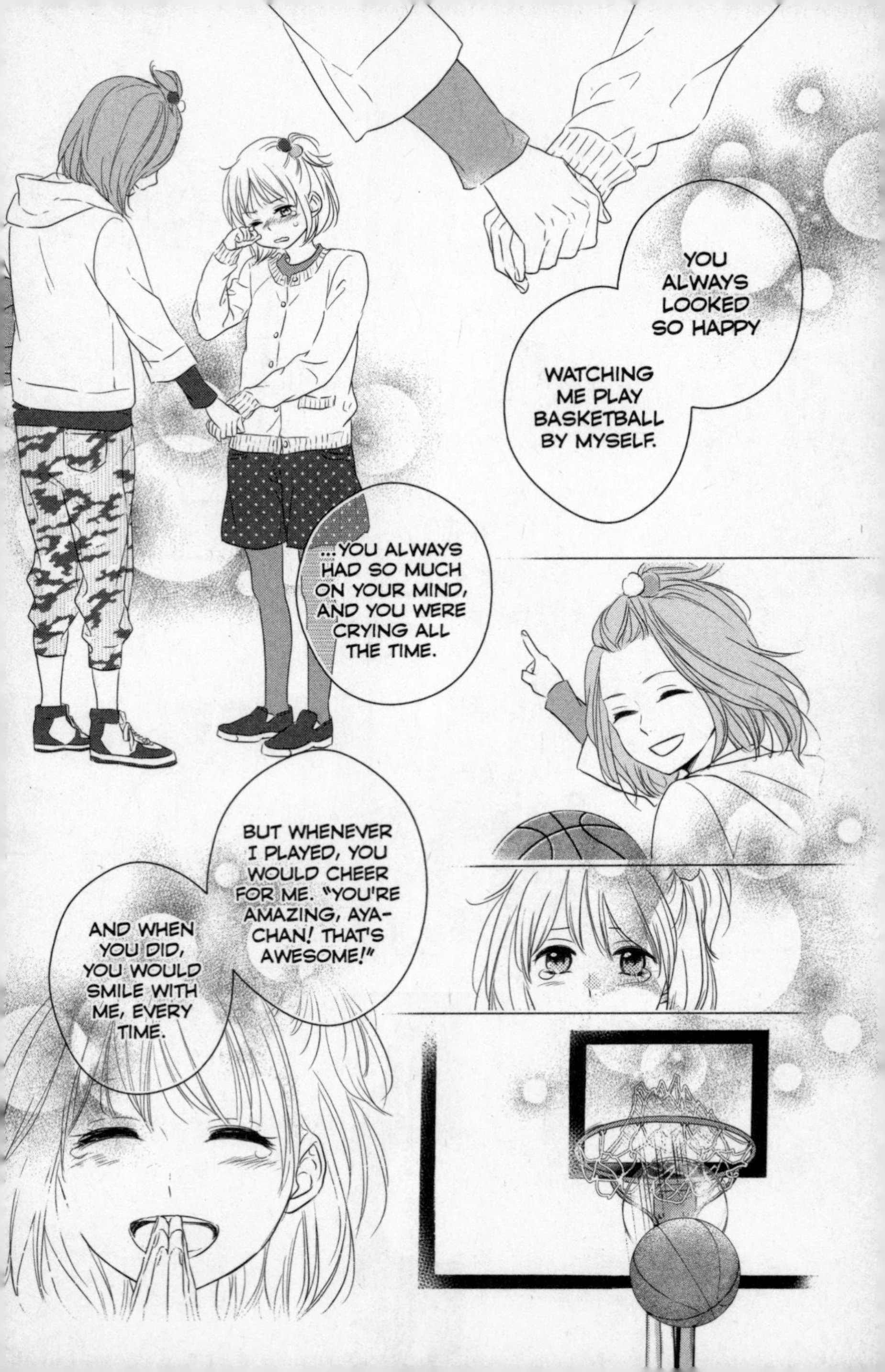
YOU ALWAYS LOOKED SO HAPPY
WATCHING ME PLAY BASKETBALL BY MYSELF.
...YOU ALWAYS HAD SO MUCH ON YOUR MIND, AND YOU WERE CRYING ALL THE TIME.
BUT WHENEVER I PLAYED, YOU WOULD CHEER FOR ME. "YOU'RE AMAZING, AYA-CHAN! THAT'S AWESOME!"
AND WHEN YOU DID, YOU WOULD SMILE WITH ME, EVERY TIME.

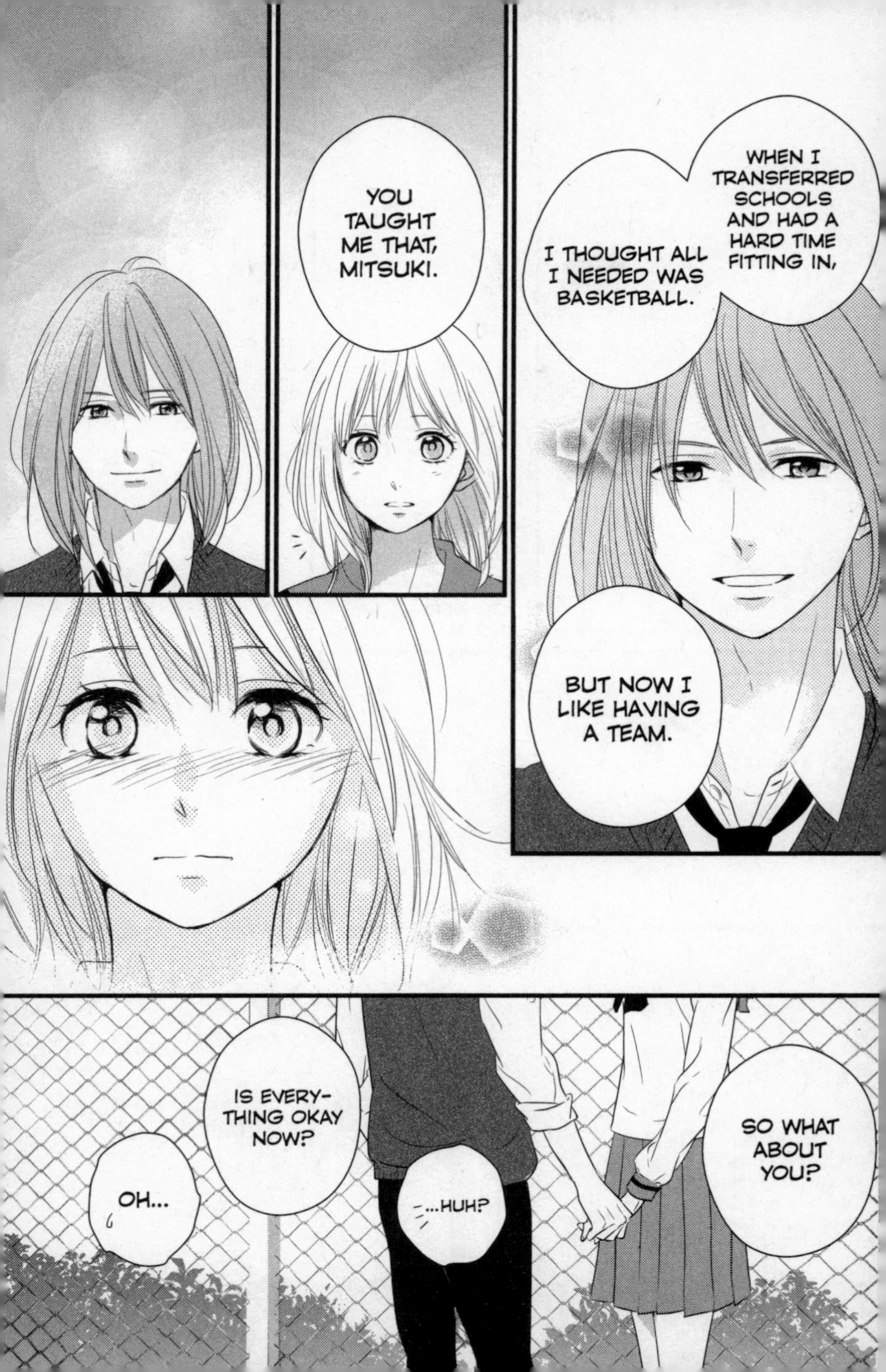
WHEN I TRANSFERRED SCHOOLS AND HAD A HARD TIME FITTING IN,
I THOUGHT ALL I NEEDED WAS BASKETBALL.
BUT NOW I LIKE HAVING A TEAM.
YOU TAUGHT ME THAT, MITSUKI.
SO WHAT ABOUT YOU?
...HUH?
IS EVERY-THING OKAY NOW?
OH...

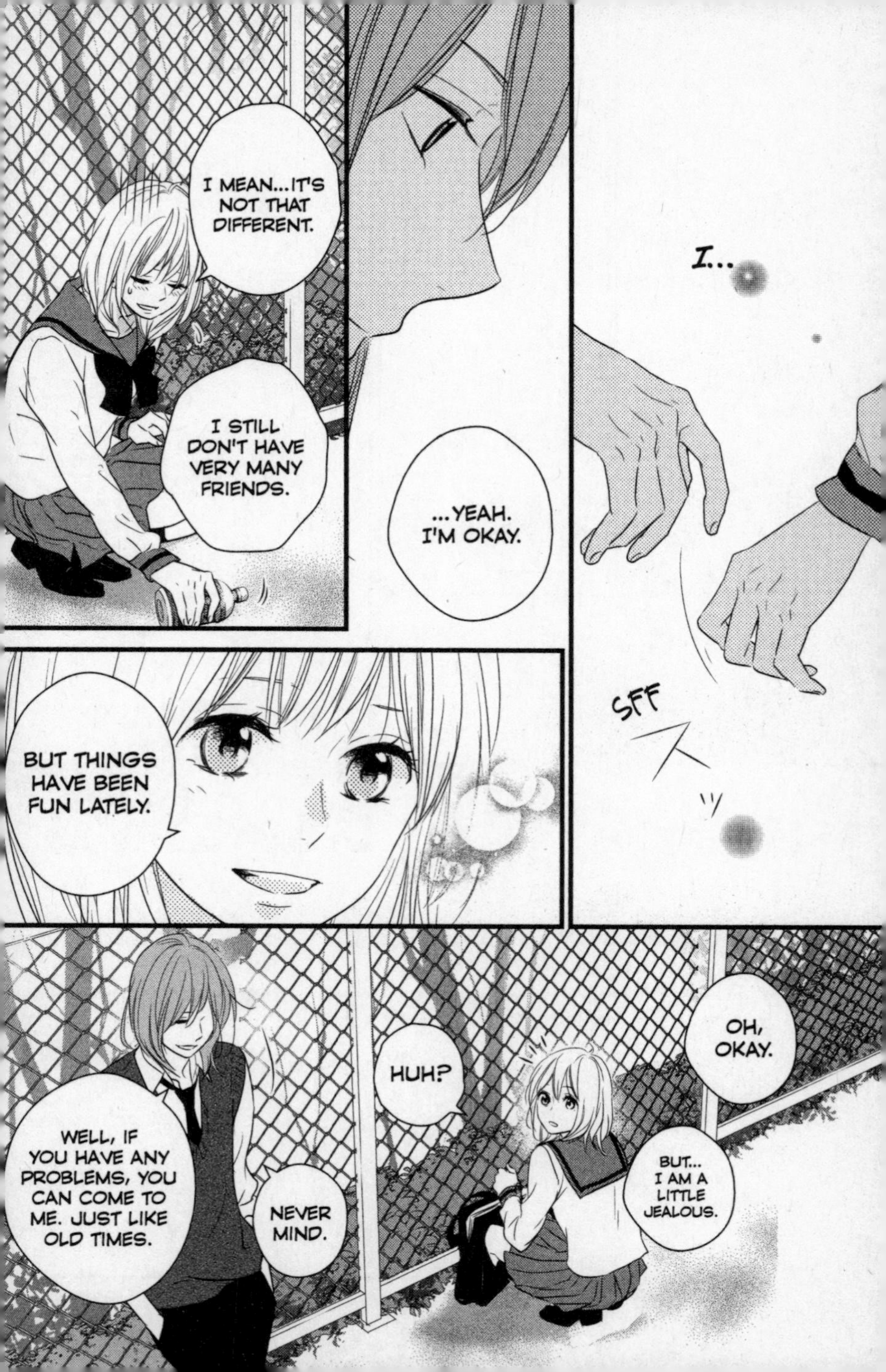
I...
SFF
...YEAH. I'M OKAY.
I MEAN...IT'S NOT THAT DIFFERENT.
I STILL DON'T HAVE VERY MANY FRIENDS.
BUT THINGS HAVE BEEN FUN LATELY.
OH, OKAY.
BUT... I AM A LITTLE JEALOUS.
HUH?
NEVER MIND.
WELL, IF YOU HAVE ANY PROBLEMS, YOU CAN COME TO ME. JUST LIKE OLD TIMES.

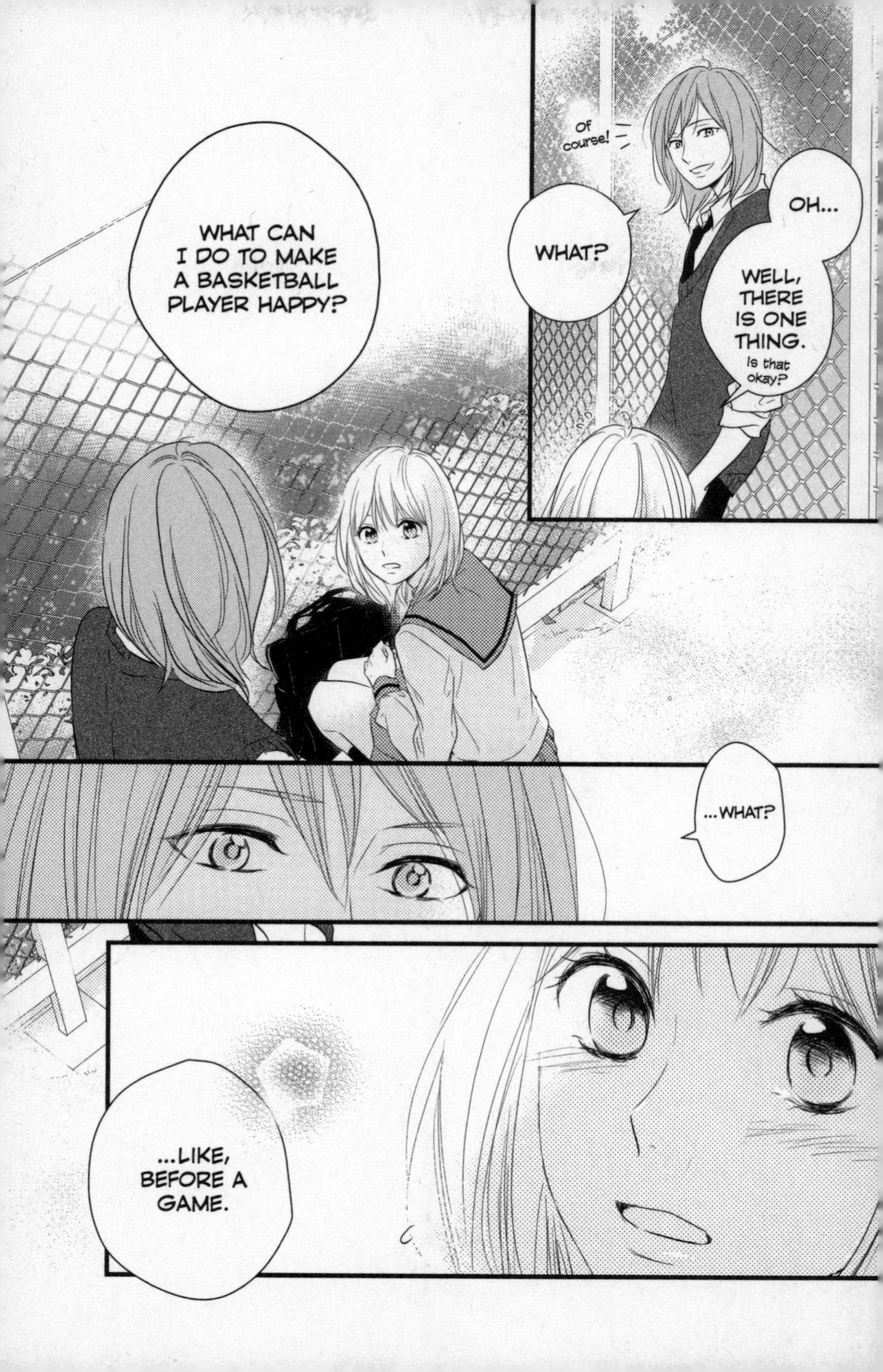
OH...
WELL, THERE IS ONE THING.
Is that okay?
WHAT?
Of course!
WHAT CAN I DO TO MAKE A BASKETBALL PLAYER HAPPY?
...WHAT?
...LIKE, BEFORE A GAME.

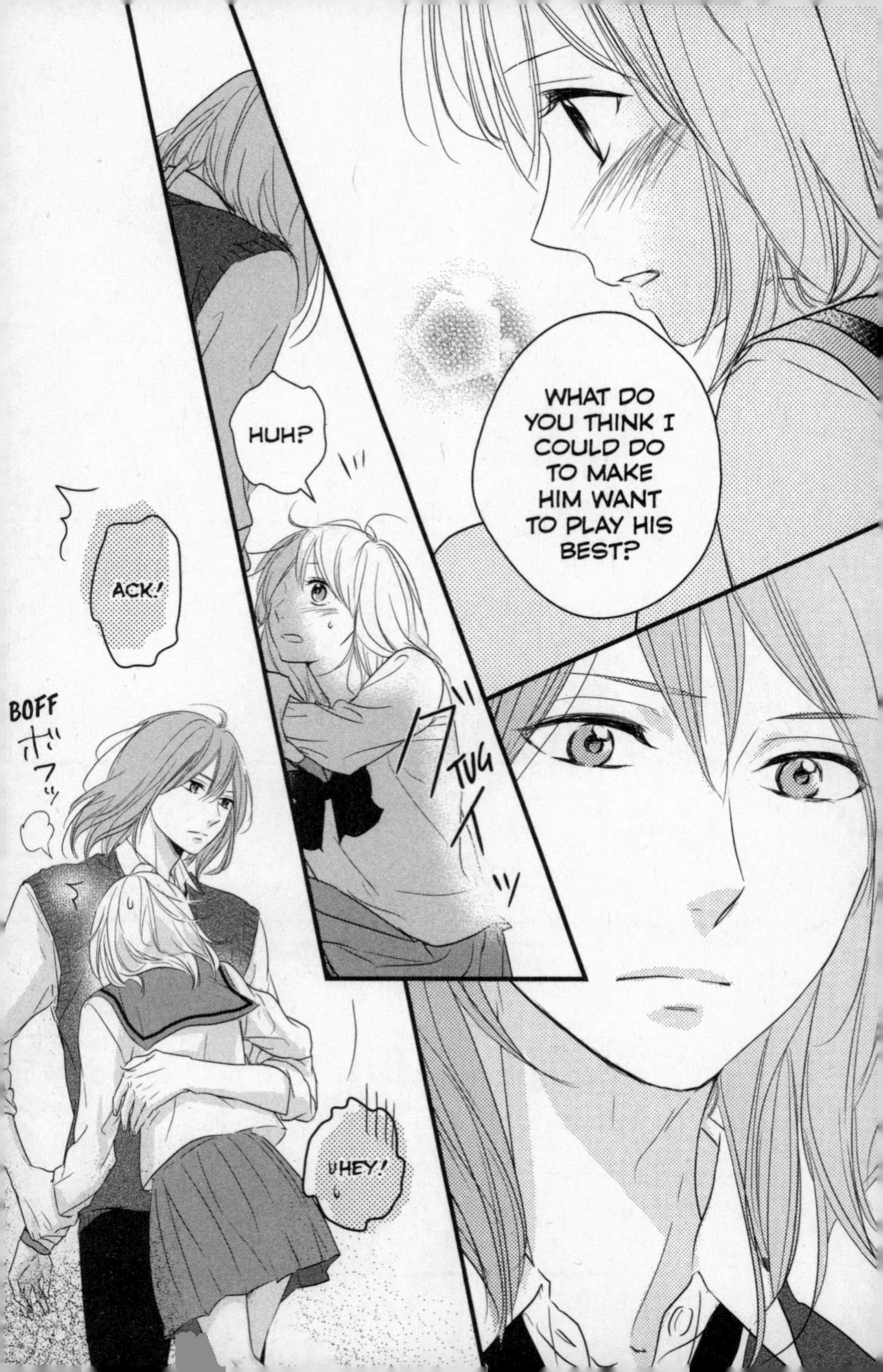
WHAT DO YOU THINK I COULD DO TO MAKE HIM WANT TO PLAY HIS BEST?
HUH?
TUG
ACK!
BOFF
ボフッ
HEY!

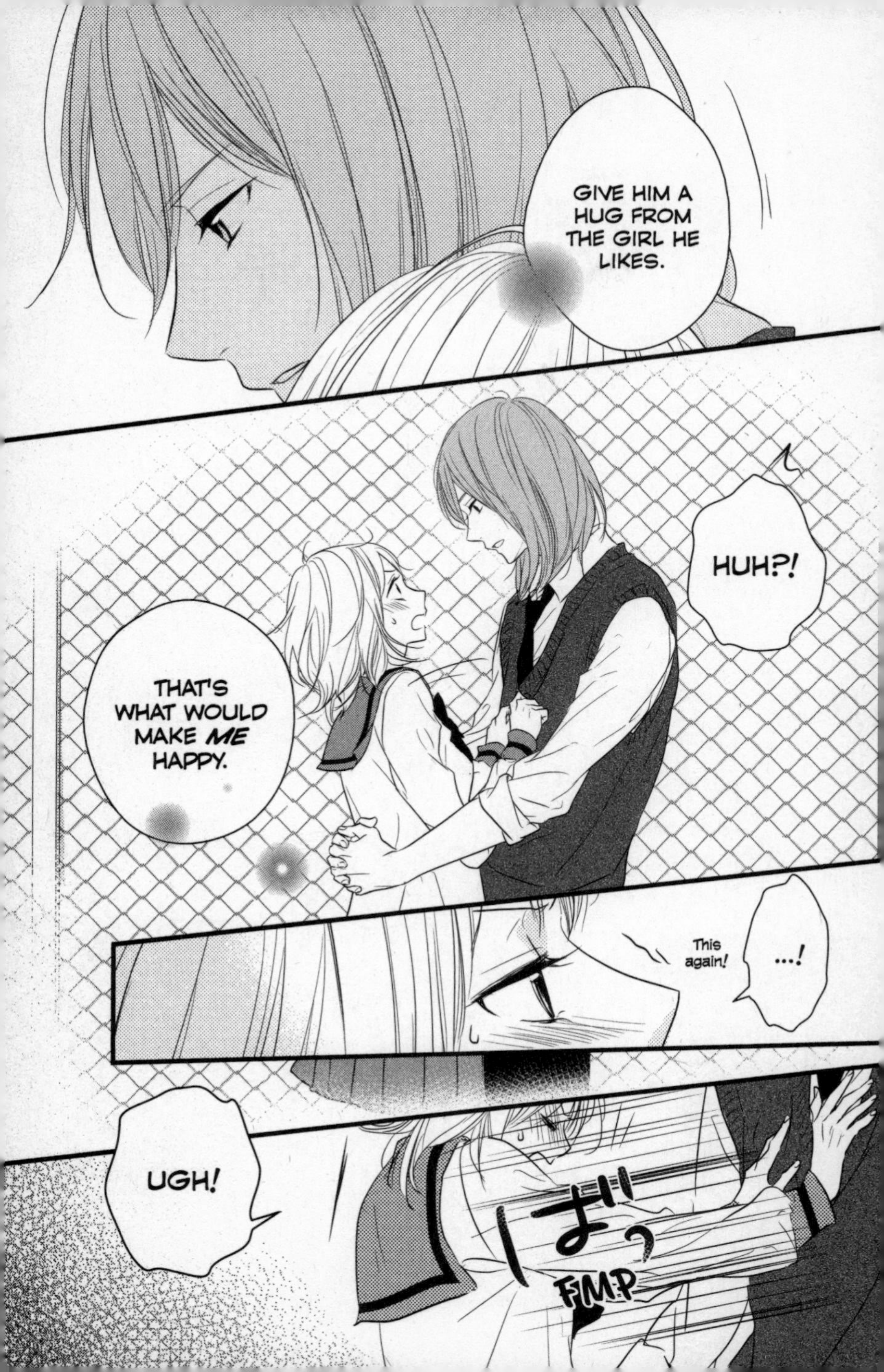
GIVE HIM A HUG FROM THE GIRL HE LIKES.
HUH?!
THAT'S WHAT WOULD MAKE *ME* HAPPY.
...!
This again!
UGH!
ぽっ
FMP

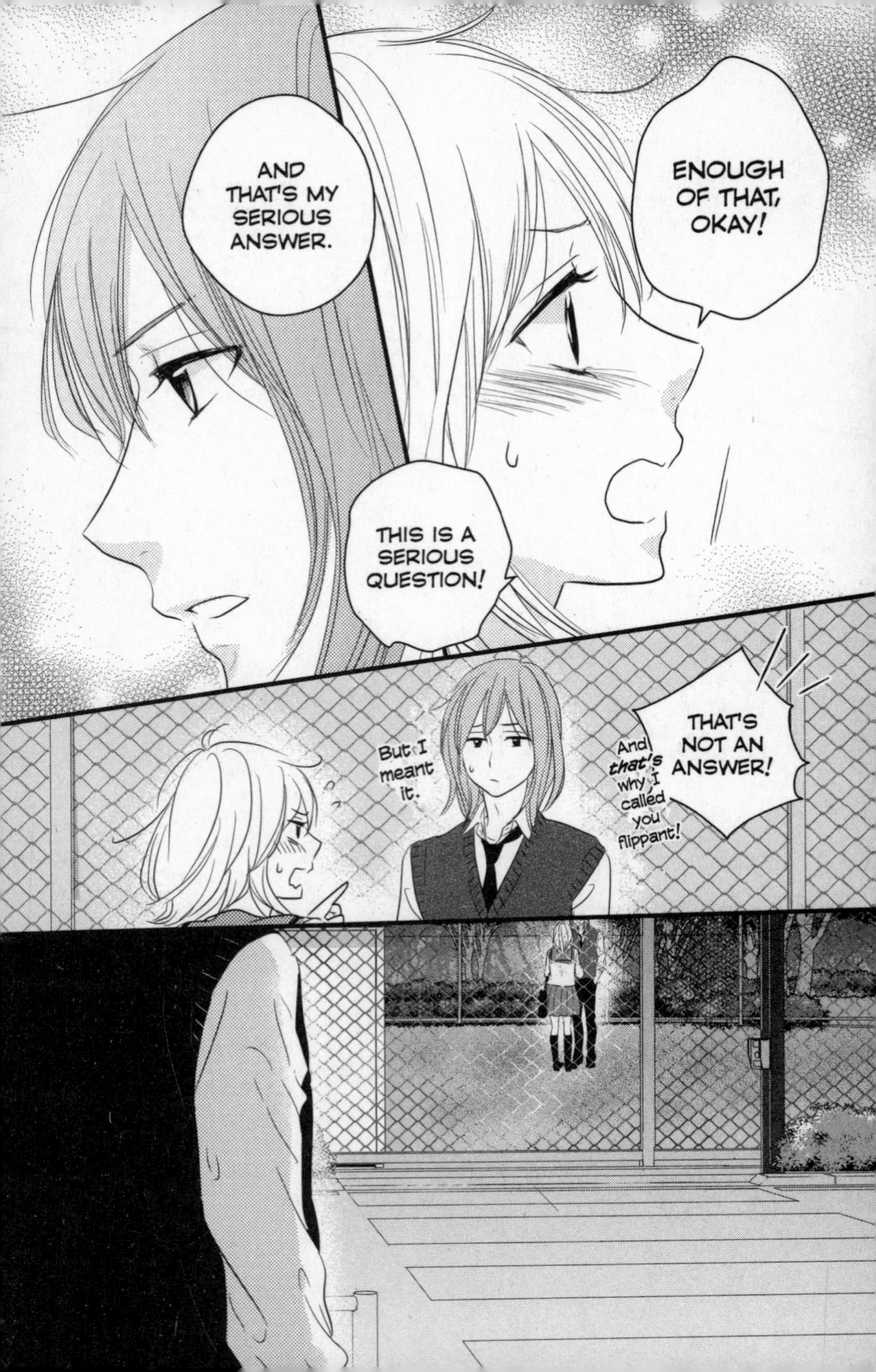
ENOUGH OF THAT, OKAY!
AND THAT'S MY SERIOUS ANSWER.
THIS IS A SERIOUS QUESTION!
THAT'S NOT AN ANSWER!
And that's why I called you flippant!
But I meant it.

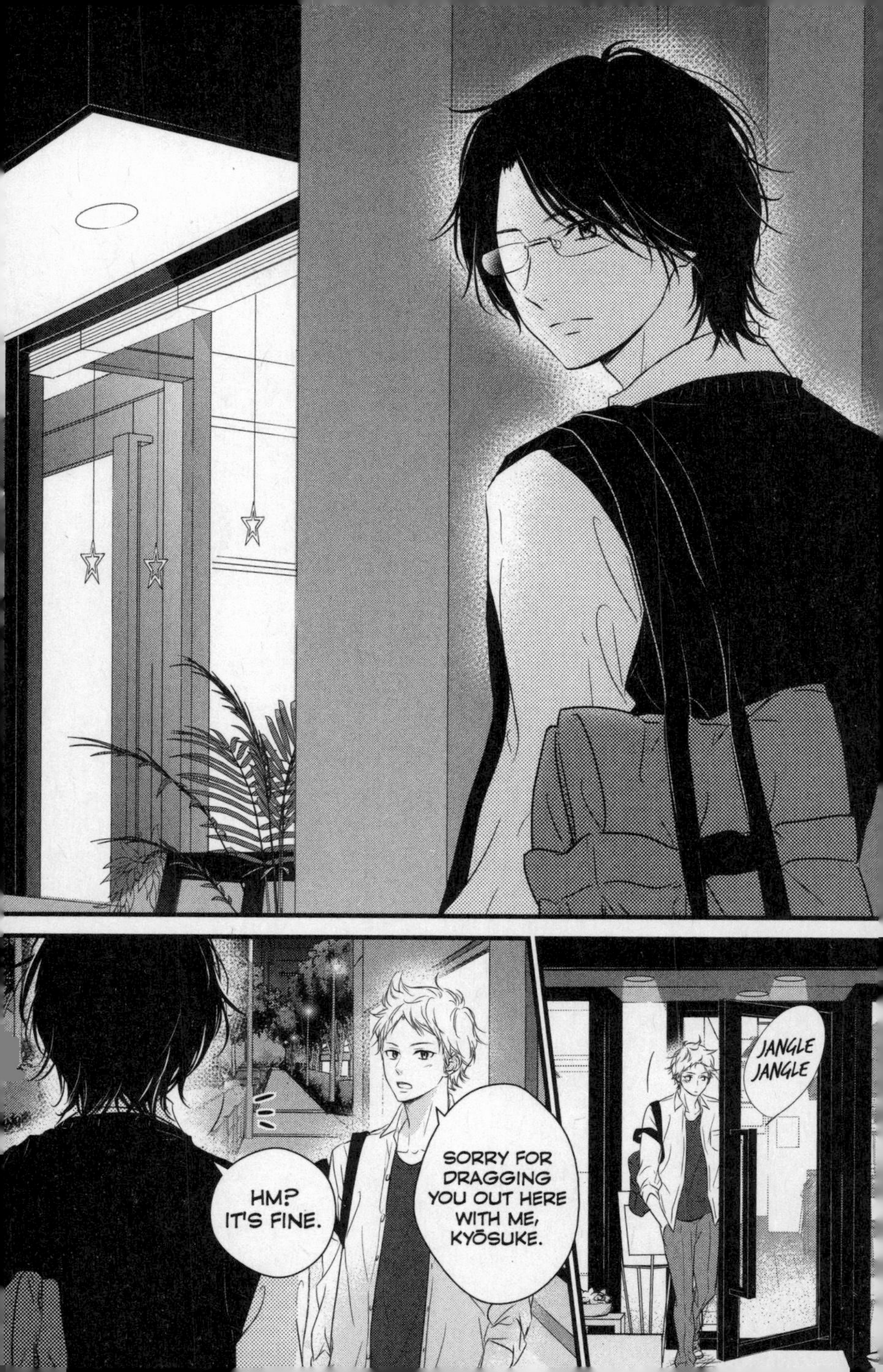
JANGLE JANGLE
SORRY FOR DRAGGING YOU OUT HERE WITH ME, KYŌSUKE.
HM? IT'S FINE.

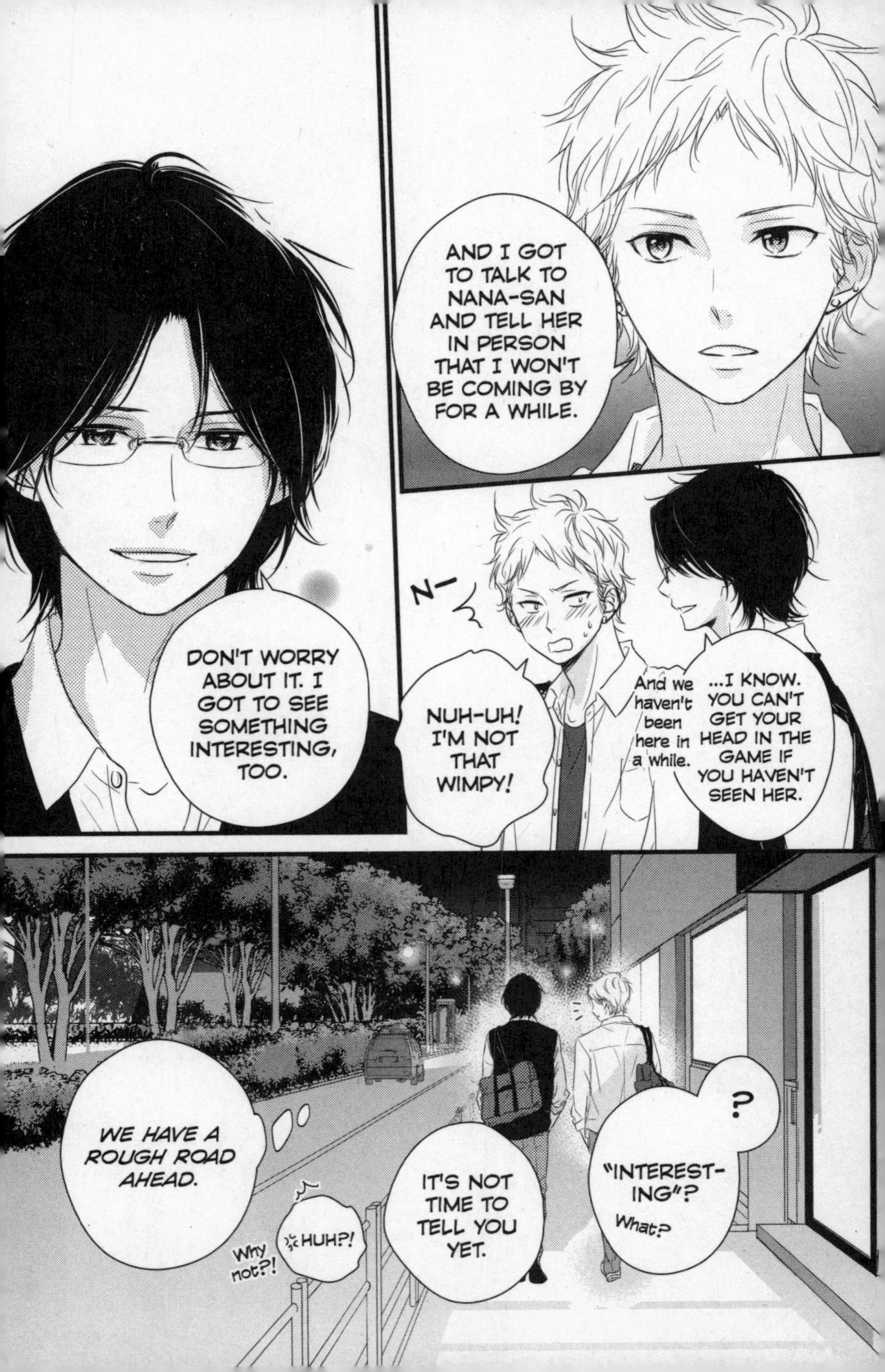
AND I GOT TO TALK TO NANA-SAN AND TELL HER IN PERSON THAT I WON'T BE COMING BY FOR A WHILE.
...I KNOW. YOU CAN'T GET YOUR HEAD IN THE GAME IF YOU HAVEN'T SEEN HER.
And we haven't been here in a while.
N-
NUH-UH! I'M NOT THAT WIMPY!
DON'T WORRY ABOUT IT. I GOT TO SEE SOMETHING INTERESTING, TOO.
?
"INTERESTING"?
What?
IT'S NOT TIME TO TELL YOU YET.
HUH?!
Why not?!
WE HAVE A ROUGH ROAD AHEAD.

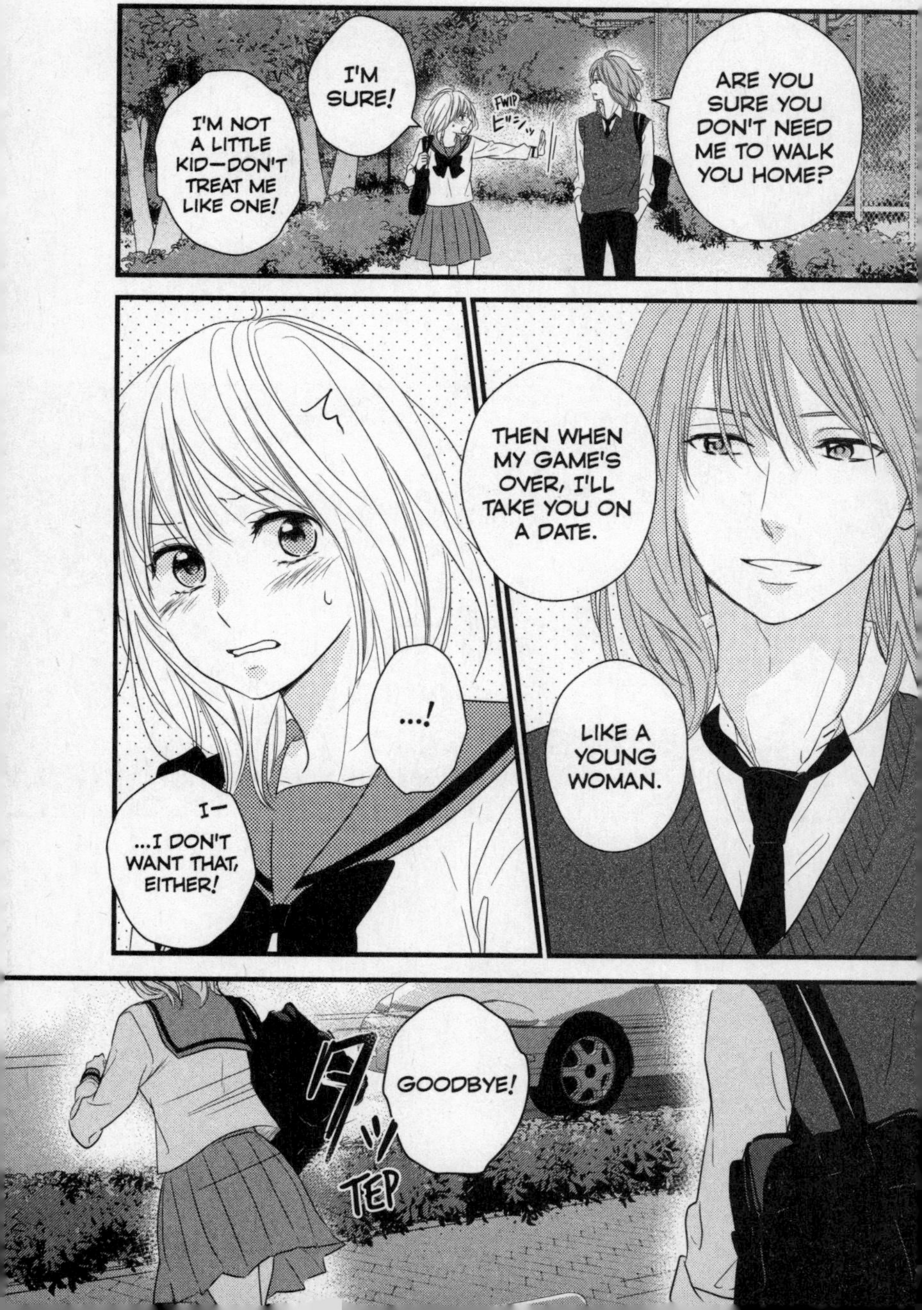
ARE YOU SURE YOU DON'T NEED ME TO WALK YOU HOME?
FWIP
I'M SURE!
I'M NOT A LITTLE KID—DON'T TREAT ME LIKE ONE!
THEN WHEN MY GAME'S OVER, I'LL TAKE YOU ON A DATE.
LIKE A YOUNG WOMAN.
...!
I—
...I DON'T WANT THAT, EITHER!
GOODBYE!
TEP

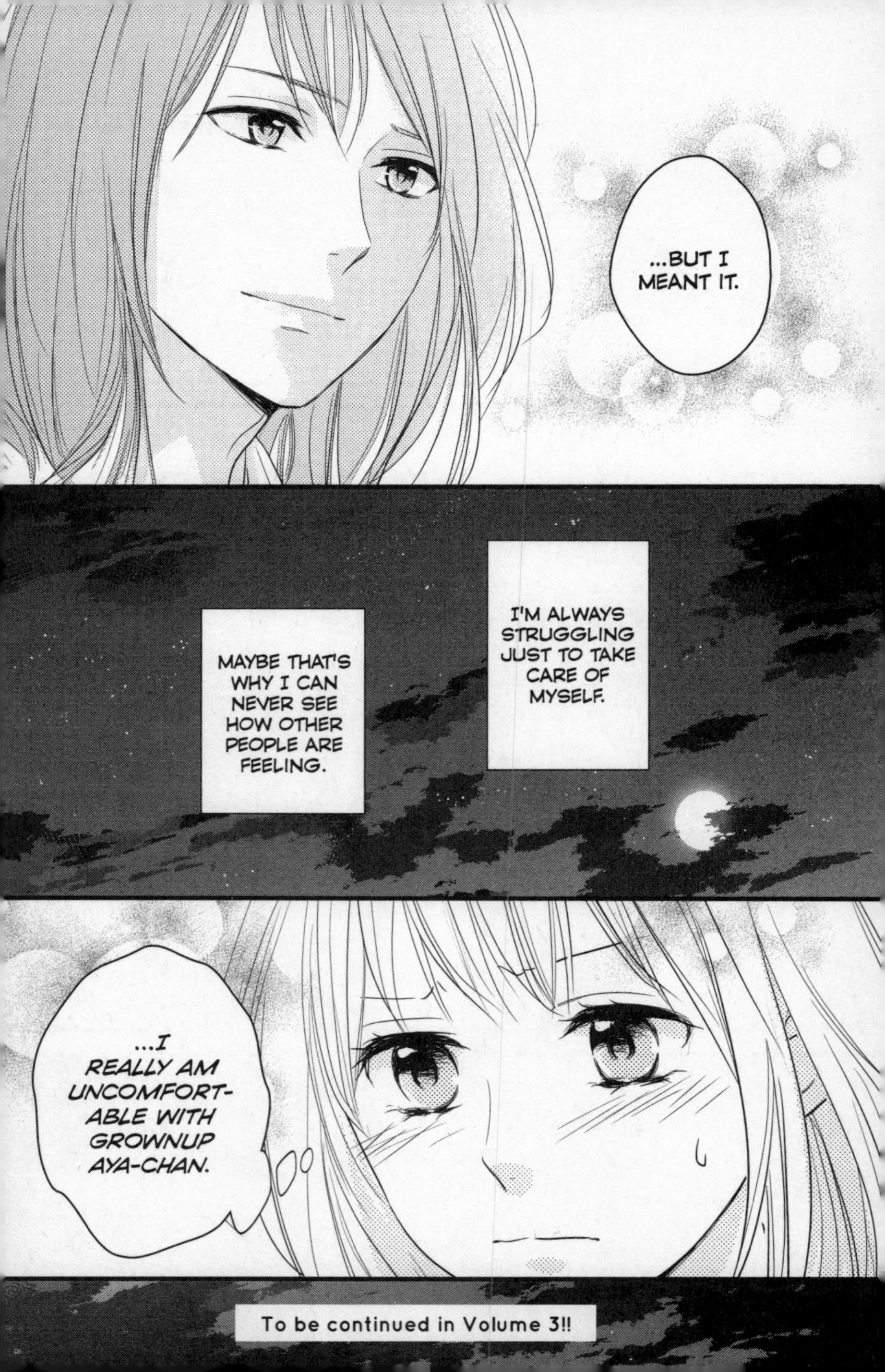
...BUT I MEANT IT.
I'M ALWAYS STRUGGLING JUST TO TAKE CARE OF MYSELF.
MAYBE THAT'S WHY I CAN NEVER SEE HOW OTHER PEOPLE ARE FEELING.
...I REALLY AM UNCOMFORTABLE WITH GROWNUP AYA-CHAN.
To be continued in Volume 3!!

Bonus Extra Manga

It Happened in the Morning

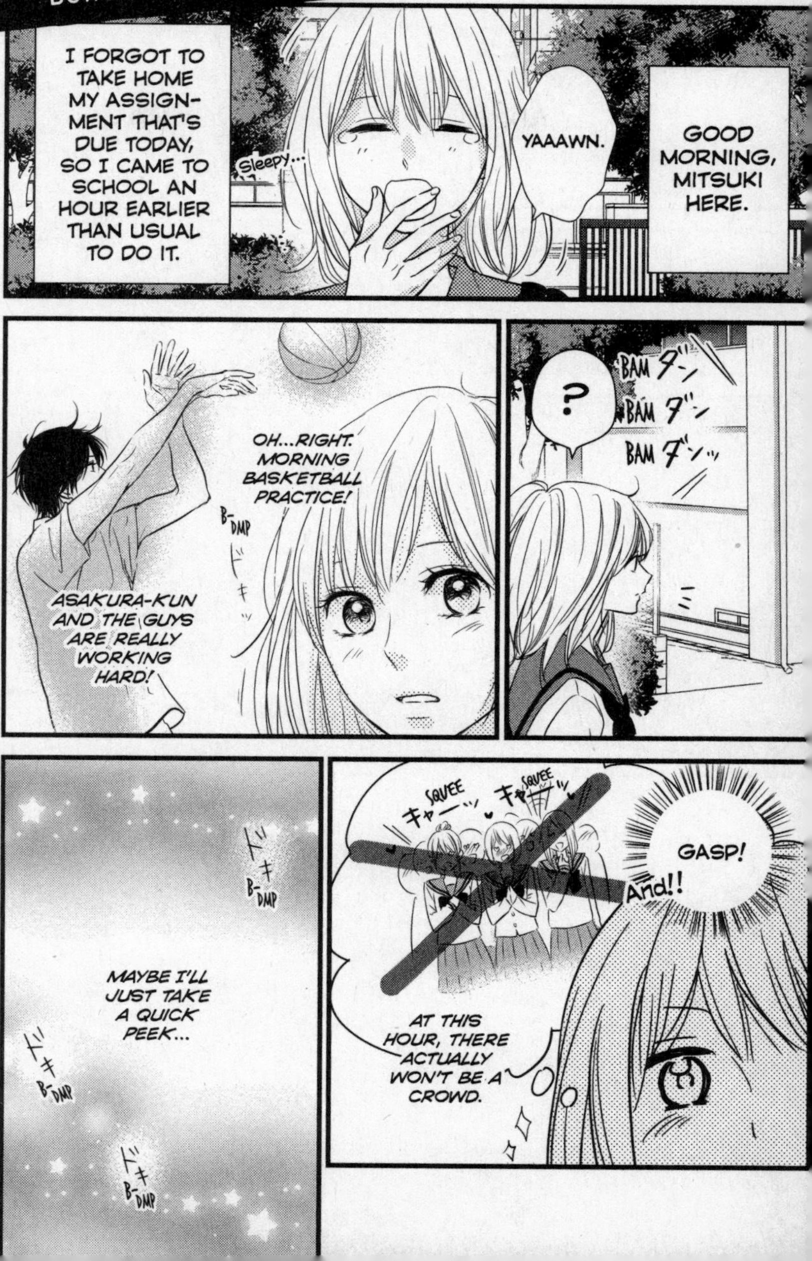
GOOD MORNING, MITSUKI HERE.
YAAAWN.
Sleepy...
I FORGOT TO TAKE HOME MY ASSIGNMENT THAT'S DUE TODAY, SO I CAME TO SCHOOL AN HOUR EARLIER THAN USUAL TO DO IT.
BAM ダン
BAM ダン
BAM ダンッ
?
OH...RIGHT. MORNING BASKETBALL PRACTICE!
B-DMP ドキッ
ASAKURA-KUN AND THE GUYS ARE REALLY WORKING HARD!
GASP!
And!!
SQUEE キャーッ
SQUEE キャーッ
AT THIS HOUR, THERE ACTUALLY WON'T BE A CROWD.
ドキ B-DMP
MAYBE I'LL JUST TAKE A QUICK PEEK...
ドキ B-DMP
ドキ B-DMP

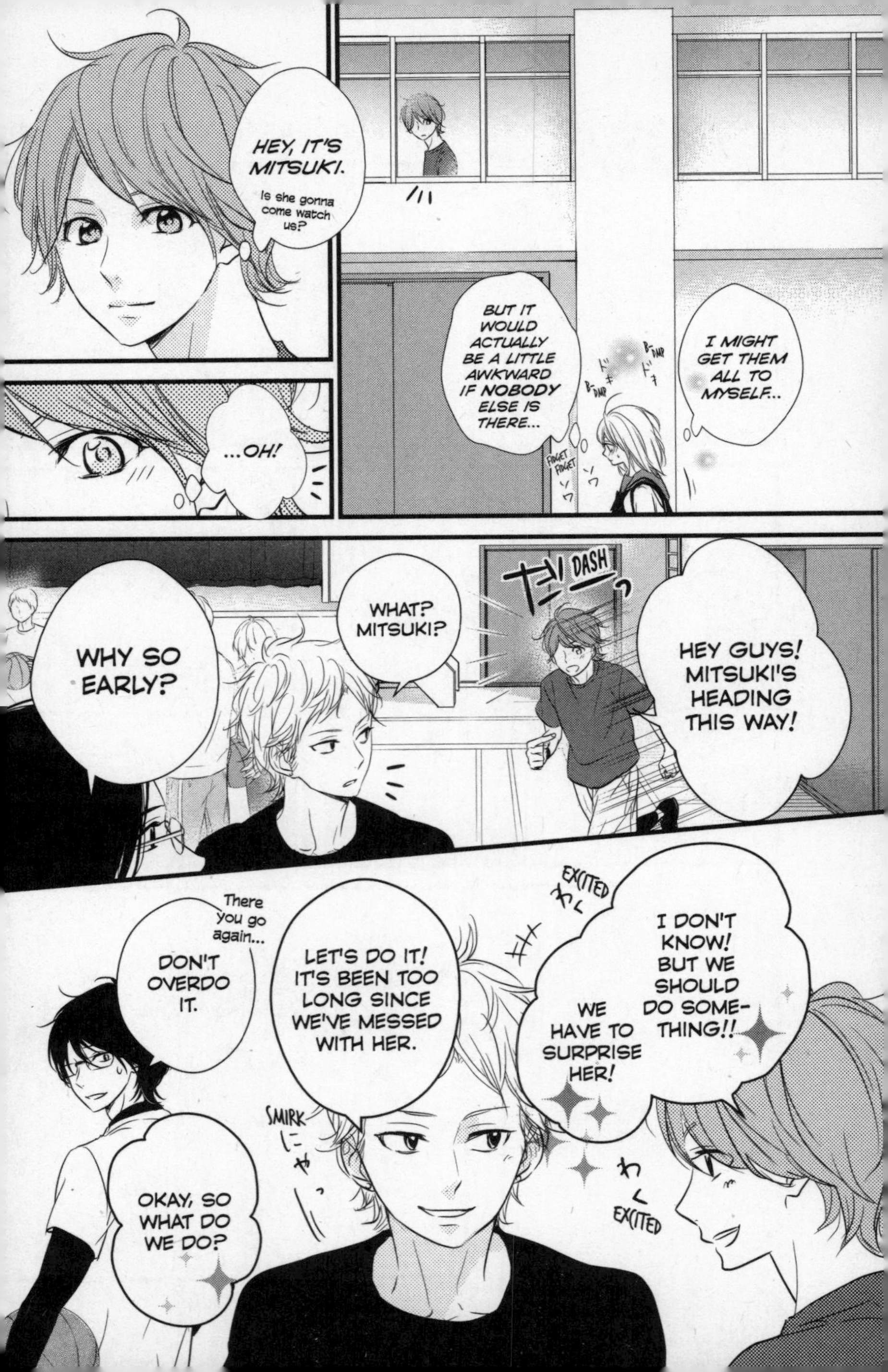
I MIGHT GET THEM ALL TO MYSELF...
B-DMP
B-DMP
BUT IT WOULD ACTUALLY BE A LITTLE AWKWARD IF NOBODY ELSE IS THERE...
FIDGET FIDGET
HEY, IT'S MITSUKI.
Is she gonna come watch us?
...OH!
HEY GUYS! MITSUKI'S HEADING THIS WAY!
DASH
WHAT? MITSUKI?
WHY SO EARLY?
EXCITED
I DON'T KNOW! BUT WE SHOULD DO SOMETHING!!
WE HAVE TO SURPRISE HER!
EXCITED
LET'S DO IT! IT'S BEEN TOO LONG SINCE WE'VE MESSED WITH HER.
SMIRK
There you go again...
DON'T OVERDO IT.
OKAY, SO WHAT DO WE DO?

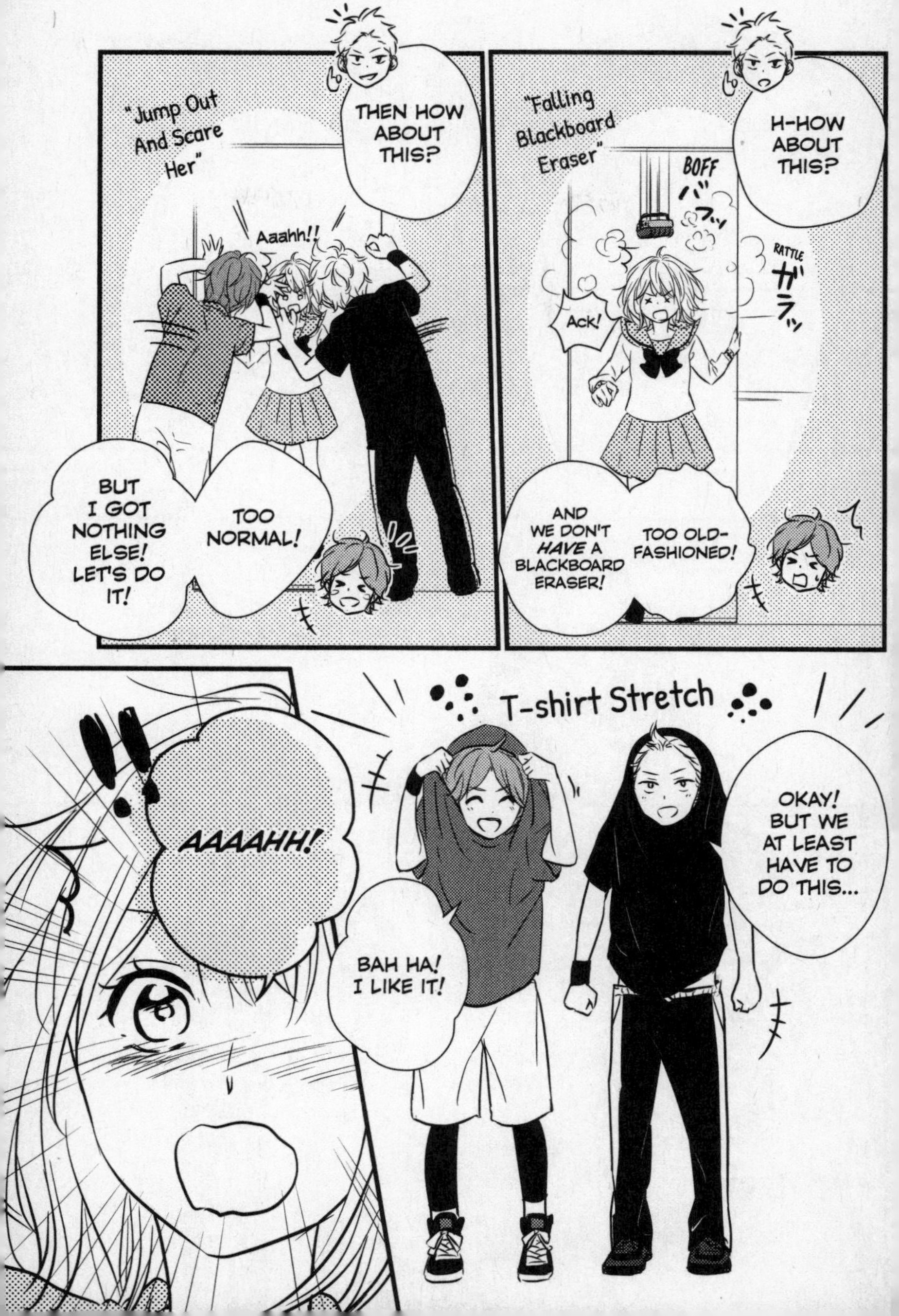
"Falling Blackboard Eraser"
H-HOW ABOUT THIS?
BOFF
バフッ
RATTLE
ガラッ
Ack!
TOO OLD-FASHIONED!
AND WE DON'T *HAVE* A BLACKBOARD ERASER!
THEN HOW ABOUT THIS?
"Jump Out And Scare Her"
Aaahh!!
TOO NORMAL!
BUT I GOT NOTHING ELSE! LET'S DO IT!
T-shirt Stretch
OKAY! BUT WE AT LEAST HAVE TO DO THIS...
BAH HA! I LIKE IT!
AAAAHH!

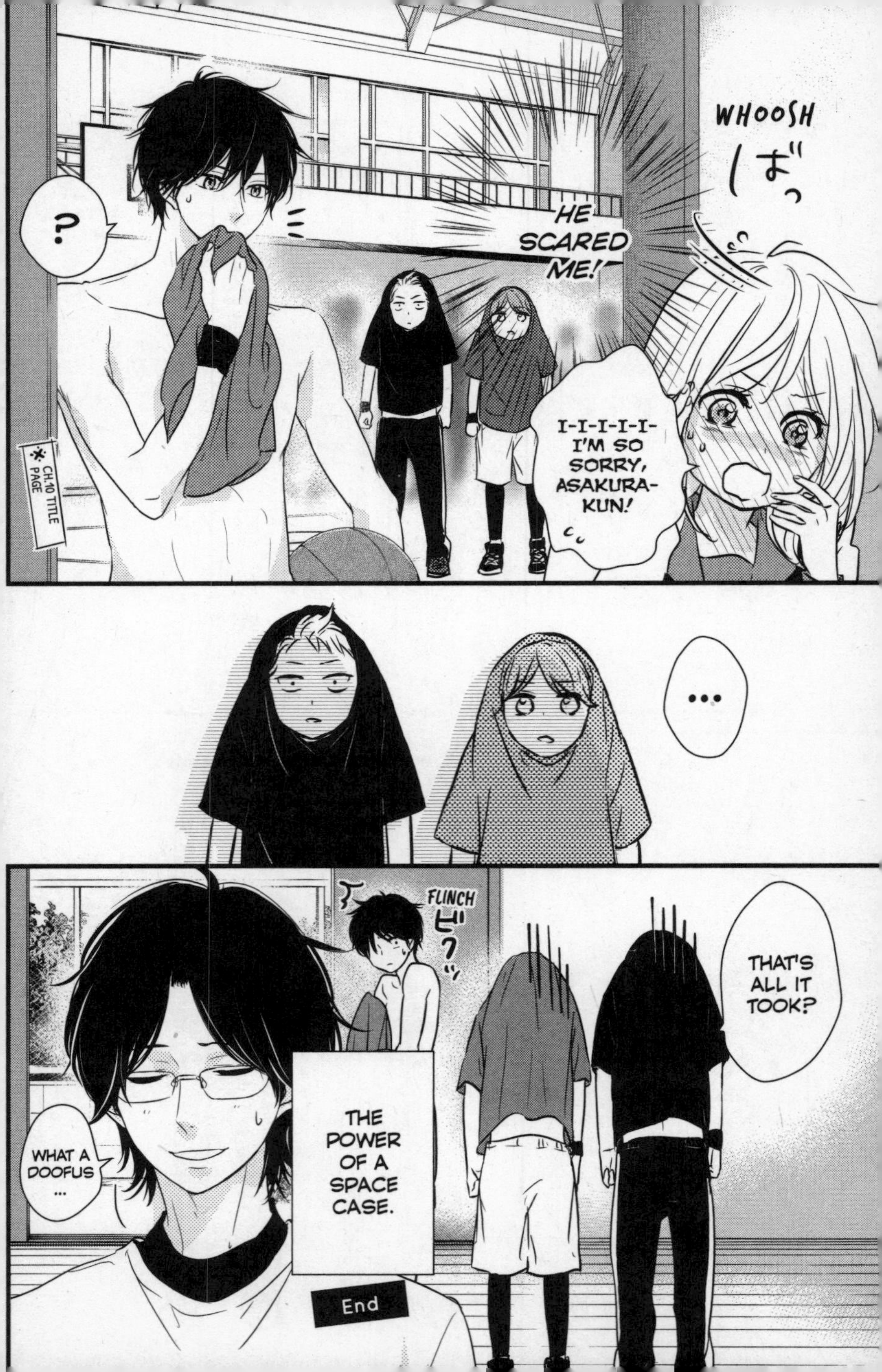
WHOOSH
ばっ
HE SCARED ME!
I-I-I-I-I- I'M SO SORRY, ASAKURA-KUN!
?
※ CH.10 TITLE PAGE
...
THAT'S ALL IT TOOK?
FLINCH
ビクッ
THE POWER OF A SPACE CASE.
WHAT A DOOFUS ...
End

Dessert December 2014 Issue Cover Draft 2

(This is the one that got used ✧✦)

Your thoughts and letters to the magazine, and your tweets and comments, are all very encouraging. Thank you very much.

I will keep doing my very best to entertain you, so

Please keep enjoying Waiting for Spring.

SPECIAL THANKS

To my editor, Editor-in-Chief Shiiigeru, everyone on the *Dessert* editorial team, the Designer-sama, everyone at the printing office, everyone who was involved in the creation of this work.
My assistants (main assistant Masuda-san, Aki-chan)
My family, and friends.

Words Cafe-sama
(The café in the series really exists in Kita Ward, Osaka)

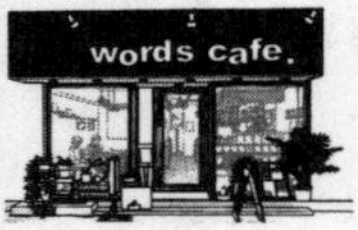
words cafe.

And to everyone who read this far, my sincerest gratitude.

January 11, 2015

Anashin

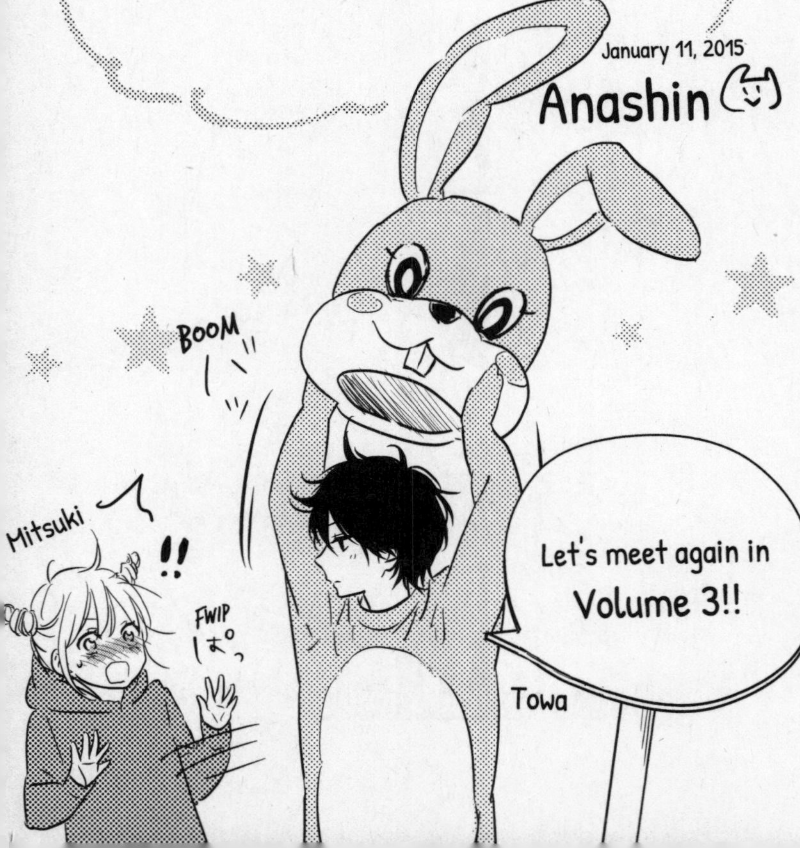
Let's meet again in Volume 3!!
Towa
BOOM
Mitsuki
!!
FWIP
ぱっ

Is It My Imagination?

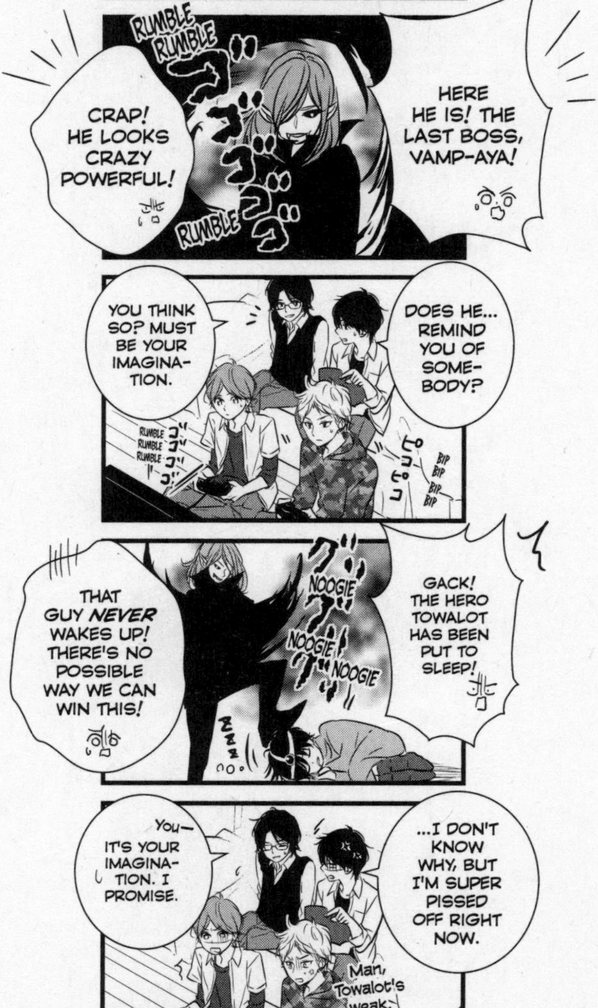
HERE HE IS! THE LAST BOSS, VAMP-AYA!
RUMBLE RUMBLE
RUMBLE
CRAP! HE LOOKS CRAZY POWERFUL!
DOES HE... REMIND YOU OF SOMEBODY?
BIP BIP
BIP BIP
YOU THINK SO? MUST BE YOUR IMAGINATION.
RUMBLE RUMBLE RUMBLE
GACK! THE HERO TOWALOT HAS BEEN PUT TO SLEEP!
NOOGIE
NOOGIE
NOOGIE
THAT GUY NEVER WAKES UP! THERE'S NO POSSIBLE WAY WE CAN WIN THIS!
...I DON'T KNOW WHY, BUT I'M SUPER PISSED OFF RIGHT NOW.
Man, Towalot's weak.
You—
IT'S YOUR IMAGINATION. I PROMISE.
Aaarrrgh! He beat us!

What's Your Special Skill?

Ryūji
SPECIAL SKILL? UH, BASKETBALL, DUH.
IS THAT ALL...?
YEAH.
Don't glare at the camera.
I THINK WE ALL KNOW ABOUT THAT, SO FOR THE NEXT PERSON, LET'S CHOOSE SOMETHING OTHER THAN BASKETBALL, OKAY!
Rui
I CAN REMEMBER A GIRL'S NAME AND FACE INSTANTLY!
AND I CAN BE FRIENDS WITH ANYBODY.
AND MY SMILE IS ADORABLE! OH, AND—
And so modest...
THAT'S ENOUGH, THANK YOU!
Kyōsuke
I CAN INSTANTLY NOTICE ANY CHANGE IN A WOMAN.
STAAARE
UM, WOULD YOU PLEASE LOOK AT THE CAMERA...
MITSUKI, YOU TRIMMED YOUR BANGS, DIDN'T YOU?
B-DMP!
Towa
I... ...
Um...
...ZZZ.
APPARENTLY HE CAN SLEEP WITH HIS EYES OPEN!

To be continued in Volume 3!!

Translation Notes

Pleeeease enjoy, page 4

In Japanese, the sound of a smile is *ni*, so it's not uncommon for people to say *ni* when posing for pictures, just like how we tend to say "cheese" in English. *Ni* is also a word for "two," so in the Japanese text, Mitsuki says "Volume 2," stretching out the *ni* (*niii-kan*) to give us a nice smile. To recreate this effect, the translators took advantage of the fact that "please" rhymes with "cheese."

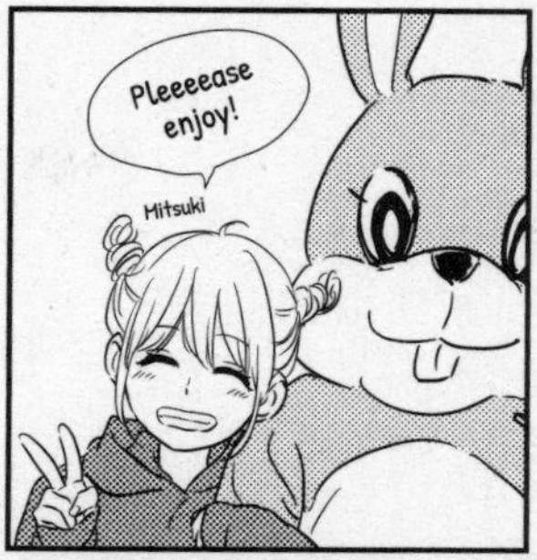
Pleeeease enjoy!
Mitsuki

What song is this?, page 86

Poor Mitsuki lives in such a small bubble that she is even unfamiliar with the international video game and anime sensation *Yo-kai Watch*. This particular song is the anime's ending theme song, "Yo-kai Exercise," which is accompanied by an animation of the characters demonstrating a calisthenic routine. Entertaining and healthy!

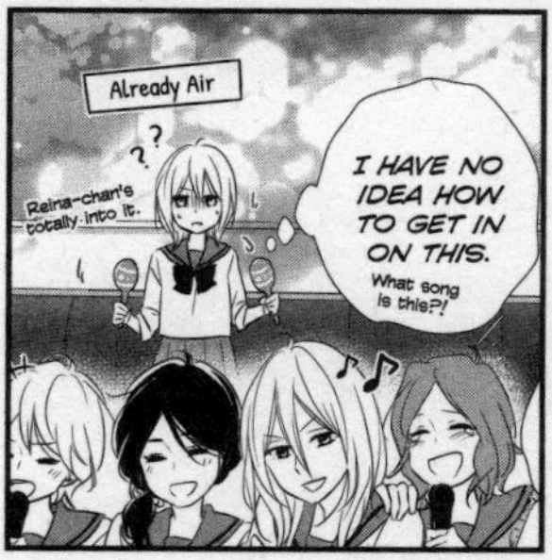
I HAVE NO IDEA HOW TO GET IN ON THIS.
What song is this?!
Already Air
Reina-chan's totally into it.

Any -nyan and every -tan, page 88

When Rui said, "Call me -nyan or -tan and I will gladly answer to it!" he was referring to two terms that are cuter versions of -chan, with -nyan having a more feline connotation (as it is also the Japanese word for "meow"). However, it's a bit of a wordplay, where *nyan demo tan demo* (nyan or tan) sounds like *nan demo kan demo* (anything and everything). The current rendering is the translators attempt to reconcile the meaning of the phrase with the pun.

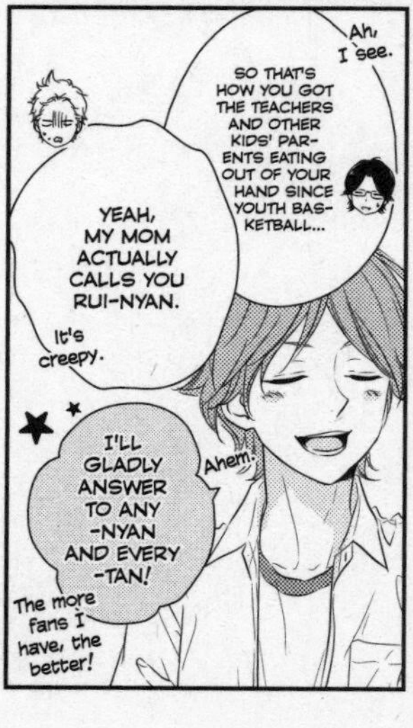
Ah, I see.
SO THAT'S HOW YOU GOT THE TEACHERS AND OTHER KIDS' PARENTS EATING OUT OF YOUR HAND SINCE YOUTH BASKETBALL...
YEAH, MY MOM ACTUALLY CALLS YOU RUI-NYAN.
It's creepy.
Ahem.
I'LL GLADLY ANSWER TO ANY -NYAN AND EVERY -TAN!
The more fans I have, the better!

The prince in his dark days

By Hico Yamanaka

A drunkard for a father, a household of poverty... For 17-year-old Atsuko, misfortune is all she knows and believes in. Until one day, a chance encounter with Itaru-the wealthy heir of a huge corporation-changes everything. The two look identical, uncannily so. When Itaru curiously goes missing, Atsuko is roped into being his stand-in. There, in his shoes, Atsuko must parade like a prince in a palace. She encounters many new experiences, but at what cost...?

The award-winning manga about what happens inside you!

"Far more entertaining than it ought to be... what kid doesn't want to think that every time they sneeze a torpedo shoots out their nose?"
—Anime News Network

Strep throat! Hay fever! Influenza! The world is a dangerous place for a red blood cell just trying to get her deliveries finished. Fortunately, she's not alone...she's got a whole human body's worth of cells ready to help out! The mysterious white blood cells, the buff and brash killer T cells, even the cute little platelets—everyone's got to come together if they want to keep you healthy!

Cells at Work!

はたらく細胞

By Akane Shimizu

Waiting for Spring volume 2 is a work of fiction. Names, characters, places, and incidents are the products of the author's imagination or are used fictitiously. Any resemblance to actual events, locales, or persons, living or dead, is entirely coincidental.

A Kodansha Comics Trade Paperback Original

Published in the United States by Kodansha Comics, an imprint of Kodansha USA Publishing, LLC, New York.

Publication rights for this English edition arranged through Kodansha Ltd, Tokyo.

ISBN 978-1-63236-517-0

Printed in the United States of America.

www.kodanshacomics.com

9 8 7 6 5 4 3 2
Translation: Alethea and Athena Nibley
Lettering: Sara Linsley
Editing: Haruko Hashimoto
Kodansha Comics edition cover design by Phil Balsman